Eating Disorders
Second Edition

Richard A. Gordon

To the memory of my father,
M. Arthur Gordon,
who taught me so much

and for Patti, Alexa, and Corinne

Eating Disorders
Anatomy of a Social Epidemic

second edition

Richard A. Gordon

BLACKWELL
Publishers

First published 1990
Reprinted 1991
First published in paperback in the USA 1992
Reprinted 1992, 1993, 1994, 1995 (twice), 1997, 1998
Second edition published 2000

2 4 6 8 10 9 7 5 3 1

Blackwell Publishers Ltd
108 Cowley Road
Oxford OX4 1JF
UK

Blackwell Publishers Ltd
350 Main Street
Malden, Massachusetts 02148
USA

British Library Cataloguing in Publication Data

A CIP catalogue record for this book is available from the British Library.

Library of Congress Cataloging-in-Publication Data

Gordon, Richard A. (Richard Allan), 1941–
    Eating disorders : anatomy of a social epidemic / Richard A. Gordon. — 2nd ed.
      p.   cm.
    Prev. ed. has title: Anorexia and bulimia.
    Includes bibliographical references and index.
    ISBN 0-631-21495-X (hbk.). — ISBN 0-631-21496-8 (pbk.)
    1. Eating disorders—Social aspects. 2. Anorexia nervosa—Social aspects.
    3. Bulimia—Social aspects.   I. Gordon, Richard A. (Richard Allan), 1941–
    Anorexia and bulimia. II. Title.
    RC552.E18G67   1999
    616.85′262—dc21   99-16396
                                             CIP

Typeset in 10½ on 13 pt Galliard
by Ace Filmsetting Ltd, Frome, Somerset

This book is printed on acid-free paper

Contents

Preface to the Second Edition

Since the publication of the first edition of this book in 1990, professional interest in and knowledge about eating disorders have continued to grow at an intense pace. There are typically over 700 publications each year on eating disorders in professional journals alone. The ongoing professional interest in these conditions reflects not only the formidable challenges that they present to the clinician but also their continued substantial incidence and prevalence in the United States and Europe and their emergence in other parts of the world as well. While there continue to be debates about just how common they are, I would take sharp issue with those who have suggested that the interest in eating disorders is largely a function of professional curiosity rather than a result of a proliferation of these problems in society.

Significant progress has been made in our understanding of basic issues in the conceptual understanding and clinical treatment of eating disorders over the past ten years. We have gained considerable understanding, among other things, about the spectrum of eating disorder diagnoses, the relationship of eating disorders to other psychiatric conditions, the role of neurobiological factors, and the impact and relative importance of risk factors such as dieting and sexual abuse in the development of eating disorders. Yet the basic argument that was advanced in the original edition of this book remains intact, namely, that one cannot understand the proliferation of these conditions in the contemporary era without an analysis of the broader sociocultural framework in which they occur. David Barlow and Mark Durand, authors of an authoritative text in the field of abnormal psychology, suggest that eating disorders are unique compared with all other psychiatric disorders in the degree to which social and cultural factors play a role in their etiology.[1]

One particularly striking phenomenon that supports a sociocultural interpretation is the emergence of eating disorders in areas of the world that were once considered relatively immune to the particular cultural influences that are described in this book. Whether we refer to such diffusion of cultural forces as globalization or Westernization, there is little question (and if there is, the reasons will be amply documented in the pages of this volume) that the impact of American and Western European attitudes towards the cultivation of bodily appearance, as well as conflicting social role expectations for women that have become a worldwide phenomenon, have been profoundly influential. Global consumerism as well as the infusion of expectations for individual achievement into societies that were formerly governed by an ethos of mutual obligation and deference to parental and societal authority seem to play a significant role. It is apparent that global capitalism brings its pathologies along with its benefits, a point that is illustrated in a particularly dramatic way by the diffusion of eating disorders.

Because the fundamental outline of the argument has remained unchanged, the basic chapter structure of the first edition has not been altered. However, thanks to an expanding knowledge base that has resulted from an explosion of research in the field, many points can now be elaborated on and new insights articulated. First, more has been learned about the diagnosis, treatment, and long-term outcome of eating disorders, and these are reviewed in chapter 2. In particular, this chapter contains new material about the prognosis, mortality rates, and medical complications of eating disorders, new findings in the neurobiology and pharmacological treatment of eating disorders, studies of the effectiveness of treatment modalities such as family therapy and cognitive-behavioral therapy, and a discussion of the new diagnosis of binge eating disorder. Second, a great deal more research has been done on the epidemiology of eating disorders, both in Western Europe and the United States and in other areas of the world as well. We have much better data on the incidence and prevalence of eating disorders in Europe and the United States, and the 1990s have seen the publication of numerous reports of eating disorders in developing nations. This work is reviewed in chapter 3. There has been intense interest in the phenomenon of sexual abuse in the eating disorders, and this issue is treated in chapter 4. Chapter 4 also examines in more detail than in the first edition research on males with eating disorders, although this continues to be a neglected and underserved population. In chapter 5, there is some consideration of the significance of the resurgence of extreme thinness in the form of the "waif" look in the 1990s. Chapter 5 also deals with the promotion and adoption of the thin ideal in cultural/geographic areas which once celebrated a larger female form. One of the most explosive areas of interest in the field of weight-related disorders has been that of obesity research. Chapter 6 examines some of the research on the epidemiology of obesity in the United States that has been published in the 1990s, as well as recent scientific and public fascination with chemical treatments of overweight. In addition, there is more discussion of the stereotyping of obesity which plays such a large role in the background of the eating disorders, particularly the issue of cultural differences in that stereotyping. Chapter 6 also includes a critical perspective on the research on the psychological consequences of dieting, new material on the research on dieting in popular culture and an expanded discussion of eating disorders in athletes. Gerald Russell once commented ruefully that he feared that the more we discuss eating disorders in public, the more common they become. Chapter 7, which deals with the social modeling of eating disorders, includes new material on the role of parental and peer modeling of eating disorders, as well as the recent debates about the possible pitfalls of prevention programs. Finally, in chapter 8, I have elaborated on some of the debates engendered by feminist perspectives on eating disorders, and particularly the questions that have been raised on the significance of the contemporary cult of beauty and appearance in women.

Throughout this new edition, I have explicitly incorporated more in the way of comparative cultural material. The tone of the book is more research-focused than the first edition, and this derives from my strong belief that the research in this field has substantially enhanced our understanding of these problems. As a result, a wide range of new references have been incorporated into this volume. Despite the widespread public interest in the eating disorders, they remain a problem that is still to some extent a hidden one or at least one that continues to be swept under the rug. This is truly remarkable, but perhaps understandable in that they reflect damage that is inflicted on the self rather than on others. In this way they contrast sharply with some of the most shocking social pathologies of our time, for example, the epidemic violence among adolescent males in the United States. And unfortunately, despite the increase in the number of patients, treatment resources for eating disorders, particularly on an inpatient or residential level, continue to decline dramatically. Any optimism expressed in the first edition of this book about the growth of the number of facilities for treatment has had to be tempered in this second edition. This is obviously a deplorable situation. It is my hope that this volume will make a contribution towards raising public awareness further about the urgency of directing needed resources towards these debilitating and sometimes deadly conditions.

Preface

My first encounter with the phenomenon of anorexia nervosa occurred in 1971, when, as an intern in clinical psychology at the Payne Whitney Psychiatric Clinic, I was asked to evaluate an anorexic patient – my very first psychiatric patient in this setting. My supervisor told me that I was very fortunate to have the opportunity to observe such a patient, as anorexia nervosa was a very rare condition and I was likely to encounter very few such patients in a lifetime of clinical practice. This particular young woman also had a secondary diagnosis of "bulimia" on her hospital form, a term which at the time was even more obscure than anorexia nervosa. The attending psychiatrist patiently explained to me the symptoms of bulimia, which he said sometimes occurred in anorexic patients. Undoubtedly, the notion that only ten years later literally thousands of college students would be engaged in a compulsive cycle of overeating and self-induced vomiting would at that time have come as a great shock to any of us.

Following my early training, I heard little about the eating disorders for several years. As a professor in a small liberal arts college, I was aware of one or two of our students who developed anorexia nervosa in the 1970s. It was not until around 1980 or 1981, however, that I began to realize that eating disorders were proliferating. At that time, I had entered into the individual practice of clinical psychology, and encountered a female college student who presented the classic picture of what is now familiar to us as bulimia nervosa. She was deeply frightened about her weight, and had found herself caught in a compulsive cycle of overeating and vomiting ("making herself sick," as she said). Unlike patients with anorexia nervosa, she was of normal weight, perhaps slightly overweight. But in other respects, her obsessive calorie counting and preoccupation with food, as well as her overwhelming fear of losing control, seemed quite similar to the mind-set of anorexic patients. After my encounter with this bulimic patient, others soon followed. As I was hardly known at that point as a psychologist with a special interest in eating disorders, it was unlikely that these patients were suddenly appearing in large numbers because of a selective referral pattern.

In 1982, I attended my first conference on eating disorders, sponsored by the Center for the Study of Anorexia and Bulimia in New York City. I wondered (as I often have done when attending specialist conferences) whether this conference would attract much interest, and certainly anticipated a small audience – perhaps 50 or 100 professionals. To my own surprise, and the apparent shock of Dr William Davis, the director of the Center for the Study of Anorexia and Bulimia and the conference organizer, several hundred health professionals appeared, filling an auditorium in one of New York's hotels. It immediately became apparent from the lectures at the conference, as well as from the remarks of the attendees, that my own sense of a sudden and dramatic increase in the prevalence of these conditions was no fluke.

This is a book about the social and cultural roots of the explosive increase in anorexic and bulimic conditions in our times. It is also a book about the larger questions of the relationships between culture and psychopathology, questions that have been of interest to me since my days as a graduate student in psychology. Increases in particular types of psychopathology signal the difficulties that certain vulnerable people have in coming to terms with the dilemmas of their culture and time. Psychological disorders require not only an understanding in term of individual factors, but also an interpretation that is social and ultimately political. It is my hope that this work will make a contribution to the understanding of these larger relationships, over and above any light that it throws on the specific question of eating disorders.

Because of the overall focus in this book, I have not devoted a great deal of attention to questions of the practical treatment of eating disorders, except in so far as such considerations are relevant to their social and cultural context. There are now a number of good articles and books on the treatment of anorexia and bulimia, the most comprehensive of which is the *Handbook of Psychotherapy for Anorexia Nervosa and Bulimia*, edited by David Garner and Paul Garfinkel. Study of this impressive volume will afford the reader an idea of the enormous scope of new treatment approaches and ideas in this field. From my own standpoint, I will be happy if a reading of my book will deepen the awareness of the practicing clinician of the importance of the social and cultural background of eating disorders. I think it is not too pretentious to hope that such awareness will implicitly affect one's approach to treatment and thinking about patients' problems; this has certainly been my experience.

A few words about terminology are in order. Technically, the precise nomenclature for the disorders that are the subject of this book are anorexia nervosa and bulimia nervosa. For the sake of readability, I sometimes refer simply to anorexia or bulimia. Strictly speaking, anorexia is a symptom (loss of appetite) that occurs in a number of psychiatric or medical conditions other than anorexia nervosa, especially depression. In this book, the term anorexia is always used as a shorthand for anorexia nervosa, unless otherwise specified. Similar considerations apply to the use of the term bulimia, which otherwise could have a number of meanings.

When it comes to referring to individuals with these problems, I have sometimes employed the terms "anorexics" or "bulimics" as a plural form. I wish it to be understood that in so doing, it is my least wish to imply a uniformity in these patients as individuals. It is true that the clinical symptoms of eating disorders are remarkably similar from one patient to the next; nevertheless, as individuals, they show an enormous diversity. As we have known since the "anti-psychiatry" critiques of the 1960s, there is an unfortunate de-individuating tendency in psychiatric terminology, which if misused can lead to pernicious consequences. My use of the terminology "anorexics" and "bulimics" is therefore strictly a matter of convenience. I profoundly hope that no one with these symptoms will be offended by it.

Finally, a word about the sensitive question of gender-linked pronouns. Throughout this book, I refer to anorexic or bulimic patients as "she." This is in large part a reflection of the overwhelming preponderance of female sufferers, a fact which is in and of itself of considerable sociocultural significance. Secondarily, I wish to avoid the awkwardness of such usages as the repetitive "he or she" or, worse, "he/she." However, I wish to make it clear at the outset that I am fully aware of the significant numbers of males with these problems, and once again sincerely hope that my use of the generic "she" will not leave them feeling discounted.

Acknowledgments

For more than two decades, Bard College has provided an ideal environment in which to exchange ideas with colleagues and students and to complete the major undertaking of a second edition despite the demands of a heavy teaching schedule. In particular, thanks go to Leon Botstein, President of Bard College, who at the outset gave enthusiastic support to the entire idea of a sociocultural analysis of anorexia nervosa and helped me gain release time from my teaching duties to make headway on the project. I would also like to thank Stuart Levine, Dean of the College, and friend and colleague, for support and advice. Thanks go to the many faculty colleagues, too numerous to mention, who supported my intellectual endeavors and are always willing to exchange ideas, and who constantly confirm the benefits of working at a small college with an open intellectual environment. Thanks in particular go to my psychology colleagues, especially Frank Oja, for enthusiastic support of my work and the time that it took as well as for stimulating discussions about psychology over the years. Thanks also to Mark Lytle for sharing his accumulated wisdom about publishing.

Others at Bard made particular contributions to the preparation of this manuscript. In particular, the library staff, particularly Jane Hyrshko but also others who have managed interlibrary loans, were almost always able to secure material for me, even from obscure journals. I would like to thank the many student assistants over the years who helped me get ahold of large amounts of material from the library and generally assisted me, especially Jennifer Ozols, Angela Bardeen, and Beata Papp. Special thanks to Beata Papp, also, for undertaking the arduous labor of recoding the footnotes in the first edition so that new references could be inserted into the second. I am very grateful to the numerous students who took a seminar in eating disorders with me almost every year over the past several years. Your questions and contributions helped shape the thinking that went into this volume.

I would like to thank the many colleagues from all over the world, too numerous to mention, whom I have continued to meet and discuss ideas with at conferences on eating disorders. Particular thanks to Leigh Cohn for his courage in starting a journal in the 1990s (*Eating Disorders: The Journal of Treatment and Prevention*) that focuses to a considerable extent on sociocultural factors in eating disorders. Thanks also to Melanie Katzman for inviting me to write the introductory chapter in a book entitled *Neurobiology in the Treatment of Eating Disorders*, edited by herself, Hans Hoek, and Janet Treasure. To be able to contribute a sociocultural chapter in such a collection was a personal honor as well as an intellectual innovation. I would like to thank the many individuals who sent me correspondence, published papers, and preprints on eating disorders from all over the world, which helped greatly, especially in writing the third chapter of this book. These include Sing Lee (Hong Kong), Chris Szabo (South Africa), Fernando Fernandez-Aranda (Spain), Armando Barriguete (Mexico), Daniel Gomez Duper (Argentina), and Giovanni Maria Ruggiero (Italy). Thanks to Harrison Pope for sending me material on muscle dysmorphia and eating disorders in males. Thanks also to Ruth Striegel-Moore for sending me reprints on her research on such various topics as eating disorders in blacks, weight concerns among lesbians, and the prevention of eating disorders. Special thanks to Anne Becker for sharing results of her research on Fiji prior to its publication.

My deepest gratitude is to all the people at Blackwell Publishers who helped to make this second edition possible. In particular, thanks to Alison Mudditt, who responded enthusiastically to my idea for a second edition and saw to it that the work was commissioned. Thanks to Martin Davies, the chief editor who oversaw the whole process, encouraged me to get the work done without pressuring me, and was always enthusiastic about my progress. Thanks to Alison Dunnett for overseeing the entire editorial process and giving clear guidelines about what was needed. And special thanks to Jenny Tyler, who not only has been an outstanding copy editor, but sensitively understood the content of the book and the nuances of the arguments and encouraged me to be clear in those places where clarity was wanting. Finally, thanks to Stella Welford, for helping to make my work familiar to an international audience by securing translations of the first edition into French, Italian, Hebrew, and Spanish.

Acknowledgments

As in the first edition, thanks goes once again to the many patients with eating disorders with whom I have the opportunity to work over the years. The struggles that you have shared with me have greatly deepened the insight that I have been able to achieve in this topic. You must remain forever anonymous, but my gratitude and respect is profound.

Finally this work would never have been completed at all without the loving support and understanding of Patti Hill Gordon, who understood and accepted the enormous investment of time and energy that a task like this requires. Thanks also to my daughters Corinne and Alexa, who have always been a great source of support and pride.

The author and publishers gratefully acknowledge the copyright holders who have given permission to reproduce copyright material. Original publication details of excerpted material are given below.

Excerpt from Roland Barthes quoted on p. 117 originally appeared in Roland Barthes, *Roland Barthes*, New York: Hill and Wang, a Division of Farrar, Straus and Giroux, 1977, p. 36.

Excerpt from P. J. V. Beumont quoted on p. 31 originally appeared in P. J. V. Beumont, "Endocrine function in magersucht disorders," in K. M. Pirke and D. Ploog (eds), *The Psychobiology of Anorexia Nervosa*, New York: Springer-Verlag, 1984, p. 121. Copyright © by Springer-Verlag Berlin Heidelberg, 1984.

Excerpt from Hilde Bruch quoted on p. 94 originally appeared in Hilde Bruch, "Four decades of eating disorders," in D. M. Garner and P. E. Garfinkel (eds), *Handbook of Psychotherapy for Anorexia Nervosa and Bulimia*, New York: Guilford Press, 1985, p. 9. Reprinted by permission of Guilford Press.

Excerpt from Hilde Bruch quoted on p. 171 originally appeared in Hilde Bruch, *Conversations with Anorexics*, New York, Basic Books, 1988, p. 150.

Excerpt from George Devereux quoted on p. 166 originally appeared in George Devereux, *Basic Problems of Ethnopsychiatry*, Chicago: University of Chicago Press, 1980, p. 29. Copyright © 1980 by George Devereux.

Excerpt from Rebecca Dresser quoted on p. 273 originally appeared in "Feeding the hunger artists: Legal issues in treating anorexia nervosa"

Acknowledgments

by Rebecca Dresser, *Wisconsin Law Review*, 2 (1984), p. 374. Copyright © 1984 by The Board of Regents of the University of Wisconsin System; reprinted by permission of the Wisconsin Law Review.

Excerpt from Sonni Efron quoted on p. 82 originally appeared in Sonni Efron, "Eating disorders go global," *Los Angeles Times*, Oct. 18, 1997, pp. A1, A9. Copyright © 1997, *Los Angeles Times*. Reprinted by permission.

Excerpt from Kathryn Harrison quoted on p. 189 originally appeared in Kathryn Harrison, *The Kiss*, New York: Random House, 1997, p. 41. Copyright © 1997 by Kathryn Harrison.

Excerpt from Marya Hornbacher quoted on p. 117 originally appeared in Marya Hornbacher, *Wasted: A Memoir of Anorexia and Bulimia*, New York: HarperCollins Publishers, Inc., 1998, p. 25. Copyright © 1998 by Marya Hornbacher-Beard. Reprinted by permission of HarperCollins Publishers, Inc.

Excerpt from Harrison G. Pope, Jr. and James I. Hudson quoted on pp. 42–3 originally appeared in Harrison G. Pope, Jr., M.D. and James I. Hudson, M.D., *New Hope for Binge Eaters*, New York: Harper and Row, 1984. Copyright © 1984 by Harrison G. Pope, Jr., M.D. and James I. Hudson, M.D. Reprinted by permission of HarperCollins Publishers, Inc.

Excerpt from Hillel Schwartz quoted on p. 140 originally appeared in Hillel Schwartz, *Never Satisfied: A Cultural History of Diets, Fantasies and Fat*, New York: Macmillan, 1986.

Excerpts from George Sheehan quoted on pp. 162–3 originally appeared in George Sheehan, *Running and Being: The Total Experience*, New York: Warner Books, 1978.

Excerpt from Irving Yalom quoted on p. 140 originally appeared in Irving Yalom, *Love's Executioner and Other Tales of Psychotherapy*, New York: Basic Books, 1989, pp. 87–8.

Every effort has been made to contact copyright holders. The publishers apologize for any errors or omissions in the above list and would be grateful to be notified of any corrections that should be incorporated in the next edition or reprint of this book.

Chapter One

Culture and Psychopathology

The Notion of an Ethnic Disorder

"The fact is that in all periods of history, mental disturbances of epidemiological significance or special fascination highlight a specific aspect of man's nature in conflict with 'the times'. . . ."[1] In the waning years of the nineteenth century, medical doctors, neurologists, and psychiatrists in Western Europe and the United States were preoccupied with a mysterious "nervous disease" that occurred mainly in women, called hysteria.[2] Hysteria was a puzzling and elusive disorder which manifested itself through a bewildering variety of somatic symptoms: paralyses, sensory disturbances such as blindness, fainting spells, even seizures. It had been known throughout recorded history, as early as ancient Egypt and later in Greece, but it had always lived a kind of shadowy existence.[3] But suddenly, in the second half of the nineteenth century, it seemed to burst onto the scene, into the forefront of medical controversy and public discussion. Although solid statistics are clearly lacking, available evidence does suggest that in fact the prevalence of hysteria during the nineteenth century actually increased, and that its heightened visibility was not simply a consequence of the increased attention that was being paid to it.[4] By the late nineteenth century, according to numerous observers, the cities in Western Europe and the United States were full of neurotics, and among these the female patients were mostly hysterics.

To clinicians in the nineteenth century, hysteria presented an exceedingly complex and baffling set of clinical problems. The symptoms were apparently physical, and indeed they often began with real physical ailments or injuries; and yet unlike typical physical symptoms, they were remarkably transient and seemed to be linked to psychological factors and emotional distress. Physical examination of patients did not in gen-

1

eral reveal pathology in local neurological systems that could account for dramatic symptoms such as paralyses and anaesthesias. More and more, psychological factors such as trauma, emotional distress, and psychological conflict were emphasized in clinical thinking, a trend that culminated in the emergence of psychoanalysis itself as a clinical discipline.[5] But what is more, hysteria was very much a social illness, a highly patterned vehicle for the expression of female distress, one that involved a significant degree of role-playing and interpersonal manipulation. Indeed these latter factors led some to doubt the reality of "hysterical complaints," a position which still has its advocates today.[6] In any case, the very character of hysterical symptoms was highly in keeping with the needs and style of the era in which they were prevalent, a period in which neurotic anxieties could still not be directly acknowledged and one in which the high drama of hysterical fainting and choking fits had credibility. Soon after the turn of the century, the prevalence of hysteria appeared to decline dramatically, and it seems clear that its eclipse was a function of the dramatic social transformations that accompanied the dawn of the twentieth century. These included significant changes in the status of women, but also an increasing degree of psychological sophistication in the general culture that assimilated the possibility that symptoms that were apparently physical could be "psychosomatic."[7]

In the second half of the twentieth century, another previously obscure disorder, which had been familiar to a small number of medical specialists for at least 100 years but which had been virtually unknown to the public, suddenly burst into public view. Anorexia nervosa, a puzzling and dangerous affliction in which a young person, typically an adolescent female, mercilessly starves herself, had been formally identified as a disease in both London and Paris during the 1870s.[8] Like hysteria, it also may have existed, although in guises that were not strictly medical, for centuries before; and also like hysteria, the characteristic behaviors may have at one point been described in terms of the language of the sacred and the spiritual.[9] In any case, by the early 1970s, anorexia nervosa had already been the subject of an extensive psychiatric literature stretching back to its modern discovery in the 1870s, and probably out of all proportion to the number of cases actually seen by practitioners.[10] It was described by one writer as a "curiousity and a rarity"; psychiatrists instructed residents that it would be unusual to see more than a small number of cases in the course of a lifetime. On the other hand, the spectacle of a young woman starving herself, sometimes to death, was enough to command intense practical and theoretical medical interest.

By the mid-1970s, though, anorexia nervosa suddenly became widely known to the American public, and by the next decade, along with its sister disorder bulimia nervosa, was being described in psychiatric publications as well as the popular press in terms such as the "psychiatric disorder of the '80s." During the late 1970s and early 1980s, anorexia nervosa was widely publicized, glamorized, and to some extent romanticized. Language such as "disorder of the '80s" reflects the fact that in the era of modern media, diseases, and particularly psychiatric disorders, can easily become fashionable and popularized, and this was indeed the case for anorexia nervosa (and to a lesser extent bulimia). Nevertheless, statistical studies as well as the experience of practitioners made it clear that anorexia nervosa had sharply increased in prevalence, in both its mild and more severe forms (a point that will be documented in the third chapter of this book). Public awareness about anorexia nervosa reached something of a high point in the early 1980s with the widely publicized death through cardiac arrest of the popular singer Karen Carpenter. Carpenter's death, which was associated with the abuse of the over-the-counter drug Ipecac, a potent emetic, thrust the shocking, self-destructive aspects of the illness starkly into public consciousness, as images of her gaunt face haunted the front pages of newspapers in the United States.

By the early 1980s, a related problem also suddenly came to public and professional attention – the eating disorder called bulimia, or bulimia nervosa. Bulimia, a pattern of binge eating followed by purging (typically self-induced vomiting), had been known by psychiatrists specializing in the treatment of anorexia to occur in the advanced stages of anorexia nervosa; however, beginning in the mid-1970s, a large number of young women (typically college students) were described who were caught in a cycle of bingeing and purging, but without the drastic weight loss that was characteristic of anorexia nervosa.[11] Similar to anorexics, though, bulimics were known to idealize thinness and to be terrified of becoming fat. Bulimia first came to widespread public notoriety in the United States through a spate of articles in the popular press, including an article in the *New York Times* in 1981 describing a study that had documented a virtual epidemic of the disorder on a campus of the State University of New York.[12] Bulimia nervosa, particularly in the form that it now presents itself, was little known prior to the 1970s, even among psychiatrists. Although the term had been used in the French literature ("la boulimie") as early as the eighteenth century to describe a pattern of overeating, and binge eating syndromes had been described throughout the nineteenth and twentieth centuries, the pattern of binge eating and attempts to compensate through purging in order to prevent weight gain is most likely a new pattern, unique to the late twentieth century. While it is clearly related in some way to anorexia nervosa (and indeed one of the first papers on the new syndrome described it as an "ominous variant of anorexia nervosa"[13]), it has become clear that it is a unique syndrome in its own right. Initial confusion about how to characterize it led to a variety of proposed names, including bulimarexia, dietary chaos syndrome, binge-purge syndrome, or simply bulimia. The term bulimia nervosa, which was initially proposed by Russell in 1979, was finally adopted by the American Psychiatric Association DSM-III-R in 1987. Most epidemiological surveys reveal bulimia nervosa to be more common than anorexia nervosa, and the weight of the evidence suggests that the incidence and prevalence of the disorder increased dramatically in the late 1970s and early 1980s (see chapter 3).

Anorexia nervosa and bulimia nervosa are termed eating disorders, and they do in fact involve abnormal patterns of eating. Nevertheless, the term eating disorder may be something of a misnomer or at least leaves out a critical element: the most central feature of these disorders is the intense pursuit of thinness and a virtually morbid dread of becoming fat. In any case, undoubtedly in response to their rising incidence, professional interest in the eating disorders grew exponentially in the 1970s and 1980s, beginning with the publication of Hilde Bruch's book *Eating Disorders* in 1973.[14] Bruch, a German-born American psychiatrist who emigrated to the United States in 1934, had been treating anorexic patients since the 1940s.[15] Her book was initially known exclusively to a psychiatric audience, although the significance of her work was already appreciated. Five years later, though, Bruch published a book for a wider readership, *The Golden Cage*, and it has been suggested that this work did much to familiarize the public with anorexia nervosa.[16] In any case, during the 1970s and 1980s, the number of clinical and research publications on eating disorders increased explosively. In 1982, a journal totally devoted to research on anorexia and bulimia, the *International Journal of Eating Disorders*, began publication; and since its inception, the number of articles appearing in it annually has grown rapidly. To give some idea of the proliferation of professional literature, a survey of the Medline index of medical literature indicated that the number of articles per year grew from 59 in 1972 to 161 in 1982.[17] This number has continued to rise rapidly throughout the 1980s and 1990s, to the point where well over 500 articles are published annually on these subjects. In the 1990s, an Academy for Eating Disorders was founded in the United States, whose members are practicing professionals as well as academic researchers. The Academy now sponsors the bi-annual International Conference on Eating Disorders held in New York City, which typically draws upward of several hundred professionals from over 20 countries worldwide. A similar conference is held in London bi-annually.

Given the increasing number of sufferers from anorexia or bulimia, the demand for treatment services, on both an inpatient and outpatient basis, has grown exponentially. Even as late as the end of the decade of the 1960s, only a small number of hospitals in the United States and Europe were known to have any experience or interest in the treatment of anorexic patients. By the mid-1980s, inpatient units devoted exclusively to the treatment of eating disorders, or at least having some specific accommodation for anorexic patients, had grown in number. In 1984, a residential facility exclusively devoted to the treatment of eating disorders opened its doors in the Philadelphia area.[18] In addition, however, therapists working in the community found themselves besieged with patients seeking help. This was especially true at university counseling centers in the US and the UK, as eating disorders on college campuses had truly become something of an epidemic by the early 1980s.[19] Most psychotherapists, whatever their training, had little or no experience or understanding of eating disorders, and found themselves confronted with symptoms that were highly intractable to familiar counseling methods. Treatment techniques developed in an atmosphere of ferment especially during the 1980s, in exciting and creative directions.[20] During the 1990s, however, at least in the United States, the treatment of eating disorders was severely affected by the increasingly stringent economic realities of health care. With hospital stays increasingly limited and outpatient psychotherapy services sharply curtailed, the ability of health care professionals to provide adequate care for eating-disordered patients has been significantly diminished.[21]

The ascendancy of eating disorders has also given rise to the emergence of self-help organizations devoted to patient and family support as well as education. Typically founded by recovered patients or a family member, these lay organizations provide referrals, support groups for families and patients, and newsletters with recent information about treatment. Some of the largest and most influential of these are the American Anorexia Nervosa Association, based in New York City; the National Association of Anorexia Nervosa and Associated Disorders, in Highland Park, Illinois; Anorexia Nervosa and Related Eating Disorders, in Eugene, Oregon; and in England, the Eating Disorders Association, in Norwich. Self-help support systems have become influential in their own right, and they reach large numbers of sufferers; and while the contemporary trend towards self-help extends far beyond the eating disorders, the very existence of these organizations for anorexia nervosa and bulimia suggests the extent to which such disorders have become a pervasive social concern.

In this book I am interested in the contemporary increase in eating disorders as not only a clinical, but also a cultural problem. Just as hysteria was a symptom of its times, one that expressed crises of identity in women in a form that was compatible with the cultural milieu of the late nineteenth century, so eating disorders have become a critical expression of dilemmas of female identity of our own time, in a period of very significant cultural transition for women. But it would be inaccurate to assert that eating disorders are simply a modern version of hysteria, both on clinical and cultural grounds. With respect to the latter, they stem from a very different set of issues to those that confronted women in the nineteenth century, and what is more they draw on a "vocabulary of discomfort" that is very much conditioned by the cultural milieu of the present.[22] In order to get a better handle on the problem, we need a framework to understand the interaction of culture, history, and psychopathology. For this purpose, I will utilize a set of concepts that have been in the literature for 40 years, but have been little utilized – the ideas of the psychoanalyst and anthropologist George Devereux. And in particular, I will utilize Devereux's specific ideas about how certain disorders become a core expression of the stresses and tensions of a particular culture or historical period – the notion of an "ethnic disorder."

Culture-bound Syndromes: The Notion of an Ethnic Disorder

The extensive writings of George Devereux on the complex relationship between culture and psychopathology have been little known to or assimilated by the psychiatric community, never mind a broader audience. And yet his work, which spanned five decades, was not only of enormous scope, but offered many seminal insights into the relationships between culture, the individual, and mental disorder, interdisciplinary problems that few have had the courage to tackle.[23] A key problem that fascinated Devereux was the relationship between the normal and the abnormal, and particularly the way in which certain psychological disorders express the core anxieties and unresolved problems of a culture. And central in his exploration of these relationships was the concept of an "ethnic disorder."

The notion of ethnic disorder was introduced by Devereux in one of his most important and provocative essays, published in 1955, on the subject of the relation of the abnormal to the normal, and then elaborated in a later application of the concept to the cultural significance of schizophrenia.[24] In the initial essay, Devereux focused on what have been known as "exotic syndromes" or "folk illnesses" – patterns of psychopathology that had been discovered by ethnologists in non-Western societies and which did not seem to be like any of the known psychiatric disorders in the West. These so-called "culture-bound syndromes" included the likes of *Amok* (a disorder of homicidal violence that occurred mainly in Southeast Asia), *Latah* (a trance-like "fright-syndrome" that was found among women in the South Pacific), and *Koro* (a syndrome that involved a delusion in a man of a receding penis, especially prevalent in southern China).[25] But Devereux's interest extended beyond the exotic topic of folk illnesses and into the domain of Western psychopathology, as was evident in his application of the concept of ethnic disorder to schizophrenia and obsessive-compulsive disorders, as they are found in the West. Devereux was a student of Greek tragedy, of religion, and of physics; ultimately, he viewed psychopathology as a way to unravel the mysteries and paradoxes of culture itself.

By the term "ethnic," Devereux meant not the narrow sense of this term as in "ethnic group" or "subculture," but rather "of a culture" or "pertaining centrally to a culture." The term ethnic disorder is probably preferable to the more frequently employed "culture-bound syndrome," a term which implies that a disorder is unique to a particular society and carries the further implication of an exotic disorder in an unfamiliar (that is, non-Western) culture. In a sense, as some have pointed out, virtually all psychiatric disorders are culture-bound, to the extent that classification systems themselves are governed by cultural modes of thought.[26] An ethnic disorder, on the other hand, is a pattern that, because of its own dynamics, has come to express crucial contradictions and core anxieties of a society. In his essays on the subject, Deveurex enumerated a number of key criteria that qualify a particular syndrome as an ethnic disorder, which we can summarize as follows:

1 The disorder occurs frequently in the culture in question, particularly relative to other psychiatric disorders.
2 Because of the continuity of the symptoms and underlying dynamics with the normal elements of the culture, the disorder expresses itself in degrees of intensity, and in a spectrum of borderline, "subclinical" forms.
3 The disorder expresses core conflicts and psychological tensions that are pervasive in the culture, but are so acute in the person who develops symptoms that severe anxiety is generated and psychological defenses mobilized.
4 The disorder is a final common pathway for the expression of a wide variety of idiosyncratic personal problems and psychological distress; people who develop the disorder can range from mildly to severely disturbed.
5 The symptoms of the disorder are direct extensions and exaggerations of normal behaviors and attitudes within the culture, often including behaviors that are usually highly valued.
6 The disorder is a highly patterned and widely imitated model for the expression of distress; it is a template of deviance, a "pattern of misconduct," providing individuals with an acceptable means of being irrational, deviant, or crazy.
7 Finally, because the disorder draws upon valued behaviors, but on the other hand is an expression of deviance, it elicits highly ambivalent responses from others: awe and respect, perhaps, but also punitive and controlling reactions to deviance. The disorder gains notoriety in the culture; it generates its own "politics."

Some Examples of Ethnic Disorders

In order to illustrate the concept of an ethnic disorder, I will discuss a few non-Western and then Western examples.

Amok is a pattern of homicidal violence that occurs among men in Malaysia, Indonesia, and New Guinea.[27] It was considered to be rather common by early ethnological observers, and although it has declined considerably in the twentieth century with the inexorable transformations brought about by a modernizing industrial economy, a few cases are still reported.[28] The explosive madness of the *Amok* usually occurs in response to an insult or an accumulation of small stresses: following an initial period of withdrawal and brooding, the subject strikes out indiscriminately against strangers and kin, often killing a number of people during an episode, and then finally lapsing into exhaustion and amnesia. During the attack, the *Amok* would typically run through the streets and countryside – hence the phrase "running amok" – and it was typical for villages and towns to keep a lance-like weapon permanently in public places in the event of encountering an "*Amok* runner."

The dynamics of *Amok* have been discussed in an analysis by John E. Carr. He suggests that the behavior is a response to a culture that demands a high degree of control over aggression and deference to authority.[29] What is more, Malaysian culture is characterized by a high degree of linguistic and cognitive ambiguity: behavioral expectations are highly explicit, and yet communication is shrouded in vagueness and abstraction. Carr suggests that *Amok* can be thought of as an "escape hatch" or "loophole" for a man who experiences intolerable distress and has no other way of discharging enormous pent-up aggression that is acutely exacerbated following an insult. The term *Amok* itself is derived from the war cry of the ferocious Malaysian medieval warrior, a revered and heroic figure in the cultural mythology. The symbolism of *Amok* is a principal reason why this pattern is a template of deviance in this culture: it is actually patterned after behaviors that are highly esteemed in the cultural traditions. Of course, it goes without saying that the behavior is greatly feared and draws an equally violent or coercive societal response. Interestingly, *Amok* also has political implications, at least historically. Early observers noted that *Amok* was considered to be an instrument of social protest against rulers who had abused their authority. It was thought of, as Carr noted, as the "ultimate veto" that each man could use as a last resort against despotic control.[30]

Even today, it has been suggested that *Amok* is given tacit social approbation – much as "Jesse James has a certain following in the United States," as one observer put it. In fact, a recent Malaysian prime minister, prior to taking office, cautioned that if Malays were made to feel disenfranchised by Chinese and Indian citizens, they might retaliate by running amok.[31]

A second example is that of *Koro*, the "shrinking-penis syndrome," found typically in men primarily in coastal southern China and other areas of the Far East.[32] The symptom is typically a delusion that the penis is receding into the abdomen, and is accompanied by feelings of panic and anxiety about impending death. The syndrome is found less commonly among females, in whom the prominent anxiety is nipple retraction or breast damage.[33] It has been suggested that the cultural origins of the symptom may have to do with sexual anxieties, particularly those that center around the masculine sense of potency, as well as archaic medical beliefs about the fatal consequences of genital retraction. The disorder is likely to occur in a neurotic individual who has suffered a blow to his self-esteem and confidence.[34] *Koro* has some interesting parallels to anorexia nervosa, in that it involves a virtually delusional sense of a bodily transformation (in the case of anorexia, that of "becoming fat") that is triggered by a blow to self-esteem. It is also of interest that this predominantly male syndrome involves a fear of becoming "smaller," while the overwhelmingly female disorder, anorexia nevosa, is centered around a dread of becoming "larger." Incidentally, like many so-called culture-bound syndromes, *Koro* also occurs in modern Western patients, although rarely. Only in the Asian subcontinent or in Southeast Asia, however, where particular culturally patterned anxieties prevail, is it an ethnic disorder.

For a Western example, we can return to nineteenth-century hysteria, with which we began this chapter. In an important paper on hysteria, the sociologist Carol Smith-Rosenberg proposed that the disorder expressed the core cultural dilemmas and social contradictions experienced by nineteenth-century women, particularly those in the middle and upper classes.[35] These included the requirement to be exaggeratedly feminine and ornamentally sexual, while at the same time being expected to follow a morally repressive and hypocritical sexual code of behavior.[36] Also, though, while much sentimental value was placed on feminine frailty, women were expected to be a beacon of moral strength, and assume total responsibility for the home and childrearing. The Industrial Revolution had served to make the middle-class woman peripheral and exclude her from public life; she was expected to accept her destiny as male helper, manager of domestic affairs, and the bearer and rearer of children. The hysterical women dramatized her power-lessness as well as her repressed sexuality through her symptoms, whose illness-like character gave her some power to passively control and manipulate her immediate situation. Hysterical symptoms exaggerated the stereotypes of femininity: they were dramatic, emotional, and con-formed to the idea of female vulnerability and weaknesses. Hysteria was clearly a social pattern, a template, a model. The symptoms were com-monly acquired through imitation, and they had a distinctly "conta-gious" character. They were a kind of exaggeration of a theatrical dramatic style that had become *au courant* in the urban cultures of Western Europe.[37] The fashionability of hysteria was reflected in the considerable notoriety the disorder attained. It was entertainment, an art form; in the 1920s, the Surrealists celebrated the "fiftieth anniver-sary of hysteria." But it also involved politics, specifically sexual politics: it offered women an opportunity to protest indirectly against male dominance. Some interpretations have even suggested that hysteria was a kind of proto-feminist revolt.[38]

As a final example, Devereux suggested that schizophrenia is a proto-type of a Western "ethnic psychosis." Devereux suggested that traits such as schizoid withdrawal and aloofness, as well as segmentation, fragmentation, affectlessness, and the blurring of reality and fantasy, were all characteristic traits of modern societies. Devereux argued that schizophrenia occurs rarely, if at all, in societies relatively uninfluenced by Western civilization.[39] While there is some evidence for this asser-tion – schizophrenia, for example, has not been detected in the remote areas of the New Guinea highlands, whereas it has a substantial inci-dence in the more industrialized area of Port Moresby – a World Health Organization study in the 1970s found schizophrenia to be widely prevalent in virtually all urban areas of the world.[40] It is increas-ingly difficult to think of schizophrenia as a culture-reactive syndrome, given the mounting evidence of the centrality of biological factors in its etiology. Nevertheless, particularly in the era of the 1960s, schizophre-nia assumed a number of symbolic meanings that gave it (temporarily) the status of an ethnic disorder. For one thing, the experience of drug-induced psychosis, which was commonplace in the 1960s, led many to readily identify with the altered state of consciousness and the transcen-dental experiences of many schizophrenics. But furthermore, the schizo-phrenic was perceived as the ultimate victim of a society in which supposedly sane people (that is, political leaders) were behaving quite crazily, a world in which the boundaries of sanity and madness were blurred. Thus the schizophrenic became a culture hero, a trend which found its ultimate expression in works such as Laing's *The Politics of Experience,* which was not only a book about schizophrenia but which served as a cultural manifesto of the period.[41] The interesting aspect of all this is that the societal turmoil of the 1960s probably had little to do with the etiology of schizophrenia. But in a symbolic sense, schizophrenia had taken on the status of an ethnic disorder.

Eating Disorders as Ethnic Disorders

In this book, we will explore the sociocultural factors underlying the ascendancy of eating disorders in our own time, using the notion of an ethnic disorder as a framework. Like hysteria, anorexia nervosa expresses symptomatically the contradictions of female identity of the present, although the nature of the problems has changed considerably since the nineteenth century. Unlike the hysteric, the anorexic does not so much mimic a physical illness (although she may move into an illness role eventually), but manipulates her food intake and becomes obsessive about her body shape and weight. Anorexics and bulimics draw upon the common cultural vocabulary of their time, through latching onto the contemporary mania about dieting, thinness, and food control that have become endemic to the advanced industrial societies. They utilize these cultural preoccupations as defenses that enable them to escape from – and achieve some sense of control over – unmanageable personal distress, most of which revolves around issues of identity. Again, similar to hysteria, anorexia and bulimia are socially patterned, the fashionable style of achieving specialness through deviance. And like hysteria, these disorders generate fascination and repugnance, simply because they are so closely tied to social contradictions experienced by all. Eating disorders are also ultimately political, since they are so closely connected with the issue of the control of the female body and the conformation to prevailing standards of beauty. Like hysteria, then, eating disorders partake in sexual politics, and they have also been taken up in the name of the feminist cause.

These are the themes that we will be exploring throughout this book. In the following chapter, we will look more closely at anorexia nervosa and bulimia as clinical disorders, and provide an overview of contemporary research on etiology and treatment. In chapter 3, the incidence and prevalence of these disorders in different countries and social groups will be examined. Chapter 4 will focus on the issue of female identity, which I will argue is at the center of the psychological conflicts underlying the eating disorders. Chapters 5 and 6 will focus on the ideal of thinness and the closely related problem of obesity, respectively, both of which are crucial to understanding the increasing incidence of eating disorders. In chapter 7, the notion that eating disorders are spread throughout the culture by a kind of psychosocial contagion will be examined. Finally, chapter 8 will take up the issue of the "politics" of eating disorders, specifically the notion that these disorders represent a particular expression of powerlessness and that the response to these patients – as well as the cultural imagery surrounding their symptoms – is conditioned by a recognition of the peculiar combination of rebellion and conformity that they express.

Chapter Two

Eating Disorders

Anorexia Nervosa and Bulimia Nervosa

*I do not remember that I did ever in all my practice see one that was
conversant with the living so much wasted . . .*

Richard Morton, *Phthisiologica*

*Vomunt et edant, edunt et vomant
(They vomit to eat, and eat to vomit)*

Seneca, *Ad Marnan*, xix

In the popular consciousness, anorexia nervosa is something relatively
new. Indeed, the disorder was unheard of by all but a few medical
specialists prior to the 1970s, when it suddenly became widely known.
But in fact, as a clinical entity, the history of anorexia nervosa probably
extends back as far as three centuries. In 1689, Richard Morton, a
religious nonconformist and English physician, reported in a massive
treatise on consumption two cases of a "wasting" disease of nervous
origins that should be considered as the first clear medical description
of anorexia nervosa. The chief symptoms described by Morton were a
radical wasting (i.e., weight loss) and loss of appetite that were not
accompanied by other typical symptoms of consumption (for example,
fever and coughing), which Morton attributed to "sadness and anxious
cares." The first patient, one "Mr. Duke's daughter," Morton described as an 18-year-old girl who was given to "continual poring upon
Books" despite her evident emaciation and was indifferent to the ex-

14

treme cold of an abnormally severe winter. Like many modern patients, the girl refused offers of treatment (which consisted of the likes of cloves bruised in wine, and stomach plasters), and soon after died following a fainting fit. Morton noted a "total suppression of her Monthly Courses from a multitude of Cares and Passions of her Mind." The second patient was a 16-year-old boy, whose "want of appetite" Morton directly attributed to "studying too hard" as well as the "passions of his mind." However, the boy followed Morton's advice to abandon his studies and pursue his health in the country, upon which he "recovered his health in great measure."[1]

Anorexia nervosa was only rarely mentioned in scattered medical reports over the next two centuries, although there were a number of "fasting girls" who achieved considerable public notoriety in England and continental Europe and who may have represented a kind of quasi-religious precursor of the condition.[2] But it suddenly became the focus of intense medical attention and controversy in the latter half of the nineteenth century, when Sir William Gull in London, and Charles Lasegue, a Parisian neurologist, simultaneously published papers in the early 1870s on a number of cases of a pattern of self-starvation that is now clearly recognizable as anorexia nervosa.[3] Gull, in fact, invented the term anorexia nervosa to distinguish the disorder, which he argued resulted from a "morbid mental state," from tuberculosis; whereas Lasegue, although clearly describing the same condition, clung to the tradition of subsuming all female neurotic disorders under the umbrella of "hysteria." These early writers noted what have become familiar hallmarks of anorexia nervosa. Gull, for example, marveled at the hyperactivity and excessive energy of his patients (all of whom were female), despite their starved condition; while Lasegue made keen observations about the anorexic's typical denial, her peculiar attitudes towards food, and her pathological family interactions. It is interesting to speculate whether Gull and Lasegue's simultaneous discoveries were responses to an actual sudden increase in the number of cases of the disorder, or whether they were redefining behaviors or symptoms that were already prevalent but had just gone unrecognized. This question bedevils virtually all discussions of psychiatric epidemiology, and is, in the absence of more solid data, essentially unanswerable. Nevertheless, it is at least plausible, on historical grounds, that there was in fact an actual increase in the prevalence of the condition at the time. Along these lines, the medical historian Edward Shorter suggested that a "first great increase in anorexia nervosa" took place as early as the beginning of the nineteenth century and reached a kind of plateau at the beginning of the twentieth century: "It was from this plateau of middling frequency in 1900 that anorexia took off in the 1960s to achieve the epidemic status it has today."[4]

The nineteenth-century literature after Gull and Lasegue made numerous references to anorexia nervosa. For example, the English physician William Playfair commented in 1888 that "I have had of late years abundant opportunities for treating many interesting cases of this kind" and they "were of very common occurrence."[5] In 1896, Freud made a passing comment to the "widespread anorexia in young girls," a phenomenon that he was soon to attribute to a sort of melancholia due to sexual underdevelopment.[6] The French neurologist Gilles de la Tourette, who is of course famous for the discovery of the tic disorder that is named after him, had seen a number of cases of anorexia nervosa and foreshadowed Hilde Bruch's categorization of anorexia nervosa into a primary and secondary type, with the primary characterized by not a loss of appetite but a determined refusal to eat.[7]

Interest in anorexia nervosa continued into the first decade of the twentieth century, particularly in France. The French psychiatrists Dejerine and Gaukler, who also attempted to distinguish between a primary and secondary form of anorexia nervosa and whose description of the primary form is eminently recognizable, commented in their textbook, which appeared in English translation in 1913, that "mental anorexia is a fact of frequent occurrence" which physicians misdiagnose at the patient's peril.[8] Pierre Janet, a French psychiatrist once considered Freud's rival but generally forgotten (although experiencing something of a revival in the late twentieth century at least among certain psychiatrists interested in post-traumatic stress disorders and dissociation), reported on a number of cases between 1903 and 1909. The most interesting of these was "Nadia," who dreaded the "fleshiness" of the female body and expressed an aversion to the female role. Janet also distinguished between a primary and secondary type of anorexia nervosa, the first of which showed a refusal to eat but an obsession with food and control.[9]

From the second decade of the twentieth century to the late 1930s, the entire subject of anorexia nervosa virtually dropped out of psychiatric discussion. This undoubtedly had to do with the ascendancy of the diagnosis of a newly discovered endocrine disease, whose symptoms were at least superficially similar to anorexia nervosa. In 1914, Morris Simmonds, a Hamburg pathologist, described a case of cachexia (wasting) that he was able to attribute to a lesion in the anterior lobe of the pituitary gland. The concept of Simmonds' Disease became enormously popular and influential, and for the next 20 years at least it was common to attribute severe cachexia and weight loss to a hypo-pituitary condition. Patients received endocrine treatments such as pituitary extracts as a result. These undoubtedly included an unknown number of patients with anorexia nervosa. It was not until the late 1930s that the very concept of Simmonds' Disease began to crumble under the weight of medical evidence and that psychiatrists and physicians were able to clearly differentiate anorexia nervosa from endocrine illness that gives rise to wasting.[10] From then on, psychological constructions of the disorder began to take hold. Nevertheless, the notion that there may be some fundamental endocrine or biological anomaly underlying anorexia nervosa has persisted until the present day (although the notion has been more influential in European than American writings).

It is possible that during the heyday of Simmonds' Disease anorexia nervosa was at least more common than may have been previously acknowledged. In the 1920s, when the ultra-slim image of the flapper dominated American fashion and her androgynous form became a symbol of the new sexual liberation among American women, there was some concern among physicians about an epidemic of self-starvation among American female college students.[11] While we have no documentation of an increase in hospital admissions for anorexia nervosa during this time, it is possible, at least, that subclinical eating disorders may have been common during this decade.

In any event, until the confusion about Simmonds' Disease was clarified in the 1930s, little progress was made in understanding anorexia nervosa as a psychiatric disorder. During the early 1940s, though, psychological theorizing about anorexia nervosa began once again in earnest, and particularly psychoanalytic interpretations, which were becoming ever dominant in American psychiatry, came to the fore. Such interpretations argued for the disorder's sexual origins, and one particularly influential paper hypothesized that anorexics were defending themselves against fantasies of oral impregnation, or against promiscuous impulses.[12] While these views have little acceptance today, psychoanalytic writings rescued the understanding of anorexia nervosa from the dreary and unenlightening speculations of a purely medical somaticism.

As long as the motivations and psychological development of the anorexic patient were ignored, there was bound to be little progress made
in comprehending the disorder. But the traditional psychoanalytic views,
which were dominant for about two or three decades, were themselves
destined to lose their influence. The exclusive focus on sexual factors,
as well as the interpretative and relatively passive approach to psychotherapy, proved ultimately of little value to anorexic patients. A more
encompassing framework was needed, one which took into account the
particular needs and developmental peculiarities of anorexic patients.

A watershed was the emergence of the work of Hilde Bruch, which
paralleled the ascendancy of eating disorders in the contemporary period. The publication of Bruch's groundbreaking book on eating disorders in 1973 signaled a major breakthrough in theory and practice, and
interestingly, it coincided with the beginning of the sharp increase in
the prevalence of anorexia nervosa and bulimia.[13] Bruch, who was
originally trained in psychoanalysis, had worked for three decades with
anorexic patients prior to the publication of her book, and had also
made some important contributions to the study of obesity in children
and adolescents.[14] *Eating Disorders* included a consideration of both
anorexia nervosa and obesity, and Bruch argued that both of these
revolved around issues of body image as well as certain characteristic
problems in psychological development. At the time of writing of the
present book, the notion of obesity as a psychological disorder remains
a problematic one; nevertheless, Bruch argued forcefully for the intimate connections between disorders of body shape and weight, and
those in which the eating function had become the focus of psychological conflict.[15]

In *Eating Disorders*, Bruch argued that anorexia nervosa had to be
understood in terms of the development of the total personality in the
context of the family, rather than through a narrow interpretation in
terms of psychosexual development. Following up on the suggestions
of some earlier writers, she proposed that there were really two types of
anorexia nervosa, a primary and a secondary form. In the primary type,
there were three distinguishing and central features that are always
present:

1   a distorted body image, which consists of the virtually delusional
    misperception of the body as fat;
2   an inability to identify internal feeling and need states, particularly

hunger, but more generally the whole range of emotions; and
3   an all-pervasive sense of ineffectiveness, a feeling that one's actions, thoughts, and feelings do not actively originate within the self but rather are passive reflections of external expectations and demands.

This third characteristic is very important, although not easy to formulate; it is a kind of lacuna at the core of the self, a sense of being "nothing," of not being an active agent in control of one's destiny. This deficient sense of self, which Bruch argued is grounded in the experiences of childhood, makes it understandable why anorexia so typically develops in adolescence, a period in which the development of a sense of autonomy, mastery, and competence is critical to achieving maturity and independence from one's parents.

The atypical form of anorexia nervosa, on the other hand, was seen by Bruch as a more heterogeneous condition. Its central feature was severe weight loss due to psychogenic factors, but in which the pursuit of thinness and a pathological deficit in autonomy were not primary. Atypical anorexia nervosa involved in a more central way than the primary form psychological conflicts that centered around the eating function ("symbolic misinterpretations of the eating function," in Bruch's language) that could stem from a whole host of underlying personality difficulties, ranging from the neurotic to the psychotic.

Bruch's distinction between primary and atypical anorexia has not been fully accepted or incorporated into contemporary diagnostic nomenclature, but a roughly equivalent category in the DSM-IV is the diagnosis of "Eating Disorder Not Otherwise Specified."[16] The latter is a rather over-inclusive category, which lacks the theoretical specificity of Bruch's notion of secondary anorexia nervosa. Nevertheless, however conceptualized, the distinction between instances of anorexia nervosa which are centered around a preoccupation with thinness and those that are driven by other factors is of some clinical and theoretical importance. For example, patients whose weight loss is not primarily driven by the pursuit of thinness may feel misunderstood by treatment approaches that stress or assume body image distortion. On a theoretical level, certain writers have stressed that the assumption that the pursuit of thinness is "primary" in anorexia nervosa may itself be culture-bound. For example, the psychiatrist Sing Lee, who has reported on a number of cases of anorexia nervosa that have appeared in Hong Kong in the period since about 1980, has suggested that roughly half of these cases do not involve the pursuit of thinness or significant body image distortion.[17] Lee suggests that the reason for this difference may have to do with the relatively low prevalence of obesity in Chinese culture and the resultant lack of passion about weight loss. This, however, does not explain why the disorder has suddenly become more common in Hong Kong, where it was virtually unknown prior to 1980. Lee suggests that despite the lack of concern about obesity, Western fashions of thinness have had an impact in Hong Kong via the images in the mass media. A further possibility is that dramatic generational changes in the values of mothers and daughters in Hong Kong may have precipitated developmental crises around autonomy in young Chinese women, psychological problems which were relatively unknown in the traditional Chinese mother–daughter relationship. And, as Bruch suggested, such developmental crises are the soil on which anorexia nervosa is likely to grow.

These developmental crises of female adolescence and young adulthood may provide a broader framework for a cross-cultural and transhistorical approach to anorexia nervosa, and in particular throw light on the patterns of emergence and recession of anorexia nervosa throughout history. Thus, in periods in which the traditional female role is relatively static and unchanging from one generation to the next, anorexia nervosa will be relatively uncommon. But in periods of intense transition in the female role, when traditional expectations are under assault, the resulting "gender ambivalence" (a phrase proposed by Brett Silverstein) leads to the types of developmental conflict that engender problems such as anorexia nervosa.[18] Such an understanding confirms DiNicola's formulation of anorexia nervosa as a "culture-change" (as opposed to the more static "culture-bound") syndrome.[19]

In addition to the formulations of Bruch, a second important theoretical conception of anorexia nervosa was advanced by the English psychiatrist Arthur Crisp.[20] Crisp, who was the director of psychiatry at St. George's Hospital in London and the originator of a seminal treatment program, also stressed the developmental nature of anorexia nervosa and its particular connection with adolescent development. However, in contrast with Bruch, who stressed the issue of autonomy, Crisp argued that the central problem for the person who becomes anorexic is the attainment of an identity, broadly conceived.

The publication of the influential *Diagnostic and Statistical Manual of Mental Disorders* in 1980[21] showed the impact of the emphasis that contemporary clinical theory placed on body image in the diagnostic definition of anorexia nervosa. The most recent version of the DSM, the DSM-IV, stipulates the following as essential diagnostic criteria:[22]

1 refusal to maintain body weight over minimum expected for age and height;
2 an intense fear of gaining weight or becoming fat;
3 a disturbance in the experience of body weight and shape, undue influence of body weight or shape on self-evaluation, or denial of the seriousness of low body weight; and
4 amenorrhea (absence of menstrual cycle for at least three months in post-menarcheal women).

Not included in this list are Bruch's notions of a deficient sense of self and the inability to recognize internal states: these, however, are probably too vague for the DSM-IV, whose authors sought operational (that is, behavioral) definitions of symptoms. The inclusion of amenorrhea, a nearly universal accompaniment of anorexia nervosa, was clearly intended to recognize the physical components of the condition. Amenorrhea is a typical consequence of significant weight loss, but in about 20 percent of cases of anorexia nervosa it begins prior to the loss of significant amounts of weight. This, among other factors, has led some to argue that anorexia nervosa involves a primary physical disorder, particularly in the hypothalamic centers of the central nervous system that control feeding and hormonal function.[23] Whether such factors are primary or secondary is at present unresolved, but there is no question that once anorexia nervosa becomes established, its physical components represent a significant part of the clinical picture.

The vast majority of anorexics are female, although the disorder does occur in males at the rate of about 5 to 10 percent of diagnosed cases.[24] This sex ratio of approximately nine females to every male seems to have remarkable consistency cross-culturally, even though a few reports have indicated a higher percentage of males. Anorexia nervosa is primarily a disorder of adolescence, with peak ages of onset at 14 and 18.[25] Nevertheless, there are some cases that begin later, in the twenties and thirties, and authentic cases of eating disorders have been documented to begin as late as the seventies.[26] At the other end of the spectrum, reports suggest that the disorder is emerging with greater frequency in younger, preadolescent children.The latter phenomenon has been attributed to increasing degrees of weight preoccupation and dieting among younger children, as well as to earlier emergence of the physical signs of puberty in females.[27]

Even though the disorder may have its onset in different age periods, most contemporary observers agree that the dynamics of adolescent development are central to understanding anorexia nervosa. In particular, the disorder is typically triggered by stresses that challenge the individual's sense of personal identity and competence, issues that are pivotal in the adolescent transition, particularly among individuals who tend to define and resolve these issues in terms of weight loss and body image. Anorexics often grow up in families in which there is an extraordinary emphasis on achievement, external appearance, and weight control, and they may be predisposed by virtue of temperament or experience to put considerable value on these. They are often compliant children who have a powerful need to please others, to "be good." Underneath a facade of good behavior, however, they typically feel weak, unworthy, and obligated to live up to what they perceive, correctly or incorrectly, as relentless demands for perfection. Any experience that challenges this rather brittle facade can greatly exacerbate underlying feelings of powerlessness. Such triggering events, for example the loss of a valued friend, failure to live up to one's personal expectations for academic or personal success, or rebuffs in personal relationships, however painful, may be able to be absorbed by many adolescents, but to the person who is vulnerable to anorexia nervosa, whose self-esteem is already fragile, they can acquire crushing intensity. The period in which such challenges to a sense of personal competence are most likely to have an impact is adolescence, since this is the era in which a person is most typically confronted with the need for independent decision-making, the challenges of sexual relationships, and the need to pursue self-chosen goals and activities. This developmental framework also makes it understandable, however, how the disorder could emerge for the first time at later ages, as these issues are not restricted to adolescents. For some individuals, the adolescent issues may have never been fully resolved, and may remain a latent vulnerability only to be triggered by a later crisis in life. Probably a significant number of later-onset cases can be accounted for by such a delayed response.

Anorexia nervosa often begins with a decision to diet, which at the outset is virtually indistinguishable from similar efforts to lose weight by countless adolescents. Such a diet may seem innocuous enough, and is rarely undertaken initially with the determination to starve oneself. However, given the anorexic's particular developmental vulnerabilities, dieting begins to yield a particularly powerful sense of control, for both internal and external reasons: internal, because it provides a sense of mastery and euphoria to a person who previously felt not only weak but depressed and empty; external, because in a culture that values thinness, the achievement of a thin body shape represents a triumph. The anorexic also derives secondary satisfactions from the manipulative power that her symptoms give her within her family or with her peers: in a situation in which she may have felt herself discounted, the refusal of food evokes a powerful response from others, an assertion of her presence that can no longer be ignored.[28] In addition to these social and psychological reinforcements, there may well be physiological factors (perhaps resulting from the state of starvation) that lock the anorexic into her emaciated and malnourished state.[29]

The Clinical Course of Anorexia Nervosa

Once set in motion, anorexia nervosa has its own characteristic development as a disease, its own internal dynamic that may be to a considerable extent independent of the factors that gave rise to it. As dieting is transformed into fasting and finally into willful starvation, the anorexic typically withdraws from ordinary activities and relationships. She will typically intensify an already excessive exercise regime, and may for a time redouble her frenetic efforts at achievement. She becomes obsessed with thoughts of food, with details of dieting and calorie counting, and with the sight of her own image in the mirror. Early in the course of the illness, anorexics often experience a kind of euphoria, akin to the famous "fasting high" described by those who fast for health reasons or by religious mystics. These experiences are typically short-lived, however. The longer the period of abstention, the more a sense of depression is likely to supervene and become the dominant mood.

Once an anorexic patient has lost a significant amount of weight and the illness has progressed to a certain point, she will typically defend her low weight with all the resources she can muster. These include various strategies of deception and secrecy, for which anorexic patients are notorious. Ingenious methods of disposing of food, for example, or hiding shocking degrees of emaciation beneath loose clothing, or using devious means of inflating one's weight before a medical examination, are not uncommon. The anorexic not only deceives others, but to a considerable extent is able persuade herself that "all is well" or that she never has felt better. Probably no disorder other than alcoholism or drug addiction is so invariably accompanied by denial. In fact, in many respects anorexia nervosa resembles an addictive disorder, in that it involves dependency on and obsessive preoccupation with an oral behavior (in this case, the negative one of food refusal) as well as pervasive denial and deception in order to maintain the "habit."[30]

By the time a person who has developed anorexia nervosa comes to the attention of clinical professionals, the disorder has in most cases progressed to a considerable degree. It is unfortunate, though understandable, that in the early stages of the illness, family members often cling to the hope that the change that has come over their offspring is a "passing phase." While in a small number of cases this may in fact be true and the developing anorexic is able to extricate herself from a downward course, in many instances the family becomes entrapped in an escalating cycle of denial and unwitting collusion. The families of anorexics are particularly vulnerable to getting caught in such a cycle, particularly those who habitually avoid emotional communication and deny the existence of psychological problems. However, whatever the contribution of the family, it must also be acknowledged that the disorder may be inherently difficult to recognize, particularly in its early stages, partly because of subtle maneuvers on the part of the anorexic to mask her weight loss but also because the self-starving behavior constitutes such a reversal of an earlier pattern of conformity and "good" behavior. Perhaps owing to the increased publicity as well as professional familiarity with the illness, it may be that in a number of instances the disorder is being recognized earlier by family members, school or medical personnel, or friends. This can only be seen as a positive trend, since early intervention is probably critical to a favorable outcome.

Unfortunately, it is still often the case that by the time the anorexic reaches the point at which the disorder is clinically identified, she has already become entrapped in a complex web of psychological attitudes and physiological sequelae associated with prolonged starvation. Such attitudes, which were documented in the famous Minnesota studies of conscientious objectors during World War II, include an obsessive preoccupation with food, withdrawal from social interactions, difficulties in concentrating, and a generalized mood of depression.[31] The physical aspects are clearly alarming from a medical standpoint. An anorexic patient, for example, presents symptoms of cachexia (emaciation), such as pallor, weakness and muscle fatigue, growth of fine body hair (lanugo), and amenorrhea. She will feel cold much of the time, and she will wear heavy clothing to enhance her sense of warmth in addition to the motive of covering over her thinness and escaping detection. She will often show heart irregularities, such as bradycardia, along with the complex dysregulation associated with malnutrition. The latter may include dangerous electrolyte disturbances, such as depleted potassium and chloride levels, disorders that place the cardiovascular system at risk.[32] While food refusal and nutrient depletion can underlie the latter, they are greatly exacerbated if a bulimic eating pattern has been established.

If weight loss has been extreme, a medical emergency has been created, typically necessitating hospitalization. Over a range of studies, anorexia nervosa has been estimated to have a fatal outcome in between about 5 and 20 percent of treated cases, a rate considerably higher than that of other psychiatric disorders.[33] The variation in mortality rates is partly attributable to differences in study populations, as well as different lengths of time over which mortality has been assessed. For example, in a 20-year followup study conducted at the Maudsley Hospital in England, at five years following treatment two out of 41 patients (4 percent) had died, but after 20 years seven (17 percent) of the original group had died.[34] These figures are typical of longer term studies, and suggest that studies that base mortality rates on, say, a five-year followup will seriously underestimate the longer term lethality of this illness. In this and other studies, at least half of the deaths result from complications associated with extreme starvation, for example, cardiovascular or circulatory failure due to nutritional deficiencies, while a significant percentage are brought about by suicide.[35] Clearly the risk of death increases with chronicity and the passage of time, a fact which underscores the urgency of early intervention.[36]

Even though the initial triggers for the disorder are most likely psychological and developmental, there is no question that once the condition becomes established, anorexia nervosa involves complex and sometimes intractable physical complications, which in turn only serve to aggravate the patient's already distressed mental state. Despite the proliferation of treatment approaches in recent years, there is not universal agreement as to the optimal mode of intervention. In general, there is a consensus that both the physical and psychological aspects of the disorder must be addressed, through a combination of nutritional rehabilitation, weight restoration, and psychotherapy. At low body weights, which are characteristic at initial clinical presentation, a program of systematic weight restoration is essential, typically in a hospital or in a residential center, and must take priority over psychotherapeutic interventions. At extremely low body weights, thinking is often distorted by metabolic factors, which makes meaningful psychotherapy difficult or impossible. Hospitalization typically involves a behavioral regimen that promotes systematic weight gain, but intensive nursing care that is sensitive to these patients' psychological needs is also essential.[37] Because medical insurance in the United States has placed increasingly stringent limits on the length of hospitalization, a tremendous part of the burden of treatment now falls on outpatient resources. This may be problematic, particularly for the weight restoration phase. Preliminary evidence suggests that patients tend to approach their ideal body weights much more efficiently in an inpatient setting. This of course has to do with the degree of control that the inpatient staff has on the patient's eating patterns. Even with frequent outpatient contacts, a "free-ranging" anorexic patient will be much less likely to comply with expectations for weight restoration when left to her own devices. This is not to say that weight gain never occurs under the influence of outpatient treatment – it sometimes does, but much less predictably so. The "down side" of hospitalization, though, is that too much emphasis may be placed on weight gain at the expense of a more comprehensive assessment and initiation of psychological treatment. Specialized eating disorder treatment units will typically do much better in offering the more complex, multi-leveled approach that is needed.

Once weight has been restored, treatment will typically consist of psychotherapy, ongoing medical followup (possibly with maintenance medication), and nutritional counseling. While there is no clearcut consensus on the optimal approach to psychotherapy, most workers in the field place emphasis on building coping and social skills, as well as dealing with the distress and adjustments associated with changes in weight and body image. Typically after some progress has been made with weight gain and food obsession no longer dominates the patient's thinking, underlying developmental and interpersonal issues can be addressed. There has been considerable interest in cognitive-behavioral modes of treatment, which help the person to replace dysfunctional habits of thought with more adaptive patterns. In an original paper on this problem, Garner and Bemis suggested that anorexics are subject to errors of thinking and cognitive biases that are similar to those found in depressed patients.[38] For example, patients tend to think in extreme dichotomies, dividing foods into "good" foods (i.e., those that lead to weight loss) and "bad" foods (those that promote weight gain). These errors can be corrected using the cognitive techniques for depression that were originally devised by Aaron Beck. The effectiveness of these interventions for anorexia nervosa, however, have yet to be assessed in large scale studies.

For younger patients still living at home, studies in England have clearly established that family psychotherapy in the period following the first hospitalization significantly improves outcome assessed at one and five years following discharge.[39] The importance of family therapy was stressed by pioneers in the treatment of anorexia nervosa, such as Bruch and Crisp. Its effectiveness presumably has something to do with the developmental dynamics of the disorder. For example, Crisp suggests that the avoidance of adolescence that is characteristic of the anorexic stance derives ultimately from conflicts in the parents about issues having to do with their own adolescence and especially with the issue of sexuality. The anorexic patient therefore is the carrier of the parents' hidden psychological problems, problems that have frequently been transformed into impasses in the parents' marital relationship.[40] Bruch emphasizes more the enmeshment of the anorexic patient with her parents, particularly her mother. Since she sees the disorder as a reflection of the patient's misdirected struggle for adolescent autonomy, she suggests that "disengagement" is perhaps the chief goal of work with the family.[41]

Despite improvements in knowledge about the disorder and its treatment, the process of recovery tends to be a difficult one, in some cases involving multiple hospitalizations and a number of failed efforts at psychotherapy. Outcome studies indicate that approximately 75 percent of anorexic patients show some degree of improvement at long-term followup, if one restricts oneself to the criterion of at least partial weight restoration. However, the outcome is considerably less sanguine if one looks at such factors as body image, food preoccupation, and ongoing difficulties with social and sexual adjustment.[42] A considerable number of former patients continue to struggle with these issues despite weight recovery. In a ten-year followup study of 76 patients treated at different centers in the United States, only 24 percent (18) of the patients evidenced a comprehensive recovery in all areas of functioning – weight, eating patterns, body image, social adjustment, menstrual function – at followup. Another 26 percent (20) of the subjects were considered to have a "good" outcome, meaning that they had fully recovered their weight and regularly menstruated, although most of these had varying degrees of body image disturbance or disordered eating. A third group, consisting of 32 percent (24) of the subjects, were judged to have an intermediate outcome, meaning that they had only partially recovered their weight and evidenced some degree of menstrual disorder and a more severe degree of other problems than the "good" group. Finally 12 percent of the anorexics had a poor outcome and 7 percent had died.[43]

There are also some serious long-term complications of anorexia nervosa. Recent studies have focused on the problem of osteoporosis, a problem which is associated with low estrogen levels and deficiencies in dietary calcium and which places patients at risk for limb fractures.[44] In a 1997 study of bone density in recovered anorexic women, 14 out of 18 showed significant reductions in bone density, as measured at the hips and spine, despite full restoration of weight and the resumption of menses for at least six months.[45] A striking finding was that the degree of bone loss was highly correlated with the length of time that the subjects had been amenorrheic. Yet it is not at all clear whether treatments such as estrogen replacement, which of course may have their own risks, can compensate for the loss in bone density.

Although the prevalence of anorexia nervosa has increased in recent years, the number of patients is still not large in absolute terms. But given the age and potential of the population which is afflicted, it represents a serious and often devastating affliction, with often tragic implications for the sufferer and her family.[46] As numerous writers have pointed out, this is an age group that should be relatively free of chronic health problems, particularly those that threaten reproductive and other functions. Despite the increased awareness of the disorder, including among physicians, there may still be a tendency to dismiss the early signs of the condition as "adolescent rebellion" or a similar appellation. The degree to which dieting is perceived as normal or even desirable in contemporary culture makes a major contribution to this problem. In this sense, not only do the social and cultural factors pointed to in this book have a role in the genesis of the condition, but, given the "normality" of dieting, they may also have a negative impact on the potential recognition of those who are in particular need of help.

While the portrait of the prognosis of anorexia nervosa that has been given would appear to be grim, outcome studies indicate that a significant number of patients – varying from 25 to 50 percent, depending on the study – do go on to make a full recovery. We have very limited understanding of why certain patients recover whereas others have a chronic and unremitting course of illness. In one of the few in-depth studies of issues of recovery, in which anorexic patients themselves were asked what specifically was helpful to them, many mentioned factors such as the need to protect a threatened marriage, or fear while pregnant of the potential harm to a fetus caused by anorexic behavior.[47] Some, but not all, patients perceived treatment to be helpful, particularly if the attitude of the therapist was a supportive and accepting one. Some felt that hospital treatment had been helpful, and in particular one mentioned being "scared straight" by the fear of further hospitalizations. Often, the involvement in a serious relationship will motivate the patient to relinquish the disorder, particularly if its maintenance threatens the relationship. Some patients also mentioned spiritual factors, particularly the experience (parallel to that reported by alcoholics) of "bottoming out" and finding, somehow, a renewed sense of faith. Obviously, much needs to be learned about factors that promote recovery. Professional treatment is not the only answer, although when conducted with a full appreciation of the complexity of the disorder, it can clearly help.

The Search for a Somatic Cause

Since the discovery of anorexia nervosa in the 1870s, considerable effort has been devoted to the identification of biological factors that may play a central role in its etiology. Such a quest for a somatic cause is understandable, given the gross physical complications of the disease. Also, because anorexics have until the relatively recent past typically been treated in medical hospitals, research into the cause of the disorder has frequently been conducted in a medical (i. e. somatic) framework. It might also be added that anorexics are notoriously difficult patients who often put up fierce resistances to treatment. The search for a "magic bullet" that would circumvent the vagaries and complexities of psychiatric intervention remains an alluring (although elusive) prospect.

Throughout the years, the anorexic's malnourished body has served as a virtual laboratory for the study of the effects of human starvation. Numerous investigations have revealed a host of physiological anomalies, including complex endocrine dysregulation, neurotransmitter deficiences, and abnormal feeding and digestive mechanisms.[48] More specifically anorexics have been shown, among other things, to evidence:

1   lowered oestrogen levels (lowered testosterone in males);
2   elevated growth-hormone levels;
3   reduced levels of neurotransmitters such as norepinephrine, serotonin, and dopamine;
4   anomalous carbohydrate metabolism;
5   abnormalities in temperature regulation; and
6   delayed gastric emptying.

A detailed review of these findings could easily fill an entire volume. But amid the welter of findings and increasingly sophisticated research methodologies, one crucial fact seems to stand out: that various physiological functions for the most part return to normal levels when weight and nutrition have been restored.[49] It is true, of course, that permanent impairments may remain in subjects after recovery (for example, menstrual reproductive abnormalities, as well as osteoporosis). But these must be considered to be consequences of the disease, not its causes.

There is also some evidence implicating a genetic factor in the etiology of anorexia nervosa. Twins studies, generally considered the most reliable method for establishing the influence of genetic factors, indicate that the concordance of monozygotic twins is significantly higher than that of dizygotic twins.[50] The fact that the concordance of monozygotic twins for anorexia nervosa is generally on the order of 55 percent, however, means that non-genetic factors must be involved in causing the disorder. An accepted interpretation of such findings is that while genetic factors create a vulnerability to the disorder, environmental factors of some sort are necessary to bring the disorder out. Of course, we have no idea at this point what the nature of a genetic predisposition to anorexia nervosa would consist of. One possibility, however, would be some vulnerability in weight-regulating mechanisms, such that when the individual loses weight beyond a certain point, it becomes very difficult to regain the weight (perhaps because weight loss is for some reason highly reinforcing). Such a model would be consistent with the sociocultural interpretation of an increase in the prevalence of eating disorders that is the theme of this book, in that in an environment in which adolescents are encouraged to diet, individuals who have a genetic vulnerability would be more likely to develop the disorder. In a culture in which there was no emphasis on dieting, on the other hand, vulnerable individuals would be unlikely to develop anorexia nervosa.

Although the possibility remains that genetic or other physiological factors lead certain individuals to be vulnerable to anorexia nervosa, present understanding seems to suggest strongly that psychological and social factors are critical in precipitating the disorder. The point was argued strongly by P. J. V. Beumont, an Australian psychiatrist, who himself has conducted biological studies:

> But does this knowledge [i. e., that derived from biological research – ed.] substantially increase our understanding of anorexia nervosa? I think not. The physical symptoms of anorexia nervosa are epiphenomena unrelated to the etiology of the illness. It is useful to know about them – but mainly to avoid unnecessary investigation of the patient. . . . Of course, the presence of physical disorder does eventually affect the patient's behavior, and to some extent a vicious circle of illness is set up. But the many elaborate schemes of interacting variables that have been proposed . . . do not really *explain* the illness. Anorexia nervosa remains basically a neurotic disturbance, leading to deviations in behavior that bring about physical dysfunction. Its treatment, albeit unsatisfactory, is psychological.[51]

Such foreclosure of the issue at this point may be premature. But even if it could be demonstrated that physiological factors are involved in a primary way in the etiology of anorexia (and I do not rule out this possibility), one central fact would still need to be explained: the dramatically increased incidence of the disease in European societies and the United States and its more recent spread to other areas of the world (see chapter 3). It would certainly seem that the most likely explanation for this phenomenon, which is the principal subject of this book, would lie in social and cultural factors.

Links with Depression, Anxiety, and Obsessive-Compulsive Disorders

Many observers have pointed to links between anorexia nervosa and other psychiatric disorders. The most frequently mentioned among these are depression, anxiety disorders, and obsessive-compulsive disorder. Symptoms of depression, such as low mood and difficulties in concentrating, are very common among anorexic patients, but it is not clear whether these are independent symptoms of a depressive disorder or, rather, typical responses to a state of starvation. Garfinkel and Garner have pointed out some clear differences between the two syndromes.[52] For example, while the fall in self-esteem in depressed patients appears to be quite general, for the anorexic patient self-esteem problems tend to be focused on issues related to body image and only later become more general, probably as a response to the struggle to overcome the disorder. Considerable interest was generated by a series of reports in the late 1970s and early 1980s that found a high prevalence of depression in the first-degree relatives of anorexics, particularly among the mothers.[53] Biologically oriented psychiatrists tend to leap on such findings as evidence for a genetic predisposition to depression, but it is equally possible to interpret such findings from a psychological and environmental viewpoint. Some anorexic patients respond favorably to antidepressant medication, although it is an error to equate the two disorders based on a drug response. For example, antidepressants have been shown to be helpful with childhood enuresis, and yet no one equates enuresis and depression. The mechanisms of antidepressants are mediated by neurotransmitters, but neurotransmitters such as norepinephrine and serotonin are implicated in many behavioral functions. Serotonin, for example, has been linked with aggression and inhibition, mood regulation, feeding activity and sleep. There is now general agreement that anorexia nervosa and depression are independent disorders, although depression may be a component of the biological or psychological predisposition to anorexia nervosa in some instances.[54]

A common clinical finding is that anorexic patients often have a history of anxiety disorders, typically prior to the onset of the eating disorder. A. H. Crisp has long suggested that an anxious temperament is a predisposition to the illness, and that self-starvation is often a massive defense against agoraphobic anxieties that preceded the disorder during early adolescence.[55] A formal study of a small group of recovered anorexics at the Western Psychiatric Institute in Pittsburgh bore this out.[56] These researchers found that 58 percent of the subjects, who were on average age 24 at the time of interview, had a childhood onset of an anxiety disorder at an average age of 10 – five years prior to the onset of the eating disorder. Especially remarkable was the fact that by far the most common anxiety disorder was social phobia, a pattern that is characterized by extreme shyness and a particularly intense fear of being humiliated or embarrassed in front of others. For anorexics, these social phobic tendencies are often expressed through an anxiety about eating with others present. By way of contrast, depression, which was also common among the subjects, appeared typically a year prior to the onset of anorexic symptoms. Other studies have showed that anxiety disorders are highly common in the first-degree relatives of anorexics.[57] Thus, anorexics may be genetically predisposed to developing anxiety disorders, although such family incidence studies do not allow us to decide between genetic and environmental influence.

In the 1990s there has been a growing interest in the possible links between anorexia nervosa and obsessive-compulsive disorder. A relationship between these two disorders was posited as early as the late 1930s, when interest in the psychological aspects of anorexia nervosa was undergoing a resurgence following the "dark ages" when it was considered to be an endocrine disease.[58] Clearly anorexia nervosa appears to have many obsessional aspects. Anorexics, for example, are preoccupied with thoughts of food and body image. They ruminate endlessly over their food intake and engage in highly ritualistic eating behavior, cutting their food into small pieces and scrupulously monitoring their caloric intake with exacting precision. They are preoccupied with control over their bodily functions, their emotions, and the environment, and they are typically highly perfectionistic, meticulous, and orderly. These features led Rothenberg, in a 1986 paper, to suggest that anorexia nervosa (and eating disorders in general) are modern manifestations of obsessive-compulsive disorder.[59] Under the influence of culturally based preoccupations with dieting and weight control, the symptoms of obsessive-compulsive disorder have been "molded" into a peculiarly modern form, those of eating disorders. Although Rothenberg's hypothesis of the cultural shaping of psychiatric disorders is consistent with the general lines of the argument put forward in this book, it is probably an oversimplification to equate eating disorders

33

with obsessive-compulsive disorder. Eating disorders have their own unique characteristics. One difference between the two, for example, is that obsessive-compulsive patients find their intrusive thoughts about dirt, violence, or sexuality to be morally repugnant and "ego-alien," whereas the preoccupations of the anorexic patient with thinness and starvation represent highly valued, "ego-syntonic" goals.

Despite the distinctions between the disorders, the parallels are compelling and have drawn a great deal of attention from behaviorally and biologically oriented researchers. For example, systematic evaluations of anorexic patients suggest that their obsessive-compulsive symptomatology is quite general and goes beyond their specific attitudes towards food and body image. A study of patients at the Western Psychiatric Institute at the University of Pittsburgh found that anorexic patients achieved scores on the Yale-Brown Obsessive-Compulsive Scale, a widely used assessment instrument, which were comparable in magnitude to the scores of a large sample of obsessive-compulsive patients. Most of the anorexic symptoms tended to be obsessions, in particular having a great fear of not saying things right or doing something embarrassing or a strong preoccupation with symmetry and exactness.[60] Similar results were found in a German sample at the University of Göttingen, with a full 37 percent of a sample of anorexic patients meeting the diagnostic criteria for obsessive-compulsive disorder.[61]

It is of considerable interest whether obsessive symptoms are simply accompaniments of the eating disorder, or whether they are in evidence prior to the development of the eating disorder and persist after recovery. Unfortunately, it is difficult to say with much precision whether obsessive-compulsive symptoms predate the disorder, as anorexic patients are not typically observed until after they become ill. Retrospective data do in fact suggest that many anorexics manifest obsessive traits as children. More clearcut are findings that well after patients recover from their eating disorders, they still manifest obsessional symptoms. In a study of 20 recovered patients, for example, the subjects still manifested strong obsessional traits, in particular a concern for order, symmetry, and exactness.[62] These findings suggest that obsessionality may be an underlying trait, and they at least raise the possibility that obsessionality may be part of the predisposition to the disorder.

It is of interest to consider these findings from a psychobiologic standpoint. Research on obsessive-compulsive disorder has strongly implicated altered serotonin metabolism as a underlying factor that

34

predisposes people to develop the symptoms of eating disorders. The reasoning that underlies this hypothesis has to do with the extraordinary efficacy of specifically serotonergic medications, such as Prozac or Luvox, in the treatment of obsessive-compulsive disorder.[63] It is remarkable, then, that research on anorexia nervosa has also unearthed evidence for altered serotonin metabolism, particularly an overactive serotonin system in the brain. These trends persist even in patients who have recovered their original body weight.[64] Interestingly, a high rate of serotonin activity is consistent with a pattern of behavioral inhibition, which is shared by both obsessive-compulsive and anorexic patients. These findings have led to the proposal that serotonergic medications may be helpful to anorexic patients, just as they have been helpful for individuals with obsessive-compulsive disorder. In some exciting initial research, it does appear that Prozac is specifically effective in helping anorexic patients to maintain their weight after it has been restored.[65] Its efficacy in helping patients at lower body weights, however, has not been established. Nevertheless, these findings should give us pause about unequivocally rejecting the possibility of biological predispositions to anorexia nervosa. They do not negate the influence of cultural factors, but once again they point to the possibility that particular biological predispositions are what may predispose certain individuals to respond to cultural pressures with illness.

Bulimic Anorexia

If an anorexic continues in a state of starvation for a long enough period of time, the pangs of hunger become intolerable and the rigid discipline of the starvation diet may be broken by a ravenous eating binge. For an anorexic, though, with her terrible fear of weight gain, nothing could be more disastrous than such an episode of gorging. The "crime" must be avenged by getting rid of the hated food, typically through self-induced vomiting, and less commonly through the consumption of frightening amounts of laxatives or redoubled efforts at starvation. Such episodes of bulimia (which means literally "ox-hunger") occur in between about 40 and 50 percent of anorexic patients, and their emergence is typically an ominous sign, making the disorder particularly resistant to treatment.[66]

Anorexic patients who develop bulimia have usually been ill longer, and it may be that bulimic urges are part of the body's normal compensatory response to prolonged starvation. The famous studies of experimental starvation in previously healthy males conducted in the 1940s showed that bulimic binges were common during refeeding and persisted for months, even years after normal weight had been restored.[67] Bulimic anorexics, however, are also typically heavier before their illness than their non-bulimic cohorts, suggesting perhaps that the body's weight-regulating mechanisms may respond more violently to starvation than they do for a patient with a leaner frame. In addition, though, there is a further distinguishing feature of bulimic anorexics, and that is that they are typically more seriously psychologically distressed than "restricting" anorexics.

Bulimic anorexics, for example, tend to have pervasive difficulty with impulse control, which manifests itself in alcohol or drug abuse, sexual promiscuity, or compulsive stealing.[68] In contrast with the classic portraits of the typical anorexic family as highly controlled, fearful of conflict, and cultivating an image of perfection, the family histories of bulimics are often replete with open conflict and turmoil. The bulimic's own relationships with others tend to be intensely dependent and emotionally stormy. Bulimic anorexics are often openly self-destructive and prone to suicide attempts or gestures.[69] This entire pattern of impulsivity, emotional instability, explosive relationships, and self-destructive behavior is what contemporary psychiatry refers to as a borderline personality disorder, although the general applicability of the borderline diagnosis to most bulimic patients has been questioned. Clearly not all bulimic anorexics are borderline personalities; but the bulimic symptoms are much more likely to emerge in these severely disturbed individuals when they develop anorexia nervosa.

Even more than anorexia, the bulimic cycle of bingeing and purging closely resembles an addictive form of behavior, and it has sometimes been compared to alcohol abuse. Indeed, a significant proportion of bulimic anorexics have a history of problem drinking or drug abuse, which may continue concurrently with the eating disorder.[70] The concept of addiction seems especially applicable to bulimia, in that the behavior pattern becomes compulsive, secretive, and the person becomes ultimately dependent on it for solving life's problems. However, it is probably important to avoid the simplistic notion put forward by some that bulimia is an "addiction to food." While bulimics may early on use food binges as a way of relieving tension, it is ultimately the vomiting that becomes the "habit" to which bulimics become enslaved.[71] Perhaps it would be best to think of the entire pattern of bingeing, purging, and intermittent starvation for which the addiction concept is relevant. When superimposed on the anorexic pattern, which already involves denial and fierce resistance to external intervention, bulimia poses formidable treatment obstacles that can tax the capacities of the most skilled clinician and treatment staff.

Bulimia was occasionally mentioned in earlier accounts of anorexia nervosa, but it appears that in the late nineteenth and early twentieth centuries it was a much less prominent part of the clinical picture of anorexia nervosa than it is today.[72] Hilde Bruch, one of the few clinicians with continuous experience with eating disorders from the 1940s to the 1980s, observed that bulimia had become an ever more prominent part of the clinical presentation of patients during her later years of work.[73] Gerald Russell, an eminent English psychiatrist, suggests that in fact the form of anorexia nervosa has changed in the second half of the twentieth century, with bulimia now a characteristic part of the clinical picture. Russell suggests that this transformation of the symptom picture of anorexia nervosa is an example of the more general phenomenon of "pathoplasticity," that is, the malleability of a disease under the influence of historical factors or altered cultural conditions.[74] The ascendancy of bulimia in the contemporary clinical picture of anorexia has yet to be accounted for, but it is likely that a number of factors are involved, including the increasing availability of low-cost, calorie-rich food, tendencies towards desocialization and fragmentation in contemporary eating patterns, and the general emergence of a cultural "style" that includes greater impulsivity and addictive patterns of behavior.

Bulimia Nervosa

Bulimia has become increasingly prominent in anorexia nervosa since it first began to be noticed in the 1940s, but beginning in the 1970s an apparently new pattern rapidly came into prominence – a cycle of binge eating and purging in a person who otherwise maintains weight above the dangerously low levels seen in anorexia nervosa. Bulimia nervosa, as this non-anorexic bingeing and purging pattern was named, is now recognized to be more prevalent than anorexia nervosa and has become a major focus of contemporary eating disorders research.

Like anorexia nervosa, bulimia nervosa may have its historical precursors. Overeating and vomiting were known to the Romans (the vomitorium, as depicted in Fellini's *Satyricon*, has become a common cultural cliche about bulimia), and one account has even suggested that Emperors Claudius and Vitellius, who both fasted extravagantly, vomited and drank excessively, exhibited some variant of bulimia.[75] However, there is no evidence that either figure was preoccupied with thinness, which is an essential feature of the contemporary pattern. It is likely, rather, that their excesses reflected the patterns of social indulgence and excess characteristic of a wealthy and decadent aristocracy. It should also be pointed out that widespread reports of self-induced vomiting in ancient cultures, which include, for example, the Egyptians, have to be understood in light of the fact that periodic purgation was recommended as a health practice by leading physicians.[76] In the Hebrew Talmud, ca. AD 400–500, the rabbinic scholars referred to a pattern that they called "boolmot," or ravenous hunger, which, in a remarkable parallel to contemporary cognitive-behavioral treatment which prescribes a diet of "forbidden" foods, they recommended be treated by sweet foods, such as honey. The Talmudists also observed that the condition excused the person from the obligation to fast on Yom Kippur ("if anyone be seized with bulimy, he is to be fed even unclean things . . .").[77] Once again, though, in the absence of a concern with thinness, it is unlikely that this was truly a parallel to bulimia nervosa.

Even in more recent medical history, the existence of bulimia nervosa prior to the twentieth century is highly doubtful, and within the twentieth century it did not emerge in full force until the 1970s. There were numerous scattered references to bulimia in the French and English medical literature from the seventeenth to the nineteenth centuries, but these were almost always to instances of ravenous overeating or insatiable appetite. The writings on anorexia nervosa by Gull and Lasegue in the 1870s made virtually no mention of bulimia, even though their descriptions of anorexia nervosa are fully recognizable. A small number of well-known case histories from early in the twentieth century show a clear similarity to bulimia nervosa. One of these, Ludwig Binswanger's famous patient, "Ellen West," evidenced a complex pattern of psychiatric symptoms, including anorexia nervosa and severe depression, and ultimately committed suicide at the age of 33. Ellen West, who killed herself in the early 1920s, was an intellectually gifted and artistic personality, whose consuming obsession with her weight, her binges with sweets and her abuse of laxatives and efforts to starve herself, read like a rich and elaborate account of the inner life of a bulimic. Interestingly, Binswanger made no mention of an eating disorder diagnosis in his case history (which was first published in 1944), despite the fact that anorexia nervosa was already well known in the psychiatric literature. Clearly, though, Ellen West suffered from other more severe psychiatric disorders, including probably either major affective disorder or schizophrenia, than is typical for a contemporary person with bulimia nervosa.[78]

A second early case history was that of the patient Nadja, written by the psychiatrist Pierre Janet in 1903. Nadja appears to have been suffering from anorexia nervosa (a diagnosis of which Janet was skeptical), but was periodically consumed with bouts of overeating followed by extremely restrictive dieting. Nadja appeared to be suffering from what is currently described as "body dysmorphic disorder," that is, a pervasive sense of being ugly and unattractive. Her preoccupation with thinness, which is very apparent in her story, appears to be one component of a much wider obsession with her appearance. Janet suggested that her problem was basically an obsessional one, but it is reasonable to argue that she also suffered from a bulimic form of anorexia nervosa.[79]

Albert Stunkard, an obesity expert, documented some striking instances of disorders resembling bulimia nervosa in the writings of a Russian-born psychiatrist, Moshe Wulff, who practiced psychiatry in Berlin, Moscow, and later in Israel.[80] In a 1932 publication, Wulff described a number of cases of what he called "food addiction." His vivid case histories are all accounts of female patients, and provide graphic descriptions of bulimic binge eating. For example, he describes one woman in her middle twenties, who, following a painful separation from her husband, described periods when

> strong drives to eat that lasted for up to three weeks alternated with short, three- to six-day-long periods of abstinence that could extend to complete fasts for the entire day. The amount that was devoured in the course of the day, particularly in the afternoons and evenings, was sometimes unbelievable. She could eat one after the other three or four meals of three or four courses each and in between them sweets, chocolate, and cookies by the poundful .... she particularly liked to buy anything

39

edible that was being sold on the street and to swallow them rapidly and greedily on the spot. She ate, moreover, in such a manner that she could hardly breathe; her abdomen protruded, then, and she liked to show it off with the observation, "Look how much I am like a pregnant woman."

During these periods of overeating, she loathed herself, felt severely depressed, and complained of " 'fat, so fat, and that is frightening.' "[81]

Stunkard notes that "unlike anorexia nervosa, which has a rich history that has been traced to the Middle Ages, bulimia seems to have burst from the blue upon modern society, and it has achieved widespread recognition in a very short period of time." He suggests that the writings of Wulff may suggest bulimia may not be as completely new as is commonly assumed. On the other hand, though, the cases he describes differ from contemporary bulimia nervosa in 1) the absence of a concern with achieving thinness; and 2) the notable absence of purging behaviors, particularly self-induced vomiting. What Wulff may well have been describing is what has become recently identified as binge eating disorder, not bulimia nervosa. Other evidence points strongly to the conclusion that while bulimia in some form may have manifested itself earlier, the disorder bulimia nervosa only emerged in epidemic proportions in the 1970s. For example, epidemiological studies at the Mayo Clinic in Minnesota and the University of Virginia strongly suggest that cases of bulimia nervosa began to appear in considerable numbers in the 1970s and that the prevalence of the disorder showed a sharp increase in the late 1970s and early 1980s.[82] The appearance of bulimia in the 1970s was not unique to the United States, as various sources indicate that patients were appearing in significant numbers around the same time in England, France, and Germany.

The first description of a series of typical cases of bulimic college students was given in 1976 by Marlene Boskind-Lodahl, then a psychologist in the counseling center at Cornell University.[83] Boskind-Lodahl described a number of female "binger-starvers" (she reported having seen 138 in all) who were high achievers but who suffered from extremely low self-esteem and were extraordinarily sensitive to male rejection. She subtitled her paper "A feminist perspective on anorexia nervosa and bulimia," but it is clear, at least in retrospect, that she was discussing women who were of mostly normal weight but experienced symptoms of bingeing and purging. She used the term "bulimarexia" to distinguish the pattern from anorexia nervosa, but this label, which

Bruch characterized as a "semantic monstrosity," was never formally adopted. Boskind-Lodahl's effort from the outset was to depathologize the behavior and suggest that it was an understandable, overconforming response to the pressures of female socialization.

Partly because Boskind-Lodahl's paper was published in a journal of feminist scholarship not widely known to the psychiatric community, her work was little noticed by professionals. The first formal clinical paper on the bulimic syndrome was published in 1979 by Gerald Russell, a psychiatrist at the Royal Free Hospital in London.[84] Entitled "Bulimia nervosa: An ominous variant of anorexia nervosa," Russell's paper described 30 patients who had a characteristic history of overeating, typically followed by self-induced vomiting, but who were of normal weight or, in some instances, significantly overweight. Russell stressed the kinship of this syndrome with anorexia nervosa, since both shared a characteristic fear of fatness and an obsessive overconcern with body shape. In fact, Russell suggested that most, if not all, of his patients had suffered an earlier episode of anorexia nervosa, although in some instances the episode had been "cryptic" (that is, transient and not noticed). On the other hand, Russell stressed that these patients were generally different from those with anorexia nervosa, particularly in their tendencies to extroversion and impulsiveness and in their greater degree of sexual activity. Russell pointed to the particular dangers of the syndrome, specifically the tendency of the bingeing and purging behavior to become habit-forming and the physical risks associated with consequences of purging, particularly depleted electrolytes. Although Russell may have been looking at a group of patients with a particularly virulent form of the disorder, his formulation of the syndrome was a classic one and remains definitive.

Throughout the 1980s, intense controversy developed about how the bulimic syndrome should be defined and diagnosed. Intense debates developed over whether binge eating was the primary symptom, over the role of purging, and over the question of how central shape and weight concerns were to the syndrome. These debates and their resolution were reflected in evolving diagnostic criteria. In 1980, the American Psychiatric Association, in its influential diagnostic manual, the DSM-III, identified the disorder simply as bulimia, and the diagnostic criteria basically described a syndrome of binge eating.[85] However, it soon became evident that this definition was unsatisfactory, as it failed to emphasize adequately the bulimics' characteristic preoccupation with weight and body image as well as their ubiquitous attempts to compensate for their binge eating. This controversy was resolved with the publication of the revised DSM-III (the DSM-III-R) in 1987, where the efforts to compensate as well as the "persistent overconcern with weight and shape" were incorporated into the newly named "bulimia nervosa." The most recent version of the manual, the DSM-IV, stipulates the following criteria for bulimia nervosa:

1 Recurrent episodes of binge eating, which consist of eating an inordinately large amount of food in a short period of time and an awareness of loss of control over eating during the episode;
2 Recurrent inappropriate compensatory behavior to prevent weight gain, particularly self-induced vomiting, misuse of laxatives or diuretics, excessive exercise or fasting;
3 Self-evaluation unduly influenced by body shape and weight;
4 Binge-eating and compensatory behaviors occuring twice a week for three months.[86]

Similar to anorexia nervosa, the number of patients with bulimia nervosa are disproportionately female, in a ratio of approximately 9 to 1. The syndrome does occur in males, but once again much less has been written about it than in females.

Diagnostic definitions are of importance for the purposes of scientific clarity, but they do not really communicate how the symptoms of disordered eating are subjectively experienced. For this, I quote the following graphic description of a bulimic episode:

> It would start to build in the late morning. By noon I'd know I had to binge. I would go out . . . to the supermarket down the block, and buy a gallon, or maybe even two gallons of maple walnut ice cream and a couple of packages of fudge-brownie mix . . . .
>
> On the way home, the urge to binge would get stronger and stronger. I could hardly drive my car because I couldn't think about anything but food. There was a doughnut shop that I passed on the way home. Almost always I'd stop the car, buy a dozen doughnuts and start munching on them even before I was walking out the door. On the way home I invariably finished all twelve doughnuts.
>
> I'd hurry up the apartment stairs with the urge for more binging growing stronger by the minute. . . . I'd hastily mix up the brownie mix

and get the brownies in the oven, usually managing to eat a fair amount of the mix myself as I was going along. Then, while they were still cooking, I ate the ice-cream. Only by constantly eating the ice-cream could I bear the delay until the brownies came out of the oven. Sometimes I'd finish the whole gallon even before the brownies were done, and I'd take the brownies out of the oven while they were still baking. At any rate, I'd start eating brownies, even though by this time I was feeling sick, intending to stop after two or three. Then it would be five or six. Pretty soon, I'd have put away about fifteen or twenty of the brownies, and then I'd be overcome with embarrassment. What if one of my roommates were to get home and see that I had eaten *twenty* brownies! The only way to disguise it, obviously, was to finish the other fifty-two brownies myself, wash the pan, and clean everything up. . . .

Seventy-two brownies later, the depression hit. I'd go to the bathroom, stick my finger down my throat, and make myself throw up. I was so good at it that it was almost automatic – no effort necessary, just instant vomiting, over and over until there was nothing coming out of my stomach except clear pale-green fluid.[87]

A person with bulimia describes high levels of tension that build up prior to a binge eating episode. Between episodes, she may eat little or at least struggle to resist eating. She will typically be obsessed with thoughts of the next binge, and these become more insistent as time goes on. This may lead her to ruminate on the details of the next anticipated eating episode, that is, what she is going to eat, where she going to get her food, where she is going to do it, and so forth. Once the binge has begun, it is as if a dam has burst. An earlier version of the DSM suggested that it is typical for bulimics to have an awareness that their eating pattern is abnormal. This is an understatement. When in the throes of an episode of bulimia, the person feels possessed, as if another personality, or something more animal in her, has taken her over. This has led some observers to use the metaphor of dissociation to describe the split that the person feels between their non-bulimic and actively bulimic periods. Once the binge begins, the person immediately feels a release of tension. But feelings of shame and guilt begin to take their toll, as well as anxiety about the feelings of bloating, which provoke the terrifying prospect of weight gain. Food, which just a short while ago was desperately sought, has now become the enemy. Vomiting now seems like the only route to relief, and indeed after vomiting the bulimic typically reports feeling clear-headed and at least momentarily calm. This situation, however, is temporary, and soon the feelings of distress with which the bulimic is living return and the cycle is repeated.

One can easily see why the bulimic cycle has been likened to an addictive pattern of behavior. The behavior is performed under a sense of extreme compulsion, it discharges profound emotional tensions and anxiety, it is powerfully reinforcing at least in the short term, and immediately after performing the act the person "swears off" and engages in a virulent struggle to resist repeating it. As in the case of anorexia nervosa, addiction can only be a metaphor, since there is no "substance" from which one can achieve abstinence, as is the case in a drug.[88] Nevertheless, there are some convincing parallels. Since the bulimic maintains a more or less normal weight, the problem, unlike anorexia nervosa, may be secretly masked beneath a facade of normality. Also unlike anorexia nervosa, which is often accompanied by unspoken feelings of pride, bulimic behavior is typically accompanied by feelings of profound shame and embarrassment. This can lead bulimics to extreme secretiveness about their behavior, and may lead them to hide their behavior by, for example, vomiting into garbage bags in their rooms to avoid detection by odors in the bathroom. The discomfort that they experience in feeling out of control is what often motivates them to disclose their problem and seek help. Even at this point, though, their feelings about getting help are typically ambivalent. They would like to reduce the sense of chaos created by the eating pattern, and yet fear that if they are treated the freedom to binge and purge will be "taken away from them." This is an uncanny resemblance to the feelings described by many alcoholics and chemically-dependent individuals. Such fears may also lead them to be highly reluctant to disclose the details of their behavior to a therapist, which in turn is likely to render treatment less effective.

Because of the mixture of shame and fear that comes to haunt the woman with bulimia, she may wait a long time after first developing the disorder before seeking help. In studies in the early 1980s, it was determined that the average time that it takes someone with bulimia to seek treatment was seven years from the onset of their symptoms. It is possible, however, with the increased publicity about eating disorders, that the time that it takes the person to seek help may be decreasing.[89]

Numerous studies, some of which will be reviewed in the following chapter, suggest that bulimia is probably several times more common than anorexia nervosa.[90] Although bulimia often begins in the high-school years, the greatest prevalence of bulimia is among college students, where the behavior has merged to some extent with socially prevalent practices of binge eating and, perhaps less frequently, experiments with purging. One study showed that bulimic college students vary widely in their degree of psychiatric disturbance, with some showing barely detectable degrees of impairment while others manifested obvious clinical disturbance.[91] Apparently, there are some instances in which bulimia is no more than an unhealthy and risky technique of weight control. The number of such "pragmatic" bulimics is unknown. But for the majority, habitual bingeing and purging becomes a way of discharging intense degrees of psychological distress. Although bulimia was occurring in epidemic proportions among students in the 1980s, it was hardly limited to them. A number of women in their twenties and thirties, many of whom are overtly successful and well-functioning, are caught in a long-term pattern of bingeing, purging, and weight obsession, which they manage to keep carefully hidden for years. The prevalence of these bulimic adult women is at present unknown, but there is little question about their existence.[92]

Bulimia nervosa, like anorexia nervosa, is probably best understood ultimately as a developmental disorder, although it tends to emerge somewhat later than anorexia nervosa. The majority of bulimics first develop their symptoms between the ages of 16 and 20 – that is, in the late years in high school and the early years of college. While it is probably an oversimplification, it could be said that whereas for anorexia the principal developmental problem is the challenge of adolescence and the psychological issues that become organized around the maintenance of a post-pubertal weight, for bulimics the central developmental impasse is the psychological separation from the family and the entry into the adult world, and particularly the challenges that these pose to the sense of personal identity.[93] Hence, the disorder rarely emerges at puberty, but rather is more likely to begin in the late high-school or early college years. Unlike anorexics, who tend to be phobic about sexuality and to avoid sexual encounters, bulimics tend to be sexually active and to be engaged in heterosexual relationships. Many have achieved a higher overall level of interpersonal maturity than anorexics, but nevertheless they tend to struggle with issues of independence and self-assertion. Their sexual and interpersonal relationships tend to be troubled, and they have particular difficulties negotiating issues surrounding intimacy and loss. Bulimic episodes are often triggered by stresses associated with relationships, particularly experiences that trigger feelings of rebuff, rejection, or isolation.

The personalities of bulimics vary widely, but clinical research has elucidated a few commonly encountered personality profiles. One of the most typical patterns is what psychologist Craig Johnson has called the "false-self," or "pseudo-independent" personality organization.[94] The false-self personality is typically on the surface a well-functioning and well-appearing young woman. Like the anorexic, she is typically an achiever in school and at work, and appears to be an independent and competent individual. Underneath the competent facade, however, she is troubled by profound feelings of neediness, dependency, and low self-esteem. This split in her identity typically resulted from a kind of childhood experience in which, because of the unavailability or disengagement of parental figures (often due to illness, depression, or addiction in at least one parent), she was expected to develop a "pseudo-mature" adaptation which left little room for the expression of either dependency or rebellion. As a result, these needs remain split off and hidden from public view, and they are precisely what is expressed in bulimic gorging and purging: it is in fact only in the privacy of the kitchen or bathroom that she can drop her facade of perfection and let herself go. The false-self type is a common pattern in bulimia, but it is not the only one. Some bulimics are more severely psychologically disturbed borderline personalities, for whom the behavior serves to ward off a threatened sense of personal fragmentation and is virtually interchangeable with a whole host of self-destructive symptoms, including alcoholism, self-mutilation, and sexual promiscuity. Such patients have typically experienced a more overtly traumatic childhood environment, one characterized by parental physical or sexual abuse. These "multi-impulsive" bulimics, as they have been called, constitute about 20 percent of the population of bulimics and present particularly demanding treatment challenges.[95] In others, bulimia has its basis in more typical adolescent conflicts. For these latter, the bulimia tends to be a more transient and superficial symptom, and therefore more easily dislodged from a therapeutic standpoint. The point is that bulimia is a final common pathway through which a variety of developmental problems can be expressed. However, all bulimics share a common central obsession with weight and body shape.

Like anorexia nervosa, bulimia can easily become a chronic pattern, and the longer the person maintains it the more difficult it is to dislodge. Bulimia, like anorexia, may also become entrenched by physiological factors once the behavior has become habitual. The chronic pattern of binge eating and purging may vastly upset the normal equilibrium of hunger and satiety mechanisms; and this dysregulation may make the intensity of both eating binges and vomiting episodes more pronounced.[96] In addition, both binge eating and vomiting may have powerful effects as immediate reinforcers – that is, in relieving states of emotional distress and tension. These "addictive" consequences of the components of the bulimic cycle may be based on physiological as well as psychological mechanisms. The point is here that like anorexia, once the bingeing and purging pattern has become established, it may be sustained autonomously by factors other than those that initially gave rise to it and adequate treatment needs to focus intensively on such self-sustaining factors.

Bulimia nervosa is still too new a condition for us to understand its long-term course, but the few followup studies that we do have tend to confirm a picture of a chronic, relapsing condition. One such study, which was conducted at the Massachusetts General Hospital in Boston, found that of 30 bulimic women who were followed up over a three-year period, only 69 percent, most of whom were exposed to various treatments, were fully recovered after a three-year period. Even for those who recovered after treatment, there was a high probability of a relapse (63 percent) within about a year and a half after recovery. Furthermore, half of those who recovered from this first relapse developed yet another episode within the first year and a half after recovery from the first relapse. Even among subjects who recovered, for many there was considerable self-consciousness about eating socially, and a number continued to engage in restrictive dieting.[97] In the first longer term study of bulimics, over 200 women who had been treated at the University of Minnesota Eating Disorders Clinic were followed up over a ten-year period.[98] While 70 percent of the patients were either in partial remission or were fully recovered ten years after they had first been seen, 11 percent met full criteria for bulimia nervosa and another 19 percent met criteria for an eating disorder not otherwise specified. Approximately 30 percent continued to engage in bingeing and purging behaviors at followup. We still do not know about the long-term health implications of sustaining bulimic behaviors over all these years, but these studies suggest that for many, bulimia nervosa remains at the very least a persistent behavioral problem that undoubtedly has a disruptive impact on one's life. The findings suggest an urgent need for improved methods of treatment and prevention.

During the 1980s, a number of effective modalities for the treatment of bulimia, at least in the short term, were developed, originally by English workers but then widely adopted elsewhere. Foremost among these is cognitive-behavioral therapy, which was developed by Christopher Fairburn at Oxford.[99] Cognitive-behavioral therapy is a relatively short-term treatment (approximately 20 sessions over four months) which encourages self-monitoring of eating behavior, provides techniques for gaining control of bingeing and purging episodes, and challenges the client's distorted ideas and thinking about her body weight and shape that are at the core of the disorder. It has been shown to be effective at bringing about improvement in a large number of controlled studies, and has been widely adopted by clinical workers in the field. More recently, Fairburn and his co-workers have shown that an approach known as interpersonal therapy is almost equally effective in reducing bulimic symptoms.[100] Originally developed as a treatment for mood disorders, interpersonal therapy focuses exclusively on patients' current interpersonal problems (for example, conflicts in relationships and major role transitions) and does not address the bulimic symptomatology directly. It is also a short-term treatment, consisting of roughly 20 sessions over a four-month period. In a controlled study comparing these two treatments, Fairburn and his co-workers found them to be equally effective in resolving the disorder, with about 70 percent of patients showing a positive response. These treatment effects have proved robust over a six-year followup period.[101]

These treatments are clearly promising, and their relatively short-term nature should encourage their adoption in the United States, particularly given the pressure of managed care to shorten the course of treatment. It is of considerable interest that interpersonal treatment, which does not address the eating disorder symptoms directly, is equally as effective as the more symptom-focused cognitive-behavioral therapy. Perhaps, as Fairburn suggests, what both treatments share is an active, problem-solving approach. The fact that patients in interpersonal treatment are able to gain considerable control over problematic areas of their life (their troubled interpersonal relationships) may give them the con-fidence to tackle their eating disorder symptoms. Psychodynamically oriented therapists have long insisted that interpersonal and emotional conflicts, particularly regarding anger and self-assertion, underlie the symptoms of bulimia. Interpersonal therapy offers a systematic and efficient approach to these problems. The choice of one treatment modality versus another may be very much a function of therapist style or patient's preference.

Another treatment approach has been developed by the London-based psychiatrist J. Hubert Lacey.[102] Lacey has developed a program that integrates psychodynamic and behavioral approaches. Specifically, it utilizes efforts at direct control over the bingeing and purging behaviors (through behavioral contracts, meal planning, and weight maintenance), but also makes a serious effort to address the underlying emotional problems, particularly anger and depression, that tend to emerge in full force only after the bulimic symptoms have been removed. The treatment protocol is also short-term (ten weeks of individual and group sessions), although the client attends monthly and then three-monthly sessions to monitor progress and reinforce gains. This approach has been shown to be highly effective, with about 85 percent of patients abandoning their eating disorder symptoms after the first ten weeks of treatment. There is some tendency for the treatment effect to weaken over time, but followup studies show that 18 months after the end of treatment 24 percent of patients are still struggling with binge eating.

A final approach to the treatment of bulimia is the use of antidepressant medications. Considerable excitement greeted initial reports by Pope and Hudson in the 1980s that claimed dramatic effectiveness for the tricyclic antidepressant medications as well as the MAO inhibitors in the treatment of bulimia.[103] Subsequently, the second generation of antidepressants (serotonergic drugs such as Prozac) have been widely used in the treatment of bulimia, and are generally considered preferable because of their less severe side-effects. Although certain patients respond very well to antidepressants, it remains unclear what the mechanism of action of these medications is in relieving the symptoms of eating disorders. The originators of antidepressant treatment argued that their effectiveness suggested that bulimia is a variant of biological depression, and that this hypothesis was supported by the elevated prevalence of depressive disorders in the first-degree relatives of bulimics. However, it is generally conceded now that this formulation was too general. While many bulimics have a history of depression, a number do not present with nor have ever had a history of depressive symptoms. Perhaps those bulimics who do respond to antidepressants are those who have a coincident predisposition to depression, the alleviation of which may also lead to an improvement of their bulimic symptoms.

Another possibility, though, is that the "antidepressant" drugs have their effect on bulimics not so much through the alteration of mood but by interrupting the cycle of bingeing and purging through the improved regulation of hunger and satiety mechanisms.[104] Disturbed serotonin regulation appears to be characteristic of bulimia, just as it is of anorexia nervosa.[105] In fact, a study of recovered bulimics at the Western Psychiatric Institute in Pittsburgh indicates that serotonin activity in bulimics appears to be heightened. Along with the persistence of altered serotonin metabolism, the bulimics in this study had similar tendencies towards obsessive traits (perfectionism, symmetry, and exactness) as well as a depressed mood that are also characteristic of recovered anorexic patients. The authors of the study suggest that people with bulimia nervosa may share with anorexics a tendency towards a high degree of anticipatory anxiety, which, they speculate, may be part of a genetic predisposition common to both conditions.

It would seem that at least on the surface, cognitive-behavioral as well as interpersonal approaches to bulimia nervosa would be more compatible with the sociocultural framework advanced in this book, simply because these approaches deal on an individual level with an internalization of the cultural factors identified: body image distortion, dieting, and interpersonal dynamics associated with identity problems, and so forth. Yet the effectiveness of medication with some patients is not at all inconsistent with a sociocultural approach. Eating disorders are a primary example of a clash between culture and biology, in which individuals respond to cultural mandates about body image and ideals of perfection by attempting to force the body to respond in a way that defies the individual's constitutional limits. The fact that this might result in a dysregulation of neurotransmitters, via such behaviors as self-starvation, binge eating, or purging, which could be corrected by medication, should not come as a surprise.

Binge Eating Disorder: A Third Eating Disorder?

While bulimia nervosa appears to be of relatively recent origin, binge eating has been known for centuries. In the earlier psychiatric literature, cases of compulsive overeating, in the absence of vomiting or other methods of purging, were described by Wulff (cited earlier) and Fenichel, who proposed that binge eating is a kind of "oral perversion" that deserves to be thought of as an addiction.[106] Albert Stunkard, who uncovered Wulff's descriptions, himself described a binge eating syndrome that is found commonly (although by no means universally) among obese patients.[107] Lindner's famous psychoanalytic case of Laura, which was published in 1949, is one of the most dramatic descriptions of binge eating in the literature.[108]

Yet it was not until the early 1990s that researchers described a binge eating syndrome distinct from bulimia nervosa. The reasons for the delayed recognition of this disorder probably have to do with the reluctance on the part of obesity researchers to associate obesity per se with an eating disorder. Evidence had accumulated in the 1970s and 1980s that many of the obese eat normally, and that there was no particular pattern of psychopathology associated with obesity. Obesity thus is defined as a medical but not a psychiatric syndrome, and there is no diagnosis in the psychiatric diagnostic system that is exclusively associated with obesity.

Yet by the early 1990s, it had become clear that a certain subgroup of obese individuals (as well as a smaller group of individuals of normal weight) do in fact have a pattern of episodic binge eating very similar to that found in bulimia nervosa. However, the fact that these individuals do not make the drastic efforts at compensation for their caloric intake that are seen among bulimics seemed to warrant designating binge eating disorder as a distinct syndrome. The DSM-IV, which was published in 1994, designated binge eating disorder a criteria set in need of further study.[109] The architects of the DSM use this general designation when a diagnosis is relatively new or when there is insufficient research or information to include it as a standard diagnosis. The diagnostic criteria were as follows:

1 recurrent episodes of binge eating;
2 binge eating episodes characterized by at least three of the following:
    i   eating much more rapidly than normal
    ii   eating until feeling uncomfortably full
    iii eating large amount of food when not physically hungry
    iv eating alone because of embarrassment about how much one is eating
    v   feeling disgusted with oneself, depressed, or very guilty after overeating;

3   marked distress regarding binge eating;
4   binge eating occurring, on average, at least two days a week for six months;
5   binge eating not associated with inappropriate compensatory behaviors.

In a series of definitive initial studies, Robert Spitzer, the architect of the DSM system of diagnosis, along with several colleagues, found binge eating disorder to be relatively common among obese individuals who were involved in a variety of weight control programs.[110] In fact, approximately 30 percent of the participants in these programs, which included university hospital programs, outpatient weight-loss and eating disorders clinics, commercial weight-loss centers, and self-help groups, received a diagnosis of binge eating disorder. Within these programs, those individuals who suffered from the disorder were more likely to be more severely overweight than those who were free of the pattern. The program that contained the highest percentage of people with binge eating disorder was Overeaters Anonymous (OA) – an astounding 71 percent. Perhaps this is understandable if one considers that a primary rationale for attending OA in the first place is a problem with compulsive overeating. OA does not define itself as a weight-loss program. The lowest prevalence among the weight-control samples was found in Jenny Craig, Inc. (15 percent). The last-named is a commercial weight-loss center not typically located in medical settings. A lower percentage of the morbidly obese are likely to enrol in such a program owing to self-selection factors. While more females than males suffered from binge eating disorder, the relative proportion of females to males (three to two) was far less skewed than that for anorexia and bulimia nervosa. Overall, those with binge eating disorder were more likely to have suffered from a past history of depression and were also more likely to have a history of repeated attempts at dieting. For individuals in the community, the prevalence of binge eating disorder was considerably lower than that found in weight-loss programs (approximately 4.5 percent), and for college students it was lower still (approximately 2.5 percent). Interestingly, Spitzer's questionnaire suggested that the prevalence of bulimia nervosa among college students was 1.2 percent, suggesting that binge eating disorder is significantly more common than bulimia nervosa, even among students!

The discovery of binge eating disorder is important in at least two ways. First, it enables the identification of a serious eating disorder and associated psychopathology in a significant percentage of the obese population. The prevalence of binge eating disorder in the general population of overweight individuals is most likely lower than the rates found in the Spitzer studies, as the latter were individuals who were seeking treatment for overweight. Nevertheless, such individuals undoubtedly have special treatment needs, in that they have a serious eating disorder over and above any medical complications or social consequences that result from obesity. Second, though, mild degrees of binge eating disorder may be closely akin to the ill-defined but important phenomenon of compulsive overeating. We have virtually no idea of the general prevalence of such problems, but given the large popular literature on the subject, it is undoubtedly a matter of serious concern. Incidentally, it should be emphasized that while binge eating disorder was first discovered among the obese, it is not necessarily limited to this group. In one of Spitzer's studies, a significant proportion (more than 50 percent) of the subjects in the community who met criteria for binge eating disorder have never been obese. However, the number of such normal-weight binge eaters was relatively small, and most likely the syndrome is highly associated with being overweight.

While people with binge eating disorder are preoccupied with their weight and the desire to lose weight, they do not appear to overvalue thinness in the way that is characteristic of bulimia nervosa patients.[111] Also, unlike individuals with bulimia nervosa, in whom intense dieting and food restriction typically precede the onset of binge eating, for people with binge eating disorder, binge eating typically precedes any attempts at dieting. Binge eaters are characteristically depressed, and it is as yet unclear to what degree their depression plays a causal role or rather is a consequence of their inability to control their eating as well as of the social stigma associated with obesity. It does appear to be the case, however, that people with binge eating disorder use food to regulate dysphoric or difficult emotions, especially anger, sadness, and feelings of inadequacy.[112]

Because of the relative recency of its discovery, binge eating disorder will not be discussed to any considerable extent in the rest of this book. However, the questions of the general prevalence of this condition, its cultural distribution, developmental antecedents, and treatment remain relatively uncharted territory and should be the subject of intense research interest in the future.

The Psychobiology of Weight Regulation

Contemporary developments in research on the mechanisms of weight regulation may have considerable bearing on our understanding of the etiology of eating disorders. Based on well-established findings such as the tendency of humans and animals to maintain a stable weight over time, despite significant fluctuations in caloric intake, set-point theory posits that a system of physiological feedback within the brain acts so as to maintain or "defend" weight at a particular level or within a certain range.[113] For a particular individual, the set-point is determined by a complex set of interacting factors, such as genetic makeup, individual weight and metabolic function, and the ongoing level of energy expenditure. Set-point mechanisms operate analogously to a thermostat, so that significant deviations in weight from the set-point (either increases or decreases) will be compensated by biological reactions that work to offset the change. Dieting, for example, triggers a slowing of metabolic rate, which then makes the utilization of food intake more efficient. This type of process may account for the tendency of anorexic patients to regain weight during a refeeding program much more rapidly than one would expect based on the amount of calories that they have consumed. Set-point also offers a conceptual explanation of the notorious difficulty that most obese individuals experience in maintaining weight loss over the long term after a period of dieting. Some modification of the set-point is possible, for example, through changes in energy expenditure brought about by exercise, or under the influence of stress or certain drugs. For any individual, however, there are limits to its alterability, beyond which more drastic physiological complications may occur. These notions may have important implications for the eating disorders, in which the effort to maintain a low body weight is pursued relentlessly and by drastic measures.

Set-point theory is not without its critics, and there are clearly a number of problems with it from a scientific standpoint.[114] However, the study of the psychobiological mechanisms of weight regulation may be crucial to an integrated framework for understanding the eating disorders. For example, it could readily account for the eating binges that follow periods of semistarvation by bulimic anorexics or bulimia nervosa patients. It might also clarify why many obese individuals who undertake radical dieting may develop a syndrome virtually indistinguishable from bulimia nervosa. More generally, the study of the pathology of weight regulation could throw light on the interactions of cultural, psychological, and biological factors in the development of anorexia or bulimia. By demanding uniformly that individuals maintain unrealistically low body weights, cultural standards could provoke certain psychologically vulnerable individuals (i.e., those with low self-esteem or who are especially susceptible to external pressures) to violate their own biological limits, thereby giving rise to the destructive psychosomatic spirals known as anorexia and bulimia nervosa.

Shape, Weight, and Personal Identity

Eating disorders are obviously complex clinical conditions, and a full understanding of them must take into account psychological, developmental, and biological factors. What unites anorexia nervosa and bulimia, however, is that they are both disorders of development that revolve around the core issues of shape and body weight, and in which the person, most typically a female, obsessively focuses on the achievement of thinness in order to solve problems of personal identity. For the anorexic, this is typically a problem that first emerges at or shortly after puberty, when the body develops its adult shape and functions and the person first confronts the typical developmental challenges of adolescence. For the normal-weight bulimic, the developmental problems are a bit more advanced, and they typically involve issues of achieving a balance between relationships and a sense of separateness, issues that typically become critical at the separation from the family and confronting the challenges of achievement and relationships of young adulthood. For both, however, the core symptom is the same – that is, an obsession with food, weight, and body shape that becomes a defensive substitute for dealing with the conflicts associated with the achievement of an identity. The term eating disorders is something of a misnomer, therefore, although eating is definitely involved in the symptoms. The essence of anorexia and bulimia, as A. H. Crisp has suggested, is "dysmorphophobia," an anxious avoidance of the challenges of life through a focus on body shape and weight. In this book, we will examine why these particular symptoms have become the most characteristic disorders of female adolescent development in our own time. Before doing so, though, it will be worthwhile to look at what is known about the prevalence and cultural distribution of eating disorders, a question that will be the subject of the next chapter.

Chapter Three

Dimensions of an Epidemic

The Epidemiology of Eating Disorders

This book is an attempt to account for the proliferation of eating disorders in the late twentieth century. In order to lay the groundwork for a sociocultural understanding of this phenomenon, this chapter will be devoted to a review of the known epidemiological facts about eating disorders. Since the first edition of this book was written, there have been extensive debates about whether or not the incidence of eating disorders has actually increased. We will be particularly interested, therefore, in studies that address this question. Moreover, since the first edition numerous reports have appeared about eating disorders in parts of the world where they were previously unknown, for example, in India, China, Africa, and South America. We will examine this globalization of eating disorders and attempt to identify some of the social factors that might be responsible for it. Finally we will examine studies of eating disorders in ethnic minorities in the US and UK, as well as research that documents the vulnerability of immigrant groups who are undergoing rapid cultural assimilation.

The Sex Ratio of Eating Disorders

If there is any one fact that would evoke nearly universal agreement, it is that the overwhelming number of people who develop eating disorders are female. This association between eating disorders and gender extends back not only to the nineteenth-century history of anorexia nervosa (all of Gull and Lasegue's patients were female, for example) but to the pre-history of the disorder – the "holy anorexics" of the Middle Ages and the fasting girls of the eighteenth and nineteenth centuries. Contemporary studies tell us with a high degree of consistency that the ratio of female to male anorexics (and bulimics) is approximately 9 to 1, and some suggest that it is even higher than this.[1] Such findings confer on the eating disorders the distinction of having the most lopsided sex ratio of any disorder known to psychiatry, even exceeding that of other strongly gender-linked conditions such as agoraphobia and depression.[2] It is a fact that holds up with remarkable consistency across cultures, having been documented in various studies of American, Western European, and Asian populations. The extremely skewed sexual incidence of anorexia nervosa and bulimia is widely acknowledged, and yet its implications for an understanding of the dramatic increase of these conditions have not yet been fully drawn. It will play a central role in the sociocultural interpretation developed in this book.

Along with the high female prevalence, it is also very important to note that male anorexics and bulimics do exist, and in clinical presentation they closely resemble female patients (with the obvious exception of symptoms such as amenorrhea).[3] Some observers have argued that male anorexics are more psychologically disturbed than their female counterparts and that their clinical presentation is atypical. This perception, however, may itself be a gendered construction, as male patients are by definition manifesting uncharacteristic sex-role behavior and therefore are likely to be viewed as 'deviant.' There has also been widespread speculation recently that eating disorders in males may also be on the increase, a trend that has been linked with a growing preoccupation among males with weight and body image. While the latter trend is undeniably real, it is not at all clear that males would be increasingly led to the same types of obsessions with thinness as those in females who develop anorexia and bulimia. For one thing, the emphasis on thinness for males is less demanding than that for females: in fact, cultural norms tend to push males in the opposite direction, of developing more imposing frames. Some recent studies have in fact revealed a syndrome relatively prevalent among males that has been called "muscle dysmorphia" or "reverse anorexia," in which a man is consumed with thoughts that he is "too small." Such a preoccupation with one's smallness, in effect the mirror image of body image distortion in anorexia nervosa, can lead to obsessive behaviors whose aim is to increase bulk.[4] In addition, however, as will become abundantly clear in later chapters, it takes a particular psychological situation, one that is much more likely to arise in females, to drive certain individuals to abuse dieting and food in the way that anorexic or bulimic patients do.

There is no question that male anorexics are a neglected group of patients. Some feel stigmatized for having a "female" disorder and the resulting sense of shame can make them reluctant to seek help. One such adolescent patient, seen by myself, had seen the family doctor, who remarked to his mother that "this problem is only something that happens to girls." Males also find it difficult to attend support groups or seek out other forms of help, for fear of such stigmatization. The extent of male anorexia, as has been suggested by some, may well be underreported. Nevertheless, there is no systematic evidence for an actual increase in anorexia and bulimia in males; in fact, the studies that have been done suggest that the proportion of females has become if anything even larger.[5]

The Rising Incidence of Anorexia Nervosa

Oscar Hill, in a paper on epidemiology, commented that prior to 1970 anorexia nervosa was considered to be a "curiousity and a rarity."[6] In fact, an American publisher resisted the idea of an English translation of a 1963 book by the Italian psychiatrist Mara Selvini Palazzoli, on the grounds that "it dealt with a rare disease of interest to too few specialists." Paradoxically, this book, which was later to become a classic in the clinical literature on anorexia nervosa, was the first in the literature to make note of the increasing literature on anorexia nervosa (in Italy).[7] The publisher's perception, however, reflected the prevailing view of the low prevalence of anorexia nervosa even as recently as the 1960s.

As we saw in the preceding chapter, anorexia nervosa may have been fairly common in the latter half of the nineteenth century. Unfortunately, though, owing to absence of epidemiological data, we may be forever in the dark as to exactly how common. Only in the latter half of the twentieth century, specifically since the 1960s, have researchers actually begun to collect more precise data about the incidence and prevalence of anorexia nervosa. If we simply use the commentary of observers at different time periods as a guide, it would appear that anorexia nervosa was fairly common in the last three decades of the nineteenth century and the first decade of the twentieth, only to go into a decline perhaps until the 1960s, when it began its ascent to epidemic proportions at least until the 1980s. As we will see from the studies that we are about to review, evidence strongly suggests an increase in the incidence and prevalence of the condition between about 1970 and 1985.[8]

At a symposium held in Germany in the mid-1960s, a number of commentators suggested that anorexia had been on the increase since World War II, in particular in Germany and Japan.[9] However, the first formal documentation of an increase did not appear until 1970, as part of an elegant monograph on the subject by a Swedish psychiatrist, Sten Theander.[10] Theander surveyed the archives of all departments, medical as well as psychiatric, of the two major university hospitals in an area of southern Sweden over the period 1930 to 1960. From these records, he unearthed 11 cases of anorexia nervosa in the first decade of the study (1933–9), 25 in the second (1940–9), and 58 in the last (1950–9). Thus, there was a virtually fivefold increase in incidence over the three decades. Theander cautioned that the apparent increase might be misleading, in that improved detection of cases and greater awareness of the disorder could be important factors contributing to it. In addition, he noted a larger number of patients from the lower social classes in the later period, which he attributed to the greater accessibility of medical care for the less affluent. It is of course also possible that the disorder was beginning to "spread" throughout the socioeconomic spectrum, a phenomenon that seems to have been in evidence in more recent studies.[11]

A number of surveys conducted in the 1970s and 1980s seemed to confirm the impression of a rising incidence. One study found, for example, a sharp increase in the number of treated cases in three different locales in the United States and United Kingdom over the decade of the 1960s.[12] From the first to the second half of the decade, the number of cases increased from 9 to 15 in Monroe County, New York (the Rochester area), from 0 to 8 in the Camberwell district of London, and from 10 to 20 in Northeast Scotland (Aberdeen and surrounding area). These communities were chosen because they had central psychiatric registers, and therefore all cases that were treated in the area by psychiatrists were reported to the register. Of course, milder cases that were never brought to the attention of psychiatrists would escape detection by such a survey. A later study of the Monroe County area showed that the trend continued into the mid-1970s, with the number of cases doubling over the period. Also, in contrast with the 1960s in which there were a small number of male cases, almost all of the new cases in the 1970s were females.[13] Continuing sharp increases in hospital admissions for anorexia in the late 1970s and early 1980s were also reported for Aberdeen.[14]

Studies outside the US and UK conducted during the 1970s and 1980s also seemed to point to an increasing incidence of anorexia nervosa. One investigation conducted in the canton of Zurich, Switzerland revealed a quadrupling in the number of hospitalized cases by decade from the 1950s through the 1970s.[15] A followup study by the same research group suggested that by the mid-1980s the incidence had leveled off, with the number of cases being treated in the mid-1980s being roughly the same as that in the mid-1970s.[16] A systematic study conducted on the island of Bornholm, Denmark over the period of 1970 to 1989 indicated that the rates were stable overall, but had increased over the last five years of the study (1984 to 1989), with a prevalence rate of 222 per 100,000 for females between the ages of 15 and 24 during the last five years of the study.[17] These prevalence rates are comparable to, although somewhat lower than, those found by Lucas in the United States (see below). In Prague, Czechoslovakia, the number of cases hospitalized for anorexia increased fivefold between 1974 and 1983.[18] In Japan, a survey of a large number of medical facilities all over the country showed that the number of patients in treatment for anorexia nervosa doubled between 1976 and 1981. Even from 1980 to 1981 alone, the total number of patients in treatment jumped from 1,080 to 1,312.[19] These trends were confirmed in a later study at a University Hospital in the Yamaguta Prefecture in Northern Japan, an area of approximately 1,200,000 inhabitants about 350 miles north of Tokyo. Over the period 1978–92, the number of patients with anorexia nervosa increased sharply over the period, from 12 new outpatients during the years 1978–82 to 26 between the years 1988 and 1992 (with even greater increases in the number of patients with bulimia nervosa).[20]

While formal epidemiological studies have not been done, an expanding literature and informal observations suggested an increasing incidence of anorexia nervosa in France,[21] Germany,[22] Italy,[23] Belgium,[24]

Norway,[25] and Spain.[26] The Eastern European countries were also not exempt from an interest in eating disorders, even prior to the breaking up of the Soviet bloc, as is evidenced from a number of clinical reports from countries such as Poland, Czechoslovakia, and Yugoslavia that appeared in the early 1980s.[27] A number of reports in the 1990s indicate an increasing number of cases in Eastern Europe following the breakup of the Soviet bloc in 1989, particularly in Czechoslovakia, Hungary, and the former East Germany. In Prague, Czechoslovakia, in particular, a report in 1998 indicated that the demand for treatment far outstripped available services.[28] Numerous publications on anorexia nervosa appeared in the former Soviet Union during the 1980s, although once again there were no reported data on an increased prevalence of the condition. When such an increase was mentioned in the literature, European and American data were cited. Most of the studies were of patients hospitalized at University Hospitals in Moscow.[29]

To return to the formal epidemiological studies, those that we have reviewed that were conducted prior to the 1990s suffered from significant methodological limitations. For example, most utilized already diagnosed cases of anorexia nervosa in existing medical records as an indication of incidence or prevalence. It is possible that some cases may have been overlooked or misdiagnosed, with the resulting prevalence figures being an underestimate of the true prevalence. A related problem lies in the fact that the basis of the diagnosis of anorexia nervosa may have varied considerably from one case to the next. A review of records using uniform diagnostic criteria would correct this problem and yet in many of the studies that have been cited, this was not done. Finally, many of the studies that we have reviewed, with the exception of those of Theander in Sweden and Willi in Switzerland, covered a relatively short period of time (ten years in most cases).

A number of studies published in the 1990s seem to have corrected for some of these problems. Probably the most important of these was conducted by Dr Alexander Lucas, a psychiatrist at the Mayo Clinic in Minnesota, itself a center long interested in the treatment of anorexia nervosa. Lucas reviewed all available medical records for both the Mayo Clinic and the surrounding community of Rochester, Minnesota (population, 60,000) over a 50-year period beginning in 1935 and ending in 1985.[30] He screened the files for a number of diagnostic terms related to anorexia nervosa, including symptoms such as amenorrhea, starvation, and weight loss. All possible cases identified in this way were then reviewed according to DSM-III-R criteria of anorexia nervosa. In this way he was able to identify a large number of patients not previously diagnosed as having anorexia nervosa. Most of those identified had never been hospitalized for their illness, and many had never received any kind of psychiatric treatment. Thus, Lucas was able to catch numerous cases in his net that would be lost in a typical psychiatric register survey.

Over the 50-year period of the study, 181 individuals who had resided in Rochester for a period of at least one year developed anorexia nervosa (166 females and 15 males). Interestingly, this corresponds fairly closely with the typical sex ratio of the incidence of anorexia nervosa (actually, at 8.1 females for every male, it is a little lower). The figures also showed some striking historical patterns. For females age 10–19, the incidence rate (the number of new cases developing per year) during the earliest period of the study (1935–9) was relatively high, but then fell to a low during the 1950s, and finally began to increase in the 1960s and rose to a peak in the early 1980s. On the other hand, the incidence rates for females between the ages of 20 and 59 remained more or less flat over the period. Of particular interest was the sharp increase in the number of cases over the period from 1980 to 1984. Specifically, the incidence rate rose from 7 cases per 100,000 population in the period 1950–4 to 26.3 in 1980–4. On the average, the incidence rate increased by 35 percent for every five-year period beginning in 1950 and ending in 1984. We shall have more to say about Lucas's findings on prevalence shortly, but suffice it to say that by the last period of the study Lucas suggested that anorexia nervosa had become the third most common health problem among adolescent females, with the first and second most common being obesity and asthma, in that order.

Lucas offered some interesting speculations about the trends in incidence over time, particularly the rather high prevalence in the earliest period of the study, the decline in the 1940s and 1950s, and the rise in incidence to a peak in the early 1980s. He suggested that changing trends in fashion over the 50-year period may account for apparent cyclical incidence of anorexia nervosa. Citing findings by Silverstein to be discussed later (see chapter 5), he points to change in the bust-to-waist ratio of female models, a measure of thinness, from a relatively low level in the 1920s and 1930s to a higher level in the 1950s and then a decline again in the 1970s and 1980s. Thus he hypothesizes that the changes in the rates of anorexia nervosa can be explained by the sociocultural pressures of body image ideals and are particularly reflected in the response of girls between the ages of 10 and 19, perhaps the most vulnerable population to such pressures. Lucas is quick to point out that only a very small percentage of this group will actually succumb to these pressures and develop anorexia nervosa. The rest are "protected" most likely by a biological mechanism that prevents them from losing excessive weight, even following stringent efforts to diet. In fact, Lucas concludes his study with a provocative speculation. He suggests that there are perhaps two types of anorexia nervosa, with differing etiologies. The first type is of largely biological origin, reflects a relatively severe form of the illness, and occurs at a relatively constant rate over time. The second type is a milder form that occurs mainly in teenagers and is triggered primarily by sociocultural pressures. Lucas hypothesizes that the biological form of anorexia nervosa is probably constant over time, whereas the environmentally influenced type gives rise to the changing incidence rates found in his and other studies.

Tilman Habermas, a psychologist at the University of Munich who himself has done historical studies on eating disorders, suggests an alternative interpretation of Lucas's data.[31] Habermas suggests that Lucas's findings of a relatively high incidence of anorexia nervosa in the late 1930s may have been an artifact of the strong research interest in the disorder at the Mayo Clinic during that period, an interest that may have affected the awareness of the illness among those who were employed by the clinic in gathering its early statistics. The ebbing of research at Mayo on anorexia nervosa during the 1950s may have led to the decline in diagnosis during that period. Habermas suggests that the most salient of Lucas's findings is the increase of new cases from the 1960s to the early 1980s, the most obvious explanation for which is the change in sociocultural factors – and particularly the increasing emphasis on thinness – in the period. Habermas is skeptical about Lucas's two-subtype formulation theory of anorexia nervosa, for which he feels there is little evidence.

A second methodologically improved study published in the 1990s was an epidemiological survey of a large area of Northeast Scotland. This study utilized the Aberdeen psychiatric case register, which covers a population area of about 550,000, to examine all inpatients and outpatients who had been treated for anorexia nervosa over a 26-year period, beginning in 1965 and ending in 1991. Like Lucas, the researchers were interested in whether cases that had originally been identified as anorexia nervosa had been misdiagnosed. Such an error would of course give a false impression about any changes in incidence rates that were detected. With these considerations in mind, they therefore reviewed the records of each patient who had received a diagnosis of anorexia nervosa, using such criteria as significant weight loss, amenorrhea, and "evidence characteristic of psychopathology." The first count of cases yielded 428 females with a register diagnosis of anorexia nervosa. However, application of the research diagnostic criteria to the original case notes revealed that only 287 (67 percent) of these could be confirmed as cases of anorexia nervosa. The authors conclude, somewhat dryly, that "the numbers of false positives are of more than sufficient magnitude to justify anxieties about accepting uncritically case register diagnosis of anorexia nervosa."[32]

Now for the crucial finding. Having identified 287 true cases of anorexia nervosa over the period, a statistical analysis revealed a sharply increasing incidence of new cases over the entire time period. The rate of increase was on the order of 5 percent a year. Viewed from another angle, the number of new cases increased between three- and fourfold over the period beginning in the late 1960s and early 1970s to the final period of the study. More specifically, the rate of new cases per 100,000 population was about 3 in 1965, while it was 15 in 1991.

The authors suggest a number of reasons for the increase. Prominent among these are the rise in the prevalence of dieting behaviors over the period, which they argue other research clearly shows to be the precursor of eating disorders. They also point to factors similar to those that are discussed in this book, namely the increasing pressures on females to compete and perform, and the way in which these new demands for individuation become translated into the quest for weight and shape control. They also mention the possibility of a link between anorexia nervosa and depression, and point to the demonstrated increasing prevalence of the latter. Despite their conviction that the increased prevalence that they observed is a real phenomenon, they still have some questions as to whether the increase in treated cases to some extent results from a greater sensitivity to the presence of the disorder by health professionals.

While these studies seem to suggest clear evidence of an increasing incidence of anorexia nervosa, other research has not been unequivocal in its acceptance of the hypothesis. For example, two epidemiological studies conducted in Denmark and the Netherlands, respectively, did not yield a conclusion of increasing incidence.[33] But these studies are not surveys of complete catchment areas, but rather examine more narrowly defined treatment populations. For example, the Danish study examined admission rates to psychiatric hospitals, while the Dutch study investigated the prevalence of the diagnosis of anorexia nervosa among primary care physicians (general practitioners, as they would be known in the US). It could be argued that neither of these is likely to reflect the actual incidence of anorexia nervosa in the general population. Counting hospital admissions only, for example, discounts the increasing numbers of anorexic patients who are treated on an outpatient basis. Using diagnoses of primary care physicians, as was the case in the study in the Netherlands, would not reflect the possibility that many cases of anorexia nervosa, particularly the milder ones, are increasingly likely to be treated by mental health workers on an outpatient basis. As a result of these considerations, it is difficult to accept the findings of these studies as a refutation of the hypothesis of increased incidence.

Doubts and Skepticism

Although the most broad-based of the studies on anorexia nervosa point to a rise in the incidence of the condition, some challenging questions have been raised about such a conclusion.[34] The first of these was the one noted in the first epidemiological study by Sten Theander, who argued that an apparent increase may be a reflection of an increased professional and public awareness of the disorder. As health professionals have become more aware of the diagnostic criteria for anorexia nervosa and have been exposed to eating disorders in their training, they are more likely to recognize the illness and less likely to attribute underweight conditions, particularly those which have no apparent medical cause, to mysterious endocrine conditions, poor eating habits, or other vague causes. This would be particularly true, for example, for pediatricians. As to possible increases in the public awareness of the condition, it could be argued that the vast amount of media exposure and public discussion of eating disorders have made families and friends acutely aware of the signs of the condition. This would facilitate an earlier and more extensive identification of cases, as those who have the condition would come forward for medical or therapeutic help at an earlier date.

Countering these arguments, one could point out that physicians and psychiatrists have long been aware of anorexia nervosa (since the late nineteenth century) and that signs and symptoms of the illness, involving as it does an alarming degree of weight loss, are not easily overlooked or misattributed. Moreover, the clinical picture of anorexia is not a vague set of symptoms that is easily confused with other conditions; to the contrary, anorexia nervosa is one of the most readily diagnosable psychiatric disorders. In addition, it could just as easily be argued that the number of cases that show up in medical statistics *underestimates* rather than overestimates the increase in prevalence. This is because surveys such as those we have described only count treated cases, which tend to be the most severe. There is good reason to think that the number of borderline cases, most of which never come to the attention of clinicians, is much greater than the number of formally diagnosed and treated ones (see below). Cases of bulimia are much more likely to be missed during medical examinations, since many bulimics are of normal weight and are highly secretive about their bingeing or purging episodes. As for increased public awareness of the condition, this may have had some impact, although it is unlikely that in clinically significant cases of anorexia nervosa some medical attention would not be sought out.

A different sort of challenge to the hypothesis of increased incidence and prevalence was raised in a 1987 study by Williams and King, published in the British medical journal *Lancet*.[35] These authors used a statistical technique used in demographic research to analyze the rates of admissions for anorexia nervosa to psychiatric hospitals in England over the period 1972–81. Their method enabled them to distinguish whether the increase was due to a change in the age structure of the population or to more contemporary factors affecting either the subjects or psychiatrists, such as changing fashion norms or altered diagnostic practices. They did in fact find a sharply increased rate of admission over the period, but their analysis suggested that this could be accounted for entirely by an 11 percent increase in the population of females between the ages of 15 and 24 over the decade. In contrast, contemporary influences did not appear to play a role. Their conclusion was that the increase in first admissions was basically an artifact of the growth in the population at risk, and that therefore any presumed epidemic of eating disorders was nothing more than a "medical myth."

That the increase in treated cases of eating disorders might be at least in part an artifact of a larger adolescent and young adult population is an intriguing suggestion and deserves further study.[36] But it is unreasonable to draw such a sweeping conclusion as that the apparent increase in eating disorders is a myth from the analysis of one particular population over a ten-year period. As Lucas's study showed, treated cases of anorexia nervosa increased from the 1960s through the mid-1980s, with a particular sharp increase from 1980 to 1985. It is doubtful that this increase, particularly in the latter period, could be accounted for by population statistics. Furthermore, while Williams and King suggest that their analysis shows that changes in fashion ideals could not have accounted for the increase in admissions over the ten-year period that they studied, few would make such an argument in the first place. Factors such as body image ideals take a longer period of time to exert their influence. Even Lucas, who is receptive to the arguments of Williams and King and skeptical about the use of the term epidemic to describe anorexia nervosa, has underscored the point that his data suggest that the incidence of the disorder has been cyclical and that sociocultural factors such as an emphasis on thinness most likely have played a role in determining the cycle.[37]

One possibility that has not been raised in the literature, however, is that while the incidence of anorexia nervosa may have risen sharply from the 1950s to the 1980s, it may have leveled off or even declined since then. While there are no epidemiological data to support such a conclusion, there is some suggestive evidence for such a trend for bulimia nervosa that will be reviewed below. Certainly such a decline, if ultimately verified, would not be incompatible with a general hypothesis about the overall cyclical incidence of this condition.

How Common is Anorexia Nervosa?

Although the weight of the evidence suggests that the incidence of anorexia nervosa has increased, estimates of its true prevalence in various populations are still difficult to come by. Epidemiologists usually state prevalence figures in terms of the number of cases per 100,000 population. Using such figures, anorexia nervosa would appear to be a rather uncommon disorder. For example, Theander, in the study cited earlier, estimated that the prevalence of anorexia nervosa in Sweden in the early 1960s was only 0.45 cases per 100,000 population.[38] The surveys in Monroe County, New York, the Camberwell district of London, and Northeast Scotland that were conducted in the late 1960s and early 1970s indicated a prevalence on average of about 1 case per 100,000 population.[39] Figures such as these hardly give the impression of an epidemic disorder.

On the other hand, these figures may be of limited value in terms of giving a realistic idea of the true prevalence of the condition. First, they were conducted relatively early in the period of interest, with Theander's being completed by 1960 and the second spanning the years from 1940 to 1960. Second, prevalence figures in terms of the number of cases per total population, even though standard, are somewhat misleading, in that the overwhelming majority of anorexic patients are females between the ages of, say, 13 and 25 (and this lower age-limit may still be too high if we consider that the number of early onset cases may be increasing). Thus, a more relevant impression of the true prevalence of the disorder would be to estimate the number of affected people relative to the population at risk. Third, given that anorexia nervosa is a potentially severe illness with the threat of mortality and chronic morbidity, and affects a portion of the population that is relatively healthy, what may appear to be a small prevalence rate may be significant from a public health standpoint.

The most widely cited estimate of the prevalence of girls at the age of risk is that from a study conducted by the psychiatrist A. H. Crisp of English secondary school students in the 1970s.[40] The figure from this study, of one case for every 150 to 200 adolescent girls, is probably the best known in the literature, and in fact a prevalence of 0.5 percent is consistent with studies of the prevalence of anorexia nervosa among American college students. Again, these rates may not seem high, but a more concrete extrapolation puts the matter into perspective. For example, the number of young women with clinical anorexia nervosa in England, using these prevalence rates, would be about 10,000; whereas in the United States the total number would be around 120,000. When we take into account the severity and potential lethality of the disorder, as well as the fact that this is a segment of the population that would be expected to be free of major health problems, then these numbers appear to be very striking and a matter of great concern. One might be hesitant to use the term "epidemic" to apply to them, but their significance is all too real.

With the publication of Lucas's study, we are in a much better position to give an estimate of the prevalence of anorexia nervosa in a small American city.[41] As we have discussed, Lucas found a steadily increasing incidence of anorexia nervosa from 1935 to 1985, with the most striking trend being a sharp increase in the number of new cases that were diagnosed between 1980 and 1985. As a prologue to his calculations of prevalence rates, Lucas states somewhat dramatically that "on Jan. 1, 1985, 99 females and six males with a history of anorexia nervosa were alive and residing in Rochester (Minnesota)." The total female population of Rochester at the time was 32,353. Based on these figures, the overall prevalence of anorexia nervosa for the general population was 306 per 100,000 for females and 22 per 100,000 for males, a ratio of approximately 12 to 1. It is of interest to compare these figures with those of Theander in Sweden in the 1960s of less than 1 per 100,000 people. But for females in the age of risk (15 to 19 in Lucas's study), the prevalence rate was an astonishing 480.3 per 100,000 persons. If these data can be extrapolated to the US population at large using 1980 census figures, then the number of anorexic women residing in the United States would be roughly 300,000 – again, a strikingly large number, given the earlier impressions of the rarity of this disease, and an alarming one from a medical or general health standpoint. Admittedly, Lucas's rates are the highest obtained in an array of epidemiological surveys, and therefore may be atypical. But on the other hand, the access of this research team to medical records and the thoroughness of their methodology lends their findings a high degree of credibility.

The Rise of Bulimia Nervosa

If anorexia nervosa, once a rare disorder, has increased in prevalence to the point where it is considered not uncommon, the sudden ascendancy of bulimic syndromes seems nothing short of spectacular. It is difficult to pinpoint exactly when bulimia nervosa came into prominence, but the publication of Boskind-Lodahl's paper on "bulimarexia" (an early term for bulimia nervosa that has fallen out of favor) suggests that the syndrome was already becoming common on college campuses in the United States by the mid-1970s.[42] Similarly, Gerald Russell's seminal paper on the bulimic syndrome in 1979, in which he coined the term bulimia nervosa, makes it clear that by this point bulimic patients were beginning to be treated in significant numbers in specialist eating disorder units.[43] It is probably the case, and certainly corresponds with this author's experience, that bulimic patients began to present for outpatient treatment in large numbers in the very late 1970s and early 1980s in North America. For example, in a study of referral rates to the Clarke Institute of Psychiatry and the Toronto General Hospital in Canada, referral rates for bulimia nervosa were as follows: 6 cases in 1978, 17 in 1979, 14 in 1980, 23 in 1981, 66 in 1982, 65 in 1983, 68 in 1984, 110 in 1985, and 140 in 1986. During the same period, the referrals for restricting anorexia nervosa remained relatively constant, fluctuating between 15 and 30 per year.[44] Essentially similar results were found in a study of the same time period in Rochester, Minnesota.[45] As Craig Johnson, a noted eating disorder researcher in the United States, said about his early attempts to do research in the late 1970s and early 1980s in the United States, "we went out to study anorexics but we found bulimics."

Could the tremendous increase in the number of bulimics seeking treatment be a matter of a previously hidden disorder "coming out of the closet"? After all, we know that the bulimic syndrome is one surrounded by considerable shame, and therefore publicity about the disorder, which began to occur in the 1980s, as well as the growing interest of clinicians in the problem, could have encouraged those who would have previously remained untreated to seek help. But these interpretations are unlikely to be true. First, it would appear that the publicity about bulimia, particularly in the major press which gave considerable space to Katherine Halmi's epidemiological study of bulimia (see below), *followed* rather than preceded the first influx of sufferers. Second, the appearance of bulimics at normal weight in large numbers was not something that clinicians were anticipating but rather came as something totally unexpected. Thus, although the bulimia diagnosis first appeared in the DSM-III in 1980, Boskind-Lodahl's and Russell's publications tell us that there were already large numbers of sufferers in the 1970s.

On historical grounds, it also seems unlikely that the apparent epidemic increase in bulimia was an illusion. It is true that certain aspects of bulimia had been noted in the earlier medical literature, and it was certainly well established as a syndrome of anorexia nervosa. As described in chapter 2, Albert Stunkard had written about a number of cases that had been described by the Russian-born psychiatrist Moshe Wulff in the 1920s.[46] Wulff's cases, though, seemed to emphasize the binge eating component of the syndrome, rather than the binge-compensation cycle and the preoccupation with thinness that characterize contemporary bulimics. While prior to the 1970s the use of vomiting was not unknown as a means of weight control, it seems implausible that large numbers of sufferers from what we now describe as a bulimic disorder would have gone unrecognized. A retrospective study of women who had been college students in the 1950s and 1960s showed that virtually none could recall any of their peers or good friends manifesting anything like the bulimia nervosa syndrome.[47] Although without epidemiological studies we will never be certain, it is likely that the phenomenon that occurred in the late 1970s and early 1980s was a new development, one that was facilitated by the convergence of a number of forces: the increasing focus on thinness among college women, the increasing anxieties about "identity" and sexuality in the wake of the social upheavals of the 1960s, and the growing trend towards disorders characterized by "impulse" (in particular, bulimia) as opposed to "self-denial."

The first epidemiological study of bulimia, carried out by Katherine Halmi and her colleagues at a summer-school registration at the State University of Purchase in New York, came as something of a shock when the results were disseminated in the press.[48] A questionnaire, which was handed out to summer-school registrants, showed that fully 13 percent of the sample "met all the DSM III criteria for bulimia." Soon after Halmi's study, Harrison Pope, a researcher at McClean Hospital in Boston, conducted an innovative survey by handing out questionnaires at random to 304 female shoppers at a suburban shopping mall.[49] Fully 10 percent of those who returned the survey reported a history of bulimia and almost 5 percent were actively bulimic at the time of the study. All of these were women in their twenties and thirties. A number of other surveys conducted by Pope and his colleagues on college campuses suggested a lifetime prevalence of bulimia anywhere from 10 to as high as 20 percent![50] It seemed that the findings of Halmi were not a fluke.

Nevertheless, it soon became clear that these studies were beset with problems. For one thing, they were almost all questionnaire-based.

Questionnaire studies have numerous drawbacks, one of the most prominent of which is that the questions posed may be relatively ambiguous. For example, a typical question in this survey was "Have you ever engaged in binge eating?" The definition of binge, particularly when one leaves it up to a respondent, is notoriously variable. For one person, it could simply mean overeating at Thanksgiving, an experience that could easily be shared by well over 50 percent of any sample; for another, it might mean something more closely approximating a symptom. A second problem is that the definition of "bulimia" utilized in the determination of prevalence rates in these studies was the rather loose and perhaps overly inclusive criteria of the DSM-III. The DSM-III defined bulimia as a syndrome of binge eating and focused on the subjective experience of abnormality of the eating pattern. It did not require, however, that the binges be followed by the typical efforts to compensate, most characteristically through self-induced vomiting, although subjects might report such a symptom. Furthermore, it did not differentiate between a subject who might have an occasional disturbing experience of binge eating and one who was having several bulimic episodes per week or even per day. Finally, the DSM-III criteria said nothing about the subject's preoccupation with weight and shape, features that are now recognized as central to the disorder. As a result of these issues, which were later clarified in the revised diagnostic criteria of the DSM-III-R, the early studies most likely resulted in significant overestimation of the prevalence rates.

One study that attempted to correct for this problem, a survey of first-year students at the University of Minnesota in 1980, compared the rates of bulimia using loose criteria (any history of bingeing and purging) and the more stringent definition.[51] Using "loose" criteria, the prevalence turned out to be around 8 percent, a figure comparable to the other college surveys; however, when it was stipulated that a subject would qualify as bulimic only if she binged and purged on a weekly basis, the percentage dropped to 1 percent. In order to see whether the prevalence of bulimia was increasing, the same researchers carried out an identical survey of first-year students three years later (in 1983).[52] Using the same stringent criteria, and adding the stipulation that in order to meet diagnostic criteria a bulimic subject should have an intense fear of becoming fat, they found that the percentage of students who were bulimic had jumped to 3 percent. The figure of 2 or 3 percent probably represents a conservative estimate of the prevalence of bulimia among college students; but even using this estimate, one can extrapolate that between 1 and 2 million young women in the United States have a clinically significant problem with bulimia. Other studies have indicated that bulimia has also become a significant problem for high-school students, at least in the United States. One survey, conducted by Craig Johnson and his colleagues at a suburban high school in the Chicago area, indicated a prevalence of bulimia of around 4 percent, a figure comparable to the estimates for college students.[53]

Since the early 1980s, a number of prevalence studies of bulimia nervosa have been carried out. Whitaker and his colleagues found the lifetime prevalence to be 4.2 percent among female high-school students in New Jersey.[54] In a study of an unusual sample whose purpose was to investigate the genetics of psychiatric disorders, Kenneth Kendler and his colleagues queried 1,176 twin pairs drawn from a twin registry in Virginia. Following the concerns about the diagnosis of bulimia from previous studies, these researchers distinguished between narrowly defined bulimia, for which subjects met the diagnostic criteria for bulimia nervosa, and broadly defined bulimia, which included narrowly defined cases and those where most but not all of the diagnostic criteria were met. They found 62 narrowly defined cases and 63 possible cases, giving lifetime prevalence rates of 2.8 percent and 2.9 percent respectively. If these rates were extrapolated throughout the age of risk (that is, the age at which subjects, some of whom were young, could develop the disorder), then the "lifetime risk rates" were 4.2 percent and 8 percent respectively. The bulimics in Kendler's sample had high rates of depressive and anxiety disorders. Statistical analysis showed that, compared with other twins in the larger sample, bulimic subjects were characterized by low paternal care, a history of dieting and weight fluctuation, low self-esteem, and an external locus of control. Consistent with the hypothesis about the recency of the bulimia problem, twins born after 1960 (about half the sample) were much more likely to receive a diagnosis than twins born before 1960. The mean age of onset of the disorder was about 20 years.[55]

Has the incidence and prevalence of bulimia nervosa increased? Based on what we know, it appears that bulimia nervosa is a disorder that first appeared in large numbers in the 1970s and early 1980s. The disorder probably began to develop in the population before it became known to clinicians. Hence the data showing a large increase in the number of cases presenting for treatment in the early 1980s probably indicate that the problem had been developing some years prior to this, perhaps beginning in the mid-1970s. The data on whether the disorder has continued to increase are more mixed. On the one hand, a study by Hans Hoek in the Netherlands indicated that the incidence of bulimia increased by about 15 percent a year over the period 1985 to 1989. This study was limited by a rather short time frame and by the fact that the incidence rates were determined by cases detected by primary care physicians. By way of contrast, a followup study to those conducted on University of Minnesota first-year students indicated that the prevalence had gone from 1 percent in 1980 to 3.2 percent in 1983 to 2.2 percent in 1986. The researchers concluded, in a 1991 publication, that "the prevalence for this disorder may have peaked and may be declining." Similar conclusions were reached by Todd Heatherton in a ten-year cross-sectional survey of students at Harvard College. While bulimia nervosa still represented a significant problem, the estimated number of students meeting diagnostic criteria declined from 7.2 percent in 1982 to 5.1 percent in 1992. Heatherton found that the prevalence of extreme dieting practices, especially fasting and the use of low-calorie, low-carbohydrate diets had undergone a significant decline over the ten-year period. Furthermore, significantly fewer women perceived themselves as overweight or wanting to lose 10 pounds, despite the fact that female students were on the average 5 pounds heavier in the second assessment.[56]

Our knowledge is still too limited to tell us whether the incidence of bulimia nervosa is currently increasing, declining, or remaining constant. What we do know is that it is a problem that conservatively afflicts a minimum of 1 million American women and a significantly larger number worldwide. Despite the publicity about bulimia and some evidence that the public discussion of the problem has led some to seek treatment, it remains an issue surrounded by an aura of shame and secrecy. Many of the studies that we have reviewed, particularly those that rely on questionnaires, are unlikely to reveal the true extent of the problem. We may simply never be able to determine this.

A Spectrum of Eating Disorders

It is possible, furthermore, that even methodologically thorough studies such as that of Lucas may underestimate the true dimensions of the eating disorders phenomenon. This is because Lucas's, as well as most epidemiological surveys, only count as "cases" those individuals who meet formal diagnostic criteria for anorexia nervosa. But such individuals may only represent the tip of the iceberg. As discussed in chapter 2, many individuals may have numerous symptoms of eating disorders, but for one reason or another fail to meet formal diagnostic criteria for an eating disorder. For example, one person may meet the diagnostic criteria for refusal to maintain body weight, body image concern, and weight phobia, but her weight loss may not meet the 15 percent level and she may continue to menstruate, if irregularly. Another may have weight loss and amenorrhea, but may have a realistic perception of her body size. From a diagnostic standpoint, such individuals are given the rather bloodless classification "eating disorder not otherwise specified (or EDNOS)." An alternative category, perhaps one which conveys the meaning better, is that of "subclinical eating disorders." On the other hand the meaning of the latter is subtly different from that of EDNOS, in that it implies a lesser degree of severity.

An early study of the phenomenon of subclinical eating disorders was undertaken by Ingvar Nylander, a Swedish psychiatrist, who surveyed a large population of high-school students in Stockholm in the early 1970s about their dieting habits, body image attitudes, and physical symptoms. Nylander found that over 50 percent of the girls had at some time "felt fat" and had undertaken rigorous dieting in order to counteract these feelings. Fully 10 percent of the 1,241 female students had experienced at least three symptoms of anorexia nervosa, such as chilliness, constipation, fatigue, amenorrhea, anxiety, and depression. Nylander concluded that "most cases of anorexia nervosa are incipient and/or mild and never come to medical attention but are spontaneously cured with increasing maturity." Her findings suggest that the symptoms of anorexia nervosa exist along a continuum of severity and that diagnosed cases represent only a small fraction of a much larger number of subclinical disorders.[57]

Studies in the early 1980s in the United States and the United Kingdom indicated that preoccupation with body image, feelings of fatness, stringent dieting, binge eating, and purging behavior had become commonplace on college campuses. For example, Button and Whitehouse conducted a survey of students at a College of Technology in England around 1980. Using an initial screening followed by an interview, they found that 5 percent of the students could be categorized as having a subclinical form of anorexia nervosa, and that a somewhat greater number scored in the "anorexic" range on the Eating Attitudes Test.[58] A more recent study of the phenomena of subclinical eating disorders was undertaken in the early 1990s by Kurth and her colleagues from the University of Michigan, who surveyed and then selectively interviewed 1,367 entering first-year female students.[59] While the prevalence of anorexia nervosa and bulimia nervosa were the typical 1 percent and 2 percent, respectively, the percentage of students who met criteria for an eating disorder not otherwise specified was a striking 13 percent. Typically, these were students who met most criteria for bulimia nervosa, except for the "frequency" criteria for bingeing and purging (twice a week for three months). In this example, the concept of EDNOS and subclinical eating disorder would roughly coincide, as the disorder in question differs from the clinical condition because it is of a lesser degree of severity. While one might be reluctant to utilize the term "epidemic" for figures such as 1 or 2 percent, one would be much more willing to do so for a figure as high as 13 percent! Furthermore, the authors classified the dieting practices of the students, and determined, using categories that reflected intensity, that 19 percent of the students were "at-risk" dieters, 21 percent "intense dieters," 23 percent "moderate dieters," 26 percent "casual dieters," a paltry 9 percent non-dieters, and 2 percent probable bulimia nervosa. In other words, if we consider intense dieting to be the principal risk factor for eating disorders, then roughly 50 percent of the sample could be viewed to be at some degree of risk.

These studies seem to support a "spectrum" notion for eating disorders. Behaviors such as continuous and sometimes stringent dieting, preoccupation with body image, and binge eating have been repeatedly shown to be commonplace, at least among college students, and more recent evidence suggests that they have become pervasive among high-school students as well, at least in the United States. However, only a small number of such individuals will go on to develop a "clinical" eating disorder, one that meets formal diagnostic criteria and that requires clinical intervention. Yet, the phenomenon of a spectrum of eating-disordered behaviors is highly congruent with the general model of an ethnic disorder that was described in the first chapter of this book. The symptoms of the disorder are continuous with attitudes and patterns of behavior that are more or less normative or at least widespread within the wider culture. But what then leads an individual to develop a clinically significant disorder? While from a diagnostic standpoint it appears to be merely the intensity or frequency of the behaviors in question (or perhaps their physical consequences, such as amenorrhea), there are almost certainly individual factors that come into play that lead the individual to adopt these behaviors to a point where they become self-destructive. For example, individuals with pre-existing mood or anxiety disorders, or a whole host of underlying psychopathologies or developmental vulnerabilities, histories of sexual abuse or familial concerns with weight control, may be predisposed to adopting such culturally sanctioned behaviors as modes of managing unbearable levels of distress. The concept of cultural influence is not primarily useful in answering the question of who *in particular* develops an eating disorder. It is critical, on the other hand, in understanding why these disorders have become pervasive.

The Global Spread of the Eating Disorders Phenomenon

The epidemiological studies that we have reviewed provide reasonably consistent evidence for an increase of eating disorders in the United States, the UK, Denmark, the Netherlands, Switzerland, and Japan. Although we lack the formal studies in other countries, it would appear from a proliferating literature and treatment units that these disorders have also become increasingly prevalent in France, Spain, Italy, Germany, and perhaps to a lesser extent in the Eastern European countries, including Czechoslovakia, Hungary, and the former East Germany. The issue is not so much a geographic one, as it is a cultural one. For example, anorexia nervosa shows a substantial prevalence among the Caucasian population in South Africa,[60] and among the upper socio-economic classes in Santiago, Chile.[61] Because of a lack of data, we know too little about the comparative incidence and prevalence of eating disorders in various countries. It is conceivable, certainly, that cultural differences could lead to variations in prevalence. An often-discussed example is that of France in comparison with the US or UK. France is widely thought of as a culinary culture, which places great value on the aesthetic value of food. Yet, on the other hand, France is the original locus of the ultra-slim fashion model, in the early years of the twentieth century. These two trends would lead us to opposite predictions about the prevalence of eating disorders. Nelly Allard, the

78

featured actress in Henry Jaglom's film *Eating*, plays the role of a French actress who interviews weight-obsessed American women at a Hollywood birthday party. Yet Allard herself admits (in her role) to a history of bulimia, and suggests that the greatest difference between the US and France on this issue may be the extent to which eating disorders are publicly discussed. Cultures may also vary a great deal in the negative stereotypes that are attributed to obesity, a factor which we will argue is an important ingredient of the proliferation of eating disorders. Only with much more complete information about cultural differences in such factors would we be able to account for cultural differences in the prevalence of eating disorders.

Despite possible cross-national differences, it seems clear that eating disorders are a phenomenon that occur throughout the Euro-American world, as well as those countries, such as Japan, that have been strongly exposed to and have actively absorbed Western cultural influences. On the other hand, it has been thought until recently that disorders such as anorexia nervosa occur rarely, if at all, in countries outside the Euro-American cultural orbit, in particular in Africa, the Indian subcontinent, or areas of Southeast Asia outside of Japan. The typical argument that was advanced in support of the low prevalence of eating disorders in such regions was an economic one. In areas in which per capita income is generally low and the food supply is limited, it is unlikely that one will find disorders whose principal symptom is voluntary self-starvation (or a bulimic "squandering" of food). Furthermore, such differences would result from the value placed on a slender body image, which is a distinctly Euro-American phenomenon, and in those areas in which food is still at a premium, fatness rather than slenderness is valued as a sign of affluence.

In an earlier version of this book, it appeared that available evidence seemed to support this general notion. For example, in the mid-1980s, the noted Indian epidemiologist Shridhar Sharma noted a very low prevalence of the disorder in India. Up until that point, for example, the *Indian Journal of Psychiatry*, which has published since the 1930s, had yet to publish a single article or report on anorexia nervosa.[62] Similarly Dr Burton Bradley, a psychiatrist who spent decades studying psychiatric disorders in New Guinea, reported never having seen a case of anorexia or bulimia there.[63] L. Bryce Boyer, an anthropologist with extensive experience with the Alaskan Eskimo, indicated that anorexia nervosa is non-existent among this population.[64] Even in those areas undergoing rapid industrialization, such as Malaysia, where anorexia was occasionally diagnosed, the relatively low incidence of the disorder, with cases apparently occurring only in the affluent Chinese population, had remained stable into the early 1980s.[65] Two cases of anorexia nervosa in African women were published in the 1980s, but both of these women had been intensively exposed to European influences through education and family.

Since the original publication of this book, however, the situation has changed. With the rapid industrialization and urbanization of large areas of the world previously isolated from Euro-American influence, and with the general globalization of culture associated with the ever-increasing influence of the mass media, a number of reports of an increasing prevalence of anorexia nervosa have appeared from areas previously considered relatively immune to such conditions. In particular, reports have emerged of an increased incidence of eating disorders in the Middle East, Africa, India and various countries in southern Asia, including Hong Kong, China, Singapore, and South Korea. In particular, a series of reports by Sing Lee, a psychiatrist based at Hong Kong University, has documented a number of cases occurring in Hong Kong throughout the 1980s.[66] Lee is not clear as to whether these cases represent an increase in the prevalence of the condition or perhaps a greater awareness of the syndrome by Western-trained psychiatrists. However, he makes a series of fascinating observations about these patients. First, the majority are from the lower socioeconomic levels of society, a fact that seems to contrast with the patterns for Western patients. Second, patients often interpret their inability to eat in terms of gastric distress (for example, symptoms of "bloating") rather than a fear of obesity. Third, and perhaps most important, over half of these patients do not suffer from body image distortion and most do not voice body image concerns. Lee suggests that these patients resemble more those seen by physicians and psychiatrists in the West in the late nineteenth century, for whom body image distortion was also not a prominent symptom. He proposes that these observations demand a reconsideration of current Western diagnostic criteria for anorexia nervosa, particularly the implicit assumption that they are universal. Rather, he suggests that anorexia nervosa may represent a characteristic reaction of adolescent females to psychological distress, but the particular features of the disorder emphasized by Western psychiatry, body image distortion and fear of obesity, are actually culturally determined. Therefore, in Lee's view, the diagnostic criteria represented by the DSM are actually ethnocentric and cannot encompass the syndromes that are seen in non-European societies.[67]

Lee buttresses his interpretation by pointing out that in Hong Kong, obesity is not the problem that it is in the West. In fact, plumpness is still perceived as representing health. There would be no particular value, he suggests, in women attaining extreme thinness as in anorexia nervosa. He suggests that the principal motivation for anorexia nervosa lies in food refusal itself, which is a way for a young person to express rejection or rebellion against their family (food is still a primary symbol of nurturance and familial control). As a result, the increased prominence of anorexia nervosa in Hong Kong may still reflect a changing and conflicted female role, with food refusal representing a battle for independence from one's family.

While Lee's argument about body image is provocative, it conflicts with other studies that he and his colleagues have carried out which show that in fact weight consciousness is pervasive among high-school and college students in Hong Kong.[68] This trend is in direct contradiction to the traditional value that the Chinese place on plumpness as a sign of health, and yet it is compatible with the pervasive influence of consumerist norms in an affluent Hong Kong. While Lee suggests that anorexia nervosa was still an uncommon condition in Hong Kong in the 1980s, it may well be that the finding of an intense degree of weight preoccupation among students in the mid-1990s will soon give rise to an increase in prevalence of eating disorders to levels comparable to those in Europe and the US. It is also possible that the lack of evident body image distortion found in patients with anorexia nervosa may represent an unwillingness to admit to such a culturally dissonant idea. In their cultural context, it might be particularly shameful to do so. It should also be kept in mind that numerous Western patients do not admit to body image distortion or "fat phobia," especially at early stages of treatment.

In addition to Hong Kong, eating disorders have gained attention in other relatively affluent South Asian societies, such as Singapore and South Korea.[69] The death of a 21-year-old, 70-pound student at the National University in Singapore in 1996 gained a tremendous amount of attention in the press. In an upscale shopping area in Singapore, a message on a t-shirt told a tale of the conflicted female consciousness about weight:

I've got to get into that dress. It's easy. Don't eat . . . I'm hungry. Can't eat breakfast. But I ought to . . . I like breakfast. I like that dress . . . Still too big for that dress. Hmm. Life can be cruel.

A survey of secondary-school student attitudes in Singapore in the 1990s showed the same pervasive body image dissatisfaction and other disturbed eating attitudes as were found in Hong Kong, with scores in some cases exceeding those of students in the US. Yet, the authors of this survey point out that despite the dramatically increased weight consciousness, the prevalence of anorexia nervosa in Singapore still remains quite low compared with that in Western countries. This they attribute to such factors as the inherently smaller body mass index of Singaporean women, the lack of pervasive obesity in the culture, the normative cohesiveness of the family, and ready availability of a cultur- ally normative healthy diet should one want to lose weight. Despite these protective factors, the authors suggest that given the high degree of body image consciousness and associated vulnerabilities of young women in Singapore, the prevalence of eating disorders is likely to increase.[70]

While there is as yet little published literature, reports also indicate a rapidly emerging problem with eating disorders in South Korea, where the forces of industrialization, urbanization, consumerism, and democ- ratization have produced an enormously rapid cultural transition. The emergence of eating disorders in Korea is particularly remarkable, given traditional attitudes towards plumpness as a requirement for marriage- ability, attitudes which held sway as recently as the 1970s. In this respect, the situation in Korea exactly parallels that of Hong Kong. Koreans can trace dramatic changes in attitudes towards food over a generation or two. Following World War II, the common question "have you eaten?" was a reflection of pervasive food shortages; to respond in the affirmative to the question was a sign of status. Now, surveys have shown that 90 percent of high-school girls, the vast majority of whom are of normal weight, feel that they are overweight. Fashion standards have become particularly stringent, with dresses of- ten being offered in only one size, the equivalent of an American size 4. The only survey of eating disorders, conducted among college students in 1990, found a prevalence rate of anorexia of 0.7 percent and bulimia nervosa of 0.8 percent. These rates, while lower than those of American or European samples, may well be rapidly increasing at the end of the decade. One psychiatrist, Kim Joon Ki, had only seen one patient prior to 1991. By 1997, he had seen over 200 patients, about half of whom were anorexic and half of whom were bulimic, in a two-and-a-half-year period since he opened a private eating disorder clinic.[71]

While eating disorders appear to have become relatively common in relatively affluent East Asian societies such as Japan, Hong Kong, Singapore, and the Republic of Korea, they have also appeared, albeit with lower frequency, in less affluent Asian countries such as China, India, Indonesia, and the Philippines. Reports of eating disorders in India began to appear in the early 1990s.[72] Despite the fact that hunger is still a public health problem for large areas of the Indian population, it must be understood that the middle and professional class in India is now quite sizable. Western-oriented fashion images are pervasive through the influence of magazines and films, and the issue of the status of women is one that resonates throughout society. Indian women report that an emphasis on weight control has been added to traditional concerns about skin lighteners and the straightness of hair. Thus it is not surprising that eating disorders have appeared with some degree of frequency, although exactly how common they are is still unknown.[73] Description of eating disorders in India have also emphasized the relative lack of body image concerns among anorexic patients, which has been attributed to the lack of conflict over the problem of obesity. However, the same qualifications apply to these assertions as were discussed regarding Sing Lee's arguments about patients in Hong Kong. In addition, Roland Littlewood has suggested that food-refusal may be driven by a different type of cultural rationale in India, in which self-sacrifice in women – as expressed, for example, in group fasting rituals – has always signified a morally sanctioned form of protest.[74]

Prior to the 1990s, eating disorders were considered to be extremely rare among Africans. In the case of Africa, this was attributed mainly to the traditional positive value placed on a large body, particularly for women, in most African societies. Largeness symbolized fertility, and the African "fattening shed," in which girls were prepared for marriage, has long been used as the starkest symbol of contrast in attitudes towards body image in Western and third-world countries. However, in a 1982 novel by Buchi Emecheta, college women in a Nigerian University were depicted as increasingly focused on the control of their weight, much to the dismay of their mothers and grandmothers, some of whom had directly experienced the traditional fattening rituals.[75] In the 1980s, four case reports of anorexia nervosa in African patients appeared in the literature, three of whom were from Nigeria and one from Zimbabwe.[76] All were individuals who were exposed directly or indirectly to European culture, through education or travel. The author of a case report on two of these patients suggested that eating disorders were probably still rare in Nigeria, but cautioned that some patients, including one whom he had seen in treatment, may consult traditional healers and may never be seen in more European-oriented medical facilities. He also points out that there remain factors within Nigerian culture that militate against eating disorders. While the fattening shed may be an artifact of the past, the Okyon people of southeastern Nigeria still require girls entering early adulthood to undertake a fat-producing diet to improve their appearance. Despite these as well as other traditional forces, the influence of European and American values in Nigeria seems to be inexorably leading to a situation in which problematic eating behaviors are becoming more common. A 1992 survey of three groups of students in Nigeria, ranging from the high-school to the graduate-school level, showed disordered eating attitudes and behaviors virtually indistinguishable in frequency from comparable Western surveys.[77] Self-induced vomiting was particularly common. Whether such tendencies will translate themselves into significant numbers of cases of clinical eating disorders remains to be seen, but such a development would not be at all surprising.

A series of reports in the 1990s suggests an increasing number of black South African women with eating disorders.[78] There had been many reports of whites in South Africa treated for eating disorders, and it seemed that in the late 1970s and 1980s, South African white school-girls did not differ at all from their European and American counterparts in their overvaluation of thinness and vulnerability to eating disorders. Prior to the 1990s, there had been no cases reported among blacks and none seen in existing treatment centers. It is possible, of course, that given the rigid segregation of society under apartheid those black individuals who did suffer from eating disorders were not seen in the established health system. From a clinical standpoint, the cases of anorexia nervosa and bulimia among black women reported on in the 1990s were indistinguishable from typical presentations of eating-disordered Caucasian patients, including characteristic disturbances in body image. Remarkably, in a 1998 study of a large number of South

African college students black students scored significantly *higher* on measures of disordered eating attitudes than their Caucasian counterparts.[79] The percentage of students who scored in the "clinical" ranges of these scales was quite similar in the two groups.

South Africa, of course, may be unique as an African nation, given the large, entrenched white minority which ruled the country until the elections in 1994. Given the power and status of the white population, one could speculate that their standards may have been particularly influential on at least certain segments of the black population. Also, given the changes since democratic election, the society has become more of a multicultural one, with boundaries between groups being much less sharply drawn. On the whole, eating disorders remain somewhat uncommon in Africa, but with increasing industrialization and Western cultural influence, their emergence may be inevitable.

Until the 1990s, eating disorders were little discussed in Latin America, with the exception of a report on 50 cases in Chile that appeared in 1980.[80] However, this too has been changing. The most notable situation is that in Argentina, and Buenos Aires in particular, in which eating disorders have been described as epidemic. Whether or not this characterization is accurate is a matter of some debate, but numerous cases of anorexia nervosa and bulimia nervosa have been treated by health professionals in the 1990s, and surveys show that the prevalence of bulimic behavior is fairly common.[81] It should be pointed out that Argentina is sometimes characterized as the most "European" of South American nations. There is an intense consciousness of appearance and fashion, and a considerable emphasis on thinness. Women report being unable to buy a dress that does not fit very tightly, and a virtual craze for cosmetic surgery in the country was reported during the 1990s. It should also be pointed out that themes of psychology and psychoanalysis have been an intense preoccupation in Argentine popular culture, and this fascination may increase the focus on and publicity about fashionable illnesses.

Eating disorders have also become more frequent in Mexico, with numerous cases being reported in the Mexico City area.[82] Fashion magazines published in Mexico put the usual contemporary emphasis on weight loss and weight control, and a rise in the number of educated young women has opened up the familiar set of vulnerabilities.

It is clear, then, that eating disorders are no longer confined to European and American populations (see table 3.1). Although they may continue to be most common among these populations, the rapid

Table 3.1   Countries reporting eating disorders

*Argentina	*Mexico
†Australia	†The Netherlands
Belgium	†New Zealand
†Canada	*Nigeria
Chile	Norway
*China	Poland
Czech Republic	*Singapore
†Denmark	*South Africa (blacks)
*Egypt	†South Africa (whites
France	*South Korea
Germany	former Soviet Union
*Hong Kong	†Sweden
Hungary	†Switzerland
*India	*Turkey
†Israel	*United Arab Emirates
Italy	†United Kingdom
†Japan	†United States

† Indicates formal epidemiological studies have been carried out
* First reports appeared since 1990

modernization and industrialization of many areas of the world, with the attendant influence of the values of the consumer economy as well as the rise in role conflicts associated with a rapidly transforming female role, make it seemingly inevitable that the problem of eating disorders will become a more global health issue. This entire phenomenon raises serious questions about the usefulness of the traditional concept of "culture-bound syndrome" as it applies to anorexia nervosa and perhaps many other disorders. The cultural patterns and forces associated with consumer economies and the modernization of sex roles appear to have a considerable degree of homogeneity, despite variations in the specifics of local traditions.

Religion, Ethnicity, and Assimilation

Despite some earlier speculations that anorexia nervosa was more prevalent in the United States among Jewish or Catholic families, there are as yet no clearly established associations between particular religious backgrounds and the development of eating disorders.[83] Clinical experience suggests, however, that anorexics frequently come from religious backgrounds characterized by strict, puritanical attitudes, particularly towards female sexuality. A. H. Crisp suggests that one source of cultural stress that may be contributing to the increase in the incidence of anorexia nervosa is the clash between such a prohibitive religious background and the far more fluid and unstructured contemporary mores regarding sexuality. Crisp cited one case of an Arab girl who felt forced to "choose" between the "liberated" morality of the contemporary culture and the highly restrictive prohibitions of her own village's Islamic tradition.[84] Such severely conflicting value choices are typical of the major identity clashes that can precipitate anorexia, and provide a context for understanding the negation of the bodily self that is so central to the disorder. Although it has been little studied, religious traditionalism, particularly those religions which prescribe fasting, such as Catholicism or Judaism, is not uncommon in the backgrounds of eating disorder patients. In some Muslim patients in England, an anorexic episode was triggered by participation in the Ramadan fast.[85] The incidence appears to be especially high in groups whose fundamentalism is perceived from within the group to clash strongly with the "looseness" of the wider culture.[86]

While there has not been a large number of studies, it appears that there is considerable variation in the incidence of eating disorders in various minority populations in the United States. On the one hand, the prevalence of eating disorders in Hispanic adolescents appears comparable to that in the white population, while the incidence in those of Asian origin appears to be somewhat lower and the prevalence in certain Native American groups appears to be quite high.[87] The minority group that has received the most attention is African Americans, probably because prior to the 1980s eating disorders were considered to be virtually non-existent in this group. This situation began to change in the 1980s, as a number of reports of blacks with anorexia and especially bulimia nervosa began to appear in the literature (one article was titled, appropriate to the uncertainty on the issue, "Are eating disorders becoming more common in Blacks?").[88] While it is generally accepted that there are now more black women with eating disorders than previously, various studies suggest that, at least among college students, the prevalence of eating disorders as well as distorted eating attitudes remains lower in the African-American than the Caucasian population. For example, in a study by Abrams, Allen, and Gray, black college students scored lower (that is to say, in a more healthy direction) on scales measuring drive for thinness and body image dissatisfaction. On the other hand, those black individuals who did score high on these measures differed from whites in that their concerns appear to be tied to actual issues of overweight, whereas for white subjects there does not appear to be any correlation between a drive for thinness and an actual weight problem. Interestingly, those black students who evidenced the most intense emulation of white cultural values – that is, the highest degree of cultural assimilation – evidenced the highest degree of eating disorder symptomatology.[89]

The persisting low prevalence of eating disorder symptomatology among young black women in the United States most likely has a cultural explanation. A 1995 community study of eighth- and ninth-grade girls conducted at the University of Arizona suggests some highly interesting reasons for the difference.[90] In comparison to their white counterparts, black teenagers placed far less emphasis on strict standards of appearance as a measure of personal worth. While many were conscious about their weight and engaged in dieting, most suggested that the criterion of weight loss was simply less central in their concept of being a good person or living up to personal ideals. Furthermore, in contrast with white adolescents, many more African-American girls placed less emphasis on external beauty as a prerequisite for personal acceptability. Rather, a greater value was placed by those interviewed on "being happy about who you are" as well as beauty being a matter of inner goodness and personal strength. African-American girls also suggested that black men prefer women who are shapely and full-figured, although they insisted that this was not their primary reason for not putting great emphasis on loss of weight. What these data imply is that in many ways these girls were more personally secure than their white counterparts, less vulnerable to external judgments and rigid standards promulgated by the mass media.

The lower prevalence of eating disorders in black women is also remarkable in light of the higher rates of obesity among black women.[91] While many black women may seek weight loss, the rationale may often be for health rather than cosmetic reasons. Obesity, or at least some degree of overweight, is not stigmatized in the black population to the same degree that it is in white culture. In any case, the data from the

Arizona study suggest the importance of variables other than the desire to lose weight as the determinant of eating disorder symptomatology, particularly the vulnerabilities to personal insecurity and conflicted identity that seem to be more typical of white, middle-class adolescents.

In contrast with the situation for American blacks, the incidence of eating disorders appears to be higher for at least some groups of Asian girls growing up in England than for their white counterparts. In a study conducted in the early 1990s, Mumford found that prevalence of bulimia among Asian schoolgirls (mostly Pakistani Muslims) living in a working-class city was several times higher (3.2 percent) than that of their white age-mates (0.6 percent).[92] This was a rather surprising finding, and was confirmed in a number of subsequent studies on similar populations. Of particular interest was the fact that the girls who were susceptible to eating disorders were those who emphasized traditional cultural values (as expressed in language and dress) and whose parents attempted to exert rigid control over their daughters. It appears that eating disorders in this group reflect the clashes in identity resulting from the collision of traditional expectations (i.e., obedience and deference to the wishes of parents) and the contemporary environment for British adolescents, which emphasizes a greater latitude of choices for girls. As one of these girls, who had developed anorexia nervosa, put it,

> "I am facing what is called 'culture clash.' Because I have been educated in England I have been taught to be independent, original, to think for myself and to be successful in my life by achieving what I aim for. In school I was prepared how to handle my life and how to stand up for myself, . . . while when I went home I was expected to be quiet, submissive, obedient and totally dependent on my parents . . . . [My parents] believe girls should not speak up and should let their parents decide what happens in their life . . . It is hard enough for me to make a decision on what I am going to do in the future without the added burden of thinking of the family and their images . . . . I will never give in to them though: there is no way I can live under their thumb."[93]

The symptoms of eating disorders characteristically represent an effort to somehow take control, and it is not difficult to envision how this type of struggle could motivate such an effort in an individual experiencing this degree of cultural conflict.

The sudden exposure of women from traditional or non-Western backgrounds to a Western cultural experience may well heighten the vulnerability to an eating disorder. A classic study of this phenomenon was conducted by Mervat Nasser.[94] Nasser compared a group of Egyptian students who had emigrated to England to study at the University of London with a group of students of the same age at the University of Cairo. While 10 percent of the students at the University of London qualified for a diagnosis of bulimia nervosa, none of the comparison group at the University of Cairo could be so diagnosed.

Nasser's findings can probably best be understood in light of a study by Furnham and Alibhai, published in 1983.[95] These authors compared three groups, one of Kenyans living in their native country, a second of Kenyans living in Britain, and a third of British Caucasians, on their respective assessments of ideal body image. They found, in accordance with their prediction, that the Kenyans in Kenya preferred a somewhat larger body shape than that preferred by the British Caucasians. Surprisingly, however, the Kenyans who had emigrated to Britain preferred an even thinner body image than did the British Caucasians. This seems to suggest not only assimilation, but also what might be called assimilation with a vengeance.

In what surely is one of the most interesting contributions to the literature on cultural assimilation and eating disorders, Kaffman and Sadeh published a report in 1989 on the greatly increased prevalence of anorexia nervosa in the Kibbutzim in Israel.[96] While there is little in the way of epidemiological data, the prevalence of eating disorders in the Israeli middle class is probably in general comparable to the levels in Europe and the United States. By way of contrast, the prevalence within the Kibbutzim was at least historically very low. The authors estimate that the prevalence of anorexia nervosa in the Kibbutzim has increased by 800 percent since 1965 and by 400 percent from the mid-1970s to the time of publication of the study. They propose that the reasons for the change have to do with significant changes in the economic and cultural life of the Kibbutz. With the economic strengthening of the Kibbutz that took place in the 1970s, food was no longer considered a scarce commodity and was no longer subject to rationing. The diet of the average Kibbutznik was comparable to that of the upper middle-class Israeli population. Meanwhile, the emphasis on communal social life that was so central to the socialist ethos of the early Kibbutz has given way to a more typical, child-centered nuclear family

90

life. Children no longer typically eat in the children's house, but rather meals are taken with the nuclear family, thus rendering eating vulnerable to the emotional reverberations that it typically takes on in the family. There has been a renewed emphasis on the mother–child relationship, and in its wake the possibility of typical problems with separation and individuation. Finally, Kaffman suggests that little emphasis was traditionally placed on the Kibbutz woman's appearance, but now "in nearly every Kibbutz the cosmetician, the hairdresser, the beautician, as well as the dietician, play an important role in the life of the woman."[97]

The vulnerability to psychiatric disorders of those who have recently immigrated into a culture with vastly different values than the culture of origin has long been a subject of interest to cross-cultural psychiatrists. While we only have a few studies of the phenomenon, it appears to be the case that young women who experience a particularly intense clash between contemporary Western values and their own traditional culture are especially vulnerable to developing an eating disorder. Disparities in expectations about female independence and sexuality as well as body image and weight control are particularly potent risk factors.

The Question of Social Class

Perhaps no characteristic is more stereotypically associated with eating disorders than that of upper socioeconomic status or more bluntly, "affluence." And yet there are serious reasons to question this association, and perhaps the time has come to discard it altogether.[98]

The notion that eating disorders are only found among the affluent was articulated over a century ago by the English physician Samuel Fenwick, who suggested that anorexia nervosa was found more frequently among the wealthy and rarely among those who have to procure their bread by daily labor.[99] The idea was reinforced by the major clinicians who labored in this field in the 1960s and 1970s. Bruch, for example, reported in her 1973 book that a disproportionate number of patients came from families of the super-rich: almost all others were from middle-class homes, and the few that were from working-class families were driven by the ethic of achievement and upward mobility.[100] Similar findings were reported by Theander in Sweden, who also

91

found that the fathers of anorexics tended to be involved in professions that made them the "guardians of traditional values": judges, headmasters, and wealthy industrialists.[101] In an English series, 77 percent of the patients were from the upper social classes, and 23 percent from the middle class. The fathers' professions included doctors, teachers, barristers, artists, businessmen, architects, stockbrokers, and accountants.[102] However, it needs to be pointed out that the patients seen by these well-known clinicians were subject to strong selection biases. Bruch, for example, was widely known as a consultant, and many of the patients who came to see her for consultation flew in from afar and had had years of previous treatment. It is understandable that this would be a highly select group.

Some of the epidemiological studies in the 1970s that were discussed earlier in this chapter also confirmed a concentration of anorexic patients in the upper socioeconomic classes. The study by Kendall, for example, which examined the number of anorexic patients in psychiatric registers in Camberwell, London, Monroe County, New York, and Northeast Scotland reported a concentration of anorexics among the higher social classes.[103] In fact, however, a significant relationship was found for only one of these districts (Camberwell), and this only contained eight patients! The authors of this study were convinced that all people who had developed anorexia nervosa would have been registered (that is, seen by a psychiatric professional), but this assumption is most likely unfounded. It neglects the differing ways in which low weight may be interpreted by different cultural and economic groups, as well as differences in the tendencies of these groups to seek professional help. Therefore, those who achieved patient status in the registry may have indeed been a select group.

A number of studies that have been carried out since the mid-1980s have failed to find an association between anorexia nervosa and higher class status, and for bulimia nervosa at least, the relationship with social class if anything appears to be in the reverse direction. For example, a study of nine communities in eastern Massachusetts, in which socioeconomic status was determined by income level, found bulimia nervosa to be more common among low socioeconomic status subjects, and the same tendency was in evidence for anorexia nervosa, although not as strongly.[104] In a retrospective study of patients with a diagnosis of anorexia nervosa in Glasgow between 1979 and 1983, the social class distribution of patients did not differ from that of the general community.[105] Studies in England of bulimic patients have found that either bulimics do not differ from the general population in their social class distribution or, if anything, there are more bulimics from the lower socioeconomic groups.[106]

It is possible, of course, that as anorexia nervosa has become better known or as social factors that were once restricted to the most affluent groups have diffused through the population (e.g., access to education, attitudes that allow for female achievement, the values of the consumer culture) the disorder has become more "democratic" with regard to social class than it was formerly. Without broader-based surveys of populations in earlier years, we will be unable to resolve this question. At any rate, the imagery of anorexia nervosa as a disorder of the "elite" that was perpetuated by some of Bruch's statements needs to be put to rest. Unfortunately, such imagery continues to be sustained in both the media and wider culture (but in some medical writings as well), and may continue to make anorexia nervosa an attractive template for the expression of distress (see chapter 7). Research seems to quite clearly support the fact that bulimia is not at all limited to those who are "affluent," and in fact may be more common in the lower socioeconomic groups.

The central issue is not income level but rather cultural values. Bruch made this point quite clearly in *The Golden Cage*, when she wrote that the emphasis on female achievement and upward mobility are universally found in the families of anorexics, whatever their income level. And it may very well be that in the societies of the late twentieth century, in which both the consumer culture and television have done much to level class distinctions in values and aspirations and to universalize the conflicting dilemmas of female identity, the class basis of eating disorders may well become a relic of the past.

Chapter Four

A Conflicted Female Identity

My own observations suggest that the changing status of (and expectations for) women plays a role [in the increase in anorexia nervosa]. Girls whose early upbringing has prepared them to become "clinging-vine" wives suddenly are expected at adolescence to prove themselves as women of achievement. This seems to create severe personal self-doubt and basic uncertainty. In their submissive way, they "choose" the fashionable dictum to be slim as a way of proving themselves as deserving respect.

Hilde Bruch, "Four decades of eating disorders"

The overwhelming majority of people who develop problems with anorexia nervosa and bulimia – regardless of nationality or social class – are female. This simple fact, which is acknowledged by virtually all researchers and clinicians, no matter what their particular theoretical persuasion, is of critical importance in a sociocultural understanding of why these problems have become an epidemic in recent times. But despite its virtually universal acknowledgment, its theoretical significance has yet to be fully appreciated.

At the outset, it is important to acknowledge the possibility that such a lopsided sex ratio may have something to do with biological differences between the sexes. There are a number of possibilities that suggest themselves. For one thing, laboratory studies show that female animals are more able to withstand starvation (that is, they survive longer) than males.[1] Such differential tolerance may have evolutionary significance. In times of food scarcity, the female's ability to tolerate starvation may have particular adaptive value in light of the female role in species propagation. This of course does not account for anorexia

94

nervosa, which occurs under conditions of relative affluence, but it makes it more understandable why females are more likely to draw upon self-starvation as a means of coping with stress. A second possible link has to do with the generally higher ratio of fat to lean tissue in females relative to males, a fact that also can be interpreted from the standpoint of evolution. Again, in periods of famine or food scarcity, it would have been advantageous to females to have reserve stores of fat tissue in order to sustain pregnancy and lactation.[2] In human cultures that emphasize the importance of thinness in women, females may experience more stress in efforts at dieting, given their greater biological propensity towards adiposity. A third possibility has to do with the relative complexity of female pubertal development, from the standpoint of hormonal functions and the intricacy of related brain mechanisms. Such differential complexity may make the pubertal process more susceptible to disruption under stress, as in anorexia nervosa.[3] And finally, it is possible that females are more vulnerable to endogenous depression. Interestingly, females tend to respond to depression with increased appetite and weight gain, while for males the reverse is true. Such differential responses may provide a bridge for the hypothesized link between eating disorders and mood disorders.[4]

Despite the possible role of biological factors in predisposing women to developing eating disorders, it seems virtually impossible to account for the gendered psychological features of these conditions without taking into account social and cultural influences. For example, anorexic patients have an enormous drive to be thin and an equally intense fear of becoming fat. It is difficult to understand the centrality of these concerns without taking into account the social and cultural pressures on women to achieve thinness, as well as the specific stigma, peculiar to Western societies, attached to fat women. As we shall see in the following two chapters, these pressures have increased significantly throughout the twentieth century, and the particular meanings that they have for women are centrally involved in understanding the eating disorders epidemic. But in addition, there are more subtle features of the psychology of eating disorders that demand an interpretation in social terms. These revolve around the nearly universal concerns of eating-disordered patients with issues of autonomy, self-esteem, achievement, and control. And this spectrum of psychological issues can be broadly understood as relating to the larger problem of the development of psychosocial identity.

The concept of identity is a difficult one, but it is critical in understanding the central problems confronted by women with eating disorders. It has received its most elaborate formulation in the writings of Erik Erikson.[5] Erikson suggests that the notion of identity relates to the individual's experience of self-cohesion, or, as he puts it, the sense of continuity and sameness in time. The development of a cohesive or "viable" identity depends on many individual and social factors, but among the most important is the individual's ability to "synthesize" or bring together the divergent and conflicting aspects of his or her social experience. The development of identity is a dynamic process, which unfolds throughout a person's life, and is influenced by a host of factors – historical and sociological conditions, the particularities of family experiences, biological predispositions, and the accidents of development. However, the most critical period for the formation of an identity is during adolescence, the period in which the individual must put together the foundations of the self laid down in childhood experience with the new demands and challenges posed by the personal and social experiences of that period. The process of identity formation is particularly susceptible to disruption by radical changes in social roles or cultural expectations. This is one reason why individuals suddenly exposed to a radically different culture – say, in a situation of migration – seem particularly vulnerable to psychological problems.[6] But it also suggests that even within the same culture, a particular group which is exposed to dramatic changes in cultural expectations – say, through a sudden change in social role – will also be highly susceptible to epidemic symptoms of identity confusion.[7]

In this chapter, I wish to apply this latter notion to an understanding of the epidemic increase in eating disorders. More specifically, I want to develop the notion that eating disorders are the extreme expression of radically altered social expectations on women that have emerged on a mass scale since about the mid-twentieth century, but particularly since the 1960s. Over a relatively short period of time, young women have encountered a new set of pressures, demanding an orientation towards achievement, competitiveness, and independence, a set of values that conflict sharply with traditional Western definitions of the female role. In a period of increased opportunities but also intensified pressures, many have found it difficult to synthesize a "viable" or "workable" identity, and suffer inwardly from a sense of fragmentation, confusion, and self-doubt.[8] What I am proposing here is that the central psychological problems experienced by patients with eating disorders, which center on issues of self-esteem, autonomy, and achievement, are a magnified reflection of much more pervasive conflicts in the wider culture about the female role. The young woman with an eating disorder therefore is the unwitting carrier of pervasive cultural crisis.

From the standpoint of the theoretical framework of this book, the person who develops an ethnic disorder, as Devereux suggested, suffers from psychological conflicts that are pervasive in the culture, but are experienced by the patient in a particularly acute form. The resulting anxiety, depression, or confusion is sufficiently severe for the person to develop symptoms, which serve as defenses against underlying psychological distress. The situation for anorexia nervosa and bulimia is parallel to that of hysteria in the late nineteenth century, which also was an expression of confusion and contradictory prescriptions in the female role.[9] The nature of the conflicts experienced by hysterical patients, however, was quite different, and had to do with the specific historical situation of women at that time. They revolved around issues of strict sexual repression, as well as blanket restrictions on female education and participation in public life. Nevertheless, the current epidemic of eating disorders is very much parallel to the wave of conversion hysteria that seemed to sweep over Europe and America in the nineteenth century. Both are expressions, appropriate to their own times, of the dilemmas of female identity, in a cultural climate in which the female role is ambiguously defined and still limited by institutionalized male control.

Female Identity in Anorexia Nervosa

So central are issues of female identity in anorexia nervosa that it is difficult to see why more has not been made of this issue in previous formulations. Most cultural interpretations of anorexia have stressed the fashion of female slenderness, which is undoubtedly of central importance in understanding the eating disorders.[10] But few have addressed the more complex issue of *why* the emphasis on thinness is so important to contemporary women, and particularly to those who develop eating disorders. More detailed study of the psychological conflicts that drive certain women to develop anorexia nervosa leads centrally to the underlying issues of identity and self-worth that cause the single-minded pursuit of thinness to be "chosen" as the principal symptom.

A central feature of anorexic patients emphasized by Hilde Bruch is that these are girls or women who grow up with a profound sense of ineffectiveness, a sense of deficiency in their ability to influence their environment and determine their own fate.[11] This lacuna in the sense of the self is a consequence of growing up in a family which places intense emphasis on achievement and performance, but simultaneously deprives the child of opportunities for self-initiated behavior or for the development of her own unique possibilities. Perhaps such a developmental course is the product of an overly compliant temperament with a parenting regime that does not sufficiently support the child's early urges towards autonomy.[12] When such a child becomes an adolescent, therefore, she is not well equipped to cope with the typical developmental demands of that period, which require a greater degree of independent functioning and autonomous choice. The events that typically trigger the onset of anorexic dieting are just those experiences that challenge the adolescent's sense of independence and self-worth: the first heterosexual relationship, the loss of a friendship, an illness, death, or separation from a valued family member, or moving away from home.[13] For those whose sense of autonomy is deficient, these rather typical developmental stresses precipitate a crisis in self-worth. In addition, many girls who develop anorexia nervosa in their early teenage years have been subjected to a particularly vicious type of social ostracism, an experience that can devastate self-confidence.[14] Dieting and weight loss, which not only bring about a positive response from others but also give the individual an experience of power that she has never before known, become quickly reinforced and then entrenched as a source of pride and perhaps even superiority.

In another model, A. H. Crisp suggests that for their own reasons, the parents have a difficult time in accepting their daughter's emerging sexual interests in adolescence. The reasons for this may vary. Perhaps the parents' own sexual relationship has become dormant, and therefore the perception of potential sexual acting-out on the part of the daughter is threatening. Crisp offers one instance in which a mother had finally tamed the father's youthful wildness, but now the daughter's emerging sexuality was perceived as a threat. The development of anorexia nervosa represents a prepubertal regression, whereby the child is able to literally annihilate the concrete physical signs of her emerging sexuality.[15]

Experience has shown that it is risky to be overly general of the nature of the "anorexic family," a lesson that was learned from schizophrenia research years ago.[16] Nevertheless, clinicians in the eating disorders field have generally accepted the notion that the developmental demands of early adolescence, which involve movements towards autonomy, sexual experimentation, and the formation of love and complex interpersonal relationships, are typically overwhelming to the child who becomes anorexic. What is usually not stated is the extent to which the characteristic experiences and problems of anorexic patients mirror and magnify common problems of female identity that have become pervasive in the wider culture. For the intense sense of ineffectiveness and exclusive focus on external expectations is the extreme version of a common developmental pattern among girls in Western societies. Studies of normal female development, which have a certain degree of cross-cultural consistency, show that despite changes in public ideology about sex roles, girls are still socialized to be pleasers and are given far less encouragement than boys to develop self-initiated and autonomous behaviors.[17] Bruch's suggestion that the mothers of anorexic patients fail to respond to their daughter's self-initiated activities and signals actually reflects a more general pattern, established by developmental research, of providing girls with significantly less "response-contingent stimulation" than is typically given to boys.[18] The orientation towards pleasing others and the intense sensitivity and responsiveness to external demands is of course consistent with girls' socialization to be nurturers, a pattern which persists, despite the changes brought about by feminism. Jean Baker Miller, in her seminal book about the dilemmas of female identity, suggests that women's self-worth and self-concept are still determined by the requirement to help and assist others, a project that requires the subordination of one's own needs to the needs and expectations of another.[19] Such a formulation is directly applicable to the core experiences of those who develop anorexia nervosa, although the latter is an extreme version of the norm.

One consequence of these patterns of socialization is that by the time a girl reaches adolescence, she is often affected by feelings of powerlessness and dependency, feelings that make it very difficult to break away from the family and establish her own life. This is especially true for anorexic patients, and it provides a direct explanation of why the disorder typically erupts in adolescence. The experiences that typically trigger anorexic dieting, experiences of loss or separation (real or anticipated), are those that present particular challenges to autonomous functioning. To the pre-anorexic teenager, whose self-esteem is highly vulnerable and sense of autonomy very fragile, such experiences can come as a crushing blow. Going on a diet, and ultimately a starvation diet, becomes a way of achieving a sense of power and independence for a person who has been painfully confronted with his or her own powerlessness. In a culture that values dieting and thinness, such a solution seems readily understandable in terms of the positive social response that it typically arouses (at least initially). But in addition, radical dieting is powerfully reinforcing for a person whose sense of power and self-control has been so compromised.

For anorexics, another factor typically comes into play, one that is at once familial and social: the intense pressure to achieve. The families of anorexics typically place an enormous value on achievement and performance. Although they are not necessarily "affluent," most are driven by middle-class values of upward mobility, performance, and the work ethic.[20] Many have a history of economic insecurity and have advanced significantly beyond the economic status of their parents. There is often a sense of anxiety in these families about maintaining their hard-won economic and social status, a concern that falls particularly heavily on the shoulders of the daughter who becomes anorexic. In addition, some studies show that in many of the families of anorexics, there has been a history of male failure or inadequacy, something that may only become apparent if one looks at the grandparents' generation.[21] In any case, there is often a mythical notion in these families that women must be strong in order to compensate for perceived male inadequacies. These anxieties are not explicitly articulated, but the young woman who develops anorexia often feels them very acutely.

It is extremely important to understand that because of their external focus and pleasing orientation, anorexics feel that their achievements in school or in athletics are a performance *for others*, not a proof to themselves of their own worthiness. In fact, one of the paradoxes of anorexia nervosa is how worthless these young women feel, despite what is often a high degree of success from an external standpoint. This is again not a unique experience, but one that is very characteristic for contemporary women. Jean Baker Miller suggests that women often get caught in a cycle of pleasing and depletion, of "doing good and feeling bad."[22] This is the consequence of an identity that is based on pleasing and supporting others, rather than behaving according to one's own needs and self-chosen goals. The entire complex of externally oriented achievement and pleasing behavior has been idealized in popular culture in the imagery of the "superwoman," the woman who "has it all" and pleases a largely masculine audience with her feminine charm and worldly accomplishments. This modernized version of the traditional notion of the "good girl" has been widely and justifiably attacked by feminists as a perversion of the ideals of female equality. Because of their own developmental experiences, anorexics seem particularly vulnerable to internalizing this distorted ideology. As Bruch pointed out, many anorexics experience the ideology of liberation as one more external demand for perfection that they feel compelled to live up to: "growing girls can experience this liberation as a demand and feel that they *have* to do something outstanding . . . . Many of my patients have expressed the feeling . . . that there were too many choices and they had been afraid of not choosing correctly."[23]

While not always explicit, anorexics sometimes openly articulate their experiences in terms of a sense of inadequacy as compared with men. Many grow up with a secret though powerful fantasy about being a boy – a "tall, long-legged prince," as one patient put it – a dream which, Bruch suggests, is typically shattered by the experience of puberty.[24] In some cases this fantasy may represent a wish to be the male child that the father either never had or was disappointed with, but in others it may be a yearning for the power that boys are perceived to have and that the anorexic feels so acutely that she lacks. For some anorexics, the slenderness and loss of curves that result from dieting represent a triumphant transformation of the female figure into that of a preadolescent boy. Casky, in an interesting treatment of these issues, suggests that the anorexic seeks an identification with an ideal of asensual intellectuality, the mythical image of the puer, an image projected onto her father, whose own frequent orientation towards and emphasis on intellectual achievement has had a powerful impact on his anorexic daughter.[25] Some anorexics are quite explicit about their resentment of suffering the social disadvantages of being female. One of Bruch's patients, Fawn, commented that "it wasn't fair as a little girl. There wasn't any way of winning. You were wrong before you started."[26] And in a wry comment on her feelings about being out of step with new standards of female assertiveness, another patient, Annette, suggested that "it would have been worse [if I had been a boy – ed.], because I would have the same ghastly peaceminded temperament and that is unacceptable in boys. At least in girls it used to be acceptable, but now it is a culturally unacceptable way of behavior. But I continue to behave like that."[27] Annette, in fact, felt that her accomplishments in school were strangely alien to her, as if they were really those of a man – and the purpose of which had been to please her father.

This desire to escape womanhood and to achieve a certain type of masculine ideal – one of intellectuality and spiritual purity – can be understood on one level in terms of familial dynamics. Many anorexics feel particularly bound by their father's expectations, and seek to disengage themselves from their own bodily feelings of femaleness – an effort that is frequently reinforced by a disturbance in their emotional connection to their mothers. However, equally important is the wider social context of these feelings. In an age in which women are thrust into a situation in which they must prove their worth through work and intellectual accomplishment, many women feel that they must prove themselves the equal of men, and for some this may mean disengaging themselves from their own femaleness, which has undergone a cultural devaluation. Anorexics carry out this purge of femaleness in a particularly radical and concrete fashion. The cultural ideal of female thinness, to which anorexics aspire to the extreme, may itself have something to do with the aspirations of women to equal power with men, an idea that will be explored further in the next chapter.

Of particular interest is the much-discussed relationship of anorexic patients with their mothers. The mother–daughter bond in these families tends to be unusually intense, and it is often a consequence of the mother's powerful identification with her daughter as a compensation for a disappointment in her relationship with her husband – a disappointment which typically is unarticulated in the service of preserving "family harmony." The mothers of anorexics have been too frequently blamed in the past for their daughter's illness, partly as a result of a long psychiatric (particularly psychoanalytic) tradition of "mother-bashing." While it is true that the mother's intense closeness and control often blocks the daughter's efforts to achieve autonomy, the social context of the mother's situation is typically not taken into account. The mothers of anorexics are, as Bruch suggested, typically talented women who sacrificed their own ambitions and careers in the service of their families. Many gave up their careers when their first child was born.[28] In effect, these were the social expectations of women from an earlier, "pre-liberated" generation. Their resulting depression and clinging to their daughters can therefore be understood not as an individual flaw, but rather as a product of their own social circumstances and experience. What makes the whole situation particularly explosive is that in the contemporary environment adolescent girls are everywhere surrounded by an ideology of independence, an ideology that can often induce its own feelings of guilt and inadequacy for not being able to "break away." This poses a particularly painful dilemma for the girl who becomes anorexic, who tends to feel a poignant sense of responsibility for her mother's well-being.[29]

Sexuality and Sexual Abuse

While it is not always the central issue, sexuality frequently plays an important role in the development of anorexia nervosa. The issue of sexuality was probably overemphasized in earlier psychoanalytic formulations, in which the resistance to food was seen invariably to represent a symbolic fear of oral impregnation.[30] However, for a number of anorexics, unwanted or problematic sexual experiences trigger the crisis in self-confidence that precipitates severely restrictive dieting. In some instances, the first sexual experience, while voluntary, is experienced as disgusting, painful, or humiliating and further lowers an already vulnerable sense of self-esteem.[31] In a certain number of cases, the experience is a more drastic instance of sexual assault or abuse. In one of the most accessible autobiographies of anorexia nervosa, Aimee Liu opened her story with an account of a preadolescent rape by two boys that took place during a holiday family visit. While Liu did not explicitly tie this experience to the development of her anorexia nervosa a few years later, it is clear that this experience of violation and bodily vulnerability was implicated in her efforts to rid her body of its emerging signs of femaleness.[32]

While estimates of the incidence of sexual abuse in the histories of eating-disordered patients have varied, there is little doubt on clinical grounds that such experiences can play a role in the genesis of an eating disorder, as Liu's experience suggests. Even a single episode of abuse, depending on its developmental timing, can have devastating impact on attitudes towards one's body and can provoke doubts and fears about one's vulnerability sufficient to motivate such a drastic response as self-starvation. By ridding her body of its femaleness, a victim may in effect defend herself from further assault and its disastrous psychological consequences. The by-now extensive clinical literature on sexual abuse suggests in general pervasive effects on body image, self-regulation, interpersonal security, and sense of personal effectiveness, all issues that resonate with the psychological characteristics of eating-disordered patients.[33] Binge eating and purging can in some instances become methods of managing intolerable levels of post-traumatic distress. Studies by the English psychologist Glen Waller have also shown that those bulimics who have a history of sexual abuse are the ones who engage in the most violent purging.[34]

On the other hand, particularly rancorous debates have raged about the frequency of sexual abuse in the eating disorders. In the late 1980s, it was common to hear assertions in the literature that anywhere from 60 to 80 percent of those suffering from eating disorders have had a history of sexual abuse. Such figures were undoubtedly overestimates that probably resulted from biased samples and overly loose criteria of sexual abuse. The dissemination of these figures sometimes had unfortunate consequences. The most notorious instance was the Holly Ramona case, in which an accused father won a legal judgment against therapists who based their treatment, which involved a "confrontation" that had disastrous implications for the family, on such inflated statistics.[35] Careful studies by researchers in the United States and England have documented that the rate of sexual abuse among women with eating disorders ranges from 15 to 25 percent.[36] This is a rate that, while higher than that in the general population, is comparable with those found in other psychiatric disorders. Such statistics should not be used to discount the relevance of sexual abuse when it does play a role in the history of an eating disorder, but they suggest that inordinate or exclusive emphasis on the role of sexual abuse in the etiology of the eating disorders should be questioned.

Theoretically, the English psychiatrist A. H. Crisp has emphasized the role of sexuality in the development of anorexia nervosa.[37] Crisp underscores the important links between female pubertal development and the development of body fat. It has been well established that the emergence of the menstrual cycle is critically connected to the development of a certain amount of body fat (the so-called "critical fat threshold").[38] In addition, experientially and socially, the development of secondary sexual characteristics, in the form of curves, is also dependent on the development of a certain degree of fatness. Thus, biologically, experientially, and socially, fatness in females is critically connected with the emergence of sexuality in adolescence. The widespread preoccupation of female teenagers with curbing bodily shape and appetite reflects an effort at the self-regulation of sexual desires, in an environment in which traditional middle-class sexual morality has unraveled. Anorexia nervosa, which Crisp suggests commonly emerges from a family background of puritanical sexual morality and anxiety about unrestrained female sexuality, represents among other things a fearful regression to a prepubertal state, in which the presence of disturbing sexual feelings has been effectively banished.

From a cultural standpoint, sexuality is an important component of the wider transformation of female identity. The general relaxation of sexual constraints that took shape in the 1960s probably has had a more powerful impact on females than on males, for whom adolescent sexual activity was formerly tolerated and perhaps even acceptable. Studies of adolescent sexual behavior in the late 1970s and early 1980s, while still few, indicate that female adolescents have in general become more active sexually and at an earlier age, and in fact differ little in their sexual experience from males.[39] Meanwhile, the cultural climate regarding sexuality has changed radically in the direction of permissiveness – and exploitation – since the 1960s. The commercial exploitation of the new atmosphere of sexual openness, including sexual explicitness in typical television fare as well as the implied sexual violence of music videos, sexualized preadolescent fashion models, and pornography, has not been pretty. In this atmosphere, it is not surprising that some vulnerable adolescent females have developed a disorder – anorexia nervosa – that represents a radical avoidance and withdrawal from the implications of sexuality. It is of considerable interest that during the same period in which eating disorders have increased, teenage pregnancy has become a problem of growing concern in Western societies, particularly in the US. As Brumberg has suggested, both anorexia nervosa and teenage pregnancy may represent two sides of the same coin, the problem of control of female sexuality in an environment in which traditional constraints and standards have crumbled.[40] And these two apparently opposite responses to the dilemma of sexual control may be tied in turn to differences in socioeconomic status, with teen pregnancy representing a hyperaffirmation of sexuality by a deprived adolescent who has no other route to a sense of power, while anorexia represents its negation in the service of newly reinforced cultural ideals of female achievement.

Body Image and the Dilemmas of the Female Adolescent

The present period is a particularly difficult one for female adolescents. Simone de Beauvoir suggested in *The Second Sex* that early adolescence is the period when girls come to the shocking realization that men have all the power.[41] While prior to adolescence girls typically experience themselves, although still children, as autonomous individuals, immediately after puberty they quickly learn the cultural truth that they do not measure up to men in social opportunities or social rewards. What is more, a girl's bodily self, or body image, undergoes a particularly dramatic change after puberty. The essential point here is not the change in her anatomy per se, which is of course relevant, but rather that the exterior of her body becomes objectified in a particular way. Attractiveness and the capacity to compel a man's attention become perhaps the most central elements of her self-esteem. Her achievements, whether academic or athletic, are less valued that those of a man. Some of these developments may be rooted in biology and evolution, but cultural attitudes have a major impact on how adolescent girls feel about themselves.

DeBeauvoir developed these ideas about half a century ago, and one could easily make the argument that conditions have dramatically changed since the formulations of *The Second Sex*. Middle-class girls have far more opportunities educationally, professionally, and athletically, and evidence indicates that girls now expect that they should be aiming at significantly greater economic independence. And yet one cannot expect centuries, even millennia, of a very narrow definition of female possibilities to be wiped out by half a century of still fairly superficial social changes. What is more, it seems that, paradoxically, with the altered notions about femininity that have been introduced by decades of feminism, the cultural definition of the female in terms of her physical attractiveness seems ever more insistent. Feminist writers have argued that this is in fact no paradox, but represents a cultural reaction against the movement of women to a greater degree of social, economic, and psychological independence.[42]

These phenomena are evident in the turmoil experienced especially by middle-school girls in the United States in the present period. As one woman put it, reflecting back on her middle-school and early high-school years, "from the seventh through the tenth grades, all we talked about was food."[43] Body image preoccupation is normal particularly at this age, the age at which young females are most vulnerable to developing eating disorders. In recent years, researchers have pointed to the dramatic loss in self-esteem and confidence that is characteristic of girls in the transition from late childhood to early adolescence.[44] The obsessive preoccupation with body image and thinness seems to be an essential factor that leads girls at this age to be vulnerable to depression, to lose interest in intellectual pursuits that they may have been formerly good at, most notably mathematics and science. We will discuss further the role that the mass media and fashion industries play in the promotion of these insecurities in subsequent chapters.

All of these considerations seem to be applicable in a particularly poignant way to adolescent girls who develop eating disorders, and anorexia nervosa in particular. The self-imposed "reduction" of the body and the annihilation of the physical changes of puberty reflects a refusal, although not one recognized as such, to comply with the objectification of the bodily self that is described by de Beauvoir, Palazzoli, and others. Since many anorexic girls are ones who carried particular talents, capacities, or potentials into adolescence, this redefinition of themselves in terms of their physical attractiveness is a particularly painful blow. Carol Gilligan and her followers, such as Catherine Steiner-Adair, have emphasized the "loss of voice" that comes so frequently with female adolescence. It is through one's appetite (or loss of appetite) that one's innermost feelings are expressed, as opposed to the confident verbal articulation of self, which was possible, only a short time ago, during late childhood and preadolescence.[45]

Bulimia: The Facade of Perfection and the Secret Self

The dynamics of bulimia, too, seem inextricably bound up with sex-role issues. An early attempt to understand bulimics from this standpoint was a 1976 paper by Boskind-Lodahl, which attempted an explicitly feminist interpretation of both anorexia nervosa and bulimia.[46] Her analysis was based on her observations of a large number of bulimic college students whom she had seen at the Cornell University student health center. One of her aims in writing the paper was a critique of the earlier psychoanalytic formulations, which suggested that all women with eating disorders are symbolically "rejecting femininity" or "refusing womanhood." In contrast, Boskind-Lodahl asserted that precisely the opposite is true. Rather than rejecting the female role, bulimics (or bulimarexics, as she called them) excessively conform to feminine stereotypes. She described her subjects as excessively pleasing, unassertive, and particularly sensitive to criticism or rejection by men. Their striving for thinness and preoccupation with their appearance represents an exaggeration, rather than a rejection, of a cultural female norm. While Boskind-Lodahl's descriptions of bulimics ring true to clinical experience, her critique of the traditional psychoanalytic formulations was somewhat misplaced, since these interpretations were about anorexia nervosa, not the bulimic syndrome. With respect to anorexia, the notion of the "rejection of femininity" has much greater applicability.

It is my experience, as well as that of others, that most bulimics have experienced some form of significant emotional deprivation in their early life.[47] For some, an illness in a parent, a parent's problem with depression or alcoholism, or preoccupation with work and career leads to the temporary (or chronic) absence or unavailability of a parental figure. In other cases, the parents are in open conflict (much more commonly than is the case in anorexia), sometimes eventuating in a separation or divorce.[48] In many instances, the chronic preoccupation of the parents with external or interpersonal problems results in the child's emotional needs being ignored. Whatever the cause, the child typically early on turns to food as a means of solace, of filling the void left by parental inattentiveness or implicit abandonment. On the surface, however, she typically cultivates a positive facade, an appearance that she "can manage." Underneath, though, she feels needy, childlike, and dependent, feelings of which she is deeply ashamed. Under no circumstances does she permit herself to reveal her primitive feelings of abandonment, sadness, and rage. These are discharged in episodes of bingeing and purging.

When compared with anorexics, bulimics typically maintain a strong conscious identification with the traditional female sex role. Unlike anorexics, a significant number of whom are sexually avoidant and inexperienced, most bulimics have a history of active sexual involvement and are oriented to pleasing males. Bulimics tend to have had an intensely ambivalent relationship with their fathers. Often, the father has been admired as a role model, and has set high standards of intellectual or professional achievement for his daughter.[49] Typically, though, the father has been extraordinarily critical or distant, and in some instances overtly abusive; in any case, he continues to be for the bulimic a figure of mystery and fascination. She remains highly sensitive to male criticism and rejection, and her relationships with men are often turbulent as a result. Nevertheless, for the bulimic the father is a powerful identification figure. In contrast with anorexics, who typically are deeply enmeshed with their mothers, bulimics often attempt to distance themselves from their mothers, whom they frequently perceive as weak and powerless. As Wooley and Wooley point out, in a period of changing sex roles in which women increasingly identify with ideals of mobility and power, bulimics reject what they see as their mother's traditionalism and lack of assertiveness; it is their father's power that they admire and idealize.[50] For bulimics, these attitudes are intimately connected with their ideas about thinness and fatness: thinness is associated with masculine power, fatness with feminine weakness.

Like anorexics, bulimics are unable to work out a satisfactory solution to the problem of identity. They are caught in the dilemma of how to integrate ambition and a need to be powerful with an identity based on pleasing, compliance, and unassertiveness. Their resolution of the problem of identity is a deep split within the self, which entails a facade of perfection, pleasing, and competence, on the one hand, and a secret self that both expresses and binds "messy" feelings of neediness, rage, and helplessness. Thinness is for them the ideal which brings together the conflicting strands of a new female identity, one which is on the one hand powerful, competent, and in control, but on the other is nurturing, submissive, and pleasing to men. Bulimics tend to be extraordinarily vulnerable to external influences, and given their intense concern with their appearance, fashion models and media figures often have a powerful impact on the standards that they feel they must live up to.[51]

As I suggested earlier, bulimia is a common stress symptom among college-age or working women, a self-destructive method of working out feelings of loneliness, anxiety, depression, or other discomfiting emotions. The contemporary college campus is an environment in which many of the new contradictory pressures confronting females seem to converge.[52] Intense academic pressures, a fluid and unstructured eating environment, the challenges of sexual relationships in an environment in which the possibility of sexual exploitation is increasingly a matter of concern, all contribute to a situation that can be overwhelming for those who are vulnerable. Of particular significance for many women who develop bulimia are their relationships with men. Many contemporary female college students (as well as males) find heterosexual relationships difficult, for a number of interrelated reasons.[53] One of the most important of these is male anxiety in response to female ambition and academic or professional competitiveness. Bulimics are particularly vulnerable to these reactions, given their intense need to be accepted as feminine and their inordinate need to please men. As a result, they will be more likely than most to suppress their own individual needs and ambitions in the service of maintaining acceptance. Associated feelings of anger and resentment tend to be taken out on the self in the form of bingeing and purging episodes. In my experience, bulimic women are especially sensitive to the subtle (and not-so-subtle) "put-downs" of females by men, particularly in situations associated with competitiveness or assertion. The relatively high prevalence of bulimia in environments that are bastions of male power – such as medical schools, or the higher levels of the corporate world – is probably understandable in terms of the ambiguities confronting women in these situations.[54] The maintenance of thinness, as well as a facade of perfection, competence, and control serves to establish an external adaptation to the demands of an environment in which one must compete and not show the softer, more vulnerable side of one's femininity. Secret rituals with food become the only avenue of expression of these carefully hidden needs and feelings.

Cultural Confusion about the Female Role

It has been the main point of this chapter to argue that the transition to a new female identity has left many young women vulnerable to developing eating disorders. The shift in contemporary Western societies to a new emphasis on female achievement and performance represents a sharp reversal from previous role definitions that emphasized compliance, deference, and unassertiveness. A new sexual ethos, in the direction of greater permissiveness and a loosening of traditional controls, has brought new problems along with it, including an increased vulnerability to exploitation and anxieties among those from conservative or traditional backgrounds. It is not my intention to argue that these changes in and of themselves are bad; this is not a conservative polemic for reversing the economic and educational gains of the past four decades. It is just that in a period of such radical cultural transition, some young women are vulnerable to becoming caught in the uncertainties and ambiguities of a drastically altered set of expectations. Most female college students, even those who are not having difficulties with food or weight control, will quietly assert that they feel vulnerable to the same problems experienced in acute form by those who develop eating disorders.

I would like to conclude this discussion with mention of two additional problems that make the attainment of female identity in the present environment difficult. The first is that the definition of the new ideal social role (and psychological identity) for women is far from clear. Most contemporary women feel that along with the increased expectations for achievement and performance, the pressure to be traditionally feminine – in the sense of being attractive, pleasing, and unassertive – is as powerful as ever before. It is the multiplicity of role demands, many of which seem to conflict with one another, which makes the contemporary situation for women so difficult. Popular culture has mythologized the notion of the women who "has it all" (that is, who performs all of these roles) in the imagery of the "superwoman."[55] The superwoman is both competent, achieving, and ambitious, and yet pleasingly feminine, sexual, and nurturing. In one popular book promoting this imagery of perfection, it is clear that in addition to fulfilling the multiple demands of modern womanhood, the superwoman devotes considerable attention to her appearance, and is meticulous in the area of weight control – she is, above all else perhaps, thin.[56] Research by Catherine Steiner-Adair in a private-school population in New York State showed that those girls who strongly identified with the ideology of the superwoman were the very ones who showed symptoms of eating disorders, while those who criticized or rejected the stereotype were relatively free of these problems.[57] Similar conclusions were drawn by a group of researchers at Yale, who found that college students with disordered eating aspired to fulfill both stereotypical male and stereotypical female ideals, while at the same time attributing enormous importance to their physical appearance.[58] Conflicts between new cultural ideals and traditional identifications were evident in a German study, in which a group of bulimic women were shown to have relatively large discrepancies between their sex-role attitudes, which were relatively progressive, and their actual behavior, which tended to be more traditional. For example, a bulimic woman might agree with an "attitude" statement such as "In a partnership, both partners should have equal rights," but also might simultaneously endorse a "behavioral" item such as "If I like someone, I give in in cases of disagreement, even if I know I am right."[59]

A second issue is that of the persisting devaluation of femininity, despite (perhaps because of?) the gains resulting from feminism and the women's movement. These cultural biases take on a number of forms. One is that despite lip-service to the contrary, female intelligence is still not respected, or alternatively is perceived as threatening to male power and dominance. Female college students are often acutely aware of this in the classroom, particularly in the hostile or dismissive reactions of male peers (and sometimes professors) to their efforts to express their opinions. In the corporation, women have experienced the phenomenon of tokenism, whereby even though they have been able to acquire a position, they have had difficulty in advancing to higher levels of management or power.[60] Thus, either female intellect and ambition are discounted, or they are perceived as too aggressive and unfeminine. This problem reinforces the dilemmas of anorexics, who have difficulty in reconciling their intellectual aspirations with their own femaleness.[61] Their solution to the dilemma – diminishing the female characteristics of the body – can be seen on one level as an internalization of cultural misogyny.

The other side of this issue is that contemporary industrial cultures also devalue the traditional female role, that of nurturance. The world outside the family places low value on nurturing activities. Consider the professions in which nurturing is a primary activity – nursing, teaching, childcare. These are not high-status occupations in contemporary society, and they are low on the ladder of remuneration. Ambitious women experience particular conflicts along these lines, as it becomes very difficult to balance the demands of a career in the extra-familial world and simultaneously to raise children. Some women have also responded to this cultural devaluation of nurturance by identifying with traditional male values of power, toughness, and control – but often only by repressing their own nurturing side. A suppression of the nurturing side of the self is a central problem for anorexic and bulimic women, who are most obviously unable to nurture (i.e. nourish) themselves.[62]

Males with Eating Disorders: A Neglected Population?

In this chapter, I have argued that women who develop eating disorders are caught in the conflicting expectations and pressures of a period characterized by a dramatic change in the female role. But what about male anorexics and bulimics? Where do they fit into the picture?

Some have argued that the number of male anorexics (and particularly bulimics) may also have been increasing. There is, however, very little documentation for this assertion.[63] Most of the evidence that we do have on this question suggests that the increase in eating disorders is particularly prominent among women, with the number of male anorexics remaining relatively constant.[64] If this were in fact the case, it would be consistent with the notion presented in this chapter that the psychological issues in the eating disorders are largely those that affect females, not males. It must be remembered, however, that evidence about male prevalence from existing epidemiological studies is rather weak. For one thing, most of the surveys of psychiatric registers that were discussed in chapter 3 only count diagnosed or treated cases. It may very well be that, given the shame felt by males with eating disorders about having "feminine" problems, males may avoid treatment to a considerably greater extent. Males with eating disorders experience considerable stigmatization, even by women with eating disorders. The latter is a common phenomenon in eating disorder treatment units or in support groups. In addition, clinicians have traditionally been more reluctant to diagnose an eating disorder in a male, and this would exert a downward bias on prevalence estimates. Finally, because of the predominance of females among eating-disordered patients, many epidemiological surveys, particularly those conducted in the community, have simply ignored the male population altogether.

All in all, the existing evidence consistently supports the notion that males constitute at most 10 percent of the eating-disordered population. A possible clue to the reason for this huge disparity lies in an intriguing study carried out by Andersen and DiDomenico.[65] These authors compared the number of articles about dieting in a representative sample of men's and women's magazines. Remarkably, the number of diet items in women's magazines were precisely ten times the number in men's. The authors suggest a "dose-response" relationship between cultural emphases and the sex ratio of eating disorders.

While males and females with eating disorders resemble each other clinically in terms of their eating behavior as well as their body image concerns, there are a number of triggering factors that appear to be more common among males. One of these is athletics, particularly those sports in which there is a strong emphasis on weight control (see chapter 6). Thus eating disorders are common among racing jockeys and particularly common among high-school and college wrestlers. "Making weight" in order to compete in a particular weight class is a common pressure for the wrestler, and starvation dieting as well as purging are sometimes employed to this end. Bulimic compensations sometimes follow. The relationship between wrestling and eating disorders in males is similar to that between ballet training and eating disorders in females. Both demonstrate the power of demands for thinness in the environment. When these affect males as intensely as they regularly do females, then males are much more likely to developing eating disorders.

A significant number of males with eating disorders are obese or overweight during childhood and adolescence. Males may be equally as susceptible as females to being teased about their weight ("Nobody likes a fat man . . . "). An interesting difference, however, is that males frequently develop eating disorders as way of coping with *actual* overweight, whereas women characteristically are responding to *perceived* overweight.[66]

One very dramatic difference between male and female anorexics is the centrality of doubts or confusion about *sexual identity* in males. In females with eating disorders, such overt concerns about being adequately feminine are far less common. While not universal, overt homosexuality or conflicts about sexual orientation are rather frequent among males with eating disorders, and in some studies up to 50 percent of male patients have shown homosexual inclinations.[67] Within the gay community itself, there is some evidence that disordered eating attitudes and behaviors, such as fear of fatness and purging, are relatively common.[68] The male gay community tends to put a premium on thinness as a criterion for attractiveness.[69]

Interestingly, while eating disorders occur among lesbians, they have been thought to be uncommon, although the literature is somewhat conflicting on this point.[71] A 1998 study of 203 lesbian women recruited from a number of settings found a prevalence of roughly 1 per cent for bulimia nervosa, 0.5 per cent for anorexia nervosa, and 5 per cent for binge eating disorder.[70] The rates for anorexia nervosa and bulimia nervosa were roughly comparable to those found in the female population at large, with the rate of bulimia nervosa perhaps being somewhat smaller. On the other hand, the rate for binge eating disorder was twice that found in the general population. These figures need to be regarded with some caution, since they were determined through the use of self-report questionnaires and not clinical interviews, and the average age of the sample (34) was somewhat older than those typically surveyed. Nevertheless, they do suggest that the prevalence of eating disorders in the lesbian community may be fairly similar to that in heterosexual females, and that for the specific symptom of binge eating it may possibly be higher. Weight preoccupation is generally viewed negatively in the lesbian community and is taken as a capitulation to heterosexual norms. Nevertheless, many lesbians have internalized gendered norms regarding thinness, and this may give rise to intense conflict in its own right.[71] Such conflict appeared to be evident in a study that compared lesbian college students to heterosexual students, which showed that while lesbian students expressed a higher degree of body satisfaction than heterosexuals, they engaged in frequent dieting as often as heterosexuals and did not differ from them in their rates of binge eating or vomiting.[72]

Recently, a number of leading clinicians who had long experience with males with eating disorders have suggested that the role of homosexuality per se may have been overemphasized. The central issue seems to be, rather, that males with eating disorders on the whole tend to be afflicted with profound doubts about their masculinity. This may or may not result in the development of homosexual inclinations. Such doubts are often rooted in problematic family experiences, particularly in difficulties that the male patient had in childhood in identifying with his father.[73] The hypothesis of uncertainty about one's maleness enables one to encompass many of the known triggers of eating disorders in males, for example, obesity in childhood or early adolescence, which may lead to teasing about being a "sissy," or a sense of not measuring up in an athletic context.

Surveys of male college students during the 1980s and 1990s indicate that on the whole, the majority of males would like to change their weight, but they are equally divided between those who want to lose weight and those who want to gain weight.[74] This may reflect a greater number of contemporary males who want to lose weight as compared with the 1960s. Nevertheless, the sizable number of men who want to gain weight reflects the continuing premium that men place on strength and muscularity. In an interesting series of studies referred to in chapter 3, Harrison Pope and his colleagues at McClean Hospital in the Boston area have identified a syndrome among bodybuilders that they call "reverse anorexia" or "muscle dysmorphia."[75] These people, most of whom are male, develop consuming obsessions that center on the idea that they are "not large enough." In Pope's view, this obsession is just as socially debilitating as an obsession with thinness, in that it leads to avoidance of social contact and obsessive absorption with the activities that will make one larger. It of course should be pointed out that such behavior would not have the reproductive consequences and other sequelae of starvation that anorexia has for females. Nevertheless, the concept of muscle dysmorphia provides a fascinating mirror image of the dynamics of anorexia nervosa in women. Perhaps our readiness to pathologize extreme behavior in women leads us to place all of our clinical emphasis on the study of eating disorders in women and to neglect what, at least from a psychiatric standpoint, may be equally dysfunctional behavior in men.

Chapter Five

The Thin Body Ideal

"But I never looked like that!" How do you know? What is the "you" you might or might not look like? Where do you find it – by which morphological or expressive calibration? Where is your authentic body? You are the only one who can never see yourself except as an image; you never see your eyes unless they are dulled by the gaze they rest upon the mirror or the lens (I am interested in seeing my eyes only when they look at you): even and especially for your own body, you are condemned to the repertoire of its images.

Roland Barthes, *Roland Barthes*

By the time I was five or so, I began to believe in some inarticulate way that if I could only contain my body, if I could keep it from spilling out so far into space, then I could, by extension, contain myself. If I could be a slip of a thing, a dainty, tidy, bony little happy thing, then the crashing tide of self within the skin would subside, refrain from excess, be still.

Marya Hornbacher, *Wasted: A Memoir of Anorexia and Bulimia*

In German, the term for anorexia nervosa is *Pubertatsmagersucht* – "mania for leanness," or to use a more contemporary metaphor, "thinness addiction." The German term is actually a much better characterization of contemporary anorexic patients than *anorexia nervosa*, which implies a "nervous loss of appetite." Many anorexics, in fact, report ravenous hunger and intense suffering from starvation, although for most, such admissions will only occur after significant weight restoration.[1] Anorexics fear that admitting to hunger will result in enforced weight gain, a prospect which induces terror. What is more, the experience of starvation can enhance feelings of martyrdom, as well as a sense of absolute control. Contemporary anorexics, though, tend to be most invested in their external appearance, which they prefer to be skeletal. Many spend hours inspecting their image in the mirror for signs of the hated moral flaw – fat. "My legs are fat," said one patient plaintively, staring at her inflated skeletal thighs as they pressed into her chair. Gerald Russell has speculated that contemporary anorexic patients are more preoccupied with body shape than their nineteenth-century counterparts.[2] This may well be the case, as references to thinness are largely missing in nineteenth-century case reports. But, then again, female patients may have been highly reluctant to tell most physicians their feelings about body weight, so closely tied as they are to issues of sexuality and therefore an indelicate subject for a physician–patient dialogue still governed by conventions of nineteenth-century prudery.[3] Even now, some patients hide their pride in their thinness until late in therapy, clinging to it like a treasured secret, fearful that a confession will lead to the ultimate catastrophe – enforced feeding.

It is undeniable, however, that most contemporary patients are highly vocal regarding their feelings about body shape. Surely one of the most intriguing puzzles of anorexia nervosa is the typical symptom of distorted body image, the perception that one is fat, an illusion that paradoxically tends to increase with worsening emaciation.[4] Anorexics (and bulimics of normal weight), when asked to adjust a televised image of themselves to accurately represent their size, or when asked to view their bodies in distorted mirrors, will typically choose a width much larger than their emaciated frames.[5] One patient reported having fleeting success in perceiving her thinness accurately, but then felt victimized by a "pumping mechanism" that made her "balloon up" as she stood before a mirror.[6] What is the significance of this bizarre distortion? Is it a delusional misperception, one that must be corrected before recovery can occur?[7] Is it the product of the deranged thinking of a starved and metabolically disregulated organism? Some have suggested that the overestimation of body size is a phenomenon analogous to the famous "phantom limb," when an amputated body part is felt to be still present (the limb in this case corresponding to the sense of the body's mass before weight loss).[8] Most likely, overestimation of body size is a "cognitive" rather than a perceptual phenomenon.[9] Anorexics will typically admit to their emaciation when confronted with its reality in a mirror, on videotape, or when urged to "break through" their denial.[10] In fact, body image overestimation is now pervasive in a culture obsessed with thinness and dieting. A number of studies have had difficulty in distinguishing anorexics from non-eating-disordered subjects in the degree of overestimation of body size.[11] Such findings have led some to argue that the criterion of body image distortion be dropped from the diagnostic criteria for anorexia nervosa.[12]

Anorexics experience their thinness as a sense of purity, of control, of distinctiveness. The angular shape, the shocking sight of bones, creates a sharp boundary between themselves and the world, insulating them from dreaded intrusions. Through her shape, the anorexic makes a powerful statement of rejection of gender expectations, in effect, "I have sharp contours, I am not soft, I do not merge with you. I have nothing to give you."[13] Some are quite explicit about the relationship of thinness to the rejection of femininity, like one patient who said "and I want to stay slender because I look more like a man. I push myself to do as much as any man can do. It's difficult to be with a woman who is strong and efficient, and I can't admit that I am not as strong as she is."[14] The famous patient, Ellen West, felt torn between an ethereal student with whom she was infatuated and the man whom she was destined to marry. She experienced her dichotomous feelings about masculine and feminine identifications in terms of the extreme polarities of her body image: "I mean my life's ideal, to be thin, continued to occupy me more than all else. I shall really become a wife only when I have given up my life's ideal."[15] The anorexic body has been likened to the pencil-thin sculptures of Giacometti, with their strange isolation, their paradoxically heightened self-definition through their minimal consumption of space, their impression of distance, their intrinsic visualizability from afar.[16] One patient offered a dramatic statement about her existential aloneness, comparing her feeling of herself with the Statue of Liberty, the "lady of the harbor . . . like the statue, untouched and untouchable, on a little island in the gray ocean, with no relationship to anybody and anything."[17]

The Increasing Cultural Emphasis on Thinness

Much evidence has accumulated now for an increasingly demanding thin-body ideal in the Western nations, particularly the United States,

119

but also in Western Europe and probably throughout the industrialized world. The idealization of thinness and the emphasis on weight control have been a part of Western culture since the early twentieth century, but it is only since World War II, and particularly since the 1960s, that dieting and thinness attained the status of a mass cultural obsession.[18] The chief bearers of the burden of the contemporary demand for thinness are women, a fact attributable to the central role of physical appearance and sexual attractiveness in women's self-esteem and social success.[19] Given the centrality of shape and weight concerns among contemporary patients with eating disorders, and given the overwhelming predominance of women in the patient population, it seems clear that the contemporary concerns with thinness must play an important role in their increased incidence.

The best-known study documenting an increasingly stringent thinness ideal was one of an important series of investigations by David Garner and Paul Garfinkel, and their colleagues. The authors studied two standards of female attractiveness, the winners of the Miss America pageant and the *Playboy* "Playmate of the Month," over a 20-year period, beginning in 1960.[20] In each case, the model became not only progressively lower in weight over the period, but also less curvaceous (as measured by the width of the hips relative to the waist). The development of this "tubular" appearance was mirrored in the world of fashion, where slender, almost boyish models, such as Jean "The Shrimp" Shrimpton and Twiggy took the fashion scene by storm in the 1960s. Meanwhile, Garner and his colleagues also documented that while the standards of thinness were becoming ever more stringent, actuarial data indicate that the average American woman had become steadily *heavier* over the same period. Taken together, these data point to a fundamental contradiction: as weight standards became more stringent, actual body weight in the population was steadily increasing. These trends persisted throughout the 1980s. On the one hand, a replication of Garner and Garfinkel's study showed a persistence of rigorous standards of thinness in *Playboy* centerfolds and Miss America contestants through 1988 (the weights of Miss America contestants actually continued to decline).[21] On the other hand, the National Health and Nutrition Examinations Surveys showed a dramatic increase in the number of people in the United States (and women in particular) who were overweight between 1980 and 1990 (from 24 per cent to 32 per cent).[22] A central hypothesis of this book is that this contradiction between cultural ideal and biological reality plays a pivotal role in the increase in eating disorders.

An interesting aspect of Garner and Garfinkel's research paradigm is the particular figures that were chosen to reflect cultural standards: the winners of the best-known (and now most notorious, in some circles) beauty pageant, and the "centerfold" of the most widely read "skin" magazine. Both of these represent body types that are idealized by a largely male audience (and both have been the justifiable target of intense feminist criticism). But are women's standards of thinness nothing more than a response to the male expectation for a certain type of body? Or are there other factors involved? A related question is, do men and women's standards for (female) thinness differ? Certainly the models of high fashion, particularly those that fill the pages of *Vogue* and *Elle*, appear to be thinner and less curvaceous than the sex symbols studied by Garner, even in the face of the decreasing weight and increasing thinness of those sex symbols.

A now classic investigation of these issues was undertaken by two researchers from the University of Pennsylvania.[23] The authors asked both male and female college students to view a series of sketches of male and female figures of varying size (they were all the same height) and to make the following rankings:

1   the figure that looked most like their own;
2   the figure they would most like to look like;
3   the figure they thought would be most attractive to the opposite sex; and
4   the opposite-sex figure that they found most attractive.

The authors also asked students to estimate what percentage of the students at the university were heavier than they were. In general, female students, in contrast with males, tended to overestimate their current weight. Furthermore, the figure that they selected as representing their current weight was consistently heavier than the one they selected as their ideal as well as the one they thought would be most attractive to men. Particularly interesting is the fact that *women's ideal figure was smaller than the one that they thought would be most attractive to men*. Apparently, then, women's weight concerns are driven by more than the effort to please men, although the latter motive is clearly important. Perhaps even more intriguing is the fact that women's estimates of the figure that would be most attractive to men were smaller than the figure that the male students actually preferred. These patterns of female preference stand in sharp contrast to those for the male students, who showed no discrepancies on the average between their perceived weights, their ideal weights, and the weights that they thought would be sexually attractive. In only one respect did the males resemble the females, and that was their misperception of the weight that would be most attractive to the opposite sex. But they miscalculated in the opposite direction from the females, choosing a *heavier* figure than the one females selected as their ideal for a man. Apparently, then, both sexes misjudge the standards of attractiveness of the opposite sex; but the overall level of body image dissatisfaction in female students is much higher than it is in males.

Popular surveys indicate that contemporary women are consumed with an obsession about their body weight. For example, a survey of 33,000 women, of varying age and employment levels, by *Glamour* magazine in the early 1980s revealed that 75 percent felt that they were too fat, even though according to conservative weight tables only 25 percent were actually overweight.[24] The particular body parts that were the targets of the greatest dissatisfaction were the thighs, hips, and stomach. Most of the respondents also reported being constantly preoccupied with their weight, with a typical comment being "there isn't a day that goes by when I don't think about it." When asked what of the following would make them happiest – "losing weight," "hearing from an old friend," "a date with a man you admire," or "success at work," 42 percent indicated losing weight, while 21 percent indicated dating and 22 percent indicated work success.

The concern about weight and shape seems to have had the greatest impact on female adolescents. This has been true at least since the 1960s, when a survey of over 1,000 high-school students in Berkeley, California revealed that 56 percent of twelfth-grade girls considered themselves to be overweight, whereas objective measurements revealed only 25 percent to be moderately or extremely overweight.[25] In contrast, most boys in the sample felt that they were underweight and therefore wanted to put on pounds. Feelings of being overweight were far more prevalent among white girls than blacks, perhaps due to ethnic differences in body image, as well as the lower socioeconomic status of the black girls. Similar concerns were voiced in a study of Swedish adolescents by Ingvar Nylander in the early 1970s.[26] As noted in chapter 3, of the 1,241 female students surveyed, over half had "felt fat" at least some of the time, and dieting was highly prevalent, particularly among the older adolescents. In addition, nearly 10 percent of the study sample reported at least three clinical symptoms of anorexia nervosa, the most common of which were fatigue, increased interest in food, depression, chilliness, constipation, anxiety, and amenorrhea. Further analysis of an American sample indicated that feelings of fatness among adolescent females are most pronounced in teenagers from middle- and upper-income families, and, at that time at least, the desire to lose weight emerged and intensified in step with the growth spurt of puberty.[27] However, during the 1980s and 1990s, the concern with weight and feelings of fatness have been seen to be increasingly prominent among much younger children, even as early as age 7. These trends are evident in studies in the United States, the UK, Australia, and Israel.[28] Such findings deeply concern workers in the eating disorders field, as reports of a growing number of preadolescent patients with anorexia nervosa and delayed pubertal development have proliferated over the same time period.[29]

The Relationship between the Idealization of Thinness and Eating Disorders: The Case of the Ballet

While standards for thinness and ideal body shape have undergone dramatic change and increasing numbers of women have become preoccupied with their weight, is there any direct evidence that this preoccupation has led to a higher incidence of eating disorders? This was the question that led David Garner and Paul Garfinkel to undertake a study of young women who were studying at professional-caliber ballet schools in Canada.[30] In the ballet, there are particularly intense pressures to attain a thin body shape, a requirement that is attributable to contemporary aesthetic standards of the art form. The ballet dancer is expected to trace out a sharp, moving contour in space. For this purpose, slight body bulges are seen as a drastic impairment. Commenting on the ideal shape for ballerinas, Agnes de Mille wrote

> Very few dancers develop the bodies of mature women; they keep lean in the hips and flat-breasted, a phenomenon remarked on by all cos-

123

tume designers. It is also the fact that the greatest performers, the women best capable of producing sensuous satisfactions, are in their bodies the least sensual. In effect they have sacrificed all organs of personal fulfillment and maintain and cherish only the means for public satisfaction, the system of bones and sinew for levitation and propulsion.[31]

Gelsey Kirkland, who in her painful autobiography reported developing anorexia and bulimia during an emotionally stressful period as the premiere ballerina of the New York City Ballet, reported that following a "watermelon feast," the revered George Balanchine tapped on her sternum and rib cage and commented "must see the bones." His recommendation: "eat nothing." Kirkland describes the ballet as being governed by a "concentration camp aesthetic."[32] It seems that ballet training provides a virtual "natural experiment" for the study of the pressure for thinness. In their study, Garner and Garfinkel compared a large group of aspiring ballerinas to a group of college students on their scores on the Eating Attitudes Test, a screening device that has been used widely in the assessment of anorexic and bulimic symptoms. Of 183 ballet students, over 30 percent obtained scores on the Eating Attitudes Test comparable to those obtained by anorexic patients, whereas only 12 percent of the college students scored in this range. Interviews with the high scorers revealed that 12 out of the 183 (6.5 percent) of the ballet students met complete diagnostic criteria for anorexia nervosa, even though none of these was undergoing treatment or had been recognized by school authorities as suffering from an eating disorder. In contrast, none of the high-scoring college students could be diagnosed as anorexic on interview; apparently their high scores reflected only a preoccupation with weight, not the full-blown clinical symptoms of an eating disorder. Furthermore, almost all of the ballet dancers had developed their anorexic symptoms after commencing their training, suggesting that the training itself with its associated thinness may have been the chief factor that triggered the eating disorder. Similar high rates of anorexic symptoms were found for a group of modeling students; that is, 7 percent of those tested met the criteria for anorexia nervosa, although half of these had developed anorexia prior to their training. As Garfinkel and Garner point out, these percentages reflect the fact that in an environment in which thinness per se is a premium for success, the rate of anorexia nervosa is about ten times greater than that which is found in a comparable age-group of females in the general population.

Garner and Garfinkel were also interested in the specific role of high performance-expectations in the development of anorexia. Could it be that the pressures of the extraordinarily competitive environment of the professional ballet school were what was triggering anorexic symptoms in so many students, rather than the specific expectations for thinness? Accordingly, they compared the ballet students with a group of students of comparable age who were studying at a professional-caliber music conservatory, which presumably presents comparably intense competitive challenges to students, but without an emphasis on body shape. The conservatory students scored much lower on the Eating Attitudes Test than the dance students, and in fact they were indistinguishable from the comparison group of college students. Thus, the specific pressure for weight control, and not just performance demands and competition in general, is a critical factor in the development of anorexia nervosa. As one final refinement, the students in the national ballet school were compared with students in college dance departments, who presumably were under less competitive pressure but were necessarily concerned with weight control. The ballet students still had much higher scores. In other words, it is the *combination* of stringent requirements for thinness with the highly competitive environment of the ballet school that significantly elevates the risk for the development of eating disorders.

The vulnerability of ballet dancers to eating disorders was the subject of a book by L. M. Vincent, a psychiatrist and former dancer.[33] Vincent depicts the ballet school and dance company as virtual hothouses of competition and performance pressure. He criticizes ballet teachers for setting dangerously low weight-standards for young students, many of whom are still physically maturing, and documents widespread starvation dieting, food faddism, and vomiting and laxative abuse among aspiring ballerinas. In the subculture of the ballet school, these "anorexic" behaviors gain a degree of social acceptability, as is evident from the following comment of one student: "You should have seen this place on Sunday nights [weighins were on Monday] . . . Nobody would eat anything past twelve noon, and the whole second floor bathroom [of the women's residence] would smell so bad that you couldn't use it."[34] One 18-year-old student, who experimented unsuccessfully with various techniques to induce vomiting (including bizarre concoctions of spices and Ipecac) "settled" finally on the use of laxatives and diuretics in order to control her weight.[35] Students tend to be extraordinarily competitive and resentful about each other's disordered eating behaviors: "A modern dancer in her mid-twenties who vomits three to four times per week recalls being 'jealous as hell' over the vomiting of her best friend and roommate before embarking on the method herself, which she has now maintained for over seven years."[36] Menstrual irregularities, along with diminished sexual interest, are not uncommon. Vincent points out that the athletic demands of the ballet are as rigorous as those of any sport, but in no other athletic activity is the *appearance* of the body so crucial to success and acceptance.

Garner and Garfinkel's findings for ballet students in Canada have been essentially replicated in studies in England, Australia, and South Africa, although with perhaps slightly lower estimates of the number of students with disordered eating. Even more disconcerting, perhaps, was a study in the 1980s that systematically documented the widespread presence of disordered eating in professional ballet companies.[37] In a major investigation that included approximately one-quarter of the female ballet dancers in North America and Western Europe, fully 15 percent of the Americans and 23 percent of the Europeans queried reported having had anorexia nervosa, while 19 percent of the Americans and 29 percent of the Europeans reported having had bulimia. This is obviously a shockingly high percentage, considerably higher than the rate found by Garfinkel and Garner in their study of ballet students. Interestingly, though, there were no cases of either anorexia or bulimia among black dancers, whose numbers were 11 of the total sample of 66. The black dancers in general indicated a higher degree of body image satisfaction, suggesting perhaps that ethnic-group differences in body image may continue to be an influence even under the rigorous standards of weight control in dance companies. The anorexic dancers were mostly from the more competitive, national dance companies, a finding that may be attributable to the higher competition pressures of these settings (although the national companies also had more rigorous weight standards and required more daily exercise).

The research on eating disorders in the ballet has led dance companies to undertake some efforts at nutritional intervention and education as well as direct advice and information about the risks of eating disorders. The results of these programs cannot as yet be determined, but preliminary studies are not encouraging. One can understand that dance educators might take up these programs with some ambivalence, since they imply a critique of standards of appearance that are inherently promulgated by the art form, but they also suggest that the culture of the dance world might be in some way inherently toxic. Public controversy about the whole issue erupted in 1997 with the death due to cardiac arrest of Heidi Guenther, a dancer in the Boston Ballet Company, whose initial weight loss was apparently triggered by a suggestion that she lose five pounds in order to be promoted to the first-tier performing company. In fairness, the directors of the company had suggested to the dancer that she not lose any more weight after her weight loss had gone far beyond that initially recommended. Nevertheless, the death of this dancer suggests that eating disorders remain a serious, potentially life-threatening problem in the highly appearance-oriented, competitive world of the ballet.[38]

The larger significance of the research on the ballet is that an increased demand for thinness, particularly in a competitive setting, greatly increases the likelihood that some individuals will develop eating disorders. It is interesting to think about these pressures in the light of gender. It has often been suggested, for example, that when men are under comparable pressures for weight control, for example as is the case among wrestlers and racing jockeys, they too will be vulnerable to developing eating disorders. Certainly, anecdotal clinical evidence suggests that this is so. Male adolescents, for example, sometimes develop anorexia when struggling to "make weight" for competitive wrestling. However, in one of the few systematic studies of such a population, a group of racing jockeys in the Newmarket and Epsom areas of England, the prevalence of eating disorders was not found to be high.[39] Perhaps the particular emphasis in the dance on the external shape of the body, along with the ethic of perfectionism and competition, makes dancers particularly vulnerable. It is also likely that, given the socialization pressures that we described in the last chapter, females will be more vulnerable to the development of eating disorders even in these high-risk environments, owing to the fact that certain of them are particularly susceptible to external demands and competition pressures.

Why Thinness?

Let us recapitulate the argument so far. It seems clear that an increasingly thin body ideal, one that is moving in the opposite direction to the realities of average body weight, has been on the ascendant from the 1960s through the 1990s. Women, particularly younger women who must compete in the sexual, academic, and occupational realms, have come under increasing pressure to lose weight and mold their bodies to an increasingly procrustean and narrow external standard. The contemporary emphasis on body shape also has to be understood in the wider context of a society that places an increasing emphasis on externals, on appearance, on image.[40] Given the "natural experiment" of the ballet, which suggests that eating disorders proliferate in an intensely competitive environment that places stringent demands on body shape, then the proliferation of eating disorders in the the 1970s and 1980s becomes readily comprehensible as a direct correlate of the increasingly thin body ideal in the wider culture.

This argument essentially restates, if in somewhat reformulated terms, previous sociocultural interpretations of eating disorders.[41] There are, however, a major problem and a major question associated with the argument. The first of these is that the evidence for the impact of body ideals on eating disorders is indirect, or, as social scientists would say, correlational in nature. The fact that the increasingly thin body ideals over a period of three decades were directly correlated with a rise in the incidence of eating disorders over the same period does not prove that one caused the other. More direct evidence is lacking and difficult to come by. We shall return to this question shortly. The second question pertains to why thinness in particular, and not some other body shape, has become the dominant body ideal, so intensely sought after, for women in our time. In previous writings, the emphasis on thinness has been treated as if it were a totally arbitrary standard, a "given," that could just as well be some other body shape.[42] But it is unlikely that such a highly valued cultural ideal, one that is felt to be of such central importance and drives many into self-destructive patterns of behavior, is arbitrary. From here, therefore, we will turn to a discussion of the historical and cultural forces which have given rise to the present value placed on thinness, a discussion that will considerably deepen our understanding of why disorders that specifically revolve around body image and thinness have become ethnic disorders at this particular time and in this particular place.

The Century of Svelte

Human cultures have placed value on a variety of body shapes. A comprehensive history of the preferred morphology of the body has yet to be written. Nevertheless, a certain amount of cross-cultural and historical evidence can begin to illuminate the origin and meanings of contemporary thinness.

Cross-cultural studies indicate that for the majority of human societies, fatness has been valued over thinness, particularly in females.[43] A common explanation for this preference is one that invokes economic determinism: in societies where resources and wealth are limited, the large body is admired because it is symbolic of wealth and plentiful supplies (particularly food). This interpretation, while probably having some validity, is also undoubtedly simplistic. For example, thinness was also desirable during Europe's Little Ice Age in the late Gothic period, as well as among the Gurage of Ethiopia, who were troubled by collective anxieties about scarcity.[44] Preferred body weight, most likely, is a complex social construction, not a simple result of economic factors. For women, in particular, one of these factors is of particular importance – the value placed on reproduction.[45] This connection is nowhere more dramatically evident than in the African institutions of the "fattening ceremony" and "fattening sheds," which at one time were pervasive throughout Eastern and Central Africa.[46] At a certain point after puberty (usually between the ages of 15 and 18), girls were intentionally overfed and then their ample bodies displayed in a ceremony that celebrated their reproductive potential and economic status. The fattening ceremonies have generally disappeared, although one writer reports observing their continued existence recently in rural Eastern Nigeria.[47] Apparently, older African women can still recall the experience of the fattening ceremony in their childhoods, but their daughters, particularly if they are university students in urban Africa, have now come under the influence of the diametrically opposite modern ideals of thinness.[48] It is important to realize, though, that the symbolic association of fatness with fertility may be a cultural intuition of a biological reality – that is, the close connection between female adiposity and reproductive capacity.[49]

In Western Europe and the United States, despite previous intimations of what was to come in the nineteenth-century fetish with the corset and ante-bellum "Steel-engraving Lady," the ideal of female thinness did not really take hold until the twentieth century, which has been dubbed by Bennett and Gurin, in their excellent book on dieting, the "century of Svelte."[50] By the end of the nineteenth century, it seems that the symbolism of thinness was strongly linked with the idea of class. In his *Theory of the Leisure Class*, for example, in which he published his famous theory of conspicuous consumption, Veblen wrote about the wives of the wealthy: "There are certain elements of feminine beauty ... which come in under this head .... The ideal requires delicate and diminutive hands and feet and a slender waist. . . . It results that at this cultural stage women take thought to alter their persons, so as to conform more nearly to the requirements of the instructed taste of the time."[51] By the first decade of the twentieth century, the fashion models of Paris had already adopted the standard of extreme thinness. As early as 1908, the *Vogue* correspondent in Paris wrote that "the fashionable figure is growing straighter and straighter, less bust, less hips, more waist, and a wonderfully long, slender, suppleness about the limbs . . . the petticoat is obsolete, prehistoric. How slim, how graceful, how elegant women look!"[52] Obesity was coming under harsh criticism, and the burden of weight control fell particularly heavily on the shoulders of women, as evidenced in the following confession in a 1907 magazine article: "The gown was neither more nor less than anticipated. But I . . . the fault was on me . . . I was more! Gasping, I hooked it together. The gown was hopeless, and I . . . I am fat."[53]

It was not until the 1920s, however, that the tubular, thin body became adopted by the mass of upwardly mobile and aspiring women. In America, the symbolism of thinness was condensed in the imagery of the flapper, whose flamboyant style, mobility, shortened skirts, and liberated sexuality shocked those who held to the lingering traditions of nineteenth-century female delicacy and heralded the democratization of new ideals of female economic and sexual independence. Bennett and Gurin suggest that the credo of the flapper was distinctly antimaternal: "I am my own sexual boss; I am in control of myself; I am not a motherly, housewifely person."[54] The flapper's boyish, androgynous body was clearly the forerunner of the tubular look that was once again to emerge in the 1960s, and it was disseminated by powerful forces that were to play an even stronger role in the contemporary period. These included the new media of communication (in the 1920s, the movies), and an emerging consumerism, which in turn was fueled by the democratization of fashion and clothing styles.[55] In the hands of the institutions of the consumer economy, though, what was originally an image of liberation and self-determination was quickly transformed into a more sophisticated instrument of external control.

The flapper, along with the entire exuberant culture of the 1920s, vanished into the abyss of the Depression and then the consuming preoccupations of World War II. In the post-war period of domestic retrenchment and suburbanization, a new emphasis on the hourglass figure, and particularly on the large-breasted female, took hold, particularly among males. In the period of Marilyn Monroe and Jayne Mansfield, the preoccupation with weight control, particularly among women, never really disappeared, but it seemed to be dampened somewhat by a period in which a number of economic, political, and international threats fueled a greater attention to pragmatic concerns. But even as early as the late 1940s, "new-wave" models were arriving in New York and appearing on the pages of *Vogue*, models who were secretly rumored to "eat nothing."[56]

The return and subsequent entrenchment of thinness in the 1960s, heralded by the sanctification of Twiggy, brought with it some new features and emphases – an extreme androgyny, almost boyish and prepubertal, a trend towards the use of younger and younger models (the huge billboard of Brooke Shields that towered over Times Square was one of the fashion symbols of the era of the 1970s), and an increased flaunting of a sexuality that carried Nabokovian overtones. The consumer culture that emerged in the 1970s (the infamous "me" decade) was obsessed with youth, haunted by the spectre of aging, and all too ready to exploit and absorb images of a free sexuality that only a decade earlier had been the symbol of the political rebellion of a "counterculture." Concretely, the emphasis on youth was driven by the enormous expansion of fashion markets for teenagers, who in the 1980s increasingly constituted a significant proportion of the consumers at American shopping malls. Meanwhile, despite the glamorization of free sexual expression and authentic selfhood ("Zena is you," one advertisement proclaimed), many women still experienced getting into a pair of designer jeans as no more liberating than the bone-crushing corsets of the nineteenth century.

By the mid-1980s, there were also some signs of a new look, one which, however, hardly denied the importance of thinness. Fashion writers exuberantly announced that "curves are back," a trend that essentially seemed to signify a movement back to a preference for larger breasts (a signal of the increasing acceptability of having children?).[57] Meanwhile, the requirement for overall slenderness remained, particularly in the hips and the waist, resulting in a body type that in some instances may even result in greater distortion. Reports were that a number of models in New York City turned to cosmetic surgery to produce the necessary modifications. A second trend, one which began in the early 1980s along with the fitness boom, was the emphasis on muscle building and strength. Even here, though, the trend was coupled with the requirement for slenderness, as was evident in the relentless stream of articles on weight control in one of the most popular American magazines on the subject (appropriately entitled *Shape*). Where these trends will ultimately lead is uncertain, but in an age of extraordinary confusion about female identity and the ever-pressing need of the fashion industry to promote new images, it seems likely that the natural spectrum of female body sizes and shapes will remain unacceptable.

In the face of proclamations about the rise of more flexible body standards, the perseveration of thinness imagery was evident in the return of the "waif" look in the early 1990s. Particularly as epitomized by the model Kate Moss but also represented by numerous others, the waif promoted vigorous debate on the fashion pages themselves as well as an angry reaction from a public now sensitized to the potentially lethal impact of thinness imagery. The look that she represented was perceived by women's advocates as regressive and reactionary (for further discussion of this point see chapter 8). The waif look may have receded somewhat in the late 1990s, but the insistent theme of thinness seems likely to have continued expression for the forseeable future.

The Marketing of Body Image Distortion

The role of commercial interests and the media in promoting contemporary body ideals should not be underestimated. In the environment of the consumer-oriented, post-industrial societies, electronic and photographic images have a potent and far-ranging influence. Given the impact and pervasiveness of this imagery, it is not surprising that disorders of body image, in which people have difficulty in seeing themselves accurately, have become rampant. The distortions that are characteristic of anorexia or bulimia are sometimes literally and concretely evident in fashion advertising. Aside from the general glamorization of thinness, some advertisements literally present female models in which the calf is larger than the thigh.[58] Such distortions in the natural proportions of the body pass virtually unnoticed and are accepted as the norm. Some high-fashion models appear to be clinically anorexic, although the extent of eating disorders among models is actually unknown. It is generally conceded that while such figures may not be sexually attractive, they have the virtue (for the fashion industry) of "looking good in clothes." To achieve a certain kind of "look" has become a paramount virtue of contemporary fashion, regardless of the consequences for the health of consumers.[59]

The overvaluation of thinness is also exploited to promote products other than those related to body adornment. In one advertisement that appeared a number of times in the *New York Times Sunday Magazine*, a full-page spread depicted an impeccably lean and shapely model in a leotard thrusting a barbell over her head, and was accompanied by the caption "She has more fat on her than our salami." The comparison of the female body with a piece of meat is buttressed (in small print) by appropriate statistics comparing the percentage of body fat on the average woman to that on the average salami. In an even more outlandish example, Hershey promoted a new slender milk-chocolate bar with the Duchess of Windsor's famous (and now notorious) dictum, "You can never be too rich or too thin." This clever promotion unwittingly intensifies the contradiction so acutely felt by anorexic or bulimic patients between the desire for calorie-rich food and the equally intense desire for thinness. This last advertisement was the target of a campaign against advertising conducive to eating disorders by the Illinois-based National Association for Anorexia Nervosa and Associated Disorders, a campaign that resulted in its withdrawal by the company.[60]

While it is exceedingly difficult to measure precisely the impact of the media, there is little question that many anorexic and bulimic patients feel directly affected by the relentless assault of commercial imagery promoting thinness.[61] In a particularly grotesque example of such intrusiveness, a certain weight-loss product (a liquid diet) was promoted via computerized mass mailings to teenagers. In the margin of the promotional text, "personalized" comments were "handwritten" (actually by machine), such as "Annette, it really works, try it." Several teenage girls in an eating disorders support group felt that the advertisement was in fact personally directed to them by someone who "knew" that they were "too fat." One mother commented, perhaps not inaccurately, that the impact of the mailing was tantamount to a "psychological assault."[62]

There have been a number of efforts to demonstrate the impact of media imagery on non-eating-disordered college students. In general, these studies have shown that exposure to a series of thin images in the laboratory leaves female subjects in particular feeling especially self-conscious and inadequate.[63] Women with eating disorders also report that being constantly inundated with images of thinness does play a role in sustaining their symptoms, and patients report feeling more affected by such imagery than non-eating-disordered women.[64] However, there is as yet no *direct* evidence for the role of media imagery in the onset of eating disorders. This has led some to be skeptical about "blaming the media" for the problem of eating disorders.[65] But given that there is very strong evidence for an intense history of weight consciousness as a predisposing factor for bulimia nervosa, it is difficult to argue that an environment that inundates women with images that make them feel insecure and self-conscious would not play a role.[66]

Because the personal matrix is what is critical to conducting therapy, it is not necessary to directly address media images in the treatment of patients. Nevertheless, there have been some experimental efforts to incorporate these concerns. Thus, for example, at an appropriate point in treatment, David Garner may ask his patients to develop an "atrocity file," in which toxic images of thinness from the media are accumulated by the patient in a scrapbook. Through discussion with the therapist of the unrealistic standards promoted by the commercial culture, the patient can potentially develop a more realistic body concept and an awareness of the distorted standards that she has internalized.[67] There is of course more to the treatment of eating disorders than the elucidation of cultural forces that have negatively impacted a patient, but it is of interest that such an approach may have therapeutic value.

While focusing on media ideals is not necessarily critical to the treatment of eating disorders, it is an important and central target of prevention programs. To promote among schoolchildren active discussion and awareness of the toxicity of media images and a critique of their implied values has at least the potential to reduce their potentially harmful effects. Whether such programs can succeed in counteracting the impact of such powerful cultural forces as the manipulative and insistent imagery of advertising remains to be seen, but they are at the very least worthy of further investigation.[68]

The Globalization of Fashion and the Globalization of Eating Disorders

While the discussion about the evolution of thinness has focused on the United States and Europe (and mostly on the former), the impact of these ideals is not limited to "The West." With a rapidly expanding international economy, the norms of the consumer culture have now had a global impact. To provide a more concrete example, British *Vogue* publishes in some 40 countries, ranging from India to Argentina to Kenya. It is virtually impossible to visit any urban area around the world without encountering ubiquitous racks of fashion and beauty magazines, some of local and some of international origin. And invariably, along with the promotion of clothes and cosmetic products, these contain articles on various methodologies to achieve weight loss. The rise of eating disorders in areas such as Hong Kong, Argentina and Chile, India, and African countries is most likely a direct correlate of the penetration of Euro-American body ideals of body image.

Unlike the Western countries, however, where the ideal of thinness has been evolving throughout the twentieth century, the impact of thinness imagery in areas outside the Western orbit has been quite sudden and dramatic. As has been suggested earlier, the traditional body ideal in most of the nations of the world until very recently was one of largeness or fatness. The sudden impact of new ideals of body size can create a great deal of tension between young people, who are most likely to adopt the new standards, and their elders, who are more likely to follow traditional norms. This type of cultural warfare has been described by Barber in his provocative book *Jihad vs. McWorld*.[69] Thus it is not surprising that in Hong Kong, for example, the development of an eating disorder in a child creates even more than the usual level of high tension within the family, since the parents are likely to see it as a complete rejection by a child of a way of life. More than one Asian student whom I have counseled, for example, has found it completely impossible to discuss the eating disorder with their parents. The subject is simply taboo.

A particularly fascinating instance of the impact of the media on attitudes toward the body in a traditional society is found in the island of Fiji. When Anne Becker, a psychiatrist and anthropologist, first conducted research in Fiji in the early 1990s, she found a far greater percentage of Fijians, and Fijian women in particular, were overweight in relation to their Western counterparts, a fact that was true at all ages, and yet the attitude of subjects towards fatness amongst themselves or others was one of acceptance or even celebration. To be fat was seen as either being strong, capable of work, or having been well fed, and kind and generous, the latter being consummate Fijian virtues. On the other hand, to be thin was viewed highly negatively, as either tantamount to being sickly and not competent or as having been the recipient of poor treatment. On tests that assessed their preference for body shapes, Fijians genuinely indicated a preference for moderately proportioned individuals, but this did not prevent even obese women from wanting, at least in some instances, to be fatter. In fact, the general attitude of Fijians towards a wide range of body shapes was one of acceptance. But if anything, fatness was preferred over thinness. Dieting, in particular, was frowned upon and viewed as a sign of self-neglect and offense to the community. No one had ever heard of an individual having anything remotely resembling an eating disorder.[70]

When Becker returned in 1998, these attitudes had undergone a dramatic change. Not only were large numbers of women, especially teenage girls, unhappy with their body size, but they were actively dieting, and on tests such as the Eating Attitudes Test, they were showing levels of distorted eating attitudes comparable to those found in Western nations (unfortunately there were no earlier test data to which to compare the more recent data, but Becker's earlier findings through interviews would suggest that the levels of disturbed eating attitudes would have been low). Over the time elapsed between Becker's first and second visits, there had been a critical change introduced into Fijian culture, that is, the introduction of television. Although there was only one commercial television station, Fijians were now exposed to the likes of programs such as "Beverly Hills 90210" and "Melrose Place." And now women, particularly young women, were beginning to show signs that they were obsessed with losing weight, that they disliked their present weight; and for the first time they had taken up dieting in earnest. This could be viewed as an informal experimental verification of the idea that the introduction of Western cultural values in a traditional culture through the mass media has a powerful effect on the development of tendencies toward eating disorders in the culture. It should be kept in mind, though, that Becker had only assessed distorted eating attitudes, not eating disorders themselves. Of the second of these, we still do not have any evidence in Fiji, but if the logic entertained here is correct, it should not be long before one sees the emergence of clinical cases of anorexia nervosa or bulimia nervosa.[71]

A Symbol of the New Female Identity

Fashion and media are not totally autonomous cultural institutions; they both create *and* reflect dominant cultural values and concerns. It would be unlikely, therefore, that the fashion and media conglomerates could successfully promote images of women of Rubensian proportions in the present social environment. Thinness sells because it amplifies emotions and values that are already latent within the populace.

A series of investigations by Brett Silverstein and his colleagues from the City University of New York serves to illuminate the connection between thinness and the dilemmas of female identity.[72] Silverstein developed a method for systematically measuring the extent to which thinness was idealized in any particular period. By sampling photographs of models from *Vogue* and *Ladies Home Journal* within a given year, in which the models wore either bathing suits or underwear, the ratio of the bust to waist width could give an accurate measure of the extent to which the preferred body ideal was "tubular," or non-curvaceous. On sampling photographs from *Vogue* from the beginning of the twentieth century to the early 1980s, Silverstein found that the bust-to-waist ratio fell from 1.95 (highly curvaceous) in 1909 to 1.1 (highly tubular) in 1925, only to rise to 1.7 in 1949 and to fall once again to about 1.2 in 1970 (where it remained for the rest of the decade).[73] So far, these results only systematically document a trend with which we are already familiar. What is of particular interest is the fact that the measure of leanness was strongly correlated with an increase in the number of women graduating from college, as well as the number of women in professional and managerial positions. Thus, the greater the number of women aspiring to male privilege and status, the greater the number involved in intellectual and vocational

137

competition with men, the more women aspire to a tubular, androgynous ideal and may be willing to virtually starve themselves to achieve this result. This is not only a phenomenon of the present, but may also have been characteristic of the 1920s, as Silverstein found a number of previously overlooked references in the popular press of that decade to epidemics of self-starvation among female students in the United States.

In further studies of contemporary college students, Silverstein found that the aspiration to thinness, as well as disordered eating, were specifically related to ambiguities regarding sex roles (and female achievement in particular) within the family.[74] For example, the more a student remembered her father as doubting her intellectual competence, the more she tended to aspire to a slender body ideal. Furthermore, female students who engaged in bingeing as well as purging more frequently recalled that (1) their parents believed that women's place was within the home, (2) their mothers were dissatisfied with their own careers, (3) the father had a disparaging view of the mother's intelligence, and (4) the father compared his daughter's intelligence unfavorably with a male sibling. Thus, for women with disordered eating, negative biases about female intellectual competence, already pervasive in the wider culture, are specifically amplified by familial attitudes, and particularly so by the negative judgments of the father. Silverstein's research thus further illuminates the relationship between disordered eating, changing sex roles, and attitudes toward female achievement. In historical periods in which women have felt under pressure to prove their intellectual ability and competence, the slender body ideal has been dominant.[75] And the reason for this is that under the persistent influence of gender bias and negative stereotypes, female curvaceousness is associated with a lack of intelligence and competence (i.e., the "dumb blonde"). But in addition, as we have seen, the roundness of the body, particularly any implications of fatness, also are closely linked with notions of fertility and reproductive capacity.[76] Thus, the aspiration to be lean and non-curvaceous also is mostly an effort to escape the patriarchal judgment (a judgment that is internalized) that "women's reproductive function defines her character, position and value." Ultimately it also represents, through the language of body shape, an emulation of the male, an effort at mimesis, one that unfortunately has self-destructive consequences and fails to solve the real issue of powerlessness.

Ethnic Disorders Revisited

We are now in a position to synthesize the arguments that have been raised in the last two chapters and to further elaborate the notion of eating disorders as ethnic disorders. In the recent period of history, women have been undergoing a vast change in their social role and, on a psychological level, in their own identities. The increasing involvement of young women in higher education and male-dominated professions has left many struggling to synthesize contradictory ideas of independence versus dependence, individual achievement versus the nurturance of others. Those who are particularly vulnerable to these conflicts internalize the prevailing ideology of body shape as an obsessive solution to the problem of identity, as a means of reducing the distress attendant upon feelings of weakness and internal conflict. Women who develop eating disorders forge a "solution" to the problem of identity by deploying a cultural symbolism of body shape that itself contains the latent, contradictory meanings of female identity. For thinness, as one group of authors suggested, is a highly potent symbol, a synthesis of the "divergent axes of nurturance and assertion."[77] Thinness is both "female" (the current ideal of sexual attractiveness) and "male" (the non-curvaceous, mobile, and active body). Like the Sinhalese phenomenon of "matted hair," which not only grows but is culturally recognized as a subject takes on the status of the "sacred" or "possessed," thinness is a symbol whose meaning is both social and personal.[78] A variety of individual experiences, conflicts, and pathologies may be expressed as anorexia or bulimia; but they all partake in this common cultural meaning.

Women with eating disorders therefore draw upon a cultural idea that has become the norm as a "defense" against particularly intense psychological, developmental conflicts (which are themselves culturally constituted). Eating disorders are ethnic disorders precisely because they magnify a culturally typical solution to a problem that is much more pervasive in the culture at large. The difference is more a quantitative than a qualitative one. The weight obsessions from which many "normal" women suffer are no more productive (and no more or less explicable) than those of the anorexic or bulimic patient, for whom they become all-consuming. Fortunately, in the usual case, their physical consequences are not so drastic as to lead them down the pathway of disease.

139

Chapter Six

The War Against Fat

Obesity, Dieting, and Exercise

What causes the most damage is not the actual weight itself, but the fear of weight.

Hillel Schwartz, *Never Satisfied*

I have always been repelled by fat women. I find them disgusting: their absurd sidewise waddle, their absence of body contour – breasts, laps, buttocks, shoulders, jawlines, cheekbones, everything, everything I like to see in a woman, obscured in an avalanche of flesh . . . . How dare they impose that body on the rest of us?

Irving Yalom, *Love's Executioner and Other Tales of Psychotherapy*

A terror of becoming fat is typically the central driving experience in the development of anorexia nervosa or bulimia. In contemporary Western societies, in which obesity is associated with significant health problems, fatness has also taken on symbolic meanings – namely, the repository of all the traits that are considered morally despicable.[1] By the time they reach elementary school, children have already absorbed the conviction, widely disseminated in the adult culture, that fatness means stupidity, laziness, slovenliness, a lack of will power.[2] Even otherwise enlightened and educated adults have difficulty in parting with the notion that these are self-evident truths about fat people. In order to penetrate more deeply into the sociocultural origins of the contem-

140

porary wave of eating disorders, we need to come to grips with our cultural obsession with fatness and the means we have adopted to combat it – dieting and exercise. But first, some discussion of the way the struggle against fat manifests itself in the eating disorders is in order.

An Intense Fear of Obesity

For anorexics, the fear of weight gain, of ballooning up, of "becoming a whale," is the spectre of the ultimate catastrophe. Many patients say openly that they would rather die of starvation than exceed their "magic number" on the scale (usually less than 100 lbs, and typically "89" or "99") by so much as a pound – with the number 100 arousing in their minds as much anxiety as any primitive taboo. The fear of fatness is the motivating force behind the food rituals, the fad diets, and the punishing exercise regimes so typical of anorexia nervosa. For anorexics, vegetarianism, new-age diets, and most recently the avoidance of cholesterol, are motivated not so much by the pursuit of health (although health ideologies may be conveniently invoked as a rationale) as they are by the dread of weight gain.[3] Meat is an object of particular avoidance, since animal fat is, in the mind of the anorexic, immediately and magically transformed into body fat.[4]

A number of anorexics begin their weight-reducing regimes in response to teasing or critical comments about adolescent overweight, or at least what is judged to be so. Even if the pre-anorexic is not heavy by objective standards (which she often is not), there is a concern with overweight, and sometimes a history of frank obesity, in the anorexic's family. In one case a 13-year-old girl began dieting after an athletic coach suggested that she might be too heavy to continue to be on a gymnastics team. The girl's father, who was himself almost frighteningly lean and highly weight-conscious, had suffered from a history of obesity in adolescence. In response to merciless teasing, he undertook a radical diet when in college through which he lost over 80 pounds over the course of a summer, a dieting success that had become a part of the family's mythology and when brought up in conversation was surrounded by considerable joking. In undertaking self-starvation herself, the daughter was emulating and replicating her father's triumph, but she was also throwing it in his face as a way of rebelling against his own

141

demands for perfection (this applied particularly to his expectations for athletic prowess, but also his own hatred of fat). The avoidance of fatness often becomes the sign of achieving a unique identity, typically in comparison with another family member. Very often, this is the mother or an older sibling, towards whom she harbors competitive or rivalrous feelings.

In the families of anorexics, a "morally bracing tone," as one writer put it, typically surrounds the topics of obesity, dieting, and physical fitness.[5] Many of these families subscribe to a highly puritanical ethic of work and self-control; fat is a symbol of sloth, of slovenliness, of self-indulgence. Ultimately, also, fat stands for the "sins of the flesh," namely sexuality – never a comfortable topic in the families of anorexics, who tend to be phobic about sensual matters.[6] Anorexics themselves internalize this contemporary version of the Protestant ethic. As one patient put it, "if you are thin they don't think that you are rich and that your life is too easy. Being fat is like the kings in the Middle Ages; they are just rich and powerful and do nothing, and everybody works for them. Looking and feeling exhausted shows that one does a lot, and without that I feel so undeserving."[7] As Bruch suggests, the characteristic hatred of fat within the anorexic family represents an "aristocratic attitude" that values being able to do without in the midst of abundance. Anorexics themselves, while not generally as critical of others as they are of themselves, reserve a particular animus for the obese. This attitude is summed up in the words of one of my patients, who recalled that "when I was anorexic, I simply couldn't stand to look at a fat person."

A struggle against obesity is even more evident in the family histories of bulimics. The percentage of the parents with a history of obesity is unusually high, particularly relative to middle-class norms.[8] In the families of bulimics, overeating is a common phenomenon, as is the use of food as a means of reducing emotional distress and solving problems. These families "move toward" food, in contrast with the families of anorexics who evidence a more avoidant attitude.[9] Bulimics often have a history of having been somewhat overweight themselves, although frank obesity is the exception. Having been teased or made to feel self-conscious about weight is a nearly universal experience for them. The bulimic's struggle with her own fluctuating weight often reflects, on a psychological level, a struggle to differentiate herself from her mother, whom for a variety of reasons she has come to disparage. Very often, she attempts to escape what she perceives as her mother's lack of power by identifying with her father, and as is typical of the eating-disordered patient, the struggle is expressed in the arena of body image. Fat, then, comes to stand for the rejected qualities of the mother, whereas thinness reflects the father's power and independence.[10] Bulimics often fluctuate widely between overweight and underweight, which is, on a psychic level, an enactment of the ambivalence and instability that surrounds these issues of gender and identity.

Obesity: Medical and Social Aspects

In the United States, in particular, the prevalence of overweight seems to be increasing at a shocking rate. The widely publicized NHANES (National Health and Nutrition Examination Surveys), which have been periodically conducted by the National Center for Health Statistics since 1960, have shown a sharp rise over the decade beginning in late 1970s and ending in the late 1980s.[11] Specifically, for adults between the ages of 20 and 74, the percentage of the population who are overweight (defined as the highest fifteenth percentile of body mass index) grew from an average of 25 percent in the period 1976–80 to 33 percent in the period 1988–91. The percentage of the total population who were overweight varied with gender and ethnic groups, with the highest rates occurring among non-Hispanic black women and Mexican-American women (almost half of the population in these latter groups were, according to the criteria of the study, overweight). However, even for those groups who showed the smallest increases (white men, black men, and white women) the percentage who were overweight also increased by a typical figure of 6 or 7 percent over a single decade. At the time of publication of the 1976–80 survey, researchers had hoped to target programs that would reduce the rate of obesity in the population by the year 2000. However, as the authors of the more recent survey acknowledged, the trend appears to be in the opposite direction. While the increase in obesity is perhaps most pronounced in the United States, it is hardly unique there. There is consistent evidence for an accelerating increase in obesity in almost all European countries, and in the UK in particular.[12]

Increasing rates of obesity appear to be endemic to the process of industrialization and are associated with a whole host of factors: relative food abundance, diets rich in fat and sugars, and especially a more sedentary life-style.[13] In food-poor, mostly rural societies in which famine is a recent memory or perhaps even a present reality, to be fat is seen as desirable, a sign of wealth and status. This association may even hold good today, for example, in India or Kenya, especially in rural areas.[14] Importantly, though, as a society becomes more affluent, the typical social-class distribution of and preference for obesity usually reverses. In the affluent societies, thinness is the symbol of status, whereas obesity becomes *déclassé*. The linkages between obesity and social class in the Western nations are not merely symbolic: a large number of studies shows the prevalence of obesity in the industrialized nations to be higher in the lower socioeconomic strata (a relationship that is particularly true for women), while the reverse relationship holds in less developed countries.[15] While the reasons for these very striking class differences are not well established, the most likely candidates are the higher caloric content of low-cost food as well as the health-consciousness and aesthetic standards associated with higher levels of education.

The intense medical interest in obesity and overweight is of course due to its association with a variety of health problems, including hypertension, coronary heart disease, diabetes, and some forms of cancer.[16] These correlations have been documented in a number of studies, particularly the large scale studies attempting to assess risk factors for coronary heart disease. Virtually all of these studies prior to the 1990s were carried out on adult male populations, but a large scale study carried out in the United States and published in 1995 confirmed that obesity carries a substantial mortality risk for women as well.[17] Also, in recent years, there is a growing concern about a sharply increasing prevalence of obesity among children and adolescents, a problem which appears to be strongly correlated with the number of hours that a child watches television.[18] Television viewing is of course an activity that includes both major life-style factors that place one at risk for obesity – sedentariness and snacking (especially on junk-food). Inactivity, however, is perhaps the most critical factor. In England, for example, the prevalence of obesity doubled in the 1980s, and yet daily energy intake and fat consumption were actually reduced during the period.[19]

Despite the understandable concerns of eating disorders professionals, who are focused on the stigmatization of fatness and the pathologies of dieting, there is little doubt that obesity is a serious medical problem, particularly for those who are morbidly overweight.[20] Nevertheless, debates have proliferated about whether the health effects of obesity have been overstated, and in particular whether they justify alarmist comments by the United States Surgeon General about the health risks of a small percentage of overweight. There are some data that suggest that moderate degrees of overweight (say 15 percent over the statistically normal weight for one's height) may not be associated with elevated risk for health problems – in fact the reverse may be true.[21] This is especially the case for women, on whom the effects of mild overweight are different than they are for men. In females, weight accumulation is distributed subcutaneously, whereas for men it results in much more medically dangerous trunkweight.[22] It is curious, therefore, that the social bias against obese women is much greater than it is against men (see below). Some have suggested that the current medical teachings about the dangers of a small degree of overweight represent the covert penetration of aesthetic standards into what should be strictly objective judgments, and even that obesity itself is a culture-bound syndrome. In support of this notion, it has been pointed out that the weight–height standards for women in the older actuarial tables were arbitrarily reduced, for reasons that were unexplained.[23]

Despite controversies about the point at which weight becomes medically problematic, as well as heated debates about the validity of standardized weight tables, the health threats of frank obesity are supported by a wealth of evidence. And because of the rapid rise in obesity in the industrialized nations, there is intense interest in understanding the underlying mechanisms that lead to excessive fatness. In the scientific community, most of the focus has been on physiological mechanisms that make certain individuals especially vulnerable. Twins studies have suggested a powerful genetic factor that may account for the fact of different degrees of fatness in people exposed to similar dietary regimens.[24] The discovery of a specific obesity gene in mice was one of the most widely publicized scientific findings of the 1990s, with pictures of an obese laboratory mouse on the front pages of the world's most prominent newspapers.[25] The Ob-gene, as it is called, in turn controls a substance called leptin, which is believed to be critical in the regulation of appetite and energy metabolism. Levels of leptin are low in the obese mouse, and perhaps these low levels, in that they imply a dysregulation of appetite, could be the chemical factor that accounts for the mouse's obesity.[26] Unfortunately, this idea does not work out in such a straightforward way, since measured levels of leptin in obese humans turn out to be *higher* than in non-obese subjects. Despite these contradictions, it is possible that an understanding of leptin will ultimately play an important role in the pharmacological treatment of obesity. Conversely, it is quite conceivable that leptin may somehow work to down-regulate appetite levels in anorexia nervosa patients, which could account for the lack of hunger experienced by these patients, their inability to gain weight, and their highly efficient use of food. Work on such possibilities is in its infancy, but it has exciting promise.

The treatment of obesity has always been enshrouded with a deep therapeutic pessimism. Nothing expresses this more clearly than a famous statement by Albert Stunkard, one of the world's most renowned obesity experts, to the effect that "most obese people won't enter treatment, most who do won't lose weight, and most who lose weight regain it." Obesity has been considered to have a worse prognosis than many forms of cancer. And yet there is room for guarded optimism in some of the new discoveries of physiological obesity research, particularly studies of hormones such as leptin and neuropeptide-Y, chemicals that may serve to regulate subtle hypothalamic mechanisms such as the body's set-point metabolism (see below). Drastic methods, such as gastric stapling, have been developed to treat the morbidly obese, but such "great and desperate cures," as they were called by Eliot Valenstein,[27] are inappropriate for those with more moderate but still significant degrees of overweight. Nevertheless, certain techniques, such as liposuction, which were once considered to be extremely hazardous, have been technically improved and have been widely adopted in the United States as a form of cosmetic surgery – to rid oneself of "love handles," for example.[28] The 1990s have also witnessed tremendous enthusiasm about the possibility of chemical treatments of obesity. The use of drugs such as fenfluramine and Redux became a medical craze in the mid-1990s, only to be ended by the detection of heart-valve defects in a significant number of patients. Their use was intended to be restricted to the seriously obese, but they were eagerly adopted by those with more modest cosmetic weight-loss goals. Fenfluramine and Redux are relatively crude serotonergic appetite-suppressants, from the standpoint of the new physiology of obesity. Undoubtedly, far more sophisticated obesity drugs are in the pipeline.

While we are mesmerized by the physiological advances in the study of obesity, it remains a truism among virtually all obesity experts that what are called life-style changes are critical in reversing a societal and what will ultimately be a worldwide trend. Decreasing activity levels, for example, will be an inevitable consequence of the spread of labor-saving devices, of electronic media, the increasing automation of labor, and other forces. The fundamental energy balance equation that governs weight changes (stored energy = consumption − expenditure) remains a reality. Nutritional and fitness education will undoubtedly play a role, but the forces that drive the fattening of the world may well overwhelm the best intentions of primary prevention programs.[29]

The Stigma of Overweight

Although the medical risks of severe obesity have been well established while those of more moderate degrees of fatness remain controversial, there is little question that obesity is a complex cultural construct loaded with an enormous amount of ideological baggage that has little to do with objective computations of mortality risk. A provocative historical study by Hillel Schwartz traced in detail the development of the anxiety about fatness in the United States from the middle of the nineteenth century to the present.[30] According to Schwartz (in an argument too complex to be recapitulated here) the evolution of our collective notions about body size reflected altered notions about the self and its appetites as we became a twentieth-century society. The new positive value placed on thinness that emerged in the early twentieth century was crucially tied to the new kinesthetic values that governed industry (efficiency experts), the arts (new dance styles that emphasized mobility), and technology (the flying machine). Concepts of efficient management were now beginning to be applied to the self and to domestic life (e.g. home economics). The ideology of obesity and dieting underwent a number of transformations and elaborations throughout the twentieth century. In the contemporary context, the concern with fatness is colored by our experience of a society which is beset by problems with overproduction, with waste, with excess world population. It reflects the increasingly difficult problem of self-management in an ever more fragmented social world that is confronted with the question of the "limits of satisfaction." Schwartz's thesis considerably broadens our understanding of why eating disorders, which are partly an expression of the struggle against obesity, would become rampant in those modern societies in which consumerism has come to a fever pitch, but which also place a particularly strong emphasis on self-reliance and self-control (particularly the United States, but also England and contemporary Japan).

In a symbolic sense, then, obesity is a mirror of our experience of not being in control of ourselves, a projection of our dysregulated appetites. Our attitudes towards fat and dieting are colored by our fantasy that in a world of excess and of undefined limits, we could eat nothing. We do not simply want to be thin, nor is our desire to reduce only a positive impulse towards "health": we *hate* our fat. The imagery of the struggle with obesity in popular culture is the imagery of warfare: "zap fat," "blast bulges," our magazine covers scream at us as we check out at the supermarket counter. The metaphor of the "burn," an apparent benefit of intense exercise, evokes the self-hating, masochistic quality of our relationship to our fat.

In contemporary Western societies, the obese have become a despised underclass, victims of discrimination in employment and social life. The moralistic stereotypes of obesity (which have never been confirmed by objective personality research) include attributions of laziness, self-indulgence, and greed. Thinness, on the other hand, has come to stand for self-control, intelligence, refinement, the civilized containment of appetites. Attitudes towards obesity have been likened to racism, in that a certain set of negative assumptions are made about personal character based on an attribute of physical appearance.[31] As is the case with racism, the assumption is made that obesity reflects a moral flaw that is basically under personal control. Interestingly, research on anti-fat attitudes suggests that they correlate with general conservatism, authoritarianism, and belief in a "just world" (the belief that people are responsible for the bad things that happen to them, that they "get what they deserve").[32] Even though systematic studies have repeatedly failed to demonstrate that the obese in general eat abnormally, the assumption that fatness is caused by ongoing gluttony is deeply entrenched. Unlike attitudes regarding race, however, which have been driven underground perhaps more than anything for reasons of political correctness, stereotyping of the obese continues to be acceptable in public discourse. Thus, baseball executive Al Campanis was immediately removed from his position following a racist characterization of the management abilities of African Americans, but fat jokes remain widely acceptable on late-night television and elicit no broad-based outrage. Campaigns for tolerance by an activist National Association for Fat Acceptance have been mounted in North America in recent years, but their impact on public attitudes is as yet uncertain. If the ideology about obesity has the profound cultural roots suggested by Schwartz, then it may take far more than public education campaigns to alter it.

As Werner Cahnman once said, in a discussion of the stigma of obesity, "one is reminded of Puritan attitudes, but even more so of the Platonic psychology, according to which the rational function of the mind is represented by the governing classes: the spirited by the military; and the appetitive by the economic. Mind and heart, that is, intelligence and courage, are then to combine to rule over the big, dull stomach."[33] Cahnman's characterization, although trenchant, omits one crucial point: the Platonic ruling class was exclusively male. And it is the particular problem of fatness of females which is so important in understanding the gender-specificity of eating disorders, to which we now turn.

Obesity in Women: Is Fat a Feminist Issue?

Despite the pervasiveness of our concern with fat, the issue of fatness is not blind to gender. In fact, the cultural stereotypes surrounding obesity have their most potent, binding effect on women. An understanding of these issues will lead us to a better understanding of the dilemmas of those who struggle most insistently and desperately against the fat woman's fate: anorexics and bulimics.

Fatness plays a critical role in female biological development. Before puberty, the percentage of body fat tissue is approximately the same in both sexes. However, during puberty the development of body fat accelerates in girls, so that ultimately, despite smaller stature when compared with adult males, women carry a greater percentage of their body mass as fat tissue. As was pointed out in chapter 4, for women the growth of fat tissue is critically connected with the emergence of the reproductive cycle. Generally speaking, the rate of obesity in adult females tends to be higher than in males, a difference that cuts across culture and social class and that may be rooted in these biological substrates.[34]

As we discussed in the previous chapter, the cultural standard for middle- and upper-class women has been one of increasing thinness. In recent decades, numerous types have been idealized by fashion: the prepubertal Twiggy in the 1960s, the less stringent but still slender models of the late 1970s and 1980s, the muscular woman of the fitness magazines, and the waif and supermodels of the 1990s. Despite variation, though, all of these types have one central feature in common – they are *not fat*. [35] Given the role of fatness in female biological development, the norm of thinness poses specific conflicts with inherent properties of female biology – it is virtually a pure instance of culture versus nature. And this conflict is exaggerated by the phenomenon noted by epidemiologists of obesity of the "socioeconomic reversal of fatness in females." In childhood, middle- and upper-class girls are usually fatter than their less affluent age-mates; but at puberty the relative degree of fatness in both groups reverses (under the influence of dieting?), so that by adulthood lower-class women are considerably fatter.[36] Girls who develop eating disorders, therefore, are caught in a struggle between the normative biological trends of female development and the rigorous cultural norms demanding thinness.

In the United States, in particular, fat women are especially stigmatized. One study showed that obese high-school seniors were typically denied college admission much more frequently than their age-mates of comparable intelligence.[37] Informally, many college admissions counselors will readily admit that an overweight female student is much more likely to "flunk an interview" than a thinner peer. Once admitted to college, obese females tend to receive less financial support from their parents. Fat women have also been subjected to pervasive discrimination in employment, and only recently have the American courts formally recognized the stigmatization of obesity as a form of legal discrimination.[38] Perhaps because of this and other social consequences, fat women tend to be downwardly socially mobile relative to their parents. Particularly in competitive settings, fat women have difficulty with acceptance: in order to prove themselves of comparable worth with men, women must conform their bodies to a more masculine shape. Of course, at the same time, some degree of "femininity" must be maintained. It is a difficult balancing act.

These patterns do show some subcultural variation, however. Among black women in the United States, obesity appears to be significantly less stigmatized.[39] This is the case even though there are some indications that black college students and teenagers aspire to thinness ideals similar to those of white students.[40] In the case of African Americans, one reason for the greater degree of tolerance for fatness may lie in the differential acceptance by black men of larger women.[41] The significantly lower stigmatization of obesity in black women is most likely a major reason for the lower prevalence of eating disorders among blacks, and this may also be the case for other minority groups. Meanwhile, though, there is clearly some suggestion of a trend towards the internalization of majority standards of thinness by minority groups, since the majority values signal higher status and power, and this process would in turn predict a rising prevalence of eating disorders.

Thus, despite some variations in cultural standards, fat is unquestionably a feminist issue. Susie Orbach, the author of a best-selling book that originally introduced this idea in the late 1970s, suggests that some women with problems of compulsive overeating may unconsciously want to be fat; it is thinness that they fear.[42] For these women, she suggests, the desire to be large represents an imagined state in which appetites could be satisfied rather than restricted, in which women would be free to "take up space" in a world which still allows them only the narrow space defined by a body whose dimensions are prepubertal. From this standpoint, it is the obese woman who is the overt rebel against the patriarchal limitation of female desire; the anorexic, by contrast, dutifully complies and even caricatures societal expectations. Caricature, though, is also a form of protest, however indirect; for the anorexic, dieting becomes a tacit hunger strike.[43] While it is certainly possible that some women may see fat as a liberating symbol, particularly those who have been trapped in a seemingly endless cycle of dieting, weight loss, and weight gain, it is unlikely that the majority of women desire fatness, even unconsciously. The social consequences of female fatness are simply too aversive. Nevertheless, from a therapeutic and political standpoint, it makes sense to attempt to destigmatize fatness, and this goal has been incorporated into a number of feminist approaches to issues of weight and body image.[44]

Dieting: An Ideology for the Self-Absorbed

In early Christianity, individuals were exhorted to counter the threat posed by bodily appetites through fasting. Contemporary societies have adopted a secular counterpart; it is called dieting. Lacking a moral vocabulary, contemporary societies have projected the notions of good and evil onto the images of our own bodies: the idea of God (the qualities of perfection, of cleanliness, of goodness) is now contained in the image of thinness; while that of the Devil (i.e. corruption by the appetite, sloth, greed) is embodied in fatness. We are actually much closer to the Puritan tradition than we are to the early Christian, particularly in our struggle for individual self-regulation and our dedication to the work ethic. The passion, the obsessiveness that surrounds the topic of dieting suggests that we are dealing with an underlying religious idea, but one which masks itself as the epitome of secular rationalism. For what could be more reasonable than wanting to lose weight?

It is interesting in this regard that dieting receives such strong emphasis among fundamentalist Christians in the United States.[45] Indeed, Christian writings on dieting have revealed the essentially moral nature of the struggle for weight control, and the way it has come to represent the struggle within the self for a sense of goodness. Reports of eating disorders in the daughters of the families of fundamentalist Christians suggest a milieu that in many respects magnifies the patterns described as typical in the general culture: an emphasis on externals and appearance, a discounting of subjectivity, a rigid, dichotomous mode of thinking about moral issues, and a gender ideology that demands that women subordinate themselves to male authority.[46]

The importance of dieting as a cultural institution is indicated by the economics of the highly variegated dieting industry. Americans spend billions annually ($30 billion is a common estimate) on diet goods and services: bariatric (i.e. weight-loss) physicians, weight-loss programs, weight spas, diet supplements and foods, and prescription and over-the-counter medications. Losing weight has become a significant component of the gross national product. Diets themselves that are promoted in popular books have become something of a designer industry, with particular methodologies going in and out of fashion like annual (or seasonal) clothing styles. A "Consumer Guide," by Theodore Berland, called *Rating the Diets*, published in the mid-1980s, offers a thorough and accessible evaluation of over 50 of the best-known plans.[47] It is interesting to view the diets as if one were a Geertzian anthropologist decoding a series of cultural "texts." Dieting is associated with the haunts of the rich and famous (the *Beverly Hills Diet*, the *Hilton Head*

Metabolism Diet, the *Palm Beach Long-life Diet),* with success and competition *(Eat to Win),* with futurism (the *Blast-off Diet,* the *21st Century Diet),* with the appeal to authority (diets entitled *Dr.—'s Diet),* even (paradoxically) with hedonism (the Diet Workshop *Wild Weekend Diet).* The dichotomous thinking of the dieter is evident in the *Fit-or-Fat Target Diet,* as is the push-button mentality in the *How to Lose 5 Lbs Fast* method. One title, *Thin Kids,* which was surprisingly given an enthusiastic review by Berland, would send a shudder down the spine of any therapist who works with eating disorders.

Diet books are often a huge commercial success. *The Beverly Hills Diet* sold well over a million copies in the early 1980s. The first book on the "Zone Diet," an extremely popular method of the 1990s developed by David Sears, sold a million and a half copies and has been translated into 14 languages. A second book, *Mastering the Zone,* was on the best-seller list for 11 weeks. Famous personages who have tried the Zone include Madonna, Bill Clinton and Howard Stern. The venerable *Dr. Atkins' Diet Revolution,* published in the early 1970s, is one of the 50 best-selling books in history. The 1990s version, *Dr. Atkins' New Diet Revolution,* was on the *New York Times* best-seller list for over 40 weeks. Diet books are obviously big business.

The journalist Malcolm Gladwell has suggested that all diet books follow a certain pattern.[48] The author begins with a personal story, almost inevitably a variation on the theme of "I was a fat kid." Then there is a moment of epiphany, when the dieter in a flash has an insight into the errors of his or her ways, and the new diet is envisioned and adopted. In short, Gladwell suggests that diet books all contain an implicit "conversion narrative." But while the personal story of the diet author is often convincing and inspirational, the underlying science is not. The Zone Diet offers a good illustration. Using a 40-year-old study, Sears argues that the key to weight loss is to reduce carbohydrates and increase protein – an idea that might have a familiar ring to chronic dieters and a particularly favored method of anorexics. Sears suggests that reducing carbohydrates succeeds in controlling insulin levels, which in turn reduces fat storage – an idea that makes little physiological sense. But furthermore, those who restrict their carbohydrates and increase their protein consumption are in fact bound to lose weight *over the short run.* This is because reduced carbohydrate intake leads to reduced water retention, while increased protein intake acts as a diuretic. In other words, weight loss will inevitably occur because of dehydration, but over a longer period of time the body's self-regulating mechanisms will work to correct the imbalance.

Sears's diet need not be singled out, since the vast majority of popular diets are supported by the same sort of questionable scientific underpinnings. In fact, many of the popular diets may provide perfectly good nutrition (with some exceptions – see the discussion of the Beverly Hills Diet in chapter 7) and most can lead to some moderate weight loss, but again in the short term. However, the secret of all the diet plans, whatever their content or scientific rationale, is the familiar use of the energy balance equation – that is, they work by reducing calories. This common denominator is masked by the targeting of one or another food group or type by a diet plan, a type of thinking that is pervasive among eating-disordered patients. But it is a commonly accepted fact among contemporary nutritionists that the key to a sensible eating plan is balance, without over- or under-emphasis of any particular food group. Eating "forbidden" foods, in fact, is an important treatment strategy in the nutritional rehabilitation of eating disorders.

Within the scientific community, and particularly those concerned with the pathologies of dieting such as eating disorders, there has been a growing chorus of voices arguing strongly that dieting is an ineffective way to lose weight, and therefore that the entire diet industry promotes a mass delusion. The data on which such arguments are based are mostly from university research clinics, which in turn have studied groups with medically serious obesity. The full version of the argument is that while varying amounts of weight can be lost on any given diet, it will almost inevitably be regained, and indeed this appears to be the case in a number of studies of the morbidly obese. Buttressing such findings is the research evidence from set-point theory, which argues that weight for each individual will typically be maintained in a certain range by physiological mechanisms, which tend to compensate for any temporary weight loss. While "resetting" can occur over a given period of time with readjustment of overall energy balance or following dramatic physiological adjustments, such as smoking cessation, it is virtually impossible to alter set-point through dieting alone. Beyond the general ineffectiveness of dieting, critics have also pointed to research that suggests that repeated cycles of weight loss and weight gain resulting from yo-yo dieting not only create metabolic hazards and risks for morbidity in their own right but also may make further weight loss difficult by creating permanent alterations in metabolic rate.[49]

Dieting has also become something of a political topic as well. Both advocates of fat acceptance as well as feminist groups angered by the diminishment of women fostered by the diet industry have contributed to a growing anti-dieting movement in the United States. Books such as *Overcoming Overeating* by Jane Hirschmann and Carol Munter and *Feeding the Hungry Heart* by Geneen Roth have advocated a non-dieting approach to weight control and emphasize the importance of attunement to internal body signals of hunger and the differentiation of such signals from states of emotional need.[50] An International Diet Coalition has attracted wide interest, along with its annual International No-Diet Day. One of the more amusing books of the anti-dieting genre is Richard Klein's *EAT FAT*, a book which, perhaps because of its outrageous title as well as its equally outrageous thesis, received widespread media coverage on its publication in 1996. Klein describes his work as a "post-modern diet book," and offers many examples of how humans have celebrated fatness throughout history, with examples from Shakespeare, Rodin's sculptures, and contemporary opera stars.[51] Klein's book, a sly work aiming to subversively undermine the puritanical ideology that underlies our culture's obsession with fatness, is sprinkled liberally with constructions such as

EAT

FAT

– a phrase reiterated like a mantra throughout the text.

It is still too early to predict the impact of scientific critique of dieting as well as the anti-dieting movement. Suggestions were made earlier that studies in the 1990s suggest that college students may be becoming a bit more balanced in their approach to food and may in some instances be rejecting radical diets. However, our ideology about fatness runs very deep and because of its linkage with more profound premises of our cultural identity will not yield easily. Despite the scientific tone of diet books, our penchant for magical thinking about the possibilities of self-improvement remains very powerful, perhaps particularly when it is cloaked in the language of science. Indeed, the rational arguments about set-point theory are notoriously ineffective with eating-disordered patients, who commonly respond to readings of set-point oriented works such as *The Dieter's Dilemma* with the comment, "I hate that book."

The Disease is Dieting

Anorexic or bulimic patients tend to be particularly vulnerable to cultural messages about dieting, which offer the promise of taking control of one's life through the alteration of body shape. Many thousands (or probably millions) of efforts at dieting are undoubtedly started and stopped, with no effect whatsoever other than a small amount of mental and material expenditure. However, the anorexic or bulimic latches on to dieting for a different purpose – to give her life direction, to obliterate emotional pain, to solve a problem of identity. Once again we come back to the idea of the defense of an ethnic disorder, drawn from the repertoire of behaviors on which a culture places great value.

The complexity of anorexia nervosa and bulimia has led many to be wary about the possible oversimplification in the view that it all simply comes down to excessive dieting. However, an important and remarkable series of studies by C. Peter Herman and Janet Polivy has suggested that the consequences of dieting, particularly when taken to extremes, may be sufficiently pernicious to account for many of the symptoms of eating disorders.[52] In their original research, Herman and Polivy invited a group of students who consistently dieted (and a group of non-dieting subjects) to their laboratory to partake in an experiment that was ostensibly a study in "taste discrimination." The subjects were initially asked to drink either one or two milkshakes, and then to fill out some rating scales on the taste of some food that was served in the laboratory. In order to complete the rating, subjects were told to "eat as much as you like." Non-dieting subjects, as expected, tended to sample less food after two milkshakes than after one. But the dieters (in Herman and Polivy's terms, "restrained eaters") surprisingly showed just the opposite trend; they ate *more* after two milkshakes than after one. Herman and Polivy suggest that non-dieters regulate their appetite according to normal cues of satiety, but the chronically deprived dieters *counterregulate* – that is, the normal control of their food intake by physiological cues of fullness is somehow disrupted by the chronic effects of dieting.[53]

The mechanism by which this dysregulation occurs was illuminated by some further studies. Dieters were divided into two groups, each of which was given an equal amount of preload, with identical caloric content; however, one group was told that the food was calorie-rich,

while the other was told that it was calorie-poor. Which group consumed more in the sham taste-discrimination task? Again, contrary to
what one would expect, it was the calorie-rich group who consumed
more food. The authors suggest the interpretation that the dieter,
having been told that she just consumed calorie-rich food, assumes that
"I blew it," that most common lament of the failed dieter. Having
blown it, the subject then throws all caution to the wind and gorges
herself on laboratory food. The effect is a cognitive and not necessarily
a physiological one: it is not so much what the dieter has eaten, as what
she thinks about what she has eaten, that triggers a counterregulatory
binge.[54]

Additional research extended the findings further. In dieters,
disinhibited eating is triggered by a lowering of mood, drinking alcohol, or the elevation of emotional stress.[55] All of these are common
triggers of binge eating among bulimics. And in one important study,
it was found that the disinhibited eating usually exhibited by dieters is
radically reduced when another subject or observer is present in the
laboratory room.[56] This corresponds well with the reports of most
bulimics that their binge eating typically takes place alone, and they are
more likely to eat normally when others are present.[57]

In an overview of their work, Herman and Polivy suggest that the
common view in the wider culture is that excessive eating is what makes
dieting "necessary." Their research, on the other hand, suggests that
the direction of causality is the other way around. To put it concretely,
it is not bingeing that causes dieting, but dieting that causes bingeing.[58]
In their words, therefore, "the disease is dieting." Herman and Polivy's
work is extremely important, especially in offering a plausible account
of the bulimic swings from gorging to starvation. It is perhaps less
useful in accounting for anorexia nervosa, except for the fact that the
longer a patient remains anorexic (that is, restrained), the more likely
she is to develop the chaotic dysregulation of eating typical of bulimia.

A significant problem with restraint theory as an account of eating
disorders is that it is based on the behavior of non-clinical subjects who
score high on the dietary restraint scale. Whether the "counter-
regulation" that these subjects show in the laboratory is an accurate
analogue of clinical binge eating remains to be demonstrated. Among
bulimic patients, while most show a history of dieting preceding the
onset of the disorder, there is a subgroup in whom binge eating begins
without prior dieting.[59] There are a number of studies, however, that

show in general that continuous dieting certainly puts a person at risk for an eating disorder. One of these followed up a large group of secondary school girls in London over a one-year period. Of 61 of these who were dieting at the initial assessment, 13 (21 percent) developed an eating disorder at followup (2 cases of bulimia nervosa and 11 "partial syndrome" or EDNOS), whereas of the original 98 non-dieters, none had developed bulimia nervosa and three (3 percent) had developed partial syndromes. In other words, the dieters had a risk of developing an eating disorder seven times that of the non-dieters.[60] Similar results were obtained in a followup study of the group of high-school girls who had been studied by Ingvar Nylander in Sweden (see chapter 3).[61]

Thus, there is consistent evidence that dedicated dieting puts one at risk for an eating disorder. Nevertheless, it is equally clear that dieting per se does not "cause" anorexia nervosa or bulimia, since the majority of the dieters in the above studies did not become eating disordered. It is apparent that only those who are vulnerable on other grounds from multiple risk factors (family history of obesity and weight concern, parental overcontrol or abandonment, personality predispositions such as high anxiety or poor impulse control, or pre-existing psychiatric disorders) will actually develop a clinical condition.[62] Nevertheless, it is apparent that without our cultural preoccupation with dieting, there would be no epidemic of eating disorders.

The Exercise Connection

Contemporary anorexics not only draw on the cultural obsession with dieting; a significant percentage become caught up in compulsive patterns of exercise. Hyperactivity was recognized as a symptom of anorexia nervosa in the earliest reports (Sir William Gull commented in 1874 that "it seemed hardly possible that body so wasted could undergo the exercise which seemed so agreeable"), but for years its role was little discussed and perhaps continues to be underestimated.[63] It was generally considered to be a secondary phenomenon – perhaps an additional method of reducing body weight or, according to some, a restless form of activity that typically accompanies starvation. Recently, though, some writers have hypothesized a more primary role for hyperactivity in the overall symptomatology and even the cause of anorexia nervosa. Laboratory research, for example, demonstrates that animals who are placed on a restricted food schedule will, if given the opportunity to run, evidence an escalating spiral of increased activity and decreased food intake – often to the point of death from starvation. These "activity anorexias" in animals suggest that a cycle of heightened activity and diminished food intake may be a characteristic psychobiological response, induced by certain environmental conditions such as diminished food availability. Extrapolating to the human situation, it may provide some insight into the process by which an escalating cycle of self-starvation and increasingly frenetic activity may become entrenched, if triggered by appropriate environmental cues. In the human situation, these cues may be interpersonal but also cultural, as in the cultural sanctions of dieting and exercise.[64]

Perhaps even more than dieting, contemporary Western cultures extol and glamorize exercise. In the United States, the fitness explosion is the contemporary expression of a long-standing national fascination with sports and physical fitness.[65] In fact, in the nineteenth century, a crusade for fitness, known as Muscular Christianity, spread from England to the United States. This movement was associated with the mass migration from rural areas to cities, and the growing concern with the relative sedentariness of urban life. Perhaps out of a renewed concern with these problems as well as a growing alarm over increasing levels of obesity and general health consciousness, throughout the 1980s and 1990s a worldwide fitness boom spread throughout the industrialized societies.[66] Exercise machines, health clubs, and the new breed of professional trainer have together constituted a growth industry that expresses perhaps even more intensely than the preoccupation with slimming the cult of the body in the consumer societies (with which of course it is connected). In the United States, some individuals have suggested that the trainer fills a role in their lives comparable with the former social function of the analyst – a kind of secular guru, who provides not only physical training but moral and spiritual guidance.[67] Television commercials in the mid-1980s touted the exercise machine as the ultimate Christmas present, and depicted as the epitome of holiday bliss an attractive and physically fit young wife comforting her perspiring husband as he groaned after yet one more repetition. A new asceticism spread through the economically anxious and competitive 1980s and 1990s, one that serves no higher moral aim but which, paradoxically, promises pleasure through self-denial.[68] The culture of fitness fits well with the anorexic's needs, particularly her quest for a sense of self-mastery and individual achievement through severe body discipline as well as a profound concern with body shape. Indeed, among other purposes that it serves, the pursuit of exercise in the broader culture is one more tool – and a particularly effective one at that – in the battle against fat.

The specific role of exercise in anorexia nervosa and bulimia, although familiar as a clinical phenomenon, has not been given sufficient study. In one of the few systematic enquiries, a group of Australian researchers found that exercise, not dieting, was the main behavior that precipitated severe weight loss in nine out of 26 cases of anorexia nervosa.[69] In these patients, the families had a general involvement with exercise, suggesting that the behavior in the patient was perhaps triggered through emulation of a parent. A case report in the *Lancet* depicted what may well become an increasingly common presentation, a masked case of anorexia nervosa presenting clinically as an exercise injury. The subject was a 30-year-old woman who complained of severe bilateral injuries to her knees. She revealed during interview that she also suffered from amenorrhea and was distressed because of her inability to bear children. It turned out that she had gone on a severe weight-reducing diet in her twenties, and when she had regained most of the weight later, she initiated a punishing exercise regime, which at first consisted of running up to 120 miles a week. At the point of seeking medical help, she complained that "exercise was taking up all of her spare time seven days a week," and that a typical day included running 5 miles, swimming 96 lengths in a full-size pool, attending an aerobic dance class (or canoeing or fencing), and doing bodybuilding exercises.[70]

The connection between exercise and anorexia nervosa is particularly evident in the high prevalence of shape and weight disorders among young athletes, a problem that has received increasing attention in the literature on sports medicine.[71] Young athletes are often expected to maintain percentages of body fat significantly below the norms for their age level, and this coupled with the intense pressures of coaches and parents as well as the demands of competition itself can lead those who are vulnerable directly into anorexia or bulimia. In fact, a 1988 survey of large numbers of elite college athletes in the United States reveals that shockingly high numbers admit to what have been called "pathogenic weight control behaviors" – prolonged fasting, vomiting, diet pills, laxatives, and diuretics.[72] These practices appear to cut across all sports, but they are especially prevalent in those activities that demand weight and/or shape control – for example, gymnastics, figure skating, and wrestling. Wrestlers, in particular, often undergo dramatic fluctuations in caloric intake as they attempt to make a particular weight class and then return to a normal weight in the offseason. While few systematic prevalence studies have been conducted, it is evident to many clinicians who see patients with eating disorders that wrestlers constitute a population at high risk for bulimia or anorexia nervosa. And interestingly, on the high-school or college level, this is a population that is exclusively male.

Female athletes, perhaps because of their general vulnerabilities to eating disorders, are especially at risk. The sports medicine field has described a "female athletic triad" – disordered eating, menstrual dysfunction, and osteoporosis – associated with substantial morbidity and mortality. A 1994 study in Norway surveyed 603 elite female athletes from the entire spectrum of sports. Of these, 117 were considered to be at risk for an eating disorder, based on an initial screening. Interviews of 105 of the latter group revealed that 92 (79 percent of the at-risk group) met full diagnostic criteria for anorexia nervosa (7), bulimia nervosa (42), and "anorexia athletica" (43). Anorexia athletica is in effect another way of saying subclinical eating disorder, with symptoms such as weight loss, delayed puberty, disturbance in body image, fear of becoming fat, caloric restriction, binge eating, purging, and compulsive exercising. As in earlier studies, the prevalence of eating disorders was highest in sports emphasizing leanness and appearance, especially diving, gymnastics, and figure skating.[73]

Of all the sports that place a premium on weight control, gymnastics is probably the one that carries the greatest risk for eating disorders. The public became intensely aware of the link between gymnastics and eating disorders following the 1992 Olympics, in which the performers were widely described in newspapers as emaciated and sad, preadolescent and yet prematurely aged. Also, the death of aspiring Olympic gymnast Christy Heinreich, whose struggle with anorexia nervosa was clearly tied to her ambitions to achieve Olympic stature, was widely publicized. In an editorial critical of the health hazards of gymnastics, *The New England Journal of Medicine* noted that the development of Olympic-level gymnasts involves "hard training, stringent coaching, and often parental pressure, ostensibly in the best interest of the child."[74] Elite gymnasts typically begin their training between the ages of five and seven years, and are often involved in rigorous, highly regimented training by the age of ten. Given the high-impact nature of the sport and demanding nature of the training, it is virtually inevitable that young gymnasts will suffer injury. Unfortunately, coaches sometimes encourage athletes to continue to exercise despite injury. Maintaining a perfectly lean, muscular appearance and low weight has become increasingly critical to success in gymnastics, and weight loss regimens are often triggered by inappropriate comments by coaches to that effect. The combination of intense achievement pressures, stringent weight demands, and the intrinsically external criteria for success (which are determined by judges) leaves young gymnasts uniquely exposed to the risk factors for eating disorders. Added to these pressures is the fact that these young athletes must often leave home and be without close parental contact for lengthy training periods during their pre-teen and early teen years. Coaches and to some extent the parents of these highly talented athletes have been singled out for a great deal of criticism in the popular press. It remains to be seen whether this growing public awareness will be enough to counteract the combination of factors, driven by huge sums of money, that lead to the vulnerability of these young girls.

Running, which in a sense was the vanguard and at one time the premier activity of the fitness boom, appears to have a particular kinship with anorexia nervosa – a link which becomes evident from the attraction that it holds as a form of exercise for anorexics.[75] A highly disciplined activity that enhances feelings of self-mastery and offers a sense of transcending the limits of the body, running for some becomes an all-consuming compulsive activity that can displace one's interest in other pursuits, particularly other people. In his highly influential book, George Sheehan suggested that through running the jogger finds his identity "because in being a runner, in moving through pain and fatigue and suffering, in imposing stress upon stress, in eliminating all but the necessities of life, he is fulfilling himself and becoming the person he is."[76] As among anorexics, running evokes feelings of identification with the ideology of asceticism and martyrdom:

> When I run the roads I am a saint. For that hour I am an Assisi, wearing the least and meanest of clothes. I am Gandhi, the young law student, trotting ten or twelve miles a day and then going to a cheap restaurant to eat his fill of bread. I am Thoreau, the solitary, seeking union with the world around

him. On the roads, poverty, chastity and obedience come naturally. [77]

As in anorexia, running provides a sense of mastery, even of perfection through body discipline, for a person who senses the world as otherwise puzzling and uncontrollable:

> Discipline in running, discipline in training comes easily. Discipline in real life is another story. The mind and the will and the imagination are not as easily controlled as the legs and the thighs, and the panting chest. Running, of course, helps. The art of running, as Eugene Herrigal wrote of the art of archery, *is* a profound and far-reaching contest of the runner with himself. And that contest should be to his perfection.[78]

Sheehan describes the struggle against fat as a never-ending war that must be fought with relentless vigilance throughout one's life. Just like anorexics, runners tend to be obsessively preoccupied with their body image, and many have an analogous habit of pinching their skin or scanning themselves to test for signs of the hated imperfections of fat. The famous "runner's high," possibly based on elevated levels of circulating endorphins, seems clearly analogous to the "faster's high" of the anorexic, which ultimately may be rooted in the same psychological and biological forces. Both seek a sense of transcendent perfection through self-denial, a narcissistic quest that is achieved through heroic asceticism. Both find the world of interpersonal relationships disappointing and unsatisfying and tend to be repelled by the comforts and excesses of affluence. In a sense, as Sours pointed out, anorexia nervosa and running may both be manifestations of the same broad changes that have taken place in middle-class culture, the seeking of a self-imposed trial of self-denial in a world in which the soul has been lost.[79]

In a remarkable publication that appeared in *The New England Journal of Medicine* in 1983, Yates, Leehey, and Shisslak described a number of patients who manifested what they called an "obligatory running syndrome," which in turn reflected, in their view, an "analogue of anorexia nervosa."[80] The authors described three men in their thirties and forties, who had began running following major life crises – in two cases the breakup of a marriage, and in a third the decline of a "polite but disappointing marriage." All three were high achievers – one a highly skilled artisan who "carved statues in exquisite detail," the second a successful architect, and the third a physicist who finished his degree because he had never been good at science and wanted to "meet the challenge." In a striking parallel with anorexics, all three had been "good boys" from achievement-oriented families in which the expression of emotion had been strongly discouraged. Each man recalled feeling overweight, "fat," and in poor health prior to beginning his running regime. All three had become totally obsessive and ritualistic about their running regimes, and had long ignored physical injuries for which they had finally sought help. One of the subjects, for example, "ran at least 10 miles a day, regardless of the weather or his state of health. He had a recurrent Achilles tendinitis and a slight limp – the result of an improperly healed stress fracture. He maintained a library of books about running and a diary of his running speed calculated in miles per hour for each hour traveled."[81] Each of the obligatory runners had an obsession with thinness. The subject above felt that his running was optimal only when he reached a very low ratio of fat to lean body mass, which he had precisely specified.

The original paper generated intense controversy, as was evident in the flood of letters to the medical journal in which the article was originally published.[82] While many of the respondents recognized and identified with the characterization of obligatory runners, a number argued that Yates had denigrated a liberating, health promoting activity (running) to the status of a pathology (anorexia nervosa). But the original article only intended to draw an analogy between the psychology of compulsive running and anorexia, not to diagnose the entire running population. Not surprisingly, a number of subsequent studies have failed to find any general tendencies towards psychopathology among runners as a whole.[83] But a later study by Yates was able to clearly identify an obligatory running syndrome in a much larger number of males and females than the original study.[84] She makes a clear differentiation between those for whom running is the equivalent of an eating disorder and those for whom it is a rigorous pattern of exercise in an otherwise healthy individual. Obligatory runners are characterized by pervasive compulsiveness as well as attitudes towards fat and body image that closely resemble pathological eating attitudes. A telltale sign of the syndrome is those who feel compelled to continue running despite severe injury. Particularly striking was the extent to which these runners admitted to severe caloric restriction and binge eating, as well as the practice of compensating for binges by adding miles to an already rigorous training schedule. "Paying the price" for one's caloric "debts" is of course a characteristic element of bulimic psychology. Running, however, particularly in moderation, is obviously a healthier activity than purging. This fact may be of some clinical significance; prescribing exercise may be one means of interrupting the bulimic cycle.

The phenomenon of obligatory running and other forms of compulsive exercise points to some issues of more general cultural significance. In contemporary societies, given the turmoil in personal relationships and the individual's growing sense of isolation, men as well as women are prone to developing addictive, obsessive solutions to the problems of life – and particularly, in our weight-obsessed society, to an insistent focus on body weight or shape. In men, these modern issues of identity are especially likely to take place in middle age, when an incipient sense of physical decline precipitates a profound threat to one's sense of competence and self-esteem. What is more, men are much more likely to emphasize activity and exercise over dieting, a choice that is more compatible with sex-role expectations. It may well be, then, that among men, problems comparable to anorexia are often masked beneath a preoccupation with exercise and sports. But the underlying issues – a weakened sense of identity and self-esteem, and obsessive quest for perfection fought out concretely in terms of health, body image, and particularly fatness – are indeed analogous.

In the late 1980s through to the late 1990s, there has been evidence in America of a decline in interest in running, at least of the fanatical sort that predominated in the 1970s and early 1980s. There is talk of a new running style, one that entails a greater sense of moderation and sociability. Two or three miles per run will do, as opposed to the ten of the obligatory runner. This trend may parallel the seeming decline in the extreme pursuit of starvation or highly restrictive dieting, with a new emphasis on healthful low-fat diets.[85] There is a strong interest in bodybuilding and "strength training," one that emphasizes not so much extreme thinness but rather a body with hard and lean contours. Meanwhile, the battle with fatness and obesity remains in place.[86] It is too early to tell what impact these changes in ideal body image will have, particularly on the prevalence of eating disorders. But the larger issue, to which eating disorders are related, remains: the problem of self-regulation in a culture of plenty, in which traditional moral ideologies have given way to the ethics of obsessionality.

Chapter Seven

The Templates of a Disease

"Don't go crazy, but if you do, you must behave as follows."

George Devereux, *Basic Problems of Ethnopsychiatry*

The deviant behavior patterns that become prevalent in a society tend to follow particular models or templates that are immediately and widely "recognized" by members of the culture. *Amok,* for example, represented a certain recognizable pattern of going crazy that was widely known in certain areas of Southeast Asia. When a person, typically a man, reached a certain point of tension or stress that was intolerable, the subsequent explosive outburst of violence was a "standardized," ready-made structure into which his homicidal rage could be discharged. Running through villages, randomly lashing out at strangers, fiercely eluding capture, the *Amok* runner followed a totally predictable (if frightening) pattern within his own culture. Everyone recognized an *Amok* and knew what to expect, not least the *Amok* runner himself. As Devereux put it, "the young Malay hopes he will never find himself in straits so desperate that only one acceptable solution remains open to him: running *amok*. He knows, however, that should such a situation arise, he *will have* to become an *amok* runner and *he will know how to* conduct himself properly."[1] Standardized patterns of psychopathology in a culture are *patterns of misconduct,* known to the actor and recognized by the observer. When it comes to enacting deviance, Devereux suggests, culture proved a directive to the effect of "Don't go crazy, but if you do, you must behave as follows."[2]

The influence of such a social model of disorder was probably involved in the spreading of the hysterical pattern in the nineteenth century. Hysteria illustrates dramatically how a pattern of deviance can be communicated by processes of social "contagion" or imitation. The hysterical patient, as Szasz once suggested, is playing the role of someone who is sick, although without being conscious of doing so.[3] The symptoms of hysteria – paralysis, blindness, anaesthesia – are readily copied or simulated, and they also offer an opportunity for the dramatization of personal problems. "Who are you copying now?," Freud queried of his famous patient, Dora. In an era in which the dramatic gesture was fashionable in the cities of Europe, hysterical symptoms could easily become the dominant model of disorder because of their consistency with a certain cultural style.[4]

But in the case of hysteria, an additional force may also have been operative, and that is the unwitting influence of healers themselves, who came to expect that a certain pattern of behavior would manifest itself. Such iatrogenic effects were clearly in evidence in the famous lecture-demonstrations of Charcot, which were widely attended not only by physicians, but also by writers, artists, and other members of the Parisian intelligentsia. Charcot formulated in detail the symptoms of an "hysterical attack," which consisted of a precise sequence of convulsions, dramatic enactments, and the like. Unbeknownst to him, however, his assistants had secretly coached the patients on precisely how to respond to his hypnotic suggestions. The patients had also learned about convulsive symptoms from being housed on the same ward as the epileptic patients. Only later did it become evident that the "stages of an hysterical attack" discovered by Charcot could only be found in Paris, an embarrassment that ultimately cost the great neurologist his scientific reputation.

Contemporary social-learning theory provides some concepts that enable a better understanding of how templates for deviant behavior are disseminated. For example, the research of Albert Bandura and his colleagues shows how easily complex patterns of behavior can be acquired by the simple observation of a "model." What is more, such imitation will be facilitated if the model is a figure of high prestige, or particularly if the model can demonstrate that his or her behavior leads to social power or the control over resources.[5] In the case of deviant behavior, or an ethnic disorder, spreading of the symptoms would be enhanced if they were modeled by figures of high prestige or visibility in the culture, or by peers (or other socially influential figures) who themselves are observed to receive positive reinforcement for their symptomatic behavior.

Anorexia by Proxy

In her last paper, Bruch suggested that within her own lifetime she witnessed the transformation of anorexia nervosa from an individual into a social disease. Even as recently as the 1960s, she suggested, cases of anorexia nervosa occurred in individuals who had never heard about the disorder: it was as if each created the symptoms anew out of the crucible of their own individual experience. But more recently, she suggested, as the disease has become more common and increasingly known, the clinical picture has undergone a subtle transformation. The classic anorexic was driven by a fierce quest for individual autonomy; what was remarkable was the clinical uniformity of the solution to a problem that each patient had struggled to come to grips with on her own. In contrast, many of today's patients had heard about the disease before becoming sick, and many had "tried it out" after seeing a television program about the disorder or doing a research project in a biology class. Also, Bruch suggested, today's patients have less resistance to social influence, and they often "cling to or compete with each other." In short, "the desire to be special or unique is expressed with less vigor and urgency, and I cannot suppress the suspicion that some of the symptoms are imitated or faked."[6] Bruch even goes as far as to suggest that the numerous programs for the treatment of eating disorders may have contributed to the socialization of the disease.

The fact that anorexia nervosa itself can be directly imitated and emulated, producing in some instances a simulated form of the illness, is evident in a report by a Washington, DC psychiatrist. Two patients, both of whom had serious neurological illnesses, loudly proclaimed that they had "eating disorders," but it turned out that in neither case was the disorder authentic. The first patient, who suffered from multiple sclerosis, first manifested her symptoms – which consisted of refusing meals and vomiting – after having been exposed to a number of anorexic patients in an adolescent ward of a hospital. Her "anorexia" was both a means of protecting herself against a very real developmental depression and a way of denying the seriousness of her own neurological disease. The second patient offered an even more blatant instance of simulation. During her hospitalization, she also was exposed to numerous anorexic patients and reported during a "rap" group that she had had a previous hospitalization for anorexia nervosa, from which she

168

stated that she had recovered through a behavior-modification program. Given the fact that she was at this point obese, she totally terrified the anorexic patients, who concluded that obesity would indeed be their fate were they to comply with the hospital's refeeding protocol. Ultimately, though, the patient confessed that her tale of previous anorexia had been fabricated. Interestingly, both of these patients were of lower socioeconomic class, and therefore to become "anorexic" was to emulate the "status" of the apparently well-heeled anorexic patients on the ward.[7]

An even more remarkable instance of such acquired anorexia was that developed by a patient who had been blind since the age of two.[8] This patient originally developed a severe depression in the context of a borderline personality, and had made multiple suicide attempts that resulted in her psychiatric hospitalization. She only developed anorexic symptoms after meeting several patients in the hospital who had the disorder. Initially, she had found these patients to be "very weird," but apparently found in their symptoms a suitable method for the enactment of her own self-destructive impulses. The disorder that she did develop was authentic, at least in comparison with the two patients we just discussed. The patient pinched herself to make sure that she was "not fat," and carried a computerized scale around with her whose voice synthesizer offered messages such as "You have gained one pound today." She thought incessantly about food, and lost considerable amounts of weight. Despite the validity of the diagnosis of anorexia nervosa, it seems unlikely that she would have developed her symptoms without suitable models. The development of a disorder of body image is particularly remarkable in her case, in that she could only receive the information about anorexia from hearing about it. We usually think of disorders of body image as contingent on the visualization of body shape. Apparently, in her case, acquired knowledge about the disorder was enough to trigger internal feelings of fatness. But beyond the special circumstances of this case, it is probably true that many patients with histrionic or borderline personalities are especially vulnerable to internalizing the dominant model of psychopathology of their own era. Thus, in the era of *The Exorcist* (in the late 1960s and early 1970s), many such patients may have more typically presented clinically as "possessed."[9] And even as late as the 1940s, many such patients still manifested "astasia-abasia," an inability to stand and inability to sit that was characteristic of nineteenth-century hysterical patients, in hospitals in New York.[10]

The preceding case histories were instances in which the disorder was a late "acquisition" and was superimposed on an already existing problem. However, the factors of imitation and competition play a role in many cases in which anorexia is the primary symptom. In particular, contemporary anorexics tend to be highly competitive, often vying to outdo each other in their degree of gauntness or the amount of food on which they can survive. Partly, this can be understood in the context of the intensely competitive atmosphere surrounding contemporary dieting, particularly among female adolescents.[11] In a culture in which the temptation to overeat has such threatening consequences to self-esteem, a disease in which one eats nothing and becomes scrawny represents the ultimate dieting triumph and therefore is likely to arouse mixed feelings of envy, resentment, and admiration. Even more mature women tend to be competitive about weight. As one writer pointed out, it is not uncharacteristic for many women, on entering a room, to quickly scan the scene to see if they are about to be shown up by an extremely thin woman.[12] Female nurses who care for anorexic patients are particularly vulnerable to these competitive feelings: "How does she do it?" is a not infrequent comment that follows a contentious interaction with a patient. Numerous articles have commented about the hostility that is often directed against thin women. Such an attitude may in part account for the frenzied speculation about whether certain actresses or models have anorexia nervosa, for example Kate Moss or the American actress Calista Flockhart (who portrays "Ally McBeal"). The producers of the latter program have done much to fan the flames of such gossip by, for example, presenting the protagonist in one episode as being so small that she falls into an office toilet.

Hilde Bruch noted an increase in competitiveness among the anorexic patients she observed in the 1970s. She provided some examples in her posthumously published *Conversations with Anorexics*. One patient, whom Bruch named "Megan – a perfect size 1," was quite literal about how she experienced her triumph in terms of contemporary fashion. Having recently gained some weight from her low of 80 pounds, she looked back wistfully at the time when she could "turn heads" by asking for a size 1 in a clothing store: "It was like the whole store, everybody was standing around, would go, 'Golly you are thin – that must be nice.' And everybody, 'Oh, that's great you can find these clothes, and everything is made for slender people nowadays, and how wonderful it must be to be thin.'"[13] Anorexia apparently commands respect in the contemporary boutique (or at least that of the late 1970s), in which women over size 8 have difficulty in finding a dress. Another patient, whom Bruch dubbed "Nora, the competitor," developed anorexia after going on a group trip over the summer during which another girl developed the illness. Having lost a large amount of weight, Nora thought about her eating in entirely competitive terms:

> I think of all the people I am competing with at school, the ones who don't eat, and then I bet they are not eating over Thanksgiving . . . . One of my friends from high school lost weight when she went to college, and when I want to eat ice cream, I think, "I bet she doesn't do it," and then I can't eat it either.[14]

Competition among peers is one essential way in which anorexic symptoms can be spread or modeled. In her autobiography, Aimee Liu reported how one of her friends, whom she had always admired for her popularity, shocked her at one point by asking her "how she did it" (i.e. lost weight). Liu's response was non-committal – she was stunned at suddenly being in a superior role with this person, whom she herself had always envied. Several months later, she was even more shocked at the sight of her formerly full-bodied friend's gauntness.[15]

The competitive aspects of anorexia are probably particularly heightened in a country such as America, in which, as Brumberg pointed out, people compete not only for success but also about diseases, particularly if they are fashionable. The frequent (and incorrect) comment that anorexia is now an "American" disease probably stems from a perception of the competitive and *au courant* aura that currently surrounds the illness.[16]

The Role of the Family and Peers

Unfortunately, the model for eating-disordered behavior may often lie within the family itself. In particular, weight preoccupation is quite characteristic within the families of eating-disordered patients, a fact that has long been known to clinicians and has been supported in numerous studies.[17] Weight preoccupation can take many forms, however, and therefore it is unlikely to manifest itself on the kind of uniform measures that are typically used in research studies. Most obviously, a parent may have had a lifelong battle with controlling weight and have been on repeated diets. Such a history may have numerous consequences. The most straightforward is a direct modeling effect, that is, that the child simply emulates the parent's behavior. Family dynamics, however, often dictate more subtle patterns. For example, the child may, in an effort to compete with and "best" a parent or sibling, diet with a vengeance. Such a pattern is not uncommon in the families of anorexics. There is also some evidence to suggest that it is not the parent's own weight preoccupation that elicits eating-disordered behavior in a child, but rather whether or not the parent is directly critical about and preoccupied with a child's weight.[18]

A more direct model is provided by a parent who himself or herself is eating disordered, even though the parent's behavior may never have been medically recognized as such. Pike and Rodin found that the mothers of eating-disordered students were themselves much more likely to have clinical levels of a drive for thinness, body image concerns, and bulimic behaviors than the mothers of non-eating-disordered students.[19] Other studies suggest that the mothers of bulimics typically weigh less than mothers of non-eating-disordered girls and have frequently been critical of their daughters' weight.[20] A different view of the issue of modeling eating-disordered behavior in the family is provided by studies of the children of anorexic and bulimic parents. Young children of active or untreated anorexic mothers, for example, are likely to show feeding disturbances and serious degrees of underweight.[21] In one report in the literature, three of the children of five bulimic mothers evidenced a frank eating disorder, characterized by low weight due to failure to thrive and difficulties in feeding.[22] However, a history of anorexia or bulimia nervosa in a parent is not necessarily determinative of such a dire outcome, particularly if the parent has achieved substantial recovery and has come to grips with her own issues about food and body image.

An often neglected factor in the social etiology of eating disorders is the influence of peers. In an study of high-school students in New York, Pike found that the presence of bulimic symptoms in friends as well as in mothers and sisters strongly increased the probability that a student would herself would be bulimic.[23] The effect of anorexic or bulimic behaviors in peers was particularly potent for ninth-grade girls, but diminished by the twelfth grade. This makes sense developmentally, as younger adolescents who are making the transition to high school are especially vulnerable to peer influence. As prevention researcher

Michael Levine has suggested, certain adolescents who have grown up in weight-toxic families, are surrounded by weight-preoccupied and perhaps eating-disordered friends, and are focused on the relentless images of thinness in the mass media, could be said to be immersed in a virtual "subculture of thinness." And it is the convergence of these factors, rather than any one in particular, that heightens the vulnerability to eating disorders both in individuals and also in groups.[24]

The Role of the Mass Media

In the present era, behavioral modeling is radically enhanced by the mass media. Much discussion has been conducted about how fashion models or television characters influence the body ideals that are so important in understanding anorexia nervosa. Less has been said, however, about how the media may influence the modeling of the disorder itself. Anecdotal evidence suggests that such influences may be important in the shaping of anorexic symptoms. In a Canadian study, one subgroup of anorexic patients developed their symptoms after the airing of a documentary program about eating disorders. Like the pseudo-anorexics described in the preceding section, these patients little resembled the classic personalities associated with eating disorders before their anorexic symptoms appeared.[25] Another report described the development of anorexia nervosa following a viewing of the television version of the popular account, *The Best Little Girl in the World*, whose protagonist was widely admired by the patient and her friends.[26] It is possible that these media accounts function similarly to fictional films about adolescent suicide, which have sometimes been followed by an elevated rate of suicide attempts.[27] Apparently, self-destructive behavior may be legitimized by the implicit glamorization of television, particularly among those who are susceptible.

While television dramas and reports have had an impact, undoubtedly the most prolific source of information about eating disorders has been the popular press – especially articles in women's magazines, but also a seemingly never-ending stream of autobiographical books. As Sours once pointed out, probably no psychiatric disorder in history has received as much publicity as anorexia nervosa. By the early 1980s, the number of articles on anorexia nervosa had mushroomed, but by the mid-1980s the focus had switched to bulimia. The spectacle of an affluent young woman starving herself to death is a fertile subject for sensationalistic journalism. The glamorization of anorexia nervosa was most blatantly evident in a mid-1970s article in *Playgirl* that identified anorexics as today's "Golden Girls," but a sensational aura is also fostered by such titles as "When dieting goes wild," "Anorexia nervosa: Dying of thinness," and "My sister and I tried to outdiet each other with some pretty scary results." Not all of this literature glamorizes, however; the ostensible purpose in many cases is to sound the alarm (for example, an article entitled "Danger! You can overdo dieting").[28] However, it is likely that much of it, even if unwittingly, may encourage identification and imitation.

Thus, for example, one article on anorexia began:

What sort of person gets anorexia nervosa? Most of them are female, young (under twenty), *bright, energetic and articulate. Good in school, good in sports, the anorexic rises to competition and achieves. She is slender, attractive, usually fun to be around.* But she worries . . . about grades, about her friends, about her looks. *Is* she getting fat? Wouldn't she look better if she lost just a few more pounds? *She is constantly dieting, becoming thinner and thinner. She talks about it all the time. She works harder and harder in gym; she is an exercise nut. Running around all day she skips meals.*[29] (emphases mine throughout)

It is difficult to imagine that many adolescents would *not* admire most of these attributes. As a result, it seems that the disorder is implicitly glamorized. A personal account by a recovered anorexic in *Seventeen* magazine described the effect:

I came across stories of anorexics and bulimics in magazines and devoured them. "When Kitty weighted eighty-six pounds, she still perceived her body as obese. After eating one chocolate chip cookie, she stayed up all night doing jumping jacks." I wanted to know how anorexics did it – how they managed to stop eating, how they got so thin. The tragedy of their stories escaped me . . . . The anorexics I read about were glamorous to me. I did not see them as pathetic; I wanted what happened to them to happen to me. It did.[30]

Autobiographical books on eating disorders have also in some instances contributed to the social modeling of the disease. Health professionals involved in the treatment of eating disorders have expressed concern with the extraordinary emphasis in many of these tracts on the detailed descriptions of symptoms, which may unwittingly provide weight-loss strategies for those who are vulnerable. An example of this possibility is the autobiography of Cherry Boone O'Neill, who describes growing up in a well-known performing family, the development of a severe anorexic disorder during her adolescence, and her subsequent recovery through psychotherapy, medication, and involvement in a Christian community. O'Neill's story is valuable in many respects, particularly her description of how a number of seemingly normal stresses – adolescent sexual anxieties, identity confusion, an enmeshed family, a number of deaths inadequately grieved, performance pressures – can, when added together, precipitate the nightmarish descent into anorexia nervosa. Undoubtedly what makes the book so vivid is the excruciatingly detailed description of the years of starvation, the punishing exercise regimes, the bizarre and secretive eating rituals (at one point, she describes eating the remains from a dog's dish), and the consumption of frightening quantities of laxatives.[31] In a subsequent book O'Neill published a sample of the many letters she received in response to her book and lectures, along with her typically sensitive and well-informed responses. Most of the letters expressed gratitude to O'Neill for bringing the disorder out of the closet and providing numerous sufferers with hope of recovery.

However, one letter indicates the potential risks of detailed symptom description, when it comes to techniques of weight control:

> When you came to Australia, I saw you on television . . . . I purchased your book in order that I might learn more about my own problems. I suffer from the "slimmer's disease", as you have probably guessed. In some ways your story helped me to better understand myself but some of the techniques you used to lose weight were unknown to me and I borrowed them. In some ways your book actually made my problem worse. I wish you hadn't gone into certain details of your illness . . . .[32]

O'Neill (to her credit) acknowledged her dismay at having unwittingly provided someone with methods for inducing emaciation, and admitted to having had misgivings from the very outset about providing detail. After apologizing, she suggested to the writer that "ultimately you must bear responsibility for your own decisions. This is part of growing up and getting well." In fairness, though, it should be pointed out that this is the only letter that O'Neill received reporting such imitation.

The social modeling of eating disorders is not limited to autobiographical accounts. Occasionally, books that are written about eating disorders with the intention of educating the public sometimes run the risk of glamorizing symptoms. For example, in *Food Fight*, a book published by Simon and Schuster in 1997 and addressed to pre-teens and adults, the author entitles one of the chapters (addressed to children) "Yum, Yum, Yum, Barf." Some subtitles include "Fierce and Committed Warrior" (describing the anorexic patient) and "Purging: The Magic Solution." Of course the author is not recommending purging to her reader, but with eating disorders one needs to choose words more carefully. In the section on the "Fierce and Committed Warrior," the author writes:

> "Not eating is all I've got," she says to herself. And she's good at it. The hunger drive is a powerful one. She's defying it, like a fierce and committed warrior.[33]

These qualities sound very admirable.

No single event did more to bring the subject of eating disorders to public awareness than the death of singer Karen Carpenter from complications due to anorexia nervosa. While Carpenter was often panned when she was alive for being banal, she has been seen as having a darker side in recent 'retro' criticism and some have suggested that she epitomized the gap between the surface of casual friendship and "good vibes" and the underlying sense of loneliness and personal alienation that was so much a part of the culture of the 1970s.[34] Carpenter's role in the social modeling of eating disorders was an ambivalent one. On the one hand, there were those to whom her struggle and early death had a certain heroic appeal. One well-known fashion model, for example, admitted on a television talk-show that despite the news of her death, she wanted to "be just like her" and deeply admired her willingness to pay the ultimate price for thinness. But the gaunt face of Carpenter that accompanied the article on her death may also have introduced some caution in the public about the dangers of extreme dieting. There was also the instance of Jane Fonda, whose long struggle with bulimia was the subject of the first chapter in her best-selling workout book.[35] Her intent was clearly to discourage others from the use of abusive methods of weight control, and rather to encourage them to adopt the fitness/health ideology of the 1980s, of which Fonda was one of the most influential proponents. But the risk of sanctioning or rationalizing purging remained, particularly by a figure whose maintenance of a youthful image in her late forties was viewed with astonished admiration by a culture obsessed with the problems of appearance and aging.

Eating disorders have been a staple of television talk-shows, which have done much to popularize a whole host of psychiatric disorders. For a period of time, it was not at all unusual for talk-shows to begin with a montage showing all the celebrities who have suffered from eating disorders. This type of presentation is at best a mixed blessing. On the one hand, it might enable someone secretly struggling with an eating disorder to feel less isolated and ashamed. But on the other the relentless associations of eating disorders with stardom can easily lead to the reinforcement of the notion that having such a problem makes one somehow elite and special. A sense of uniqueness is often one of the secret "rewards" of developing anorexia nervosa, and the reinforcement of such an idea by the presentations in the mass media can only make a negative contribution to the motivation to relinquish the disorder.

The Pitfalls of Prevention Programs

The prevention of eating disorders is a worthy but so-far elusive goal. If the arguments that have been raised in this work have any validity, then programs that aspire to preventing eating disorders in effect must attempt to counteract the impact of an entire culture. This is obviously a daunting prospect.

While the design and evaluation of prevention efforts are in their infancy,[36] researchers have become aware of the fact that in some instances prevention programs may unwittingly and paradoxically provoke the very symptoms that they are attempting to prevent. This effect was demonstrated in a study of a brief intervention program at Stanford University.[37] The authors of this study suggested that the protocol of the program, which consisted of a single 90-minute session in which recovering anorexic and bulimic patients provided information and told their stories to small groups of students, was typical of similar programs that have been instituted in numerous universities in the United States. Students who participated in the brief intervention of this program were assessed before the intervention took place, one month after the intervention, and then again three months after the intervention. Interestingly, students who participated in the intervention showed a slight *worsening* of their eating disorder symptoms after the intervention, although when they were assessed again after three months, these deleterious effects appeared to disappear. Comparable results were found in a study in Oxfordshire, England.[38] Groups of 13- and 14-year-old secondary-school students were exposed to an intervention consisting of one 45-minute session a week for eight weeks. The sessions consisted of teaching information about eating disorders and the risks of dieting, but also encouraged more direct participation than the Stanford study, with students engaging in self-monitoring of their eating patterns, role-playing exercises, and other experiential methods. While students showed improved attitudes towards weight and shape immediately following the eight-week program, their attitudes returned to their pre-intervention levels at six-month followup, and the students actually showed greater dietary restraint at followup than they had before the program. The lack of a control group in the Oxford study makes it impossible to say whether the observed changes reflected the impact of the intervention, as opposed to developmental factors or external influences.

Those concerned with eating disorders prevention have been understandably concerned with the negative image of prevention resulting from the widespread publicity about the Stanford program.[39] It might be added, also, that the extent of the negative effects of these programs was quite small. Therefore, it is possible that rather than being actively harmful, they were merely ineffectual. Nevertheless, these studies should lead us to be cautious about the kinds of interventions that might be helpful. In particular, the "lecture-format" of the Stanford approach may be particularly unhelpful, perhaps comparable to the failure of the "just-say-no" approach to drug-abuse prevention. In addition, though, as the researcher in the Stanford program pointed out, a particular problem with eating disorders prevention is the susceptibility of listeners to the seductive appeal of the recovered patients' stories, particularly in the context of the powerful culture of thinness. This problem was exacerbated by the apparently slender but healthy appearance of the recovered patients who gave the lecture, leaving the impression that perhaps eating disorders are not so dangerous after all and might even be beneficial in achieving the holy grail of thinness.

Getting Skinny with the Stars: The Case of the Beverly Hills Diet

In a sense, the entire culture of diet books is a breeding ground for eating disorders. Anorexics and bulimics are often avid readers of diet books, and often weave them directly into the fabric of their symptoms. This is an issue that has been given little systematic study, but it is an impression from clinical experience that is widely shared. In light of the research reviewed in the last chapter on restrained eating, though, this should come as no surprise. Particularly conducive to eating disorders are diets that suggest severe caloric restriction, or that implicitly or explicitly encourage bingeing. The rice diet, which has a respectable history in the treatment of medical obesity, used to crop up occasionally in the history of anorexic patients. Often, it was utilized by a parent or sibling in a struggle against obesity. A prescription for bulimia seems implicit in the Diet Workshop's Wild Weekend Diet, which recommends 800 calories per day during the week and 2,100 plus on the weekend; in the concise formulation of Theodore Berland, "sparse during the week; pig-out on the weekend." This diet is intentionally structured to follow the renunciation-to-indulgence cycle of the typical working week; it presents a tantalizing instance of how disturbed eating may be a magnification of "normal" contemporary eating patterns (see below).[40]

But undoubtedly the most notorious example of a prescription for eating disorders is that of *The Beverly Hills Diet*, a book that sold over a million copies in the early 1980s and, in this author's experience, was used at the time as a manual by a number of patients in the early stages of their disorder.[41] This tract encouraged the use of large amounts of fruit (it dictates eating nothing but fruit for the first few days), and propounded a pseudoscientific notion of "conscious combining," which translates into consuming large amounts of food, such as fruit, that will "cancel out" the fattening effect of other foods. The overall purpose, as one critique suggested, was to make binge eating possible through the liquefaction of foods that would otherwise produce "fat." The author of *The Beverly Hills Diet* expressed unabashed enthusiasm about the elimination of foods that would compromise skinniness: "If you have loose bowel movements, hooray . . . Keep in mind that pounds leave your body in two main ways – bowel movements and urination. The more time you spend on the toilet, the better."[42] She raised a hypothetical reader's rhetorical question: "Won't I be living in the bathroom after eating all that fruit?" Her answer: "Hopefully, but probably not . . . ."[43]

The Beverly Hills Diet was initially heralded as the final solution to the problem of fat, as is evident from the cover story of an issue of *Harper's Bazaar* which proclaimed it "the diet phenomenon of the 1980s" and went on to intone: "A unique, boldly original new food program, now sweeping across the US, has already been tried and tested in Beverly Hills among the movie stars, the trend-setters and the ultra-body conscious."[44] The author herself had, with all due modesty, proclaimed it "the skinny voice of America, the diet conscience of the world." The publication of the book soon generated some devastating critiques, however. One article in the *Journal of the American Medical Association*, whose authors reported seeing a number of Beverly Hills Dieters who had suffered from dizziness, headache, and fatigue, pointed out that the plan was built on a virtually grotesque misunderstanding of the physiology of digestion.[45] The most blatant example was the author's assertion that "As long as food is fully digested, fully processed through the body, you will not gain weight. It is only undigested food, food that is 'stuck' in your body for whatever reason, that accumulates and becomes fat." As the critics pointed out, precisely the opposite is true – only digested food can be absorbed and so transformed. The author gives evidence of a kind of magical thinking that is characteristic of anorexics: the "feeling" of fat (i.e. being full) is confused with a change in body shape.

Even more devastating was a critique by obesity experts Susan and O. Wayne Wooley.[46] The Wooleys comment that the author has written a virtual handbook for anorexic behavior: "the spectre of starvation haunts the pages of *The Beverly Hills Diet*." With its virtual obsession with every mouthful of food (documented by complicated charts scheduling every morsel of intake), its suggestion of hyperactivity associated with reduced food intake ("three little grapes and you're ready to run a mile"), its association of hunger and an empty stomach with feelings of moral purity, the Beverly Hills Diet represents "an unwitting transla-

180

tion of the anorexic's delusional system into the jargon of pop culture and pseudo-science."[47] Repeatedly, it equates the feeling of fullness after meals with "being fat," and it engages in typical dichotomous thinking, the morality of body shape: the world is divided up into "fatties" and "skinnies." The diet guru, with a metaphor that could beautifully articulate the panicked feelings of countless anorexic patients, describes the scale as "that little mechanical device that has more effect on us than the atom bomb," and, in another passage, as "your non-judgmental lover." And in a fantastic formula for body image distortion, she asserts "the scale forces us to see and feel ourselves as we really are . . . ." Particularly virulent, the Wooleys suggest, is the author's tacit encouragement of bingeing (with enough "conscious combining," you can eat anything you want) and purging (the praise of catharsis described above). In fact, the diet "marks the first time an eating disorder – anorexia nervosa – has been marketed as a cure for obesity. It is a case of one disease being offered as a cure for another." Consistent with the premise of this chapter about the social modeling of eating disorders, the Wooleys suggest that it represents "a form of direct training in anorexic behavior," the "mass-marketing of anorexia nervosa."[48]

In addition to its covert prescription of eating-disordered behavior, the Beverly Hills Diet also represented something else: the assimilation of eating disorders to the culture of narcissism and tinsel. The author made no secret about the adoption of the diet by the rich and famous. Indeed, not only was it adopted by more and more celebrities, but "the chanteuse set was singing its glories."[49] In a sense, the philosophy of this book represents the fulfillment of the trend described by Bruch: the assimilation of a disorder that once represented a solitary quest by a few isolated individuals obsessed with self-discipline to the chaotic and impulse-ridden life-style of the self-indulgent.[50] Indeed, as the author promised, "Once you are perfect, you have your choice of *everything* . . . Now you can go to bed at night feeling good about yourself . . . Now you can keep your eyes open when you pass the mirror . . . and make love with the lights on."[51] In the words of one of the converts to the diet, "I did it and I'm totally in love with myself."[52]

The Beverly Hills Diet seems at this point like an artifact of the extreme dieting mania of the 1970s and early 1980s. Because it both reflected and perhaps made its own contribution to triggering the wave of eating disorders of that period, it offers a good illustration of a socially (or at least commercially) sanctioned "template of deviance."

While in the late 1990s this type of extreme fad dieting probably has fewer adherents, the author has not given up. In 1996, *The New Beverly Hills Diet Born Again Skinny* was published, followed in 1997 by *The New Beverly Hills Diet Little Skinny Companion.*[53] Perhaps in response to criticism, the author has included some animal protein in her 35-day menu plan, whereas in the original diet the first ten days only allowed fruit. However, the underlying psychology remains intact. The author suggests that her readers sing the following lines to the tune of "Love is a Many Splendored Thing": "Thin is a many-splendored thing. When your hipbones show, your cheeks will glow, and your heart will sing." And again, the idea of having it all while slimming down: "Cheesecake and cheekbones, hamburgers and hipbones." This is still a fad diet, which prescribes mostly fruits which induce diuresis via urination. As one skeptical reader put it in a review on Amazon.com, "starvation or lack of proper nutrition will have the same weight loss effect . . . Dieters, beware!"

While it is difficult to know, enthusiasm for this type of diet seems to have waned. *The Zone Diet,* perhaps the most popular diet book of the 1990s,[54] advocates a more balanced nutritional approach, even though, as we pointed out earlier, its physiological basis has also been questioned. As Heatherton's study of students' dieting habits seems to indicate, students describe themselves as seeking out "healthy" "low-fat" diets and many more in the 1990s reject the low-calorie approach as well as fasting than was the case in the 1980s.[55] It is still too early to tell whether this new moderation will have an effect on the incidence and prevalence of eating disorders. The population continues to get fatter and the idealization of thinness has certainly not come to an end, but the stringency of standards that characterized the latter in the 1970s and 1980s may be giving way to a more moderate and tolerant attitude towards body size.

The Socialization of Bulimia

A striking fact about bulimia is that, compared with anorexia, it is relatively easily learned, or acquired.[56] This may partially account for the greater heterogeneity of bulimic patients and the relative difficulty of locating a characteristic "bulimic personality." As we suggested earlier, the bulimic cycle may range from a temporary experiment in weight control by an otherwise psychiatrically "normal" subject, to an addictive "stress" syndrome used to discharge emotional tension much in the same way as alcohol, or in the extreme to a masochistic behavior that is used to hold together a tenuously organized borderline personality. The flexible assimilation of bulimia to all of these very different conditions is a function of its social "availability," its visibility as a template of deviance.[57]

In the 1980s, bulimic behavior became so common on college campuses that it had the character of a fad, comparable, as Susie Orbach suggested, to pot-smoking.[58] Bingeing and purging seemed to sweep like a brush-fire through college dormitories, almost like one of the famous epidemics of mass hysteria. One student from a large university in the northeastern United States reported that in her dormitory, one floor had become known as the "bulimic floor": residents of the floor were eyed suspiciously when entering a bathroom, whose odor evoked images of the Roman vomitoria. A particularly astonishing development, also, is the emergence of bulimia as a group activity. Patients sometime report "trying it with a friend"; notes are compared, particularly techniques of purging. Perhaps even more shocking are reports of the practice of collective bulimia in sororities. One student recounted that in a prestigious college in the western USA, it was common for her sorority sisters to "pig out" at a fraternity house, and then return to the sorority and vomit together in the bathroom. The sorority is a breeding ground for eating disorders, given the emphasis of most sorority sisters on social life, the resulting preoccupation with physical appearance, and, of course, the competition. In a systematic study of two sororities, Crandall found that binge eating was the norm rather than the exception, and in one, greater degrees of binge eating were associated with higher degrees of popularity. Furthermore, binge eating tended to be concentrated among certain networks of friends, in a pattern that suggested a high degree of social influence.[59]

In speaking about such "social" bulimia, the question has been raised whether such activity should be dignified with clinical status. One writer argued strongly that "fad bulimia" should be clearly distinguished from the authentic clinical pattern; the distinguishing features of the former are its superficiality and its transience.[60] The distinction may in some instances be difficult to make in practice, although it is unlikely that most fad bulimics will ever appear for treatment. The existence of fad bulimia is one probable reason why some reports that make claims that 20 or 50 percent of college women have an eating disorder are most likely inflated. This is not to minimize the clinical problems that do exist.

The acquisition of the bulimic pattern from social models is evident in the reports of clinical patients, most of whom report having heard about it from a friend, or reading about it in a magazine article.[61] One patient even claimed that she got the idea from an inquiry by a doctor into her weight-control practices.[62] Patients typically describe being "initiated" into the practice by a friend, a sibling, or in one case, the patient's mother. Such learning by imitation does not of course account for or explain the clinical disorder; for this, one must understand the predisposing factors (personality, mood disorder, weight history) that led the person to incorporate and finally become addicted to such self-abusive behavior. But these data do suggest that social factors provide the model or template for the particular form that the symptomatic behavior takes.

The magazine articles, books, and television talk-shows that we discussed previously with regard to anorexia nervosa are if anything more contributive to bulimia. Purging techniques, in particular, are eagerly snapped up by those who are vulnerable. Particularly astonishing, though, has been the appearance of printed material directly advocating the adoption of bulimia. An advertisement in the *New York Times* in 1987 (printed, ironically, on the "Health" pages) promoted a book called *Responsible Bulimia,* to be obtained by mail order.[63] The advertisement claimed that the author had safely practiced bulimia for several years, which had enabled him to eat freely, control his weight, and preserve his health through dental care and medical monitoring. Bulimia, the advertisement claimed, was an age-old health practice, sanctioned by the ancients (the latter part of the claim is questionable, as Roman physicians criticized the practice). The book, whose cover depicted the handsome and well-dressed author holding two large plates of food, makes a case for bulimia as an alternative to drastic medical options for the control of obesity, with which the author had struggled. Statements such as the following would cause any therapist who has worked with eating-disordered patients to cringe and would be flatly rejected by any person who has suffered the torment of bulimia nervosa:

> I recently read an article which talked about some women who have been bulimic for 30 years. The therapists felt it a great tragedy that there

were people who had suffered for 30 years with bulimia. I would say "congratulations" to these women. They are heroines in my eyes. They have been enjoying the hunger-free thin life for 30 years, and have managed to survive with their health intact.[64]

Completely ignoring Jane Fonda's reports of years of suffering and ultimate denunciation of bulimia, he writes "If such a health conscious female like Jane Fonda can use bulimia for several years, then perhaps it is just further indication that bulimia is not necessarily the degrading, irresponsible practice which the eating disorder people would have us believe."[65] When he sent me the book, the author included a personal communication indicating that he had now (six months after the appearance of the advertisement in the *New York Times*) totally reversed his position, that he was convinced that bulimia was "physically destructive" and "emotionally devastating," and that he now strongly discouraged its use.[66] It is not known how many people were affected by *Responsible Bulimia* or the monthly newsletter published by the author before his epiphany. Unfortunately, those who saw his advertisement were not the beneficiaries of his retraction. One would hope that all of those who had ordered the book would have received a letter similar to the one that was sent to me.

Responsible Bulimia may well have been an artifact of the cultural extremism of the 1970s and 1980s. It is unlikely that the advocacy of bulimia as a way of life would gain many adherents now. Twenty years of negative publicity about the destructive impact of this behavior and the havoc that it can wreak on a person's emotional and physical health have given bulimia, and eating disorders in general, a far more negative image than they had when the public first became familiar with them. From the standpoint of those concerned with the public health implications of eating disorders, this can only be a good thing, but it remains to be seen what the impact of newer attitudes will be on the actual incidence and prevalence of these conditions.

Eating Disorders are Disorders of Eating: The Anorexic– Bulimic Conflict

The social patterning of eating disorders can also be viewed in broader perspective, in relation to issues about food, eating styles, and weight

185

control in the advanced industrial societies. In the food-abundant, urban cultures of the West, food has become a pervasive symbol of affluence and the contemporary ethic of pleasure-seeking. In contemporary societies, as Roland Barthes pointed out, virtually every situation has become an occasion for eating – working, driving, television watching, and of course socializing.[67] At the same time, though, contemporary eating has become radically desocialized and individualized; collective eating rituals, particularly the family meal, have undergone a radical decline.[68] In fact, in the United States, very little eating is taken at regularly scheduled "meals." We have become a culture of "grazers" or "foragers"; snacking, usually in the form of irregularly scheduled episodes with unpredictable nutritional intake, has replaced the tradition of three-meals-a-day.[69] These trends are particularly in evidence on college campuses. Students tend to eat irregularly, with meal-skipping a way of life for many.[70] These trends, which were documented in the 1980s, only seem to have increased in the 1990s. Meanwhile, snack food – particularly of the high-carbohydrate, high-calorie type – is everywhere available, in the bookstore, in the student center, even in designated areas in the library. The fast-paced life of the professional has also resulted in new eating styles, under pressure of the chronic shortage of time. A book on nutrition by a respected researcher devotes some space to the problem of satisfactory eating and nutrition when at professional conferences.[71] In the highly pressurized, sometimes frenetic academic or professional environment, it is therefore not surprising that disorders of alimentation have become common; to some extent, they directly reflect the desocialization of contemporary eating patterns. In this sense, eating disorders are not only reflections of cultural preoccupations with shape and weight; they also mirror the general disorganization of social eating per se.

In the advanced industrial societies, food is a consumer product, elaborately packaged, promoted, and marketed with all the tools of modern consumerism. Eating, even excessive eating, is therefore good for business, particularly the food business. McDonald's seeks to plan the location of its restaurants in the United States such that any consumer is only an average of eight minutes away from a Big Mac. Fast food, which symbolizes perhaps better than anything else the desocialization of eating, has long been at the vanguard of the globalization of American culture. The appearance of a McDonald's in Moscow in the late 1980s was one of the first cultural harbingers of the demise of the Soviet Union and the advent of the golden arches in Beijing and Shanghai heralded the onset of capitalism in China. As food has been transformed into one of the "designer" products of the affluent society, its forms have proliferated. The contemporary consumer who seeks ice-cream is confronted at the supermarket with a choice between Häagen-Dasz, Tofutti, Ice Milk, or just plain old Sealtest; at the ice-cream factory, between Heavenly Hash, Rocky Road, Peach Brandy, or Plain Vanilla. Food, in fact, has now become a medium of fashion, ranging from discount to upscale. Consumer-oriented food advertising, particularly in the traditional women's magazines, has been likened to pornography, with its glossy depiction of the untouchable, its evocation of forbidden fantasies of indulgence.[72] Food advertising continues to be aimed largely at women, who, despite the public imagery of liberation, are apparently still considered responsible for its preparation. This selectivity provides one further reason, over and above considerations of shape and weight, why eating disorders, and particularly the problem of "compulsive overeating," are more prevalent in females.[73] Food is a sanctioned and legal form of oral gratification, apparently safer than alcohol and certainly more acceptable than drugs. In any case, the widespread prevalence of binge eating in the United States, particularly among college students, is symptomatic of a society in which the problem is not one of starvation, but rather of surplus.[74] It is not surprising that a book called *The Joy of Pigging Out* was displayed in the windows of local bookstores; it is in fact symptomatic of the times.[75]

Our culture has also developed a distinctly paranoid attitude towards food, mostly resulting from the widely publicized results of scientific studies of health and nutrition and the anxieties that they engender. And in the 1990s, much of that anxiety has centered on one element in particular, and that is fat. The concern with the linkages of fat content to heart disease, colon and breast cancer, and other ailments has now replaced the obsession with cholesterol of the 1980s (which has now been divided into a good and bad type). Low-fat foods have become the holy grail of the shopper, the primary yardstick about whether one is "eating healthy." The reading of food labels with a special eye for fat content has become one of the rituals of contemporary supermarket shopping. Food producers have taken advantage of these concerns with the marketing of "low-fat" products, even though in some instances the distinction between a low-fat and regular product may be a distinction without a difference.[76] A frenetic search continues in the food industry for a synthetic fat substitute that retains the taste and texture of real fat while actually reducing the amount of nutrient fat.

Of course the fat content of food is not identical to fat on the body, although it is undoubtedly the case that a high-fat diet may ultimately lead one to be heavy. Nevertheless, one gets the sense that the health concerns about fatness are widely linked in people's minds with the cosmetic anxieties about weight (in fact, one might argue that they are somehow unconsciously equated).

Thus, while overconsumption is encouraged by an economy whose hunger for profits seems limitless, the ultimate contradiction that leads us back to eating disorders is the simultaneous demand, also economically promoted (but by a different industry), to be thin – a requirement which, as we have seen, is critically involved in the proliferation of anorexia nervosa and bulimia. To return to the argument of Hillel Schwartz (see chapter 6), the problem of obesity (but to which we can now add those of anorexia nervosa and bulimia) must ultimately be traced to the problem of self-regulation in societies in which alienated production and consumption have run riot. To experience the pleasures of plenty while eating nothing is the fantasy of the normal contemporary dieter, but one which reaches obsessional proportions for the person with an eating disorder. Ultimately, the social modeling of eating disorders must be understood in terms of this "anorexic–bulimic" conflict, which seems to be entrenched in the very fabric of contemporary life.[77]

Chapter Eight

The Cultural Politics of Eating Disorders

The dizzy rapture of starving. The power of needing nothing. By force of will I make myself the impossible sprite who lives on air, on water, on purity.

Kathryn Harrison, *The Kiss*

The symptoms of an ethnic disorder, according to Devereux, invariably represent a kind of social negativism, an unstated rebellion against prevailing cultural expectations. They signify, he suggests, a society's "disavowal of itself," the negation of its most cherished explicit ideals. Paradoxically, though, such antisocial behavior may be secretly admired and revered, perhaps because others within the culture secretly identify with the symptomatic person's dilemma.[1] After all, the sorts of conflicts which occur in a person who develops an ethnic disorder are much more widespread than the actual number of individuals who manifest symptoms. The social response to the person with an ethnic disorder, therefore, is typically an ambivalent one, a mixture of admiration, fear, and hostility. Like any deviant, society attempts to bring back such individuals "into the fold" through various mechanisms of social control – with varying degrees of success.

An anthropological account by Littlewood and Lipsedge proposes that ethnic disorders (they use the more traditional term "culture-bound syndromes") reflect the efforts of certain individuals of inferior status – typically defined by age or sex – to protest against or otherwise escape from their oppression by the more powerful. Such protests are typically not consciously acknowledged, nor labeled as such; they reflect what the anthropologist Victor Turner has called "the power of the weak" – in psychiatric terms, manipulation.[2] By taking on the identity of a deviant, the symptomatic person is able to indirectly punish or at least gain some degree of control over those who are more powerful than herself, even though her behavior is simultaneously self-destructive. Because the rebellion is indirect and unarticulated, such efforts typically do not result in a fundamental change in the status quo, and invariably result in the relegation of the deviant to a marginal status or an alternative identity. They do afford the deviant some measure of escape from what is experienced as an intolerable situation. In preindustrial societies, such deviant behavior was not necessarily identified as illness, but was often "mystically rationalized" – for example, as "possession."

An example of these psychosocial dynamics can be found in the Zar cults of Ethiopia. Certain women, who were suffering at the hands of abusive or exploitative husbands, would become members of such cults and engage in a spectrum of intolerable and outrageous behaviors: frenzied dancing, dressing as men, sometimes brandishing weapons. Since possession by Zar spirits had cultural credibility, substantial sums of money or possessions could be extracted from the errant husband by the healers of the Zar cults. Meanwhile, the woman herself could escape from a punishing marital situation by assuming the alternative identity of the Zar, which had a certain degree of social status, and she might even ultimately attain the stature of a healer.[3] Importantly, as is typical for such mystically rationalized rebellion, the societal order of male dominance was not fundamentally altered by the adoption of a Zar identity. Within limits, though, the phenomenon of Zar possession enabled some unlabeled protest against and escape from a social situation of powerlessness.

According to Littlewood and Lipsedge, in contemporary Western societies, such manipulative and disguised protests are typically enacted through psychiatric disorders or "mental illness" – the "scientistic" equivalent of mystical rationalization.[4] And since women continue to suffer the limitations of inferior social status and a relative lack of power, it should come as no surprise that the majority of ethnic disorders in the West occur predominantly among females. Such considerations may also partly account for the fact that females continue to constitute a disproportionate number of psychiatric patients. Ethnic disorders such as conversion and somatization disorders, agoraphobia, and now anorexia nervosa, whose prevalence has been and continues to be overwhelmingly female, have therefore been the characteristic expressions of female powerlessness from the late nineteenth century to the present. Hysteria, as we have seen, represented a strategy of coming to grips with the socially prescribed dependency and passivity that was central to the nineteenth-century female sex role: through becoming hysterical, a woman both rebelled against, and yet exaggerated, this stereotype. The "secondary gains," which played such a central role in hysterical symptoms, represented the "escape from obligations" with which so many women felt burdened, as well as the achievement of some degree of power through the woman's passive tyrannization of the household and her capacity to frustrate the physician.[5] Similarly, agoraphobia, a disorder which involves a phobic avoidance of public spaces, public transportation, and crowds, can in many instances be seen as a metaphoric encapsulation of the situation of the dependent and unassertive wife (indeed, it is sometimes referred to, somewhat inaccurately, as "housewife's disease"). Studies of the family dynamics of agoraphobics, many of whom are young married women with small children, suggest that the symptom can be viewed as a strategy by which a woman could effectively dominate her husband, by commanding his presence and aid, while simultaneously conforming to role expectations of dependency.[6] In such an imbroglio, the husband continues to maintain his dominant position; social reality has not fundamentally changed.

In this context, eating disorders such as anorexia nervosa and bulimia nervosa can be understood as the most recent in a long tradition of stereotyped expressions of "female distress." In this chapter, we will explore their political dimensions.

Some Historical Forerunners: Holy Anorexics, Hunger Artists, and Hunger Strikers

The use of self-starvation as a tool of manipulation and control over self and others actually has a long history, and it is a tactic that has been especially deployed by women. J. Hubert Lacey, an English psychiatrist, has suggested that the story of St Wilgerfortis, who lived around the tenth century AD, presents some striking parallels to anorexic behavior. Wilgerfortis (literally "strong virgin"), the daughter of a Portuguese king, starved herself when confronted with the prospect of marriage to a brutal king of Sicily.[7] As a consequence of her resulting emaciation, the marriage arrangement was broken off by the suitor, upon which her father had her crucified. Apparently, Wilgerfortis's plight echoed that of countless young women, as cults based on her martyrdom sprung up all over Europe. Interestingly, it was customary to make an offering of food at the shrines dedicated to her memory. In his recounting of the legend, Lacey speculates that a dark area in an English statue of Wilgerfortis (St Uncumber) represented a beard, which suggests the symptomatic lanugo (body hair) of anorexia nervosa. This notion has been disputed by other scholars, who argue that the dark area represents a veiled crucifix.[8] More problematic is Lacey's assertion that Wilgerfortis, like contemporary anorexic patients, was "fearful of the implications of sexuality" associated with her adolescence. Unlike contemporary patients, the saint's conflict was hardly an internalized one. Rather, her self-starvation was much more literally a weapon that enabled her to fend off sexual enslavement.

The story of Wilgerfortis is shrouded in historical uncertainty, and is probably of interest mainly for its mythic implications. More credible historically are the numerous instances of self-starvation among women in the late medieval and postmedieval period in Europe, many of whom were ultimately sanctified by the Church. These women, who have been called "holy anorexics" by Rudolph Bell in his startling work on the subject, in many ways strikingly resembled contemporary anorexics, despite the vast cultural divide between the medieval and the modern world.[9] Like contemporary patients, most began their fasting in adolescence (although some began later), typically in order to resolve an acute sense of self-doubt and unworthiness and as a solitary quest for a sense of spiritual and moral perfection. Their radical ascetic behavior, which reduced their bodies to an asexual and non-reproductive state, made them unsuitable for marriage and was typically in defiance of parental expectations for an arranged marriage or at least a conventional life. In fact, Caroline Bynum has suggested that the highly unconventional and masochistic behavior of these women served as a subtle reproach to their families, many of whom were part of a secular and materialistic mercantile class and were embarrassed by their daughters' fanatical asceticism and religiosity.[10] As Bynum points out, the fasting of these holy women went far beyond conventional religious practices of the time, which, unlike those of early Christianity, were more circumscribed by an ethos of moderation.[11]

Of particular interest is the sexual politics of these early instances of self-starvation. Most of these women were unwilling to accept the conventional limitations of the female role, and aspired to something higher. And yet the notion of spiritual autonomy or authority for women in the Church was totally unacceptable. The radical abstinence of these women aroused considerable suspicion among the male clergy, and they were typically monitored carefully by their male confessors. Despite their spiritual and moral accomplishments, and the sometimes reluctant admission of their virtue by male authority, it was impossible for these women to gain official acceptance in the Church on an equal footing with their male confessors. Rather, as Bynum suggests, they fashioned an alternative religious identity, a kind of charismatic lay priesthood, one which was elaborated in distinctly female metaphors of bodily suffering and nurturance.[12] Like many contemporary anorexics, these holy women starved themselves but gave to others, often literally in the form of feeding the poor. These women often had a following, but their admirers were not typically drawn from the ranks of the official Church, but rather from the lay public, many of whom identified with their sense of suffering and charismatic inspiration. It is a somewhat similar situation to contemporary anorexics, who evoke a sympathetic response from their feminist interpreters (who tend to work outside the clinical establishment) as well as the lay public, while the (mostly male) clinical establishment remains skeptical of any redeeming features of their behavior.

Although there are striking parallels between medieval and modern anorexia, it is important to note the differences. A vast gulf separates the medieval and modern world, and therefore we should expect that the meaning of self-starvation would differ. Most striking is the fact that contemporary anorexics starve themselves in the pursuit of a particular external body shape, a wholly secular goal that seems at least superficially to have little in common with the moral and spiritual ideals of a Catherine of Siena.[13] Medieval fasters expressed themselves through a rich and elaborate spiritual vocabulary, which was drawn from the magico-religious world view of medieval Christianity. Today's anorexics have no comparable language for the expression of moral or spiritual conflict, a fact that may have something to do with their widely noted inability to articulate their inner experiences while they are ill. Yet, even among modern anorexics, who speak in terms of control and thinness, there is an echo of the struggle of the medieval holy woman for a sense of purity and perfection, as well as the impulse to nurture others while depriving themselves. And one extraordinarily gifted anorexic woman – the celebrated and intellectually notorious Simone Weil – articulated an alternative Christian vision, replete with metaphors of food and eating, that is reminiscent of the nearly heretical visions and formulations of medieval fasters.[14]

Although holy anorexics may have used food refusal as a tactic of power, their protest had to be carefully cloaked in the guise of religious self-denial. A more blatantly manipulative use of self-starvation can be found in the fasting practices of ancient India. Fasting was an integral part of the Hindu tradition (as it remains today), but it was also put to more openly secular purposes. For example, it was common practice in the villages of ancient India for a man who was owed a debt to entrench himself in front of the tent of the debtor and fast until the debt was repaid.[15] It has been suggested that such "masochistic blackmail" may have prefigured the triumphant use of fasting by Gandhi, which became the ultimate symbol of passive resistance by the Indian nation against British authority. As Gandhi himself pointed out, though, such tactics cannot be effective unless the authority against which one protests is susceptible to moral blackmail. In his words, "one cannot fast against a tyranny."[16]

Hunger strikes, of course, represent the quintessentially political use of self-starvation. Historically, the hunger strike has been employed by the socially oppressed, as a means of embarrassing or humiliating those in control and ultimately extracting concessions from them. The hunger strike is a powerful symbolic tool, which typically evokes a sympathetic, or at least a guilty, response in those who identify with the hunger striker's plight. And although historically the hunger striker is invariably from the ranks of the oppressed, it is interesting that throughout history the vast majority of political hunger strikers have been male (the one exception is that of the suffragettes).[17] Women's fasting, on the other hand, has typically only been permissible in religious or psychiatric contexts. Apparently, even when they are from the downtrodden, it is more acceptable for males to engage in direct aggression – even when it takes a passive form. For women, the protest must remain veiled in a mystical or symptomatic language. Anorexia nervosa, of course, falls in this latter category.

By the nineteenth century, fasting had become totally secularized in the figure of the hunger artist, whose public feats of asceticism gained considerable notoriety in Europe and the United States.[18] Unlike hunger strikers or saintly maidens, hunger artists had no moral or religious agenda. Rather, their food refusal was a sheer act of will and self-control for its own sake, a public spectacle devoid of moral content. The fascination with hunger artists coincided almost exactly with the emergence of anorexia nervosa as a recognized disease, although the latter remained obscure in the public consciousness until about a hundred years later. Nevertheless, as Kafka's story suggests, the inner psychology of the hunger artist and the anorexic were virtually identical – the narcissistic pursuit of perfection through the mastery of appetite.[19] And, as Hillel Schwartz points out, the public interest in hunger artists, which parallels in many ways the contemporary fascination with anorexia nervosa, grew out of an increasing unease with the problem of self-control in a society in which greed, accumulation, and consumption were already running rampant.

In the early twentieth century, the suffragettes became the first women to utilize self-starvation as a direct form of political protest. It is probably overextending a metaphor to argue, as Showalter has, that the suffragettes "brilliantly put the symptoms of anorexia to work in the service of a feminist cause."[20] The suffragettes' hunger strikes were hardly motivated by a sense of personal or interpersonal conflict. Nevertheless, it may not be totally accidental that the intrafamilial protest of the anorexic seemed to anticipate the hunger strikes of the suffragettes, in a period in which debates about the rights of women had moved to the forefront of public consciousness. Perhaps, as Showalter suggests, it is possible to view nineteenth-century anorexia as well as hysteria as a kind of proto-feminist revolt, but one which for the individuals involved could not be articulated in anything other than a symptomatic vocabulary. In view of the central role that female identity conflicts play in contemporary eating disorders, it is possible that similar parallels may hold in the late twentieth century. This makes it understandable why contemporary feminists have seen the problems of the anorexic or bulimic woman as uniquely symbolic of the contemporary female dilemma.[21] Of course, most anorexics are not feminists, nor can the women's movement be held responsible for their situation.[22] In fact, it could be argued that the process of recovery from an eating disorder, which requires a more tolerant acceptance of the body as well as the development of a "self-respecting identity" (Bruch's phrase), itself involves the emergence of an implicitly feminist consciousness.

195

Addiction to Control

Fasting, as generations of mystical seekers and health faddists have known, yields an enormous sense of exhilaration, purity, and spiritual power. Feelings of lightness, of enhanced sensory clarity, of transcending the ordinary compulsions of the body can drive the faster into escalating the heroic efforts at self-denial. Fasting became popular in the 1970s (and had something of a revival in the 1990s) not fundamentally as a technique of dieting (although medical fasts for the obese came into vogue during the period), but as a technique of getting high, one of many popularized alternatives to psychedelic drugs. Health cultists are familiar with the potentially addictive lure of fasting, and typically prescribe strict time limits for the duration of a fast, knowing that without such an external structure, the faster may push the process beyond the boundary of physical and psychological safety.[23]

The sense of enthrallment yielded by fasting is ultimately rooted in physiological processes. But for the person predisposed to developing anorexia nervosa, fasting has an especially powerful psychological appeal, even though it is initially hit upon virtually by accident. Before an anorexic begins dieting, she feels secretly enslaved, dependent, and manipulated. As dieting turns into fasting, it begins to yield an exhilarating sense of power and independence. One of Bruch's patients, Betty, explained that "losing weight was giving her power, that each pound lost was like a treasure that gave her power. This accumulation of power was giving her another kind of 'weight,' the right to be recognized as an individual."[24] Generally, it is only later, when starvation becomes chronic or bulimia supervenes, or when it dawns on her that thinness and food refusal bring no real power, that the euphoria gives way to depression. And although the fasting may be perpetuated by endogenous, physiological factors, the sense of empowerment that derives from food refusal is critical to understanding why an anorexic patient will defend her starvation so radically, as if her life depended on it.

The anorexic stance has been likened to the classic posture of asceticism, in which the total subjugation of appetite yields a transcendent sense of perfection and purity.[25] For most patients, though, it is an asceticism that is not embedded in an explicit philosophical, moral, or religious context. It is more a purely psychological defense mechanism,

196

common and to some extent adaptive among adolescents, but exaggerated in anorexics to the point of obsession. Anorexics deny themselves in order to become unencumbered of the uncertainties and vulnerability that are unavoidable accompaniments of relationships with others. They are driven to the behavior almost wholly from a sense of intolerable dependence and enmeshment. Some writers have noted an explicit preoccupation among many anorexics with religious themes; most, however, can only articulate their quest in terms of a secular goal, that of attaining a particular external body shape. But as one observer noted, "the asceticism of anorexia nervosa may appear perverse rather than good, debased rather than noble, foolish rather than heroic, but even in its most misguided forms it may contain within itself an ineradicable element of the numinous."[26]

The Politics of the Family

The fierce struggle for self-control and a sense of power in anorexia is actually rooted in a profound sense of powerlessness. And this core feeling is rooted in the experience of the eating-disordered patient in the family. It is the imbalance of power in the family, and the resulting profound deficiency in the child's capacity for independent self-assertion, that leads to such radical measures of self-control in adolescence or later. Probably no symptom has a greater capacity to drive family members to distraction than a determined effort on a child's part to starve herself. But the noisy battles and vituperative clashes that take place over the issue of food once the anorexic patient becomes ill are often a symptomatic expression of a power struggle that had been latent, although suppressed, from early on.[27]

Family therapists have done much to illuminate the dynamics of power in the families of anorexics. Salvador Minuchin, for example, suggests that the family dynamics of anorexia are typical of those that more generally give rise to "psychosomatic" symptoms, such as gastrointestinal disorders or psychologically aggravated asthma attacks.[28] Such families tend to be excessively "enmeshed," fearful of the implications of individuality, unable to openly express conflicts and differences. In the families of anorexics, the child who develops symptoms becomes "triangulated" into the parents' relationship, which is loaded with unresolved conflict. Conflict between the parents is typically denied and detoured through the anorexic, who is therefore unable to achieve individuation. The dynamics of enmeshment are compounded by the fact that these families typically find the world beyond the family a fearful place. In many instances, only a dramatic ritual will have the power to free the anorexic from the grip of this powerful centripetal dynamic. The most notorious and dramatic example offered by Minuchin was the "family lunch session," in which the therapeutic team engenders a "therapeutic crisis" by joining the family and patient for a common meal. Such an encounter may take some of the charge out of the battles over food, by defining the meeting as "just having lunch" and by diverting the discussion along pathways other than the patient's eating. But, conversely, it may confront the issue head on by prescribing that the parents get the patient to eat. The almost inevitable failure of the parents to force the anorexic to eat exposes the absurdity and futility of the struggle. The anorexic's refusal to eat casts a certain spell over the family, and deflects attention from more fundamental issues and conflicts. This is a major reason why, in addition to its obviously life-threatening nature, the parents and siblings become totally focused on and preoccupied with the symptom. Such a dramatic intervention can in some instances trigger a startling improvement in the identified patient's eating behavior.[29]

The issue of power is also central in the work of the Italian psychiatrist Mara Selvini Palazzoli, who has treated large numbers of anorexic patients through family therapy in Milan, Italy. In a paper addressing cultural factors, Palazzoli noted a steady increase in the number of anorexics since World War II, which she attributed to the emergence of a consumer-oriented, affluent society, an increasing degree of child-centeredness among middle-class families, and the contradictory situation of women under the increased pressure from emancipation. However, in order to understand any particular case, these broad social pressures must be understood within the specific context of the individual family. According to Palazzoli, it is typical in the families of anorexics for the parents' relationship to be characterized by rancor, bitterness, and deep resentments of each partner by the other. These conflicts have never been admitted to, but rather covered over by a facade of harmony and deflected through an excessive solicitousness towards the children. Such minute attention to every single aspect of a child's needs may be appropriate or at least tenable prior to adolescence but it is completely inappropriate for adolescents. Adolescents' developmental needs are to become relatively autonomous of parental control and to reformulate values that are inevitably critical of those of the prior generation. It is this reorganization of the structure of the family at adolescence that the families of anorexics are particularly unable to negotiate. Palazzoli suggests that one important reason why anorexia is so much more common in girls is that, despite contemporary social rhetoric of emancipation, girls continue to be subjected to a much greater degree of parental control than boys. When an anorexic begins dieting, and as her weight loss begins to be noticed and commented upon by her parents, she quickly finds that starving herself is a way of "bringing her parents to their knees," even though inwardly she feels more out of control than ever. This is the point at which hospitalization and eventually psychotherapy typically begins.[30]

In a later work, Palazzoli adopted the metaphor of the "game" to describe these familial dynamics.[31] Game implies a situation that is rule-governed, but also involves the dynamic unfolding of interaction patterns in time. Anorexics and bulimics conduct power struggles over the issues of food and eating; and it is only in the affluent societies, in which food is readily available and offered, that such "games with food" can occur.[32] In one typical case, which Palazzoli characterizes as a "psychotic family game," the anorexic perceives her father as weak and submissive to her mother's demands and manipulations. This is actually a misperception on her part, since the father's helplessness is only surface: he "passively controls," while the mother "actively controls." The "dieting ploy" or "silent hunger strike" is a way of showing the father how to "get at" or retaliate against the mother. In effect, the symptom states, in an enactive language, "look, this is how you can get to her, this is the way to drive her crazy." This is of course not only a game built on a false premise, but one with potentially deadly consequences.[33]

Therapy in such families must involve a deft and expert deployment of counterpower by the therapist, a set of tactical maneuvers that could match the dramatic ploys of any primitive shaman. Family therapy techniques have the aura of ritual drama, of shamanistic countermagic. The "problem" may be radically redefined or "reframed," "prescriptions" or "injunctions" may be delivered by the therapist, or the symptom itself may be paradoxically mandated. The latter technique, initially formulated by Palazzoli and her colleagues, was dramatically illustrated in a case report by Peggy Papp, an American family therapist. Papp works with a "consultation group," which issues oracular injunctions from behind a one-way mirror. In this particular case, that of a 21-year-old anorexic girl, it was suggested to the family that the therapists were reluctant to prescribe change, particularly for the anorexic to gain weight too rapidly, for fear that if she gained curves and began to menstruate, her father would feel "increasingly isolated in a family of women" and the parents' estrangement would be intensified. The purpose of this seemingly outrageous prescription, which stands conventional therapeutic wisdom on its head, is to expose the intimate connection of the symptom with the family system and thereby dramatically reveal its function. And while cautioning an anorexic against gaining weight may seem virtually unethical, the therapist is only telling the patient and the family to do what it is already doing, in effect mirroring to the family its secret truth; the instruction comes at first as a shock, a joke. But, at least in this particular case, the anorexic began to eat and appeared soon after with a significant weight gain.[34] In her newer work Palazzoli suggested the use of what she calls the "invariant prescription": the parents are directed to go out together as a couple, to refrain from discussing their evening together with the children, and to take careful notes on their children's reactions.[35] The results achieved by these measures are reported to have been dramatic; and of course, what has happened is that the problem of the excessive overinvolvement of the parents with the children has been directly dealt with, by prescribing behavior on the part of the parents that demands disengagement. Through enacting the prescription, the deadlock in which the anorexic symptom has become entrenched is broken.[36]

Power issues are also critical in the family dynamics of bulimic anorexia and bulimia nervosa. In these families, conflict and strife are typically much more out in the open than in the families of restricting anorexics. In this often explosive atmosphere, problems with alcohol and drug abuse or compulsive overeating and obesity are commonplace. Despite the presence of overt conflict, the open communication of feelings is often difficult. In these families, separation is as difficult as is being together; it is as if a knot of ambivalence holds the family together. Bulimia nervosa patients internalize this powerful ambivalence about relationships, which is typically evident in their own pattern of intense involvement and withdrawal. For bulimics, a critical or sometimes overtly abusive father typically plays a particularly important role in their development; they often perceive their mothers as weak and ineffectual, or otherwise unable to cope with the father. Root, Fallon, and Friedrich, in an important work on the family therapy of bulimia, propose a feminist understanding of the experience of victimization and sense of powerlessness that is so common among bulimics.[37] The inability to leave home, so critical in the emergence of bulimic symptoms, typically is the culmination of a familial pattern of generations of female difficulties with achieving independence.

Bulimic symptoms themselves are often a covert means of striking back, a symptomatic expression of rage. In some cases, the bulimic's devouring of a family's food supply is a barely masked retaliation for her sense of victimization. In one instance, a 17-year-old, who was the recipient of sexual harassment and physical punishment from her alcoholic father as well as a lack of support from her mother, struck back by bingeing regularly on all of the food in the kitchen late at night. When her young brother and sister awoke in the morning before school, they had no food to eat. In this case, the manipulative tactic hardly seems subtle, but the patient felt that her eating episodes were "out of her control." The mother was enraged with the daughter's provocative behavior, but felt helpless in the face of her "illness." In other instances, vomiting, in addition to whatever psychological purposes it serves, becomes a violent form of retaliation for what is experienced as abusive parental intrusion. One 15-year-old, for example, felt abused, harassed, and embarrassed by her father's unruly dog, who served as a surrogate for her father's own anger and sexual frustration towards his wife. The daughter, who maintained a carefully cultivated facade of physical attractiveness and goodness, fought back by vomiting into garbage bags that she kept hidden in her room. This was an unacknowledged expression of feelings of rage, disgust, and powerlessness. In this case, a parental divorce led to a marked lessening of the bulimic symptoms.

As in anorexia nervosa, the bulimic's quest for power is ultimately self-destructive. But unlike anorexia, the symptom often remains hidden beneath a facade of normality. In contrast with the emaciated anorexic, whose appearance shocks others into responding, the bulimic's abusive food habits are often only known to herself. The ultimate "power" that resides in her symptom is in the rewards of the compliments that she receives for her thinness; and unfortunately, it is this feedback that unwittingly reinforces the symptom and contributes to its chronicity.

The Cultural Politics of a Disease: Illness as Metaphor

The symptoms of an ethnic disorder exaggerate cultural values to the point of caricature; they are thus both an affirmation and a disavowal of a society's esteemed ideals. Because of this dual function, the response to those with ethnic disorders is typically an ambivalent one. On the one hand, they are seen as pariahs, rebels, or deviants; but on the other, they evoke responses of admiration, envy, even awe. In Devereux's characterization, ethnic symptoms are typically "antisocial social behaviors." Like any deviant behavior with a negative sign, the patient tends to evoke controlling and punitive responses from others. But precisely because these rebellious behaviors represent antisocial tendencies that are latent within everyone, they may be secretly admired and even imitated:

> Cultural materials that represent society's basic disavowal of itself are also precisely the ones that troubled individuals synthesize and give expression to by their behavior – and do this in a manner that can earn them society's approval or its disapproval. These antisocial social values . . . permit the individual to be antisocial in a socially approved and sometimes even prestigious manner.[38]

The fact that anorexics sometimes evoke admiration was evident in a query into the responses of the friends and relatives of a number of anorexic patients.[39] Most showed concern or alarm regarding the patient's low weight. Surprisingly, though, more positive than negative comments were voiced about the patient's condition. Typical remarks were "she is fashionable," "slender," or "in control." One respondent (a boyfriend of the patient) went so far as to say that "she is triumphant." Terms such as "gaunt" and "haggard" were much less frequently utilized. The authors of this study were dismayed by the implications. Such barely masked glorification of the patient's thin appearance and "control" could easily be reinforcing and thus serve to reduce her already tenuous will to recover. In the literature, in fact, there have been a number of reports in which a patient's recovery has been covertly resisted or sabotaged by a parent, who fears that weight gain will make the patient "fat."[40] Some parents may even carry a secret, perverse pride that their child has an "elite" affliction.

202

The glamorization of anorexia nervosa is not surprising in that the disorder "embodies" cultural ideals such as slenderness, self-control, and achievement. This enmeshment of anorexia with positive values makes it more understandable why it has become a widely imitated template of deviance in societies which hold these values dear. In an environment in which many fashion models border on anorexia, it is not surprising that the disorder itself has become "fashionable." Many anorexics themselves have testified to the secret gratifications afforded by a condition to which people respond with such admiration and envy. Thus, Aimee Liu commented to a friend who also was anorexic, "They're in awe of us. It sounds insane, but maybe it's something like [being a] celebrity. Everybody wants to be thin, after all. Right? Including the doctors, our mothers, and our friends. We've achieved what they can't. They're jealous. They want to take it away from us."[41] The romanticization of anorexia also makes it understandable why, for some patients, the disorder becomes such a central part of their identity. As one of Bruch's patients remarked, she could never give up her illness because without it she would be "nothing."[42] Such an overidentification with the illness has unfortunately become common among eating-disordered patients, and represents a further stage in the socialization of the disease. And while it is understandable that a person with such painfully low self-esteem might feel strengthened by identifying with a glamorous affliction, the glamorization of eating disorders and its internalization by vulnerable individuals can obviously place significant obstacles in the way of the process of recovery.

Bruch once commented that anorexics command respect because of the universality of the human fear of famine. Individuals who starve themselves voluntarily evoke both awe and terror; in this sense the power of the anorexic to astonish her friends and the hunger artist to mesmerize his or her spectators are highly parallel. Perhaps this response is limited to food-abundant cultures, in which the spectre both of obesity and of the waste of resources become prominent. Many anorexics in fact identify explicitly with the "wretched of the earth," and their food refusal becomes a token of rebellion against the values and attitudes of middle-class affluence. For the vast majority, though, these ideas are typically not translated into political action; rather, they remain as justifications for an exclusively personal rebellion.

The unfortunate projection of a heroic mythology onto anorexia nervosa is reminiscent of Sontag's discussion of the status of tubercu-

losis in nineteenth-century Europe. In *Illness as Metaphor,* Sontag
points out that tuberculosis was a quintessential romantic symbol,
carrying such meanings as refinement, sensitivity, a higher nature.[43] In
comparison, one thinks of one group of psychiatrists who characterized their anorexic patients as "pale, angel-faced gamins."[44] Interestingly, tuberculosis also was a disease of the young, which often resulted
in death. In the nineteenth century, the symbolism of death was
centrally linked with romantic ideology of aestheticism and sensitivity.
In addition, like anorexia nervosa, tuberculosis was a disease of thinness (albeit involuntary, in the case of tuberculosis), with the wan
appearance of the consumptive carrying the significance of aristocratic
sensitivity and refinement.[45] The consumptive body "burned itself
up" or "wasted away with passion"; and yet, this imagery was one of
essentially passive vulnerability. Similar meanings may have been attached to the thinness sought by nineteenth-century anorexics.[46] Over
the course of the twentieth century, however, the connotations of
thinness seem to have changed. As noted above, contemporary
anorexics are noted for their heroic exercise, their self-discipline, their
"control." Such imagery seems more appropriate to competitive societies, in which a changing female role has placed a new emphasis on
female activity and achievement.

Although anorexia may be glamorized and romanticized, particularly in its earlier stages, the disorder eventually evokes reactions of
horror, shock, and revulsion. Indeed, what is initially a hyperaffirmation
of cultural demands ultimately turns into a hateful parody (the "antisocial social behavior" described by Devereux). Not only is it frightening,
but there is something distinctly hostile and intimidating about the
emaciation of the anorexic, as if she were somehow saying to the world
"You want me to be thin, I'll show you what thin is." It has been
pointed out that many anorexics are involved in caricature, in mockery,
in impersonation, typically directed at members of the immediate family.[47] But the anorexic's grotesquely reduced body can also be seen as
an implicit critique of the absurdity of the cultural obsession with body
shape. Just as the hysteric's bodily gyrations and pantomimes were a
kind of parody of nineteenth-century images of female sexuality (Charcot called them "les attitudes passionelles"), so the anorexic's emaciation serves as a kind of caricature of modern culture's unrealistic demands
for thinness. From this standpoint, it could be said that one of the
cultural functions of anorexia has been the provocation of a discourse

about the hazards of dieting, just as hysteria in a sense provoked a critique of sexual repression.[48]

In the 1990s, the glorification of extreme thinness seems to have undergone something of a decline. In an era haunted by the spectre of AIDS, wasting diseases of any type may have lost a great deal of their lustre. Also, as anorexia nervosa has become better known either through the mass media or direct personal experience, its negative aspects, particularly its potential chronicity and lethality, seem to have become more central in the way people view the disorder. It is possible that familiarity with anorexia nervosa may lead people to be more hesitant about such practices as starvation dieting, and this in turn may lead to a decline in its prevalence.[49]

Ethnic disorders, as Devereux suggested, always involve social negativism, rebellion. The negative reactions provoked by an anorexic patient can partly be seen by her refusal to cooperate and conform with normative social expectations. By starving herself, the anorexic totally rejects the ultimate tokens of affluence and success – plentiful food. Nothing could be a greater affront to a middle-class family's pride in the fruits of its efforts, particularly given the role that food typically plays in these families.[50] Also, anorexics typically are accused of "refusing to grow up" or "refusing to be a woman," the latter being the classic formulation of the earlier psychoanalytic literature. But, as feminist writers have pointed out, such a formulation, while perhaps literally true, is implicitly judgmental, in that it accepts normal femininity as unproblematic.[51]

Nevertheless, in clinical contexts, there is no question that anorexics can be the most provocative and even intimidating patients. The resulting anxiety, frustration, and anger have often provoked extreme countermeasures in treatment, a response that can have disastrous consequences. The imagery of battle and power struggle that surrounds the history of the treatment of anorexic patients is reflected in the following call to arms by a noted English psychiatrist:

> When encountered in its extreme form, these patients are formidable adversaries, giving and expecting no mercy. The doctor may well falter and quail, compromising with them, and in effect allowing them to dominate their treatment and continue their downward path unchecked. To succeed with these patients a doctor must be as ruthless as they are, confine them to bed and force them to obey.[52]

The game that anorexic patients play with death is the ultimate stimulus for drastic medical intervention. Doctors find themselves in the position in which the ultimate responsibility of the physician – that of preserving life – is challenged by a patient who typically stubbornly refuses intervention and claims that she is "just fine." The situation is inevitably complicated by the perplexing question about the extent to which the patient's starvation is voluntary.[53] Anorexics are notorious among hospital staff for their deceitful and manipulative behavior, which includes finding all sorts of ingenious ways of disposing of food, filling their pockets with weights or drinking large amounts of water prior to weighing, secretly doing pushups in their rooms, despite admonitions to the contrary. Perhaps it is this combination of intractability and deceitfulness that accounts for the nightmarish list of psychiatric austerities in the earlier history of the treatment of anorexia: forced tube feeding, electroshock, even leucotomy. Even the more benign and less invasive techniques of behavior modification, which have reported a high success rate in promoting short-term weight gain, came under fire by writers such as Bruch, who argued that any technique that deprives a patient of her sense of autonomy undermines progress in the long run.[54]

The power struggles and contentiousness that characterize the treatment relationships between the anorexic patient and her doctors are somewhat reminiscent of the rancorous relationship between the hysterical patient and her Victorian physician.[55] In the case of anorexia nervosa, as in hysteria, there may often be a subtext, an undertone, of sexual politics, a struggle between the authoritative male physician and the rebellious (although ultimately powerless) female patient. This is not to say that only female therapists should treat anorexics, since they too can easily become enmeshed in control issues.[56] The point is that as long as the treatment situation is defined in terms of a power struggle and an effort by the doctor to overwhelm and subdue the disease, it is bound to fail. "Getting the anorexic to eat," whether by forced feeding or by the more subtle tactics of behavior modification programs, is never a sufficient treatment in and of itself. What is critical is a full appreciation of the anorexic's ambivalent feelings about control, what Lawrence has called the "control paradox." As Lawrence points out, the anorexic is typically viewed as overemphasizing control; but what is typically unappreciated by such a view is that she also feels profoundly out of control, powerless.[57] It is of course the ultimate irony that a disease that grows out of a sense of personal weakness and external domination in the family ultimately replicates the struggle for control on the stage of the treatment situation.

In the present climate, the politics of treatment may also lead the therapist to err in the opposite direction. Therapists who approach the treatment of anorexia nervosa through a strong feminist framework may perceive (and perhaps identify with) the patient as a victim of societal oppression. This may in turn lead to a dogged "hands-off" attitude towards the patient's eating and weight-related behavior. Such an approach, presumably justified by the ethics of non-interference, can sometimes lead to a dangerous neglect of the hazardous consequences of low body weight. In addition, all therapists, whether male or female, must examine their own attitudes towards shape and weight, which are inevitably culturally influenced. There may be a tacit sanction of a weight that is lower than what is healthy for the patient, or (and this can particularly be a problem for female therapists) competitive feelings about the patient's body weight.

In an enlightening discussion of the dynamics of power in the thera-peutic relationship, Angelique Sallas suggests that the most important first step in treatment is to communicate clearly to the patient that the therapist is to change only the symptom.[58] It is critical for the therapist to convey to the patient the idea that her search for control is valid; it is only the means that she has chosen that are ineffective, and self-defeat-ing. No effective treatment of the eating disorders can ignore the symptom, which has such destructive and potentially life-threatening consequences. If an anorexic patient is about to starve to death, there is little point in attempting psychotherapy. In fact drastic medical inter-vention, for example in the form of intravenous hyperalimentation, may be the only viable alternative. However, without an appreciation of the patient's sense of powerlessness and search for self-esteem, treat-ment is doomed to failure from the outset.

The Politics of Bulimia

A curious fact is that while bulimia is probably far more prevalent than anorexia nervosa, it has received much less popular attention than ano-rexia nervosa, and when the subject does come up, it is often an object of fun. The behavior was satirized in an episode of *Saturday Night Live*, and stand-up comics have derided the existence of bulimia in a world in which people are starving. Bulimia is viewed as self-indulgent behavior (not to mention disgusting), and it is implicitly assumed that binge eating or vomiting are completely under voluntary control. What is more, given the general competitiveness surrounding the issue of weight control, the bulimic's practice of "eating her cake and heaving it too" is viewed as a form of cheating. In contrast with the perception of rigorous self-discipline, for which the anorexic is admired, bulimics therefore tend to be disdained and misunderstood. Negative attitudes towards bulimics are unfortunately shared by some clinicians. Among these was the otherwise impeccably objective Hilde Bruch, who lamented the passing of classical anorexia nervosa and the ascendancy of bulimia:

> They make an exhibitionistic display of their lack of control or discipline, in contrast to the adherence to discipline of the true anorexics . . . . The modern bulimic is impressive by what looks like a deficit in the sense of responsibility. Bulimics blame their symptoms on others; they may name the person from whom they "learned" to binge, in particular those who introduced them to vomiting . . . from then on, they behave as completely helpless victims. Though relatively uninvolved, they expect to share in the prestige of anorexia nervosa. Some complain about the expense of their consumption and will take food without paying for it. They explain this as due to "kleptomania," which indicates, like "bulimia," an irresistible compulsion that determines their behavior.[59]

Bruch's attitude towards bulimics appears to be somewhat harsh. Of course, it is true that the bulimic is much more impulsive than the ascetic, restricting anorexic. But this is not a moral flaw, something deserving of condemnation. The impulsiveness of bulimics also seems to coincide with cultural changes, in that contemporary society encourages consumption and overeating, and is also more supportive of an undisciplined, impulsive life-style. Bulimic behavior has much more in common with the addictions than it does with the obsessional conscientiousness characteristic of anorexia nervosa. The shift in the wider culture to a more narcissistic and impulsive ethos may have a great deal to do with the ascendancy of bulimia, and the decline of what Bruch calls "true" primary anorexia nervosa.

Because bulimic behavior is viewed either as self-indulgent or as under voluntary control, the seriousness of the problem has tended to be disregarded. In New York State, for example, it is still difficult to obtain insurance coverage for the hospital treatment of bulimia, whereas anorexia nervosa patients will more readily be admitted, particularly if they meet low weight criteria.[60] In a way, the status of bulimia resembles the mostly discarded (but still persistent) stereotypes of alcoholism, which asserted that the behavior is under voluntary control; as such it is interpreted as a moral defect. People often say to the bulimic, "Why don't you just stop?," completely neglecting the possibility that those who have a problem with bulimia have no such ability to quickly relinquish their symptoms with a simple exertion of "will power."

Unlike anorexia, therefore, bulimic behavior is not praised or seen as "special"; quite the contrary. Nevertheless, the bulimic also obtains unwitting reinforcement of her behavior, but by a somewhat different pathway than the anorexic. The bulimic who manages to maintain a low weight is invariably complimented for her thinness. One patient remarked that men began to notice her and respond to her whenever her weight dropped below a certain point. Of course, such a response tends to reinforce not only bingeing and purging activity, but also the secrecy with which the behavior is maintained. Aside from the few that proudly announce their problem, most bulimics feel profound shame and embarrassment about their behavior. The positive social reinforcement for their low weight often places profound practical obstacles that oppose progress in treatment.

When compared with anorexia nervosa, the politics of bulimia represent something of a retreat. Through her extreme thinness, the anorexic makes a public statement, one which is perceived as a protest, a rebellion. The power struggles between the anorexic and those around her testify to the political character of the anorexic symptom. In contrast, the bulimic woman, even after her symptoms have developed, tends to be outwardly compliant and conforming. Her protest has gone underground, so to speak, her anger at her situation secretly discharged through the violence of bingeing and purging rituals. Feminist writers seem to have much more readily identified with the anorexic than the bulimic woman: the anorexic presents a posture of defiance, the bulimic one of capitulation.[61]

However, more attention needs to be paid to the much more pervasive problem of bulimia, which, while perhaps not as immediately life-threatening as anorexia nervosa, carries the potential for serious long-term health problems. From the standpoint of gender, it can be argued that bulimia represents in an especially critical way the difficulty that many women have in achieving the satisfaction of their emotional needs. Food and nourishment are especially linked for women with the idea of caring.[62]

For the bulimic women, the ambivalence about one's own emotional needs that affects women in the wider culture is felt in a particularly poignant way.[63] The "solution" to the problem of identity fashioned by the bulimic is to develop a split between her external facade of self-control and pleasing femaleness, on the one hand, and the neediness, anger, and "messiness" of her kitchen and bathroom rituals, on the other. The delicate balance between the controlled external self and the out-of-control secret self is tenaciously maintained. One of the primary functions of psychotherapy for the bulimic is to provide a relationship in which she can allow herself to be nurtured. Her difficulty in allowing this to happen is precisely why the psychotherapy of bulimics is often characterized by "stops and starts." Group therapies (or less formal support groups) are particularly helpful for bulimics. The sharing of experiences in groups does much to overcome the painful isolation and secrecy in which the bulimic is entrapped. And the identification with other women who have had highly similar social experiences, even though individually diverse, is inherently empowering.[64]

Eating Disorders and the Politics of Fashion

Perhaps through the work of psychologists who have exposed the cultural roots of eating disorders, anorexia nervosa and bulimia are strongly linked in the public's mind with images of thin women in fashion and entertainment industries.[65] And among these, the fashion industry has come under particular fire for its role in fueling the mania for thinness. The issue came to a head in the 1990s both in England and the United States when the waif supermodels such as Kate Moss burst onto the scene. *British Vogue* reported being inundated with angry letters following the publication of the first spread of pictures of Moss in the early 1990s, one which depicted her in Lolita-like poses that flirted on the borders of child pornography. Large posters of Moss, which adorned New York City bus stops during 1992, were often covered with graffiti by protesters that said "feed me." One group of mental-health workers and parents, calling itself BAM ("Ban

Anorexic Marketing"), organized protests about the marketing of anorexic-like models, including a Sprite model called "The Skeleton," and made the rounds of the major talk-shows in the United States in 1994.

Stung by the criticism, fashion writers attempted to respond through a series of articles on the subject of eating disorders. A piece in *Harper's Bazaar*, which focused specifically on waif supermodels, suggested that perhaps the critics were only envious of Kate Moss's natural thinness.[66] Moss herself has always insisted that she has no eating disorder, and that in fact she loves to eat ice cream. "These models eat like horses" is a common description in the fashion press of the eating behavior of waifs. Of course these rather lame defenses miss the point. The debate is not about whether this or that supermodel has an eating disorder, but rather the impact of relentlessly promoting these perhaps uniquely proportioned individuals as the ideal. The "sour grapes" argument concocted by *Harper's Bazaar* is really another form of the old saw about feminists being unattractive. Young adolescents are among the most avid consumers of the images in fashion magazines, and any health care professional who works with teenagers with eating disorders can attest to the fact that these images are influential. To ward off the fact that one may be promoting potentially toxic images with the argument that the model herself is healthy is hardly an adequate response.

A later piece in *Vogue* took a more subtle tack.[67] *Vogue* seized on doubts within the professional community itself that "the media" play a causal role in eating disorders. Such questions have arisen, in this author's view, for at least two reasons. First, it is extraordinarily difficult to demonstrate the impact of global factors such as advertising imagery on the development of psychological disorders in individuals, and the impact is not a simple causal one in any case. An analogy may help here. While both alcohol and cigarettes have been massively marketed in the past, only a minority of individuals who have been exposed to such marketing will develop alcoholism or tobacco addiction. Few outside the alcohol and tobacco industries would argue against the notion that alcohol or cigarette advertising plays a role in the development of addiction (this is a principal reason why such advertising has been subjected to stringent legal limits), and yet virtually no one would make a simple causal argument about the influence of "the media" when it comes to these substances. I would suggest that the promotion of dieting and thinness in advertising be understood in a parallel fashion. Some individuals, in response, may attempt dieting, but such a project will typically be self-limiting and that will be the end of it. For others, though, who are predisposed for other reasons, the impact of thinness imagery may be quite toxic, even lethal.

In addition to emphasizing the individual factors that cause eating disorders, *Vogue* brought up testimony of anorexic patients who deny that the media played any role in the development of their condition. The thrust of the comments of one of these was that "it was my own fault and only I have the responsibility to fix it." Fair enough, but again such statements are somewhat beside the point. Of course, recovery from an eating disorder is ultimately one's personal responsibility (although the capacity to resist the imagery with which one is inundated may be a component of the strengths that one acquires), but such facts do not exonerate the fashion media from actively fostering a climate that mesmerizes the public with a narrow and unrealistic body ideal.

Fashion insists that it is not a public trust but a business, and of course one cannot argue with the latter point. Nevertheless, so are the alcohol and tobacco industries, but this has not prevented their regulation because of the health threats posed by their products. Perhaps the causal linkage between fashion images and eating disorders is mediated by too complex a chain of events and therefore can never be isolated to the same extent as the influence of toxic substances. Despite the fact that the fashion industry is in a position to do what it wants, it does, like any other industry, have a public responsibility with regard to the safety of its products. Perhaps, also, in the absence of self-regulation by fashion, economic and demographic forces will themselves bring about change. Specifically, recent reports suggest an attempt on the part of a number of designers to market clothes to a broader spectrum of adolescents, including those of larger sizes.[68] Such a shift is an obvious response of the marketplace to the demographic reality that the average weight of adolescents has in fact increased. But it has also been suggested that the pervasiveness of eating disorders education in health curricula in the public schools has had some impact on the destigmatization of heavier children.

Eating Disorders and Female Empowerment

Perhaps the ultimate irony is that, to quote Minuchin, "in a society in which the new woman's consciousness promises a change in the relationship between the sexes, we are seeing more and more anorectics."[69] Ironic, indeed. According to Kim Chernin, the contradiction is not accidental, but rather represents a situation in which the female role is indeed changing, but, perhaps in response, the patriarchal ideals of body size are imposed ever more insistently. Indeed, as Chernin points out, contemporary female consciousness itself is polarized into two camps. The first, that of feminism, utilizes such metaphors as the "expansion" of consciousness, the "enlargement" of female possibilities, the "widening" of female horizons; while the second, the culture of dieting, speaks of "reduction," of "narrowing," of becoming "smaller." Chernin suggests that the marketing of the thinness ideal reflects a conspiratorial effort to keep women in their place, in a period in which female assertiveness threatens the perpetuation of male control. But, as she herself points out, women can also be seen as colluding in their own oppression, as most (and especially anorexics or bulimics) have internalized the misogynistic hatred of female fatness.[70]

A similar, if less psychologically sophisticated, argument was put forward by Naomi Wolf in her widely read book *The Beauty Myth*.[71] Wolf insists that the enormous growth in the various industries that sell products that presumably enhance female beauty is almost perfectly coincident with rise of the women's movement since the 1960s. According to Wolf, the marketing of extreme thinness is only one component of a much broader assault on women's consciousness by an industry that is determined to divert their thinking from more relevant issues about themselves. The hidden agenda of the beauty industry, therefore, is the control and ultimately the enslavement of women. Wolf writes in an impassioned style and on at least one level her argument hits home. It does seem that the marketing of beauty products entices women, especially young women, to focus too much of their productive energies on perfecting their physical appearance, and this of course includes the issue of weight. However, it is somewhat doubtful that the rise of the multinational beauty industry reflects a conspiracy on the part of anxious males to keep women in their place. The beauty industry rose to multinational status at the same time as the entertainment industry (films, movies, recordings), the computer industry, and pharmaceutical industries. Is the preoccupation of boys with video games, for example, an attempt on the part of the game-makers to keep boys in their place? I doubt it. Nevertheless, as Wolf suggests, there is something problematic about the way in which female adolescents are led to place too much emphasis on their appearance, and as I have argued in this book, there is at least something retrograde about the cult of thinness in particular.

The politics of eating disorders ultimately revolves around the politics of gender. The contemporary epidemic of these conditions is a reflection of the ambiguities of female identity in a period of change and confusion. Perhaps as women are able to achieve real power in the world, and the size and shape of their bodies are no longer taken to be the true measure of their worth, eating disorders will sharply decline in incidence. Already, at the century's end, there is speculation that the crest of the wave of eating disorders has passed. But given the ongoing relentless cultural preoccupations with shape, weight, and identity, it is difficult to foresee a future in which symptoms that revolve around the control of the female body will disappear. Undoubtedly, a century from now, eating disorders and our current preoccupation with them will appear as quaint as nineteenth-century hysteria appears to us now. But who knows what other vocabulary of discomfort will take their place?

Notes

Preface to the Second Edition

1 D. H. Barlow and V. M. Durand, *Abnormal Psychology: An Integrative Approach*, 2nd edn (Boston: Brooks/Cole, 1999), p. 237.

Chapter One   Culture and Psychopathology

1 E. H. Erikson, *Life History and the Historical Moment* (New York: W. W. Norton, 1975), p. 22.
2 For a discussion of the central role of hysteria in nineteenth-century psychiatry, see G. Drinka, *The Birth of Neurosis* (New York: Simon and Schuster, 1984), ch. 4; I. Veith, *Hysteria: History of a Disease* (Chicago: University of Chicago Press, 1965); and H. Ellenberger, *The Discovery of the Unconscious* (New York: Basic Books, 1970).
3 Veith, *Hysteria*, chs 1 and 2.
4 J. Goldstein, "The hysteria diagnosis and the politics of anticlericalism in late nineteenth century France," *Journal of Modern History*, 54 (1982), pp. 209–39.
5 J. Breuer and S. Freud, *Studies in Hysteria*, first published 1896 (New York: Pelican Books, 1974).
6 T. Szasz, *The Second Sin* (New York: Anchor Books, 1974), p. 105.
7 The diagnosis (or at least the terminology) of hysteria has itself been banished from the diagnostic nomenclature, for good reason. The term "hysteria" is derived from the Greek word for "uterus," suggesting the ancient historical association of hysteria with women. This etiological significance of the uterus was not put to rest until the nineteenth century, with the emergence of the new clinical theories of Freud and Janet. The contemporary diagnostic system, as represented by the DSM-III and DSM-IV, substitutes the terminology of "conversion disorder," which is

itself considered a suspect derivative of early psychoanalytic concepts of the conversion of emotional into physical energy. Conversion disorders are considered to be quite rare in Western cultures, and contemporary research on these conditions is virtually non-existent. In a unique account, however, Elaine Showalter has proposed that conversion disorders are still pervasive, but present in dramatically different forms than their nineteenth-century predecessors. Specifically, Showalter suggests that such diverse conditions as multiple personality disorder, chronic fatigue syndrome, Gulf War Syndrome, and what has been called "false memory syndrome" are all variants on hysteria. What unifies all these "hystories" is a narrative of personal distress that cannot be expressed or legitimized through direct verbalization, but generate a "following" because they are stories that dramatize the common problems of certain social groups. Showalter's account is provocative, but it is doubtful that such a broad grouping of what is an extremely heterogeneous group of problems will have clinical utility. A further problem is that some of these conditions, such as Gulf War Syndrome and chronic fatigue syndrome, may turn out to have demonstrable physical causes, while others (e.g., multiple personality, false memory syndrome) quite obviously have no physical source. See E. Showalter, *Hystories: Hysterical Epidemics and Modern Media* (New York: Columbia University Press, 1997).

8   See W. W. Gull, "Anorexia nervosa," *Transactions of the Clinical Society (London)*, 7 (1874), pp. 22–8, reprinted in *Evolution of Psychosomatic Concepts. Anorexia Nervosa: A Paradigm*, ed. R. M. Kaufman and M. Heiman (New York: International Universities Press, 1964), pp. 132–8; C. Lasegue, "De L'Anorexie Hysterique," *Archives Generale de Medicine*, 385 (1873); also reprinted in Kaufman and Heiman, *Evolution of Psychosomatic Concepts*, pp. 141–55.

9   Historical discussions of a pattern of self-starvation in medieval women in many ways similar to anorexia are contained in R. Bell, *Holy Anorexia* (Chicago: University of Chicago Press, 1985); and C. Bynum, *Holy Feast and Holy Fast: The Religious Significance of Food to Medieval Women* (Berkeley: University of California Press, 1987). The "fasting girls" that appeared in the seventeenth through nineteenth centuries, who also may have been the antecedents of modern anorexics, are discussed in J. J. Brumberg, *Fasting Girls: The Emergence of Anorexia Nervosa as a Modern Disease* (Cambridge, MA: Harvard University Press, 1988).

10 A point made by Hilde Bruch in an excellent review of the pre-1970 literature. See Bruch, *Eating Disorders: Obesity, Anorexia Nervosa and the Person Within* (New York: Basic Books, 1973), ch. 9.

11 The first American paper on normal-weight bulimia was that of M. Boskind-Lodahl, "Cinderella's stepsisters: A feminist perspective on anorexia

nervosa and bulimia," *Signs: The Journal of Women in Culture and Society*, 2 (1976), pp. 342–56. It was followed by a seminal English publication by G. F. M. Russell, "Bulimia nervosa: An ominous variant of anorexia nervosa," *Psychological Medicine*, 9 (1979), pp. 429–48.

12 "Eating binges," *Time*, 116 (1980), pp. 94; "Eating their cake and heaving it too," *McCleans*, 83 (1980), pp. 51–2; "A subtler relative of anorexia is gathering victims," *New York Times*, Jan. 25, 1981, p. C1.

13 Russell, "Bulimia nervosa."

14 Bruch, *Eating Disorders*. Actually, psychiatric interest in eating disorders was beginning to grow in the 1960s, although eating disorders were still virtually unknown to the public. An international symposium was held in Germany in the mid-1960s, which was attended by Bruch as well as clinicians from various European countries as well as Japan.

15 An appreciative biography of Bruch by the wife of her nephew was published in 1996. See J. H. Bruch, *Unlocking the Golden Cage: An Intimate Biography of Hilde Bruch* (Carlsbad, CA: Gurze Books, 1996).

16 H. Bruch, *The Golden Cage* (New York: Vintage, 1978). Written in a highly lucid, direct and yet elegant style, this book is virtually required reading for any beginning student of anorexia nervosa and contains many clinical insights that are still highly pertinent. Bruch had begun to incoporate some of the new insights about the implications of the psychology of starvation and its implications for anorexia nervosa. She also formulated the multidimensional approach to treatment that has become the norm. The approach to individual psychotherapy that she describes is the foundation of a more cognitive approach to these patients, emphasizing correction of patients' erroneous thinking about food, weight, and self. Its major limitation is that it reflects a rather class-bound patient base, but this may have been reflective of the demographics of eating disorders at the time as well as Bruch's position as a consultant of international stature.

17 G. F. M. Russell, "The changing nature of anorexia nervosa: An introduction to the conference," *Journal of Psychiatric Research*, 19 (1985), pp. 101–9.

18 The Renfrew Center. See "Eating disorders: New treatments," *New York Times*, Sept. 2, 1985, p. 22.

19 During the 1980s eating disorders became one of the most significant health issues for contemporary students and have been the target of prevention studies funded by insurance companies. Support groups for students with eating disorders proliferated. See, for example, E. Greene, "Support groups for students with eating disorders," *Chronicle of Higher Education*, March 5, 1986, pp. 1, 30. Also, see L. C. Whitaker and W. M. Davis (eds), *The Bulimic College Student: Evaluation, Treatment, and*

Prevention (New York: The Hayworth Press, 1989.

20 See D. M. Garner and P. E. Garfinkel (eds), *Handbook of Psychotherapy for Anorexia Nervosa and Bulimia* (New York: Guilford Press, 1985) for a valuable collection of works by some of the major figures in the field. A second and updated edition appeared in 1997: D. M. Garner and P. E. Garfinkel (eds), *Handbook of Treatment for Eating Disorders*, 2nd edn (New York: Guilford Press).

21 The impact of diminishing economic resources, particularly under the managed care practices of the US health care system, have been eloquently discussed in an article by Susan Wooley. See S. Wooley, "Managed care and mental health: The silencing of a profession," *International Journal of Eating Disorders*, 14 (1993), pp. 387–402.

22 P. Bart, "Social structure and vocabularies of discomfort: What happened to female hysteria?" *Journal of Health and Social Behavior*, 9 (1968), pp. 189–93.

23 Among Devereux's more important works were *Mohave Psychiatry and Suicide: The Psychiatric Disturbances of an Indian Tribe* (Washington, DC: Smithsonian Institution Press, 1961); *From Anxiety to Method in the Behavioral Sciences* (Paris and the Hague: Mouton, 1967); *Ethnopsychoanalysis: Psychoanalysis and Anthropology as Complementary Frames of Reference* (Berkeley: University of California Press, 1978).

24 G. Devereux, "Normal and abnormal" and "Schizophrenia: An ethnic psychosis, or schizophrenia without tears," in *Basic Problems of Ethnopsychiatry* (Chicago: University of Chicago Press, 1980), pp. 3–71 and 214–36.

25 The term culture-bound syndrome was originally invented by the psychiatrist P. M. Yap (see "Mental diseases peculiar to certain cultures: A survey of comparative psychiatry," *Journal of Mental Science*, 97 (1951), pp. 313–27) and a literature on the subject developed that has been somewhat on the periphery of mainstream psychiatry. A more recent collection of essays on these disorders is given in R. C. Simons and C. C. Hughes (eds), *The Culture-bound Syndromes: Folk Illnesses of Psychiatric and Anthropological Interest* (Dordrecht, Holland: D. Reidel Publishing Company, 1985).

26 In recognition of the significance of culture-bound syndromes, the DSM-IV (1994) has included an appendix with an "Outline for Cultural Formulation and Glossary of Culture-Bound Syndromes." The DSM authors note that "some disorders have been conceptualized as culture-bound syndromes specific to industrialized culture (e.g., Anorexia Nervosa, Dissociative Identity Disorder), given their apparent rarity or absence in other cultures" (American Psychiatric Association, DSM-IV: *Diagnostic and Statistical Manual of Mental Disorders* (Washington, DC: American Psychiatric Association, 1994), p. 844. Generally, however,

the DSM approach to diagnosis has been criticized for being overly parochial and neglectful of cultural context (see, for example, G. Valliant, "The disadvantages of the DSM-III outweigh its advantages," *American Journal of Psychiatry*, 141 (1984), pp. 542–5). Perhaps the relegation of cultural issues to an appendix of the DSM-IV is reflective of this trend.

27 For a general discussion of the *Amok* syndrome, see the essays in Simons and Hughes (eds), *The Culture-bound Syndromes*, pp. 197–264.

28 J. Teoh, "The changing psychopathology of *Amok*," *Psychiatry*, 35 (1972), pp. 345–51.

29 J. E. Carr, "Ethno-behaviorism and the culture-bound syndromes: The case of Amok," in Simons and Hughes, *The Culture-bound Syndromes*, pp. 199–223.

30 J. E. Carr, in "Ethno-behaviorism," p. 202.

31 E. Tan, "Amok: Its worldwide occurrence," summarized in *Transcultural Psychiatric Research Review*, 26 (1989), pp. 137–40.

32 P. M. Yap, "Koro: A culture-bound depersonalization syndrome," *British Journal of Psychiatry*, 111 (1965), pp. 43–50. A number of papers on *Koro* are found in Simons and Hughes (eds), *The Culture-bound Syndromes*, pp. 151–96. Relatively recent *Koro* epidemics, from the 1960s through the 1980s, have been described in India, China, Singapore, and Thailand.

33 A. N. Chowdhury, "Koro in females: An analysis of 48 cases," *Transcultural Psychiatric Research Review*, 31 (1994), pp. 369–80.

34 Bartholomew, however, has suggested that the social epidemics of *Koro* have little to do with psychopathology, but rather should be understood as collective delusions. See R. E. Bartholomew, "The medicalization of exotic deviance: A sociological perspective on epidemic Koro," *Transcultural Psychiatry*, 35 (1998), pp. 5–38.

35 C. Smith-Rosenberg, "The hysterical woman: Sex roles in 19th century America," *Social Research*, 39 (1972), pp. 652–78.

36 S. Freud, "'Civilized' sexual morality and modern nervousness," *Sexuality and the Psychology of Love*, ed. P. Reiff (New York: Macmillan, 1963).

37 Ellenberger, *The Discovery of the Unconscious*.

38 An argument formulated in E. Showalter, *The Female Malady: Women, Madness, and English Culture, 1830–1980* (New York: Pantheon Books, 1985). The idea of hysteria as proto-feminism originated in a fascinating paper by D. Hunter, "Hysteria, psychoanalysis, and feminism: The case of Anna O," *Feminist Studies*, 9 (1983), pp. 465–88.

39 G. A. Devereux, "A sociological theory of schizophrenia," in *Basic Problems of Ethnopsychiatry*, pp. 185–213. Devereux's speculations on this issue were borne out, although interpreted quite differently, in a wide-

ranging epidemiological survey by the biologically oriented psychiatrist E. Fuller Torrey. See E. F. Torrey, *Schizophrenia and Civilization* (New York: Brunner Mazel, 1979).

40 For a review of the WHO study and related findings, see A. Jablensky, "Schizophrenia: The epidemiological horizon," in *Schizophrenia*, ed. S. R. Hirsch and D. R. Weinberger (Oxford: Blackwell Scientific, 1995), pp. 206–52. The data on New Guinea are given in E. F. Torrey, R. R. Torrey, and R. R. Peterson, "The epidemiology of Schizophrenia in Papua, New Guinea," *American Journal of Psychiatry*, 131 (1974), pp. 567–73.

41 R. D. Laing, *The Politics of Experience* (New York: Random House, 1967).

Chapter Two   Eating Disorders

1 R. Morton, *Phthisiologica: Or a Treatise on Consumptions* (London, 1689). Morton's work and life are discussed further in S. Bhanji and V. B. Newton, "Richard Morton's account of 'nervous consumption,'" *International Journal of Eating Disorders*, 4 (1985), pp. 589–95, and in J. A. Silverman, "Richard Morton, 1637–1698: Limner of anorexia nervosa: A tercentenary essay," *Journal of the American Medical Association*, 250 (1983), pp. 2830–2.

2 The debate over fasting girls is discussed at length in J. J. Brumberg, *Fasting Girls: The Emergence of Anorexia Nervosa as a Modern Disease* (Cambridge, MA: Harvard University Press, 1988), ch. 3. Brumberg sees this controversy in terms of the struggle for credibility between the religious and scientific interpretations of the seemingly "miraculous" behavior of surviving without food. For further discussion of the fasting maidens, see W. Vandereycken and R. van Deth, *From Fasting Saints to Anorexic Girls: The History of Self-Starvation* (New York: New York University Press, 1994).

3 See chapter 1, n. 8.

4 E. Shorter, "The first great increase in anorexia nervosa," *Journal of Social History*, 21 (1987), pp. 69–96. For further discussion of anorexia nervosa in the nineteenth century, see E. Shorter, *From the Mind Into the Body: The Cultural Origins of Psychomatic Symptoms* (New York: The Free Press, 1994), esp. ch. 6.

5 W. Playfair, "Note on the so-called 'anorexia nervosa,' " *Lancet*, April 28, 1888.

6 *The Standard Edition of the Complete Psychological Works of Sigmund Freud*, tr. and ed. James Strachey, vol. 1, *Pre-Psychoanalytic Publications* (London: Hogarth Press, 1953), pp. 200–1.

7 G. de la Tourette, *Traite clinique et therapeutique de l'hysterie*, 3rd edn

(Paris: Plor, Nourit, 1895).

8 J. Dejerine and E. Gaukler, *The Psychoneuroses and their Treatment*, 2nd edn, tr. S. E. Jellife (Philadelphia and London: J. D. Lippincott, 1913).

9 P. Janet, *The Major Symptoms of Hysteria* (London: Macmillan, 1907).

10 J. A. Sours, *Starving to Death in a Sea of Objects* (New York: Jason Aronson, 1979), pp. 209–10.

11 B. Silverstein, B. Peterson, and L. Perdue. "Some correlates of the thin standard of bodily attractiveness for women," *International Journal of Eating Disorders*, 5 (1986), pp. 895–905.

12 J. V. Waller, R. M. Kaufman, and F. Deutsch, "Anorexia nervosa: A psychosomatic entity," *Psychosomatic Medicine*, 2 (1940), pp. 3–16.

13 H. Bruch, *Eating Disorders: Obesity, Anorexia Nervosa and the Person Within* (New York: Basic Books, 1973).

14 H. Bruch, *The Importance of Overweight* (New York: W. W. Norton, 1957).

15 The trend of contemporary thinking is to question the entire notion of thinking about obesity as a primary psychiatric disorder, the latter having reached the height of its popularity in the 1950s. The strongest critique of the "obesity-as-a-neurosis" argument has been put forth by Susan C. Wooley and O. Wayne Wooley. See, for example, S. C. Wooley and O. W. Wooley, "Should obesity be treated at all?," in *Eating and Its Disorders*, ed. A. J. Stunkard and E. Stellar (New York: Raven Press, 1984), pp. 185–93.

16 American Psychiatric Association, *DSM-IV: Diagnostic and Statistical Manual of Mental Disorders* (Washington, DC: American Psychiatric Association, 1994).

17 S. Lee, T. P. Ho, and L. K. G. Hsu, "Fat phobic and non-fat phobic anorexia nervosa: A comparative study of 70 Chinese patients in Hong Kong," *Psychological Medicine*, 23 (1993), pp. 999–1017.

18 B. Silverstein and D. Perlick, *The Cost of Competence: Why Inequality Causes Depression, Eating Disorders and Illness in Women* (New York: Oxford University Press, 1995). See also J. R. Bernporad, "Self-starvation through the ages: Reflections on the prehistory of anorexia nervosa," *International Journal of Eating Disorders*, 19 (1996), pp. 217–38; and M. A. Katzman and S. Lee, "Beyond body image: The integration of feminist and transcultural theories in the understanding of self-starvation," *International Journal of Eating Disorders*, 22 (1997), pp. 385–94.

19 V. F. DiNicola, "Anorexia multiforme: Self-starvation in historical and cultural context," *Transcultural Psychiatric Research Review*, 27 (1990), pp. 245–86.

20 A. H. Crisp, *Anorexia Nervosa: Let Me Be* (London: Academic Press, 1980).

21 American Psychiatric Association, *DSM-III: Diagnostic and Statistical Manual of Mental Disorders* (Washington, DC: American Psychiatric Association, 1980).

22 American Psychiatric Association, *DSM-IV*.

23 Hypothalamic dysfunction in anorexia nervosa has been particularly strongly emphasized by English writers. See, for example, G. F. M. Russell, "The present status of anorexia nervosa," *Psychological Medicine*, 7 (1977), pp. 363–7. For an interesting discussion of the possible relationships between hypothalamic dysfunction and clinical symptoms, see R. C. Casper, "Hypothalamic dysfunction and the symptoms of anorexia nervosa," *Psychiatric Clinics of North America*, 7 (1984), pp. 201–13. Casper argues that hypothalamic involvement is probably implicated in the fact that symptoms such as hyperactivity, body image distortion, euphoria, and a fear of fatness gradually intensify as weight loss progresses. If these symptoms were purely psychological, they would probably precede the disorder, rather than intensify with starvation.

24 See, for example, K. M. Bemis, "Current approaches to the etiology and treatment of anorexia nervosa," *Psychological Bulletin*, 85 (1978), pp. 593–617; P. E. Garfinkel and D. M. Garner, *Anorexia Nervosa: A Multidimensional Approach* (New York: Brunner Mazel, 1982), pp. 103–4.

25 K. A. Halmi, R. C. Casper, E. D. Eckert, S. C. Goldberg, and J. M. Davis, "Unique features associated with the age of onset of anorexia nervosa," *Psychiatric Research*, 1 (1979), pp. 209–15.

26 Garfinkel and Garner, *Anorexia Nervosa*, p. 103.

27 A. J. Hill, E. D. Draper, and J. Stack, "A weight on children's minds: Body shape dissatisfaction at 9-years old," *International Journal of Obesity*, 18 (1994), pp. 383–9; R. Bryant-Waugh and B. Lask, "Annotation: Eating disorders in children," *Journal of Child Psychology and Psychiatry*, 36 (1995), pp. 191–202.

28 In this sense, anorexia nervosa may be seen as an adaptive response to both cultural demands and personal distress. For an illuminating discussion of this point, see C. L. Johnson, R. A. Sansone, and M. C. Chewing, "Good reasons why young women would develop anorexia nervosa: The adaptive context," *Pediatric Annals*, 21 (1992), pp. 731–7.

29 P. Garfinkel and A. S. Kaplan, "Starvation-based perpetuating mechanisms in anorexia nervosa," *International Journal of Eating Disorders*, 4 (1985), pp. 651–67. Casper has suggested that the state of starvation also leads to a high state of behavioral activation, which then becomes highly reinforcing. See R. Casper, "Behavioral activation and lack of concern, core symptoms of anorexia nervosa?," *International Journal of Eating Disorders*, 24 (1998), pp. 381–94. Endorphins have been hypothesized to play a role in the physiological perpetuation of anorexia nervosa, but

the status of this hypothesis is as yet uncertain. See H. F. Huebner, *Endorphins, Eating Disorders and Other Addictive Behaviors* (New York: W. W. Norton, 1993).

30 The analogies between anorexia nervosa and addictions have been made in G. I. Szmuckler and D. Tantam, "Anorexia nervosa: Starvation dependence," *British Journal of Medical Psychology*, 57 (1984), pp. 303–10. See also M. Bachmann and H. Rohr, "A speculative illness model of overeating and anorexia nervosa," *Psychological Reports*, 53 (1983), pp. 831–8; and Huebner, *Endorphins*. Addiction models for eating disorders have been severely criticized, however. For a discussion of some of the problems, see K. Bemis, "'Abstinence' and 'non-abstinence' models for the treatment of bulimia," *International Journal of Eating Disorders*, 4 (1985), pp. 407–38. One especially difficult problem is the question of what the anorexic (or bulimic) person is addicted to. This cannot be food, for then the "cure" would be itself anorexia nervosa. Therefore addiction models require the invocation of such notions as "addiction to starvation," which, while analogous in several respects to the behaviors found in other addiction, is ultimately a metaphor.

31 A. Keys, J. Brozek, A. Henschel, O. Mickelsen, and H. L. Taylor, *The Biology of Human Starvation*, 2 vols (Minneapolis: University of Minnesota Press, 1950).

32 For discussions of the medical complications of anorexia nervosa, see A. S. Kaplan and D. B. Woodside, "Biological aspects of anorexia nervosa and bulimia nervosa," *Journal of Consulting and Clinical Psychology*, 55 (1987), pp. 645–53; D. W. Ploog and K. M. Pirke, "Psychobiology of anorexia nervosa," *Psychological Medicine*, 17 (1987), pp. 843–9; and C. W. Sharp and C. P. L. Freeman, "The medical complications of anorexia nervosa," *British Journal of Psychiatry*, 162 (1993), pp. 452–62.

33 Garfinkel and Garner, *Anorexia Nervosa*, pp. 341–2. A review of studies of mortality rates found that the annual mortality rate of those with anorexia nervosa was 12 times the annual death rate due to all causes for females 14–24 years old in the general population and twice that for female psychiatric inpatients. See P. F. Sullivan, "Mortality in anorexia nervosa," *American Journal of Psychiatry*, 152 (1995), pp. 1073–4.

34 G. F. M. Russell, "The prognosis of eating disorders: A clinician's approach," in *The Course of Eating Disorders: Long-Term Follow-up of Anorexia and Bulimia Nervosa*, ed. W. Herzog, H.-C. Deter, and W. Vandereycken (New York: Springer-Verlag, 1992), pp. 198–213.

35 Suicide accounts for roughly 25 percent of the deaths from chronic anorexia nervosa. See, for example, S. Theander, "Chronicity in anorexia nervosa: Results from the Swedish long-term study," in Herzog, Deter, and Vandereycken, *The Course of Eating Disorders*, pp. 214–28. Sudden

deaths due to circulatory or cardiovascular failure are documented in J. M. Isner, W. C. Roberts, S. B. Heymsfield, and J. Yager, "Anorexia nervosa and sudden death," *Annals of Internal Medicine*, 102 (1985), pp. 49–52.

36 That reduced mortality might be associated with early, aggressive intervention seems to be evident from a 20-year study at St George's Hospital in London, which found a 20-year mortality of treated patients of 4 percent, a figure lower than most other studies. See A. H. Crisp, J. S. Callender, C. Halek, and L. K. G. Hsu, "Long-term mortality in anorexia nervosa: A 20–year follow-up of the St. George's and Aberdeen cohorts," *British Journal of Psychiatry*, 161 (1992), pp. 104–7.

37 A point that is particularly well articulated by A. E. Andersen, C. Morse, and K. Santmyer, "Inpatient treatment for anorexia nervosa," in *Handbook of Psychotherapy for Anorexia Nervosa and Bulimia*, ed. D. M. Garner and P. E. Garfinkel (New York: Guilford, 1985), pp. 311–43.

38 D. M. Garner and K. M. Bernis, "Cognitive therapy for anorexia nervosa," in *Handbook of Psychotherapy for Anorexia Nervosa and Bulimia*, ed. D. M. Garner and P. E. Garfinkel (New York: Guilford Press, 1985), pp. 107–46. A reformulation of the cognitive approach is C. G. Fairburn, R. Shafran, and Z. Cooper, "A cognitive behavioral theory of anorexia nervosa," *Behavior Research and Therapy*, 37 (1999), pp. 1–13. The use of cognitive-behavioral methods in inpatient settings has been described in A. Andersen, W. Bowers, and K. Evans, "Inpatient treatment of anorexia nervosa," in *Handbook of Treatment for Eating Disorders*, ed. D. M. Garner and P. E. Garfinkel (New York: Guilford Press, 1997), pp. 327–48.

39 G. F. M. Russell, G. I. Szmuckler, C. Dare, and I. Eisler, "An evaluation of family therapy in anorexia nervosa and bulimia nervosa," *Archives of General Psychiatry*, 44 (1987), pp. 1047–56. For a five-year followup, see I. Eisler, C. Dare, G. F. M. Russell, G. Szmuckler, D. le Grange, and E. Dodge, "Family and individual therapy in anorexia nervosa: A 5-year follow-up," *Archives of General Psychiatry*, 54 (1997), pp. 1025–30.

40 A. H. Crisp, "Anorexia nervosa as a flight from growth: Assessment and treatment based on the model," in Garner and Garfinkel, *Handbook of Treatment for Eating Disorders*, pp. 248–77.

41 H. Bruch, *The Golden Cage* (New York: Vintage, 1978), ch. 5.

42 An early review of outcome studies, with a discussion of the problems in recovery criteria, is given in L. K. G. Hsu, "The outcome of anorexia nervosa: A review of the literature (1954 to 1978)," *Archives of General Psychiatry*, 37 (1980), pp. 1041–6. A more recent review by the same author is L. K. G. Hsu, "Critique of follow-up studies," in *Psychobiology and Treatment of Anorexia Nervosa and Bulimia Nervosa*, ed. K. A. Halmi

(Washington, DC: American Psychiatric Press, 1992), pp. 125–50.

43 E. D. Eckert, K. A. Halmi, P. Marchi, W. Grove, and R. Crosby, "Ten-year follow-up of anorexia nervosa: Clinical course and outcome," *Psychological Medicine*, 25 (1995), pp. 143–56.

44 N. A. Rigotti, S. R. Nussbaum, D. B. Herzog, and R. M. Neer, "Osteoporosis in women with anorexia nervosa," *The New England Journal of Medicine*, 311 (1984), pp. 1601–5. N. A. Rigotti, R. M. Neer, C. J. Skates, D. B. Herzog, and S. R. Nussbaum, "The clinical course of osteoporosis in anorexia nervosa," *Journal of the American Medical Association*, 265 (1991), pp. 1133–8. A. E. Andersen, P. J. Woodward, and N. LaFrance, "Bone mineral density in eating disorder subgroups," *International Journal of Eating Disorders*, 18 (1995), pp. 335–42.

45 A. Ward, N. Brown, and J. Treasure, "Persistent osteopenia after recovery from anorexia nervosa," *International Journal of Eating Disorders*, 22 (1997), pp. 71–4. Similar findings were reported in B. Siemers, Z. Chakmakjian, and B. Gench, "Bone density patterns in women with anorexia nervosa," *International Journal of Eating Disorders*, 19 (1996), pp. 179–86.

46 An extremely poignant and informative account of the experience of families is given in B. P. Kinoy, *When Will We Laugh Again? Living and Dealing with Anorexia Nervosa and Bulimia* (New York: Columbia University Press, 1984).

47 L. K. G. Hsu, A. H. Crisp, and J. S. Callender, "Recovery in anorexia nervosa: The patient's perspective," *International Journal of Eating Disorders*, 11 (1992), pp. 341–50.

48 For an extensive review, see Garfinkel and Garner, *Anorexia Nervosa*, ch. 4 ("Hypothalamic and Pituary Function"); also, an excellent collection of papers is contained in K. M. Pirke and D. Ploog, *The Psychobiology of Anorexia Nervosa* (New York: Springer-Verlag, 1984). See also the various papers cited in n. 32 above. For a discussion of the impact of anorexia nervosa on neurotransmitter function, see M. Fava, P. M. Copeland, U. Schweiger, and D. Herzog, "Neurochemical abnormalities of anorexia nervosa and bulimia nervosa," *American Journal of Psychiatry*, 146 (1989), pp. 963–71.

49 Garfinkel and Garner, *Anorexia Nervosa*, ch. 4. An issue of particular concern, however, that has emerged in recent research is the possibility of enlarged brain ventricles and reduced gray matter, effects that persist after recovery. See, for example, E. K. Lambe, D. K. Katzman, D. J. Mikulis, S. H. Kennedy, and R. B. Zipursky, "Cerebral gray matter volume deficits after weight recovery from anorexia nervosa," *Archives of General Psychiatry*, 54 (1997), pp. 537–42.

50 A. J. Holland, N. Sicotte, and J. Treasure, "Anorexia nervosa: Evidence for

a genetic basis," *Journal of Psychosomatic Research*, 32 (1988), pp. 561–71.

51 P. J. V. Beumont, "Endocrine function in magersucht disorders," in Pirke and Ploog, *The Psychobiology of Anorexia Nervosa*, p. 121.

52 Garfinkel and Garner, *Anorexia Nervosa*, pp. 21–2.

53 D. P. Cantwell, S. Sturzenberger, J. Burroughs, B. Salkin, and J. K. Green, "Anorexia nervosa: An affective disorder?," *Archives of General Psychiatry*, 34 (1977), pp. 1087–93. E. S. Gershon, J. R. Hamovit, J. L. Schreiber, E. D. Dibble, W. H. Kaye, J. I. Nurnberger, A. Andersen, and M. H. Ebert, "Anorexia nervosa and affective disorders associated in families," in *Childhood Psychopathology and Development*, ed. S. B. Guze (New York: Raven Press, 1983), pp. 279–86.

54 M. Strober and J. Katz, "Do eating disorders and affective disorders share a common etiology? A dissenting opinion," *International Journal of Eating Disorders*, 6 (1987), pp. 171–80.

55 A. H. Crisp, *Anorexia Nervosa*.

56 A. L. Deep, L. M. Nagy, T. E. Weltzin, R. Rao, and W. H. Kaye "Premorbid onset of psychopathology in long-term recovered anorexia nervosa," *International Journal of Eating Disorders*, 17 (1995), pp. 291–8.

57 M. D. Schwalberg, D. A. H. Barlow, S. Alger, and L. Howard, "Comparison on bulimics, obese binge eaters, social phobics and individuals with panic disorder on comorbidity across DSM-III-R anxiety disorders," *Journal of Abnormal Psychology*, 101 (1992), pp. 675–81.

58 H. D. Palmer and M. S. Jones, "Anorexia nervosa as a manifestation of compulsive neurosis: A study of psychogenic factors," *Archives of Neurology and Psychiatry*, 41 (1939), pp. 856–60.

59 A. Rothenberg, "Eating disorder as a modern obsessive-compulsive syndrome," *Psychiatry*, 49 (1986), pp. 45–53.

60 W. H. Kaye, T. Weltzin, and L. K. G. Hsu, "Anorexia nervosa," in *Obsessive-Compulsive-Related Disorders*, ed. E. H. Hollander (Washington, DC: American Psychiatric Press, 1993), pp. 49–70.

61 A. Thiel, A. Broocks, M. Ohlmeier, G. E. Jacoby, and G. Schussler, "Obsessive-compulsive disorder among patients with anorexia nervosa and bulimia," *American Journal of Psychiatry*, 152 (1995), pp. 72–75.

62 N. M. Srinivasagam, W. H. Kaye, K. H. Plotnicov, C. Greene, T. E. Weltzin, and R. Rao, "Persistent perfectionism, symmetry, and exactness after long-term recovery from anorexia nervosa," *American Journal of Psychiatry*, 152 (1995), pp. 1630–4.

63 W. Kaye, K. Gendall, and M. Strober, "Serotonin neuronal function and selective serotonin reuptake inhibitor treatment in anorexia and bulimia," *Biological Psychiatry*, 44 (1998), pp. 825–38.

64 T. D. Brewerton, H. A. Brandt, M. D. Lessem, D. L. Murphy, and D. C.

Jimerson, "Serotonin in eating disorders," in *Serotonin in Psychiatric Disorders*, ed. E. F. Coccaro and D. L. Murphy (Washington, DC: American Psychiatric Press, 1990), pp. 127–52.

65   W. H. Kaye, "Anorexia nervosa, obsessional behavior and serotonin," *Psychopharmacology Bulletin*, 33 (1997), pp. 335–44.

66   Garfinkel and Garner, *Anorexia Nervosa*, pp. 42–4, 51.

67   Keys, et al.,*The Biology of Human Starvation*.

68   See P. E. Garfinkel, H. Moldofsky, and D. M. Garner, "The heterogeneity of anorexia nervosa: Bulimia as a distinct subgroup," *Archives of General Psychiatry*, 37 (1980), pp. 1036–40; and R. C. Casper, E. D. Eckert, K. A. Halmi, S. C. Goldberg, and J. M. Davis, "Bulimia: Its incidence and clinical importance in patients with anorexia nervosa," *Archives of General Psychiatry*, 37 (1980), pp. 1030–4.

69   Garfinkel and Garner, *Anorexia Nervosa*, p. 46. For a study of the characteristically distressed patterns of interaction in the families of bulimic anorexics, see L. L. Humphrey, "Structural analysis of parent–child relationships in eating disorders," *Journal of Abnormal Psychology*, 95 (1986), pp. 395–402.

70   See, for example, J. Brisman and M. Siegel, "Bulimia and alcoholism: Two sides of the same coin?," *Journal of Substance Abuse Treatment*, 1 (1984), pp. 113–18. Also R. L. Pyle, J. E. Mitchell, and E. D. Eckert, "Bulimia: A report of 34 cases," *Journal of Clinical Psychiatry*, 42 (1981) pp. 60–4; C. Bulik, "Drug and alcohol abuse by bulimic women and their families," *American Journal of Psychiatry*, 144 (1987), pp. 1604–6.

71   C. Johnson and R. Larson, "Bulimia: an analysis of moods and behavior," *Psychosomatic Medicine*, 44 (1982), pp. 341–51.

72   H. G. Pope, J. I. Hudson, and J. Mialet, "Bulimia in the late nineteenth century: The observations of Pierre Janet," *Psychological Medicine*, 15 (1985), pp. 739–43.

73   H. Bruch, "Four decades of eating disorders," in Garner and Garfinkel, *Handbook of Psychotherapy for Anorexia Nervosa and Bulimia*, pp. 7–18.

74   G. F. M. Russell, "The changing nature of anorexia nervosa: An introduction to the conference," *Journal of Psychiatric Research*, 19 (1985), pp. 101–9.

75   P. Crichton, "Were the Roman emperors Claudius and Vitellius bulimic?," *International Journal of Eating Disorders*, 19 (1996), pp. 203–7.

76   M. Nasser, "A prescription of vomiting: Historical footnotes," *International Journal of Eating Disorders*, 13 (1993), pp. 129–31.

77   A. Stone, *The Fate of Borderline Patients* (New York: Guilford Press, 1990), p. 139. Attributed to Dr R. Winchel of New York State Psychiatric Institute.

78   L. Binswanger, "The case of Ellen West. An anthropological-clinical study,"

in *Existence: A New Dimension in Psychiatry and Psychology*, ed. R. May, E. Angel, and H. F. Ellenberger (New York: Basic Books, 1958), pp. 237–64.

79 P. Janet, *Les obsessions et la psychasthénie* (Paris: Germer Baillière, 1903), vol. 1, section 5.

80 A. Stunkard, "A description of eating disorders in 1932," *American Journal of Psychiatry*, 147 (1990), pp. 263–8.

81 Ibid., p. 266.

82 K. S. Kendler, C. Maclean, M. Neale, R. Kessler, A. Heath, and L. Eaves, "The genetic epidemiology of bulimia nervosa," *American Journal of Psychiatry*, 148 (1991), pp. 1627–37; T. J. Soundy, A. R. Lucas, V. J. Suman, and L. J. Melton, "Bulimia nervosa in Rochester, Minnesota from 1980 to 1990," *Psychological Medicine*, 25 (1995), pp. 1065–71.

83 M. Boskind-Lodahl, "Cinderella's stepsisters: A feminist perspective on anorexia nervosa and bulimia," *Signs: The Journal of Women in Culture and Society*, 2 (1976), pp. 342–56.

84 G. F. M. Russell, "Bulimia nervosa: An ominous variant of anorexia nervosa," *Psychological Medicine*, 9 (1979), pp. 429–48.

85 American Psychiatric Association, *DSM-III*.

86 American Psychiatric Association, *DSM-IV*.

87 H. G. Pope and J. I. Hudson, *New Hope for Binge Eaters* (New York: Harper and Row, 1984), pp. 12–13.

88 See K. Bemis, " 'Abstinence' and 'non-abstinence' models."

89 T. Habermas, "Possible effects of the popular and medical recognition of bulimia nervosa," *British Journal of Medical Psychology*, 65 (1992), pp. 59–66.

90 Pope and Hudson, *New Hope for Binge Eaters*, pp. 33–6.

91 D. E. Garner and M. Olmstead, "The significance of self-induced vomiting as a weight-control method among non-clinical samples," *International Journal of Eating Disorders*, 5 (1986), pp. 683–700.

92 Some interesting case histories of professional women with bulimia are described in S. Squire, *The Slender Balance* (New York: Pinnacle Books, 1983). Inquiries published in women's magazines in both the United States and Germany elicited large numbers of such apparently well-functioning bulimics. See C. L. Johnson, M. Stuckey, L. Lewis, and D. Schwartz, "Bulimia: A descriptive survey of 316 cases," *International Journal of Eating Disorders*, 2 (1982), pp. 1–16.

93 See, for example, Sours, *Starving to Death in a Sea of Objects*, pp. 349–50; and M. P. P. Root, P. Fallon, and W. N. Friederich, *Bulimia: A Systems Approach to Treatment* (New York: W. W. Norton, 1986), pp. 72–5.

94 See C. L. Johnson and M. E. Conners, *The Etiology and Treatment of Bulimia Nervosa* (New York: Basic Books, 1987), pp. 120–2.

95   M. W. Wiederman and T. Pryor, "Multi-impulsivity among women with bulimia nervosa," *International Journal of Eating Disorders*, 20 (1996), pp. 359–65; J. H. Lacey, "Self-damaging and addictive behaviour in bulimia nervosa: A catchment area study," *British Journal of Psychiatry*, 163 (1993), pp. 190–4.

96   S. C. Wooley and O. W. Wooley, "Intensive outpatient and residential treatment for bulimia," in Garner and Garfinkel, *Handbook of Psychotherapy for Anorexia Nervosa and Bulimia*, pp. 395–6.

97   M. B. Keller, D. B. Herzog, P. W. Lavori, I. S. Bradburn, and E. M. Mahoney, "The naturalistic history of bulimia nervosa: Extraordinarily high rates of chronicity, relapse, recurrence and psychosocial morbidity," *International Journal of Eating Disorders*, 12 (1992), pp. 1–10.

98   P. K. Keel, J. E. Mitchell, K. B. Miller, T. L. Davis, and S. J. Crow, "Long-term outcome of bulimia nervosa," *Archives of General Psychiatry*, 56 (1999), pp. 63–9.

99   C. G. Fairburn, "Cognitive-behavioral treatment for bulimia," in Garner and Garfinkel, *Handbook of Psychotherapy for Anorexia Nervosa and Bulimia*, pp. 160–92.

100 C. G. Fairburn, "Interpersonal therapy for bulimia nervosa," in Garner and Garfinkel, *Handbook of Treatment for Eating Disorders*, pp. 278–94.

101 C. G. Fairburn, P. A. Norman, S. L. Welch, M. E. O'Conner, H. A. Doll, and R. C. Peveler, "A prospective study of outcome in bulimia nervosa and the long-term effects of three psychological treatments," *Archives of General Psychiatry*, 52 (1995), pp. 304–12.

102 J. H. Lacey, "Time-limited individual and group treatment for bulimia," in Garner and Garfinkel, *Handbook of Psychotherapy for Anorexia Nervosa and Bulimia*, pp. 431–57.

103 Pope and Hudson, *New Hope for Binge Eaters*, pp. 12–13.

104 For an interesting study of this hypothesis, see T. D. Geracioti and R. A. Liddle, "Impaired cholecystokinin secretion in bulimia nervosa," *The New England Journal of Medicine*, 319 (1988), pp. 683–8.

105 W. H. Kaye, C. G. Greeno, H. Moss, J. Ferstrom, M. Ferstrom, L. R. Lilenfeld, T. E. Weltzin, and J. Mann, "Serotonin activity and psychiatric symptoms after recovery from bulimia nervosa," *Archives of General Psychiatry*, 55 (1998), pp. 927–35. The authors point to other research from twins and family studies that suggest that anorexia nervosa and bulimia nervosa tend to cluster in families and twin pairs. Of course it is possible that such findings represent common environmental concerns with weight and body shape.

106 O. Fenichel, *The Psychoanalytic Theory of Neurosis* (New York: Norton, 1945). For a discussion of Wulff's contribution, see Stunkard, "A description of eating disorders in 1932."

107   A. Stunkard, *The Pain of Obesity* (Palo Alto, CA: Bull Publishing Co., 1976).

108   R. Lindner, *The Fifty-Minute Hour* (New York: Holt, Rinehart, and Winston, 1955).

109   American Psychiatric Association, *DSM-IV*, pp. 729–31.

110   R. L. Spitzer, M. Devlin, B. T. Walsh, D. Hasin, R. Wing, M. D. Marcus, A. Stunkard, T. Wadden, S. Yanovski, W. S. Agras, J. Mitchell, and C. Nonas, "Binge eating disorder; A multidimensional field trial of the diagnostic criteria," *International Journal of Eating Disorders*, 11 (1992), pp. 191–203; R. L. Spitzer, S. Yanovski, T. Wadden, R. Wing, M. D. Marcus, A. Stunkard, M. Devlin, J. Mitchell, D. Hasin, and R. L. Horne, "Binge eating disorder: Its further validation in a multisite study," *International Journal of Eating Disorders*, 13 (1993), pp. 137–53.

111   M. D. Marcus, "Adapting treatment for patients with binge eating disorder," in Garner and Garfinkel, *Handbook of Treatment for Eating Disorders*, pp. 484–93.

112   C. F. Telch and W. S. Agras, "Do emotional states influence binge eating in the obese?" *International Journal of Eating Disorders*, 20 (1996), pp. 271–80.

113   For discussions of some of the experimental evidence for set-point theory, see R. E. Keesey, "A set-point analysis of the regulation of body weight," in *Obesity*, ed. A. J. Stunkard (Philadelphia: W. B. Saunders, 1980), pp. 144–65, and R. E. Keesey and S. W. Corbett, "Metabolic defense of the body weight set-point," in Stunkard and Stellar, *Eating and Its Disorders*, pp. 87–96. An extremely accessible and yet thorough discussion of the basis and implications of set-point theory is contained in W. Bennett and J. Gurin, *The Dieter's Dilemma* (New York: Harper and Row, 1982).

114   For example, the precise physiological mechanism of the set-point, or "appestat," has yet to be determined. The entire concept is an inference from various behavioral findings in animals and humans.

Chapter Three   Dimensions of an Epidemic

1   See K. M. Bemis, "Current approaches to the etiology and treatment of anorexia nervosa," *Psychological Bulletin*, 85 (1978), pp. 593–617 for a review.

2   See I. Al-Issa, *The Psychopathology of Women*, (Englewood Cliffs, NJ: Prentice-Hall, 1980) for a review of the sex prevalence of various disorders.

3 See, for example, H. Bruch, *Eating Disorders: Obesity, Anorexia Nervosa and the Person Within* (New York: Basic Books, 1973), pp. 285–305; D. W. Scott, "Anorexia nervosa in the male: a review of clinical epidemiological and biological findings," *International Journal of Eating Disorders*, 5 (1986), pp. 799–820; A. E. Andersen, *Males with Eating Disorders* (New York: Brunner Mazel, 1990).

4 H. G. Pope, A. J. Gruber, P. Choi, R. Olivardia, and K. A. Phillips, "Muscle dysmorphia: An underrecognized form of body dysmorphic disorder," *Psychosomatics*, 38 (1997), 548–57.

5 See, for example, the study by Jones et al. that shows that the proportion of female anorexic patients actually rose in the 1970s over the previous decade. (D. J. Jones, M. M. Fox, H. M. Babigan, and H. E. Hutton, "Epidemiology of anorexia nervosa in Monroe County, New York: 1960–1976," *Psychosomatic Medicine*, 42 (1980), pp. 551–8.) A selective increase in the percentage of female patients has also been reported by P. E. Garfinkel and D. M. Garner (see *Anorexia Nervosa: A Multidimensional Approach* (New York: Brunner Mazel, 1982), pp. 103–4), and confirmed in studies at the Mayo Clinic at Rochester, Minnesota.

6 O. W. Hill, "Epidemiologic aspects of anorexia nervosa," *Advances in Psychosomatic Medicine*, 9 (1977), pp. 48–62.

7 The quotation is from M. S. Palazzoli, "Anorexia nervosa: A syndrome of the affluent society," *Transcultural Psychiatric Research Review*, 22 (1985), pp. 199–204. The book by Palazzoli is *Self-Starvation*, originally published in Italian in 1963; published in English in London in 1974, and in the USA (New York: Jason Aronson) in 1978.

8 The two key terms concepts used by epidemiologists are *incidence* and *prevalence*. Incidence refers to the number of new cases developing in a designated period of time, typically per year, and it is typically specified for a particular population. Because it reflects changing patterns in the onset of a disease, the incidence of a disorder provides essential information about the planning of services. During periods in which an epidemic is occurring, the incidence should of course increase rapidly. Prevalence, on the other hand, refers to the percentage or proportion of the population that has a particular disorder. *Point prevalence* refers to the proportion of cases per unit population at a particular point in time, say, when a survey is conducted, whereas *lifetime prevalence* refers to the proportion of the population that had ever had a disorder.

9 W. Von Baeyer, "The meaning of sociopathological factors in the anorexia nervosa syndrome," in *Anorexia Nervosa*, ed. J. E. Meyer and H. Feldmann (Stuttgart: Verlag, 1965), pp. 150–3. See also K. Ishikawa, "Ueber die Eltern von anorexia-nervosa-Kranken," in the same volume, pp. 154–6.

10   S. Theander, "Anorexia nervosa: A psychiatric investigation of 94 female patients," *Acta Psychiatrica Scandinavica Supplement*, 214 (1970), pp. 1–194.

11   M. C. E. Gard and C. P. Freeman, "The dismantling of a myth: A review of eating disorders and socioeconomic status," *International Journal of Eating Disorders*, 20 (1996), pp. 1–12.

12   R. E. Kendall, D. J. Hall, A. Hailey, and H. M. Babigan, "The epidemiology of anorexia nervosa," *Psychosomatic Medicine*, 3 (1973), pp. 200–3.

13   Jones et al., "Epidemiology of anorexia nervosa in Monroe County, New York".

14   G. Szmuckler, C. McCance, L. McCrone, and D. Hunter, "Anorexia nervosa: a psychiatric case register study from Aberdeen," *Psychological Medicine*, 16 (1986), pp. 49–58.

15   J. Willi and S. Grossman, "Epidemiology of anorexia nervosa in a defined region of Switzerland," *American Journal of Psychiatry*, 140 (1982), pp. 564–8.

16   J. Willi, G. Giacometti, and B. Limacher, "Update on the epidemiology of anorexia nervosa in a defined region of Switzerland," *American Journal of Psychiatry*, 147 (1990), pp. 1514–17.

17   A. K. Pagsberg and A. R. Wang, "Epidemiology of anorexia nervosa and bulimia nervosa in Bornholm County, Denmark, 1970–1989," *Acta Psychiatrica Scandinavica*, 90 (1994), pp. 259–65.

18   F. Faltus, "Anorexia nervosa in Czechoslovakia," *International Journal of Eating Disorders*, 5 (1986), pp. 581–5.

19   An increase in the number of anorexia nervosa patients in Japan since World War II was first noted by Ishikawa (see n. 9 above), who attributed the increase to changes in the traditional family structure. More recently, see H. Suematsu, H. Ishikawa, T. Kuboki, and T. Ito, "Statistical studies on anorexia nervosa in Japan: Detailed clinical data on 1,011 patients," *Psychotherapy and Psychosomatics*, 43 (1985), pp. 96–103.

20   T. Nadaoka, A. Oiji, S. Takahashi, Y. Morioka, M. Kashiwakura, and S. Totsuka, "An epidemiological study of eating disorders in a northern area of Japan," *Acta Psychiatrica Scandinavica*, 93 (1996), pp. 305–10.

21   French writings on anorexia nervosa have been prolific, and have made particularly strong contributions along phenomenological lines. A selected list of titles from the period beginning in 1970 includes E. Kestemberg, K. J. Kestemberg, and S. Decubert, *Le Faim et Le Corps* (Paris: PUF Edition, 1972) (a psychoanalytic treatise); P. Jeammet, "Psychogenic thinness and mental anorexia," *Revue Pratique*, 92 (1982), pp. 257–72; F. Lang and H. Rousset, "Anorexia nervosa: Disease with a future," *Lyon Medicale*, 3 (1984), pp. 357–63; M. Laxenaire and P. Marchand, "Anorexia nervosa: has it changed?" *Annales Medico-Psychologiques*, 140 (1982), pp. 448–53; S.

Consoli and P. Jeammet, "Epidemiology of mental anorexia," *Semaine de Hospitaux*, 60 (1985), pp. 2139–43. The latter is a review of mostly American and British studies.

22 The German literature on anorexia nervosa is extensive. A short list of some representative recent titles includes M. Gerlinghoff, "Anorexia nervosa," *Munchener Medizinische Woschenschrift*, 129 (1987), pp. 89–90; M. Fichter, *Magersucht and Bulimia* (Berlin: Springer-Verlag, 1985); R. Bonenberger and G. Klosinski, "Parent personality, family status and family dynamics in anorexia nervosa patients with special reference to father–daughter relations (a retrospective study)," *Z. Kinder Jugenpsychiatry*, 16 (1988), pp. 186–95; M. Gerlinghoff, "Disorders of the maturation process and psychosexual development of anorexic patients," *Schweiz. Arch. Neurol. Psychiatr.*, 139 (1988), pp. 61–73; and K. Engel and D. Hohne, "Prevalence of anorectic behavior in a normal population: An epidemiologic study with conclusions and treatment in anorexia nervosa," *Z. Psychosom. Med. Psychoanal.*, 35 (1989), pp. 117–29. In the last-named study, the authors found anorexic symptoms to be relatively common in a non-clinical population, with significant cases occurring at the rate of 1 to 2 percent. A somewhat earlier German literature on anorexia nervosa stressed social and anthropological factors in the disease, as well as its broader human implications. For example, an early article by E. Bilz ("Anorexia nervosa: a psychosomatic syndrome from a paleoanthropo-logical viewpoint," *Bibliotheca Psychiatrica*, 14 (1971), pp. 219–44) compared the feeding behavior of anorexics with that of the solitary honey bear, in contrast with the more organized behavior of baboon troops; that is, as a regression to snacking or foraging behavior, which is more primitive and asocial than communal feeding organized around meals seen in the apes. See also V. A. Massing and W. Beckers, "A discussion of the origins and increase in pubertal anorexia," *Z. Psychosom. Med. Psychoanal.*, 1 (1974), pp. 53–9, for a discussion of sex-role conflicts in anorexic patients.

23 In Italy, M. Selvini Palazzoli, whose innovative approaches to family therapy have had a worldwide influence, noted in the 1970s a steady increase in the number of cases since World War II. An overview of her work, with speculation about the reasons for the rising incidence, was given in *Self-Starvation*.

24 In Belgium, extensive work with anorexia nervosa patients has been reported in a series of publications by Walter Vandereycken and his colleagues. See, for example, W. Vandereycken and R. Pierloot, "Long-term outcome research in anorexia nervosa," *International Journal of Eating Disorders*, 2 (1983), pp. 237–42; W. Vandereycken, E. Kog, and J. Vanderlinden, *The Family Approach to Eating Disorders* (New York: Spectrum Books, 1987).

25   K. G. Gotestam and W. S. Agras, "General population-based epidemiological study of eating disorders in Norway," *International Journal of Eating Disorders*, 18 (1995), pp. 119–26.

26   Dr Fernando Fernandez-Aranda of the Hospital of the University of Bellvitge in Barcelona reports that in 1988, there were about 25 new eating-disordered patients per year referred for treatment (90 percent with anorexia nervosa, 10 percent with bulimia), whereas in 1998 there were 360 new cases per year (40 percent anorexia nervosa, 60 percent bulimia nervosa), a more than tenfold increase. The approaches to treatment at this center have been described in F. Fernandez and V. Turon, *Eating Disorders: Handbook for Treatment* (Barcelona: Masson, 1998).

27   See, for example, A. Kasperlik-Zaluska, B. Migdalska, M. Kazubska, and T. Wisniewska-Wozniak, "Clinical, psychiatric, and endrocrinological correlations in 42 cases of anorexia nervosa," *Psychiatria Polska* (Warsaw), 15 (1981), pp. 574–83; A. Banas, A. Januszkiewicz-Grabias, P. Radziwillowicz, "Multifactorial aspects of eating disorders," *Psychiatria Polska*, 32 (1998), pp. 165–75; J. Sutovec and V. Frank, "Body image in patients with mental anorexia," *Ceskosloveriska Psychiatrie* (Prague), 78 (1982), pp. 180–4; Z. Lopicic-Perisic, S. Popovic-Deusic, and S. Filipovic, "Therapy of mental anorexia," *Psihijatrija Danas* (Belgrade), 13 (1981), pp. 91–5.

28   H. Papezova, A. Yamamoto and E. Dragomirecka, "Eating disorders – Sociocultural differences in therapy availability and course of the illness," presented at Eighth New York International Conference on Eating Disorders, April 1998.

29   An early Soviet paper on anorexia nervosa, with clinical descriptions virtually identical to those described in the US, the UK, and Western Europe, was G. Ushakov, "Anorexia nervosa," in *Modern Perspectives in Adolescent Psychiatry*, ed. J. G. Howells (New York: Brunner Mazel, 1971). A review of the world literature, with passing reference to native cases and the current "intense interest" in the problem (presumably in the Soviet Union), was M. V. Korkina and V. V. Marilov, "The contemporary state of the problem of anorexia nervosa," *Zhurnal Nevropathologii I Psyikhiatrii*, 74 (1974), pp. 1574–83. More recently a series of papers has been published by M. V. Korkina, V. V. Marilov and others, whose work is at Patrice Lumumba University Moscow. See, for example, M. V. Korkina, V. V. Marilov, M. A. Tsivilko, and M. A. Kareva, "Anorexia nervosa in males," *Zhurnal Nevropathologii I Psyikhiatrii*, 79 (1979), pp. 1562–8; M. V. Korkina, et al., "Distorted self-perception and eating behavior of patients with anorexia nervosa," *Zhurnal Nevropathologii I Psyikhiatrii*, 86 (1986), pp. 1813–19 and "On the special case of the pathology of drive in schizophrenic patients with anorexia nervosa," *Zhurnal*

Nevropathologii I Psyikhiatrii, 86 (1986), pp. 1689–94. Epidemiological data are not given, but samples of over 100 patients at this one center have been studied.

30   A. R. Lucas, C. M. Beard, W. M. O'Fallon, and L. T. Kurland, "50-year trends in the incidence of anorexia nervosa in Rochester, Minn.: A population-based study," *American Journal of Psychiatry*, 148 (1991), pp. 917–22.

31   T. Habermas, "In defense of weight phobia as the central organizing motive in anorexia nervosa: Historical and cultural arguments for a culture-sensitive psychological conception," *International Journal of Eating Disorders*, 19 (1996), pp. 317–34.

32   J. M. Eagles, M. I. Johnston, D. Hunter, M. Lobban, and H. R. Millar, "Increasing incidence of anorexia nervosa in the female population of Northeast Scotland," *American Journal of Psychiatry*, 152 (1995), pp. 1266–71.

33   The Danish study referred to is S. Nielsen, "The epidemiology of anorexia nervosa in Denmark from 1973 to 1987: A nationwide register study of psychiatric admission," *Acta Psychiatrica Scandinavica*, 81 (1990), pp. 507–14. For a study with an opposite conclusion (i.e., increasing incidence), see P. Munk-Jorgensen, S. Moller-Madsen, S. Nielsen, and J. Nystrup, "Incidence of eating disorders in Danish psychiatric hospitals and wards 1970–1993," *Acta Psychiatrica Scandinavica*, 92 (1995), pp. 91–6. The Dutch study is H. W. Hoek, A. I. M. Bartelds, J. J. F. Bosveld, Y. Van der Graaf, V. Limpens, M. Maiwald, and C. Spaaij, "Impact of urbanization on detection rates of eating disorders," *American Journal of Psychiatry*, 152 (1995), pp. 1272–8.

34   An argument that the data do not support an increase in incidence is presented by E. Fombonne, "Anorexia nervosa: No evidence of an increase," *British Journal of Psychiatry*, 166 (1995), pp. 462–71. The author reviews various studies, many of which are methodologically incompatible, and concludes, conservatively, that taken together they do not support the hypothesis of an increased incidence. The incompatibility of these studies, however, weakens the conclusion of the review. A more extensive critique is offered by S. van't Hoft, *Anorexia Nervosa: The Historical and Cultural Specificity: Fallacious Theories and Tenacious Facts* (The Netherlands: Swets and Zeitlinger, 1994). Despite marshalling strong arguments against the existing data, the author overstates the case by arguing that because of the educational advances of women since the 1960s, psychiatrists *expected* to see an increase in the condition and thus the interpretations of the epidemiological data were self-fulfilling prophecies. This argument seems untenable in the face of the evidence.

35 P. Williams and M. King, "The 'epidemic' of anorexia nervosa: Another medical myth?," *Lancet*, Jan. 24, 1987, pp. 205–7.

36 A similar conclusion was drawn by Nielsen in a epidemiological study in Denmark; see S. Nielsen, "The epidemiology of anorexia nervosa in Denmark from 1973 to 1987: A nationwide register study of psychiatric admission," *Acta Psychiatrica Scandinavica*, 81 (1990), pp. 507–14.

37 A. R. Lucas, "The eating disorder 'epidemic': More apparent than real?," *Pediatric Annals*, 21 (1992), pp. 746–51.

38 Theander, "Anorexia nervosa."

39 Jones et al., "Epidemiology of anorexia nervosa in Monroe County, New York."

40 A. H. Crisp, R. L. Palmer, and R. S. Kalucy, "How common is anorexia nervosa? A prevalence study," *British Journal of Psychiatry*, 128 (1976), pp. 549–54.

41 See Lucas et al., "50-year trends in the incidence of anorexia nervosa in Rochester, Minn."

42 See M. Boskind-Lodahl, "Cinderella's stepsisters: A feminist perspective on anorexia nervosa and bulimia," *Signs: The Journal of Women in Culture and Society*, 2 (1976), pp. 342–56.

43 G. F. M. Russell, "Bulimia nervosa: An ominous variant of anorexia nervosa," *Psychological Medicine*, 9 (1979), pp. 429–48.

44 D. M. Garner and C. G. Fairburn, "Relationship between anorexia nervosa and bulimia nervosa: Diagnostic implications," in D. M. Garner and C. G. Fairburn, *Diagnostic Issues in Anorexia Nervosa and Bulimia Nervosa* (New York: Brunner Mazel, 1988), pp. 56–79.

45 T. J. Soundy, A. R. Lucas, V. J. Suman, and L. J. Melton, "Bulimia nervosa in Rochester, Minnesota from 1980 to 1990," *Psychological Medicine*, 25 (1995), pp. 1065–71. In this study, the findings were highly parallel to those in Toronto, with the incidence increasing sharply from 7.4 per 100,000 in 1980 to 49.7 per 100,000 in 1983 and then remaining constant at about 30 per 100,000 throughout the rest of the decade.

46 A. Stunkard, "A description of eating disorders in 1932," *American Journal of Psychiatry*, 147 (1990), pp. 263–8.

47 M. Rosensweig and J. Spruill, "Twenty years after Twiggy: a retrospective investigation of bulimic-like behaviors," *International Journal of Eating Disorders*, 6 (1987), pp. 59–66.

48 K. A. Halmi, J. R. Falk, and E. Schwartz, "Binge-eating and vomiting: A survey of a college population," *Psychological Medicine*, 11 (1981), pp. 697–706. See also chapter 1, note 12.

49 H. G. Pope, Jr., J. I. Hudson, and D. Yurgelun-Todd, "Prevalence of anorexia nervosa and bulimia among 300 suburban women shoppers," *American Journal of Psychiatry*, 141 (1984), pp. 292–4.

50 H. G. Pope, Jr., J. I. Hudson, and D. Yurgelun-Todd, "Prevalence of anorexia nervosa and bulimia in three student populations," *International Journal of Eating Disorders*, 3 (1984), pp. 45–51.

51 R. L. Pyle, J. E. Mitchell, E. D. Eckert, P. A. Halvorson, P. A. Neuman, and G. M. Goff, "The incidence of bulimia in freshman college students," *International Journal of Eating Disorders*, 2 (1983), pp. 75–85.

52 R. L. Pyle, P. A. Halvorson, P. A. Neuman, and J. E. Mitchell, "The increasing prevalence of bulimia in freshman college students," *International Journal of Eating Disorders*, 5 (1986), pp. 631–41.

53 C. Johnson, C. Lewis, S. Love, and M. Stuckey, "The incidence and correlates of bulimic behavior among a high school population," *Journal of Youth and Adolescence*, 13 (1984), pp. 15–25.

54 A. Whitaker, J. Johnson, D. Shaffer, J. L. Rapoport, K. Kalikow, B. T. Walsh, M. Davies, S. Braiman, and A. Dolinsky, "Uncommon troubles in young people: prevalence estimates of selected psychiatric disorders in a nonreferred adolescent population," *Archives of General Psychiatry*, 47 (1990), pp. 487–96.

55 K. S. Kendler, C. MacLean, M. Neale, R. Kessler, A. Heath, and L. Eaves, "The genetic epidemiology of bulimia nervosa," *American Journal of Psychiatry*, 148 (1991), pp. 1627–37.

56 T. F. Heatherton, P. Nichols, F. Mahamedi, and P. Keel, "Body weight, dieting, and eating disorder symptoms among college students, 1982–1992," *American Journal of Psychiatry*, 152 (1995), pp. 1623–9.

57 I. Nylander, "The feeling of being fat and dieting in a school population," *Acta Sociomedica Scandinavica*, 3 (1971), pp. 17–26.

58 E. J. Button and A. Whitehouse, "Subclinical anorexia nervosa," *Psychological Medicine*, 11 (1981), pp. 509–16.

59 C. L. Kurth, D. D. Krahn, K. Nairn, and A. Drewnowski, "The severity of dieting and bingeing behaviors in college women: Interview validation of survey data," *Journal of Psychiatric Research*, 29 (1995), pp. 211–25.

60 N. Ballot, "Anorexia nervosa – a prevalence study," *South African Medical Journal*, 27 (1981), pp. 992–3.

61 H. Pumarino and N. Vivanco, "Anorexia nervosa: medical and psychiatric characteristics of 50 patients," *Revista Medica de Chile*, 110 (1982), pp. 1081–92.

62 Shridhar Sharma, personal communication.

63 Burton Bradley, personal communication.

64 Cited in C. P. Wilson, *Fear of Being Fat* (New York: Jason Aronson, 1983).

65 N. Buchrich, "Frequency of presentation of anorexia nervosa in Malaysia," *Australian and New Zealand Journal of Psychiatry*, 15 (1981), pp. 153–5.

66 See S. Lee, "Anorexia nervosa in Hong Kong: A Chinese perspective," *Psychological Medicine*, 21 (1991), pp. 703–11; S. Lee, T. P. Ho, and L. K. G. Hsu, "Fat phobic and non-fat phobic anorexia nervosa: A comparative study of 70 Chinese patients in Hong Kong," *Psychological Medicine*, 23 (1993), pp. 999–1017; A. M. Lee and S. Lee, "Disordered eating and its psychosocial correlates among Chinese adolescent females in Hong Kong," *International Journal of Eating Disorders*, 20 (1996), pp. 177–184.

67 S. Lee, "Review of 'Transcultural aspects of eating disorders: A critical literature review by Cindy Davis and Joel Yager,'" *Transcultural Psychiatric Research Review*, 30 (1993), pp. 163–8.

68 A. M. Lee and S. Lee, "Disordered eating."

69 For the following material on South Korea and Singapore, I am indebted to a well-researched article in the *Los Angeles Times* by Sonni Efron, "Eating disorders go global," *Los Angeles Times*, October 18, 1997, pp. A1, A9.

70 L. P. Pok and C. S. Tian, "Susceptibility of Singapore Chinese schoolgirls to anorexia nervosa – Part I (psychological factors)," *Singapore Medical Journal*, 35 (1994), pp. 481–5.

71 Information on South Korea in this paragraph comes from Efron, "Eating disorders go global."

72 S. K. Khandewal, P. Sharan, and S. Saxena, "Eating disorders: An Indian perspective," *International Journal of Social Psychiatry*, 41 (1995), pp. 132–46.

73 T. N. Srinivasan, T. R. Suresh, and J. Vasantha, "Emergence of eating disorders in India. Study of eating distress syndrome and development of a screening questionnaire," *International Journal of Social Psychiatry*, 44 (1998), pp. 189–98.

74 R. Littlewood, "Psychopathology and personal agency: Modernity, culture change and eating disorders in South Asian societies," *British Journal of Medical Psychology*, 68 (1995), pp. 45–63.

75 B. Emecheta, *Double Yoke* (London: Ogwugwu Afor, 1982).

76 A. Nwaefuna, "Anorexia nervosa in a developing country," *British Journal of Psychiatry*, 138 (1981), 270; T. Buchan and L. D. Gregory, "Anorexia nervosa in a black Zimbabwean," *British Journal of Psychiatry*, 145 (1984), pp. 326–30; O. O. Famuyiwa, "Incidence of anorexia nervosa in two Nigerians," *Acta Psychiatrica Scandinavica*, 78 (1988), pp. 550–4.

77 L. K. Oyewumi and S. S. Kazarian, "Abnormal eating attitudes among a group of Nigerian youths: I Bulimic behavior," *East African Medical Journal*, 69 (1992), pp. 663–6.

78 C. Szabo, M. Berk, E. Tiou, and C. W. Allwood, "Eating disorders in black South African females," *South African Medical Journal*, 85 (1995), pp. 588–90.

79   D. Le Grange, C. F. Telch, and J. Tibbs, "Eating attitudes and behaviors in 1,435 South African Caucasian and Non-Caucasian college students," *American Journal of Psychiatry*, 155 (1998), pp. 250–4.

80   Pumarino and Vivanco, "Anorexia nervosa."

81   L. Bay and C. R. Herscovici, "Anorexia nerviosa: 34 casos con asistencia multidisciplinaria de enfoque sistemico," *Archivos Argentinos de Pediatría*, 86 (1988), pp. 137–48; C. R. Herscovici and L. Bay, "Favorable outcome for anorexia nervosa patients treated in Argentina with a family approach," *Eating Disorders: Journal of Treatment and Prevention*, 4 (1996), pp. 59–66; R. Zukerfeld, R. Zukerfeld, and S. Qiroga, "Binge eating and psychopathology in 207 university women in Buenos Aires," paper presented at Eighth New York International Conference on Eating Disorders, April 1998.

82   Dr Armando Barriguete, personal communication, 1998.

83   Bruch, *Eating Disorders*.

84   A. H. Crisp, *Anorexia Nervosa: Let Me Be* (London: Academic Press, 1980), p. 62.

85   B. R. Bhadrinath, "Anorexia nervosa in adolescents of Asian extraction," *British Journal of Psychiatry*, 156 (1990), pp. 565–8.

86   Eating disorders appear to be particularly common among fundamentalist Christian groups in the United States. See, for example, K. Lampson Reiff, "The fundamental flaw: Christianity and eating disorders," presented at Sixth National Conference on Anorexia Nervosa and Bulimia sponsored by the National Anorexic Aid Society, Columbus, Ohio, October 1987. See also T. Sitnick and J. Katz, "Anorexia nervosa in ultra-orthodox and hasidic girls: A question of tradition," presented at Eighth New York International Conference on Eating Disorders, April 1998.

87   These comparisons are based on M. Crago, C. M. Shisslak, and L. S. Estes, "Eating disturbances among American minority groups: A review," *International Journal of Eating Disorders*, 19 (1996), pp. 239–48. Specifically, Rosen et al. found that among the Chippewa in Michigan, a significant percentage were trying to lose weight and among these, fully 24 percent were using purging (L. W. Rosen, C. L. Shafer, G. M. Dummer, L. K. Cross, G. W. Deuman, and S. R. Malmberg, "Prevalence of pathogenic weight-control behaviors among Native American women and girls," *International Journal of Eating Disorders*, 7 (1988), pp. 807–11). The prevalence of eating disorder diagnoses among Native American groups, however, remains unknown. Since some groups, such as the Pima in Arizona, suffer from extraordinary degrees of obesity, it seems likely that many may be vulnerable since they cannot escape the idealization of thinness in the dominant, white culture.

88   L. K. G. Hsu, "Are eating disorders becoming more common in Blacks?"

International Journal of Eating Disorders, 6 (1987), pp. 113–24.

89 K. Abrams, L. Allen, and J. Gray, "Disordered eating attitudes and behaviors, psychological adjustment and ethnic identity: A comparison of Black and White female college students," *International Journal of Eating Disorders*, 14 (1993), pp. 49–57.

90 S. Parker, M. Nichter, N. Nichter, N. Vuckovic, C. Sims, and C. Ritenbaugh, "Body image and weight concerns among African American and White adolescent females: Differences that make a difference," *Human Organization*, 54 (1995), pp. 103–14.

91 See ch. 6, n. 11.

92 D. B. Mumford, A. M. Whitehouse, and M. Platts, "Sociocultural correlates of eating disorders among Asian schoolgirls in Bradford," *British Journal of Psychiatry*, 158 (1991), pp. 222–8.

93 Ibid.

94 M. Nasser, "Comparative study of the prevalence of abnormal eating attitudes among Arab female students of both London and Cairo Universities," *Psychological Medicine*, 16 (1986), pp. 621–5.

95 A. Furnham and N. Alibhai, "Cross-cultural differences in the perception of female body shapes," *Psychological Medicine*, 13 (1983), pp. 829–37.

96 M. Kaffman and T. Sadeh, "Anorexia nervosa in the Kibbutz: Factors influencing the development of a monoideistic fixation," *International Journal of Eating Disorders*, 8 (1989), pp. 33–55.

97 Ibid., p. 35.

98 In this I am in agreement with M. C. E. Gard and C. P. Freeman, "The dismantling of a myth: A review of eating disorders and socioeconomic status," *International Journal of Eating Disorders*, 20 (1996), pp. 1–12. The authors buttress a thorough critical review of the existing literature with a finding of a high prevalence of eating disorders among a young, homeless population.

99 S. Fenwick, *On Atrophy of the Stomach and on the Nervous Affections of the Digestive Organs* (London: Churchill, 1980).

100 Bruch, *Eating Disorders*, p. 81.

101 Theander, "Anorexia nervosa."

102 P. Dally, *Anorexia Nervosa* (London: William Heinemann Books, 1969).

103 Kendall et al., "The epidemiology of anorexia nervosa."

104 H. G. Pope, R. F. Champoux, and H. L. Hudson, "Eating disorders and socioeconomic class: Anorexia nervosa and bulimia in nine communities," *Journal of Nervous and Mental Disease*, 175 (1987), pp. 620–3.

105 K. M. Leighton and H. R. Millar, "Anorexia nervosa in Glasgow," *Journal of Psychiatric Research*, 19 (1985), pp. 167–70.

106 B. M. Dolan, C. Evans, and J. H. Lacey, "Family composition and social

class in bulimia: A catchment area study of a clinical and comparison group," *Journal of Nervous and Mental Disease*, 177 (1989), pp. 267–72; B. M. Dolan, J. H. Lacey, and C. Evans, "Eating behaviour and attitudes to weight and shape in British women from three ethnic groups," *British Journal of Psychiatry*, 157 (1990), pp. 523–8.

Chapter Four   A Conflicted Female Identity

1   See "Sex differences in death, disease, and diet," appendix B in K. B. Hoyenga and K. T. Hoyenga, *The Question of Sex Differences: Psychological, Cultural and Biological Issues* (Boston: Little, Brown, 1979). The greater female tolerance for starvation was known as early as the twelfth century, where Heloise argued that "nature herself has protected our sex with a greater power of sobriety. It is indeed known that women can be sustained with less nourishment, and at much less expense, than men" (cited in C. Bynum, *Holy Feast and Holy Fast: The Religious Significance of Food to Medieval Women* (Berkeley: University of California Press, 1987), p. 387).

2   A. S. Beller, *Fat and Thin: A Natural History of Obesity* (New York: McGraw-Hill, 1977). This book contains a great deal of information about fatness, particularly from an evolutionary and anthropological perspective.

3   Katherine Halmi, personal communication.

4   E. Frank, L. L. Carpenter, and D. J. Kupfer, "Sex differences in recurrent depression: Are there any that are significant?," *American Journal of Psychiatry*, 145 (1988), pp. 41–5.

5   See E. H. Erikson, *Identity, Youth and Crisis* (New York: W. W. Norton, 1964); and *Life History and the Historical Moment* (New York: W. W. Norton, 1975).

6   B. Malzberg, "Are immigrants psychologically disturbed?," in *Changing Perspectives in Mental Illness*, ed. S. Plog and R. B. Edgarton (New York: Holt, Rinehart, and Winston, 1969), pp. 395–421.

7   H. B. M. Murphy, "Culture and schizophrenia," in *Culture and Psychopathology*, ed. I. Al-Issa (Baltimore: University Park Press, 1982).

8   See, for example, L. Komarovsky, *Women in College* (New York: Basic Books, 1985); also J. L. Bardwick, *In Transition* (New York: Holt, Rinehart, and Winston, 1979).

9   C. Smith-Rosenberg, "The hysterical woman: Sex roles in 19th century America," *Social Research*, 39 (1972), pp. 652–78.

10   For example, D. M. Schwartz, M. G. Thompson, and C. L. Johnson, "Eating disorders and the culture," in *Anorexia Nervosa: Recent Develop-*

ments in Research, ed. P. L. Darby, P. E. Garfinkel, D. J. Garner, and D. V. Coscina (New York: Alan R. Liss, 1983), pp. 83–95.

11   H., Bruch, *Eating Disorders: Obesity, Anorexia Nervosa and the Person Within* (New York: Basic Books, 1973), pp. 254–5. This is one of the three core deficiencies in anorexia nervosa cited by Bruch, the others being a disturbance of body image of delusional proportions and an inability to accurately perceive internal need states.

12   M. Strober, "Disorders of the self in anorexia nervosa: An organismic developmental paradigm," in *Psychodynamic Treatment of Anorexia Nervosa and Bulimia*, ed. C. Johnson (New York: Guilford, 1991), pp. 354–76.

13   H. Bruch, *The Golden Cage* (New York: Vintage 1978), ch. 4 ("How It Starts").

14   C. L. Johnson, R. A. Sansone, and M. C. Chewing, "Good reasons why young women would develop anorexia nervosa: The adaptive context," *Pediatric Annals*, 21 (1992), pp. 731–7.

15   A. H. Crisp, "Anorexia nervosa as flight from growth: Assessment and treatment," in *Handbook of Treatment for Eating Disorders*, 2nd edn, ed. D. M. Garner and P. E. Garfinkel (New York: Guilford Press, 1997), pp. 248–77.

16   For a useful discussion of this point, see J. Yager, "Family issues in the pathogenesis of anorexia nervosa," *Psychosomatic Medicine*, 44 (1982), pp. 43–59.

17   J. Block, *Sex Roles and Ego Development* (San Francisco: Jossey Bass, 1985).

18   Ibid.

19   J. Baker Miller, *Towards a New Psychology of Women* (Boston: Beacon Press, 1976).

20   Bruch, *The Golden Cage*, p. 25.

21   R. Slade, *The Anorexia Nervosa Reference Book* (New York: Harper and Row, 1984), ch. 8.

22   Miller, *Towards a New Psychology of Women*.

23   Bruch, *The Golden Cage*, p. ix (original emphasis).

24   Bruch, *Eating Disorders*, p. 98.

25   N. Casky, "Interpreting anorexia nervosa," in *The Female Body in Western Culture*, ed. S. Suleiman (Cambridge, MA: Harvard University Press, 1986).

26   H. Bruch, *Conversations with Anorexics* (New York: Basic Books, 1988), p. 108.

27   Bruch, *Conversations with Anorexics*, p. 126.

28   Bruch, *The Golden Cage*, p. 27.

29   The dilemmas for girls of "breaking away" in the contemporary environment are further discussed in a little noticed essay by Suzett Finkelstein,

"Eating disorders: Why women and why now?," in *Women and Depression: A Lifespan Perspective*, ed. R. Formanek and A. Gurian (New York: Springer Publishing, 1987), pp. 101–18.

30 J. V. Waller, R. Kaufman, and F. Deutsch, "Anorexia nervosa: A psychosomatic entity," *Psychosomatic Medicine*, 2 (1940), pp. 3–16.

31 P. J. V. Beumont, S. F. Abraham, and K. Simson, "The psychosexual histories of adolescent girls and young women with anorexia nervosa," *Psychological Medicine*, 11 (1981), pp. 131–40; M. W. Wiederman, T. Pryor, and C. D. Morgan, "The sexual experience of women diagnosed with anorexia nervosa or bulimia nervosa," *International Journal of Eating Disorders*, 19 (1996), pp. 109–18.

32 A. Liu, *Solitaire* (New York: Harper and Row, 1979).

33 For overviews, see S. A. Wonderlich, T. D. Brewerton, B. S. Dansky, and D. W. Abbot, "Relationship between childhood sexual abuse and eating disorders," *Journal of the American Academy of Child and Adolescent Psychiatry*, 36 (1997), pp. 1107–15; and C. Zlotnick, L. Hohlstein, M. T. Shea, T. Pearlstein, P. Recupero, and K. Bidadi, "The relationship between sexual abuse and eating pathology," *International Journal of Eating Disorders*, 20 (1996), pp. 129–34.

34 G. Waller, "Sexual abuse and the severity of bulimic symptoms," *British Journal of Psychiatry*, 161 (1992), pp. 90–3.

35 The story of this case, along with detailed testimony of expert witness, is vividly described in Moira Johnston, *Spectral Evidence. The Ramona Case: Incest, Memory, & Truth on Trial in Napa Valley* (New York: Houghton Mifflin, 1997). While the author appears to side with the accused (and legally vindicated) father in the story, the account shows that it is difficult, if not impossible, to resolve an account of "recovered memory" in a courtroom. The plaintiff, Holly Ramona, was still convinced of the veracity of her memories at the end of the trial and did not recant her accusation. Discussion of the implications of this case for the treatment of eating disorders are given in H. G. Pope and J. I. Hudson, " 'Recovered memory' therapy for eating disorders: Implications of the Ramona verdict," *International Journal of Eating Disorders*, 19 (1996), pp. 139–45.

36 S. L. Welch and C. G. Fairburn, "Sexual abuse and bulimia nervosa: Three integrated case control comparisons," *American Journal of Psychiatry*, 151 (1994), pp. 402–7; H. G. Pope, B. Mangweith, A. B. Negrao, J. I. Hudson, and T. A. Cordas, "Childhood sexual abuse and bulimia nervosa: A comparison of American, Austrian, and Brazilian women," *American Journal of Psychiatry*, 151 (1994), pp. 732–7. The latter cross-cultural study found sexual abuse was reported at no higher rates than for women in the general population in these three countries. The authors concluded that sexual abuse is not a specific risk factor for bulimia ner-

vosa. This does not rule out a role for sexual abuse in certain cases, however.

37 A. H. Crisp, *Anorexia Nervosa: Let Me Be* (London: Academic Press, 1980); also "The psychopathology of anorexia nervosa: getting the 'heat' out of the system," in *Eating and its Disorders*, ed. A. J. Stunkard and E. Stellar (New York: Raven Press, 1984), pp. 209–34.

38 R. E. Frisch and J. MacArthur, "Menstrual cycles: Fatness as a determinant of minimum weight for height necessary for their maintenance and onset," *Science*, 185 (1974), pp. 949–51.

39 J. P. Curran, "Convergence toward a single sexual standard?" in *Exploring Human Sexuality*, ed. D. Byrne and L. A. Byrne (New York: Harper and Row, 1977), pp. 194–200.

40 J. J. Brumberg, *Fasting Girls: The Emergence of Anorexia Nervosa as a Modern Disease* (Cambridge, MA: Harvard University Press, 1988), pp. 270–1.

41 S. de Beauvoir, *The Second Sex* (New York: Vintage Books, 1952).

42 See, for example, K. Chernin, *The Obsession: Reflections on the Tyranny of Slenderness* (New York: Harper and Row, 1981); N. Wolf, *The Beauty Myth: How Images of Beauty are Used Against Women* (New York: Dutton, 1991).

43 See A. M. Klein, "Fat talk: Body image among adolescent girls," in *Many Mirrors: Body Image and Social Relations*, ed. M. Sault (New Brunswick, NJ: Rutgers University Press, 1994), pp. 109–31.

44 M. Pipher, *Reviving Ophelia: Saving the Selves of Adolescent Girls* (New York: Ballantine Books, 1995).

45 C. Gilligan, N. P. Lyons, and T. J. Hanmer (eds), *Making Connections: The Relational Worlds of Adolescent Girls at the Emma Willard School* (Cambridge, MA: Harvard University Press, 1990).

46 M. Boskind-Lodahl, "Cinderella's stepsisters: A feminist perspective on anorexia nervosa and bulimia," *Signs: The Journal of Women in Culture and Society*, 2 (1976), pp. 342–56.

47 See, for example, W. J. Swift and R. Letven, "Bulimia and the basic fault: A psychoanalytic interpretation of the binging-vomiting syndrome," *Journal of the American Academy of Child Psychiatry*, 23 (1984), pp. 489–97; C. L. Johnson and M. E. Conners, *The Etiology and Treatment of Bulimia Nervosa* (New York: Basic Books, 1987), ch. 6.

48 See Johnson and Conners, *Etiology and Treatment*. These authors characterize the family environment of bulimics as typically "disengaged, chaotic, highly conflicted and neglectful. Family members use indirect and contradictory patterns of communication, are deficient in problem-solving skills, are non-supportive of independent behavior, and are less intellectually and recreationally oriented than the families of normal controls,

despite their higher achievement orientations. These family characteristics generally result in children feeling disorganized, disconnected, insecure, and anxious" (p. 137). In line with the theme I am elaborating in this chapter, Johnson and Conners remark that "Despite the high risk loading of both biological and familial factors, if the child were able to lean on a consistent and stable structure within the sociocultural milieu she might be able to compensate for the lack of structure within her immediate family. Unfortunately, particularly for young women, the broader sociocultural context simultaneously exacerbates feelings of instability and, ultimately, suggests a pathological adaptation to that instability" (p. 138).

49   M. Boskind-White and W. White, *Bulimarexia* (New York: W. W. Norton, 1983); H. Steiger, J. VanderFeen, C. Goldstein, and P. Leicher, "Defense styles and parental bonding in eating-disordered women," *International Journal of Eating Disorders*, 8 (1989), pp. 131–41. The latter found the father–daughter bond to be disturbed for all types of eating-disordered women.

50   S. Wooley and O. W. Wooley, "Ambitious bulimics: Thinness mania," *American Health*, October 1986, pp. 68–74.

51   The heightened self-consciousness and sense of "fraudulence" experienced by bulimic women was documented in R. H. Striegel-Moore, L. R. Silberstein, and J. Rodin, "The social self in bulimia nervosa: Public self-consciousness, social anxiety and perceived fraudulence," *Journal of Abnormal Psychology*, 102 (1993), pp. 297–303.

52   For an interesting discussion of the particular vulnerabilities to bulimia created by campus life, see L. J. Dickstein, "Current college environments: Do these communities facilitate and foster bulimia in vulnerable students?," *Journal of College Student Psychotherapy* (Special Edition: The Bulimic College Student: Evaluation, Treatment, and Prevention), 3 (nos 2, 3, 4) (1988–9), pp. 107–34.

53   L. Komarovsky, *Women in College* (New York: Basic Books, 1985).

54   See, for example, C. H. Deutsch, "The dark side of success," *New York Times*, Sept. 10, 1986, p. C1 for a discussion of the after-hours addictions of a number of high-flying corporate women. Interesting anecdotal descriptions of bulimic professionals are contained in S. Squire, *The Slender Balance* (New York: Pinnacle Books, 1983). The prevalence of bulimic syndromes among medical students is documented in D. Herzog, M. Pepose, D. K. Norman, and N. A. Rigotti, "Eating disorders and maladjustment in female medical students," *Journal of Nervous and Mental Disease*, 173 (1985), pp. 734–7. For an interesting discussion of the issues and a case history, see L. R. Barnett, "Bulimia as a symptom of sex-role strain in professional women," *Psychotherapy*, 23 (1986), pp. 311–15. Barnett suggests that "bulimarexia may represent the ambivalence

toward filling the sociocultural stereotype of femininity and asserting her personal power in a world that rewards hypermasculinity." As she points out, the most devastating insult that male colleagues or teachers can deliver to a female medical student is that she is "behaving like a nurse."

55 The notion of the "superwoman" was introduced by the journalist Ellen Goodman. See *Close to Home* (New York: Simon and Schuster, 1979). A "manifesto" of this ideology is contained in a book by Cosmopolitan editor Helen Gurley Brown, *Having It All* (New York: Pocket Books, 1982).

56 Brown, *Having it All*.

57 C. Steiner-Adair, "The body politic: Normal female adolescent development and the development of eating disorders," *Journal of the American Academy of Psychoanalysis*, 14 (1986), pp. 95–114.

58 C. Timko, R. H. Striegel-Moore, L. R. Silberstein, and J. Rodin, "Femininity/masculinity and disordered eating in women: How are they related?" *International Journal of Eating Disorders*, 6 (1987), pp. 701–12.

59 W. Rost, M. Neuhaus, and I. Florin, "Bulimia nervosa: Sex role attitude, sex role behavior and sex role related locus of control in bulimarexic women," *Journal of Psychosomatic Research*, 26 (1982), pp. 403–8.

60 R. M. Kanter, *Men and Women of the Corporation* (New York: Basic Books, 1977).

61 M. Lawrence, "Women, education and identity: thoughts on the social origins of anorexia," *Women's Studies International Forum*, 7 (1984), pp. 201–9.

62 The conception of anorexia as a problem in nurturance has been sensitively discussed by S. Levenkron, "Structuring a nurturant/authoritative psychotherapeutic relationship with the anorexic patient," in *Theory and Treatment of Anorexia Nervosa and Bulimia: Biomedical, Sociocultural and Biological Perspectives*, ed. S. W. Emmet (New York: Brunner Mazel, 1985, pp. 234–5. See also A. Lehman and J. Rodin, "Styles of self-nurturance and disordered eating," *Journal of Consulting and Clinical Psychology*, 57 (1989), pp. 117–22.

63 It is, however, likely that some male anorexics and bulimics go unrecognized, both because health professionals are reluctant to diagnose eating disorders and because eating-disordered males may be reluctant to come forth with "female" problems. See A. Andersen and A. D. Mickalide, "Anorexia nervosa in the male: an underdiagnosed disorder," *Psychosomatics*, 24 (1983), pp. 1066–75.

64 See D. J. Jones, M. M. Fox, H. M. Babigan, and H. E. Hutton, "Epidemiology of anorexia nervosa in Monroe County, New York: 1960–1976," *Psychosomatic Medicine*, 42 (1980), pp. 551–8.

65 A. E. Andersen, and L. DiDomenico, "Diet vs. shape content of popular

male and female magazines," *International Journal of Eating Disorders*, 11 (1992), pp. 283–92.

66 A. Andersen, "Eating disorders in males," in *Eating Disorders and Obesity: A Comprehensive Handbook*, ed. K. D. Brownell and C. G. Fairburn, (New York: Guilford, 1994), pp. 177–82.

67 Studies that have found high levels of homosexuality among eating-disordered males include D. B. Herzog, D. K. Norman, C. Gordon, and M. Pepose, "Sexual conflict and eating disorders in 27 males," *American Journal of Psychiatry*, 141 (1984), pp. 989–90; M. M. Fichter and C. Daser, "Symptomatology, psychosexual development and gender identity in 42 anorexic males," *Psychological Medicine*, 17 (1987), pp. 409–18; J. A. Schneider and W. S. Agras, "Bulimia in males: A matched comparison with females," *International Journal of Eating Disorders*, 6 (1987), pp. 235–42; and D. J. Carlat, C. A. Camargo, D. B. Herzog, "Eating disorders in males: A report on 125 patients," *American Journal of Psychiatry*, 154 (1997), pp. 1127–32. The latter accumulated information on 125 male patients over a 13-year period and found that 42 percent were either homosexual or bisexual. On the other hand, other studies have found much lower percentages of homosexuality among males with eating disorders, such as R. Olivardia, H. Pope, B. Mangweth, and J. I. Hudson, "Eating disorders in college men," *American Journal of Psychiatry*, 152 (1995), pp. 1279–85. The latter was a community study, and it is possible that gay males are over-represented in clinic samples. On the other hand, it is perhaps less likely that gay males would respond to a survey in which subjects are recruited by advertisement, such as the above.

68 J. Yager, F. Kurtzman, J. Landsverk, and E. Wiesmeier, "Behaviors and attitudes related to eating disorders in homosexual male college students," *American Journal of Psychiatry*, 145 (1988), pp. 495–7.

69 M. D. Siever, "Sexual orientation and gender as factors in socioculturally acquired vulnerability to body dissatisfaction and eating disorders," *Journal of Consulting and Clinical Psychology*, 62 (1994), pp. 252–60.

70 K. Hefferman, "Eating disorders and weight concerns among lesbians," *International Journal of Eating Disorders*, 19 (1996), pp. 127–38.

71 S. E. Beren, H. A. Haden, D. E. Wilfley, and R. H. Striegel-Moore, "Body dissatisfaction among lesbian college students: The conflict of straddling mainstream and lesbian cultures," *Psychology of Women Quarterly*, 21 (1997), pp. 431–45.

72 S. A. French, M. Story, G. Remafedi, M. D. Resnick, and R. W. Blum, "Sexual orientation and prevalence of body dissatisfaction and eating disordered behaviors: A population-based study of adolescents," *International Journal of Eating Disorders*, 19 (1996), pp. 119–26.

73 A detailed developmental account of the "gender dysphoria" hypothesis,

with richly detailed case histories, is given in J. A. Schneider, "Gender issues in male bulimia nervosa," in Johnson, *Psychodynamic Treatment of Anorexia Nervosa and Bulimia*, pp. 194–222.

74 A. Drewnowski and D. K. Yee, "Men and body image: Are males satisfied with their body weight?," *Psychosomatic Medicine*, 49 (1987), pp. 626–34.

75 The concept of reverse anorexia was described in H. G. Pope, D. L. Katz, and J. I. Hudson, "Anorexia nervosa and reverse anorexia among 108 male bodybuilders," *Comprehensive Psychiatry*, 34 (1993), pp. 406–9. Muscle dysmorphia is described in H. G. Pope, A. J. Gruber, P. Choi, R. Olivardia, and K. A. Phillips, "Muscle dysmorphia: An underrecognized form of body dysmorphic disorder," *Psychosomatics*, 38 (1997), pp. 548–57.

Chapter Five   The Thin Body Ideal

1 The experience of starvation in anorexics is beautifully described by Hilde Bruch, in *The Golden Cage* (New York: Vintage 1978), ch. 1.

2 G. F. M. Russell, "The changing nature of anorexia nervosa: An introduction to the conference," *Journal of Psychiatric Research*, 19 (1985), pp. 101–9.

3 See M. Poovey, "Scenes of an indelicate character: the medical treatment of Victorian women" *Representations*, 14 (Spring 1986), pp. 137–68. Poovey's discussion is mostly directed towards the atmosphere of anxious silence surrounding the obstetrical examination, but it could well apply to the sensitive topic of body weight. Some evidence for the hidden preoccupations of some nineteenth-century anorexics with body weight and the lack of attention of physicians to same is presented in J. J. Brumberg, *Fasting Girls: The Emergence of Anorexia Nervosa as a Modern Disease* (Cambridge, MA: Harvard University Press, 1988), p. 159.

4 The literature on body image distortion is extensive. For examples from clinical cases, see H. Bruch, *Eating Disorders: Obesity, Anorexia Nervosa and the Person Within* (New York: Basic Books, 1973), ch. 6; for an overview of the research literature through 1982, already prolific, see P. E. Garfinkel and D. M. Garner, *Anorexia Nervosa: A Multidimensional Approach* (New York: Brunner Mazel, 1982), ch. 6.

5 For a complex study of body image distortion using both methods of measurement, see G. F. Huon and L. B. Brown, "Body images in anorexia nervosa and bulimia nervosa," *International Journal of Eating Disorders*, 5 (1986), pp. 421–39. These researchers raised some of the complex distinctions between perceiving the body as fat versus "feeling"

that it is fat. One study found that the degree of size overestimation is even greater in normal-weight bulimics than anorexics. See S. W. Touyz, P. J. V. Beumont, J. K. Collins, and I. Cowie, "Body shape perception in bulimia and anorexia nervosa," *International Journal of Eating Disorders*, 4 (1985), pp. 259–65.

6 Bruch, *Eating Disorders*, p. 90.

7 Ibid.

8 S. C. Wooley and O. W. Wooley, "Intensive outpatient and residential treatment for bulimia," in *Handbook of Psychotherapy for Anorexia Nervosa and Bulimia*, ed. D. M. Garner and P. E. Garfinkel (New York: Guilford Press, 1985), p. 398.

9 R. M. Gardner and C. Moncrieff, "Body image distortion in anorexics as a non-sensory phenomenon: A signal-detection approach," *Journal of Clinical Psychology*, 44 (1988), pp. 101–7.

10 R. A. Pierloot and M. E. Houbon, "Estimation of body dimensions in anorexia nervosa," *Psychological Medicine*, 8 (1978), pp. 317–24. These researchers confronted patients with their mirror image and urged them to give more accurate estimations than the initial tests. See also A. H. Crisp and R. S. Kalucy, "Aspects of the perceptual disorder in anorexia nervosa," *British Journal of Medical Psychology*, 47 (1974), pp. 349–61, who urged the patient to "drop your guard for a moment and tell me again how wide you really judge yourself to be." For a therapeutic use of body image confrontation using videotape, see E. Gotheil, C. E. Backup, and F. S. Cornelison, "Denial and self-image confrontation in a case of anorexia nervosa," *Journal of Nervous and Mental Disease*, 148 (1969), pp. 238–50.

11 K. Halmi, S. Goldberg, and S. Cunningham, "Perceptual distortion of body image in adolescent girls: Distortion of body image in adolescence," *Psychological Medicine*, 7 (1977), pp. 253–7; E. Davies and A. Furnham, "Body satisfaction in adolescent girls," *British Journal of Medical Psychology*, 59 (1986), pp. 279–87; F. Fernandez, M. Probst, R. Meermann, and W. Vandereycken, "Body size estimation and body dissatisfaction in eating disorder patients and normal controls," *International Journal of Eating Disorders*, 16 (1994), pp. 306–10.

12 C. Bergh and P. Sodersten, "Anorexia nervosa: Rediscovery of a disorder," *Lancet*, May 9, 1998, pp. 1427–9.

13 M. Lawrence, "Anorexia nervosa: The control paradox," *Women's Studies International Quarterly*, 2 (1979), p. 94.

14 H. Bruch, *Conversations with Anorexics* (New York: Basic Books, 1988), p. 125.

15 L. Binswanger, "The case of Ellen West: An anthropological-clinical study," in *Existence: A New Dimension in Psychology and Psychiatry*, ed. R. May, E. Angel, and H. F. Ellenberger (New York: Basic Books, 1958), p. 251.

16 This connection was first pointed out by Hilde Bruch. Also, see T. Habermas, "On the meaning of thinness in the body experience of anorexics – illustrated with the sculptures of A. Giacommetti," *Psychther. med. Psychologie*, 36 (1986), pp. 69–74.

17 H. Bruch, *Conversations with Anorexics*, p. 157.

18 An extraordinarily rich and amusing history of weight preoccupation in the United States, which deals extensively with turn-of-the-century material, is H. Schwartz, *Never Satisfied: A Cultural History of Diets, Fantasies and Fat* (New York: Macmillan, 1986). An excellent historical discussion of the evolution of the thin-body ideal is contained in W. Bennett and J. Gurin, *The Dieter's Dilemma* (New York: Harper and Row, 1982), ch. 7. The already intense preoccupation with dieting in the 1950s is discussed in G. Walker, "The great American dieting neurosis," *New York Times Magazine*, Aug. 23, 1959.

19 For an overview, see R. Freedman, *Beauty Bound* (Lexington, MA: D. C. Heath and Company, 1986); also T. Cash and L. Janda, "The eye of the beholder," *Psychology Today*, December 1984, pp. 46–52.

20 D. Garner, P. E. Garfinkel, D. Schwartz, and M. Thompson, "Cultural expectations of thinness in women," *Psychological Reports*, 47 (1980), pp. 483–91.

21 C. V. Wiseman, J. J. Gray, J. E. Mosimann, and A. H. Ahrens, "Cultural expectations of thinness in women: An update," *International Journal of Eating Disorders*, 11 (1992), pp. 84–9.

22 R. J. Kuczmarski, K. M. Flegal, S. M. Campbell, and C. L. Johnson, "Increasing prevalence of overweight among US adults: The national health and nutrition examination surveys, 1960 to 1991," *Journal of the American Medical Association*, 272 (1994), pp. 205–11.

23 R. Fallon and P. Rozin, "Sex differences in perception of desirable body shape," *Journal of Abnormal Psychology*, 94 (1985), pp. 102–5.

24 "Feeling fat in a thin society," *Glamour*, February 1984, pp. 198–201, 251–2.

25 R. L. Huenemann, L. R. Shapiro, M. C. Hampton, and B. W. Mitchell, "A longitudinal study of gross body composition and body conformation and their association with food and activity in a teenage population," *American Journal of Clinical Nutrition*, 18 (1966), pp. 325–38.

26 I. Nylander, "The feeling of being fat and dieting in a school population," *Acta Sociomedica Scandinavica*, 3 (1971), pp. 17–26. The dieting subjects in this study were at elevated risk for an eating disorder, as indicated in a followup study several years later. See K. Schleimer, "Dieting in teenage schoolgirls: A longitudinal prospective study," *Acta Paediatrica Scandinavica Supplement*, 312 (1983), pp. 1–54. This issue is discussed at greater length in chapter 6.

27 S. M. Dornbusch, J. M. Carlsmith, P. D. Duncan, R. T. Gross, J. A. Martin, P. L. Ritter, and B. Siegel-Gorelick, "Sexual maturation, social class, and the desire to be thin among adolescent females," *Developmental and Behavioral Pediatrics*, 5 (1984), pp. 308–14.

28 "Girls, at 7, think thin, study finds," *New York Times Health Section*, Feb. 11, 1988. See also A. J. Hill, E. Draper, and J. Stack, "A weight on children's minds: Body shape dissatisfactions at 9-years old," *International Journal of Obesity*, 18 (1994), pp. 383–9; A. J. Hill, S. Oliver, and P. J. Rogers, "Eating in the adult world: The rise of dieting in childhood and adolescence," *British Journal of Clinical Psychology*, 30 (1991), pp. 346–8; S. H. Thompson, S. J. Corwin, and R. G. Sargent, "Ideal body size beliefs and weight concerns of fourth-grade children," *International Journal of Eating Disorders*, 21 (1997), pp. 279–84; K. Rolland, D. Farnill, and R. A. Griffiths, "Body figure perceptions and eating attitudes among Australian schoolchildren aged 8 to 12 years," *International Journal of Eating Disorders*, 21 (1997), pp. 273–8.

29 See R. Bryant-Waugh and B. Lask, "Annotation: Eating disorders in children," *Journal of Child Psychology and Psychiatry*, 36 (1995), pp. 191–202. These authors report a sharp increase in the referral of preadolescent children with eating disorders at Great Ormond Street Hospital for Children in London in the early 1990s (10 with anorexia nervosa in 1991, 17 in 1992, 25 in 1993, and 25 in the first six months of 1994). They point out that most preadolescent children do not meet the formal diagnostic criteria for eating disorders (for example, a preadolescent who has not started menstruation cannot have amenorrhea), and yet most could be described in the following general terms: "a disorder of childhood in which there is an excessive preoccupation with weight and shape, and/or food intake, and accompanied by grossly inadequate, irregular or chaotic food intake." The growing preoccupation of younger children with thinness and dieting would seem to implicate cultural factors in obvious fashion.

30 Garfinkel and Garner, *Anorexia Nervosa*, pp. 112–17.

31 A. De Mille, *And Promenade Home*, quoted in L. M. Vincent, *Competing with the Sylph* (New York: Berkeley Books, 1979).

32 G. Kirkland, *Dancing on My Grave* (New York: Doubleday, 1986), pp. 55–6.

33 Vincent, *Competing with the Sylph*.

34 Ibid., p. 78.

35 Ibid., p. 79.

36 Ibid., p. 79.

37 L. H. Hamilton, J. Brooks-Gunn, and M. P. Warren, "Sociocultural influences on eating disorders in professional female ballet dancers," *In-*

ternational Journal of Eating Disorders, 4 (1985), pp. 465–78.

38 J. Dunning, "Dancing with death: Eating disorders and ballerinas," *New York Times*, July 16, 1997.

39 M. B. King and G. Mezey, "Eating behavior of male racing jockeys," *Psychological Medicine*, 17 (1987), pp. 249–53.

40 C. Lasch, *The Culture of Narcissism* (New York: Warner Books, 1979).

41 See, for example, D. M. Schwartz, M. G. Thompson, and C. L. Johnson, "Anorexia nervosa and bulimia: The sociocultural context," *International Journal of Eating Disorders*, 1 (1982), pp. 23–35, and Garfinkel and Garner, *Anorexia Nervosa*, ch. 6.

42 The one major exception to this statement is the writing of Arthur H. Crisp. See, for example, Crisp, *Anorexia Nervosa: Let Me Be* (London: Academic Press, 1980), ch. 5.

43 C. S. Ford and F. A. Beach, *Patterns of Sexual Behavior* (New York: Ace Books, 1951).

44 Schwartz, *Never Satisfied*, p. 338; W. Shack, "Hunger, anxiety, and ritual: Deprivation and spirit possession among the Gurage of Ethiopia," *Man*, 6 (1971), pp. 30–43.

45 H. Powdermaker, "An anthropological approach to the problem of obesity," *Bulletin of the New York Academy of Medicine*, 36 (1960), pp. 286–95.

46 A. Mazrui, *The Africans: A Triple Heritage* (Boston: Little, Brown, 1986), pp. 127–8.

47 P. Crispin, "The essence of fattening," *Democratic Weekly* (Lagos), July 29, 1984.

48 These issues are portrayed novelistically in Buchi Emecheta, *Double Yoke* (London: Ogwugwu Afor, 1982).

49 A. S. Beller, *Fat and Thin: A Natural History of Obesity* (New York: McGraw-Hill, 1977), ch. 3.

50 Bennett and Gurin, *The Dieter's Dilemma*, ch. 7. The Steel-engraving Lady is discussed in L. Banner, *American Beauty* (New York: Basic Books, 1983). A fascinating and provocative discussion of the corset, one that runs against contemporary feminist interpretations, is D. Kunzle, *Fashion and Fetishism: A Social History of the Corset, Tight-Lacing and Other Forms of Body Sculpture in the West* (Totowa, NJ: Roman and Littlefield, 1982). The author suggests that some women who wore corsets were also anorexic; like some contemporary patients (and perhaps even some beauty pageant contestants), self-starvation may have been a "practical strategy" to conform to stringent clothing dimensions.

51 T. Veblen, *The Theory of the Leisure Class* (New York: Macmillan, 1899), pp. 148–9.

52 Quoted in V. Steele, *Fashion and Eroticism* (New York: Oxford University Press, 1985), p. 227.

53 "On growing fat," *Atlantic Monthly*, March 1907, pp. 430–1 (quoted in Brumberg, *Fasting Girls*, p. 340).

54 Bennett and Gurin, *The Dieter's Dilemma*, p. 208.

55 S. Ewen and E. Ewen, *Channels of Desire: Mass Images and the Shaping of the American Consciousness* (New York: McGraw-Hill, 1982).

56 Walker, "The great American dieting neurosis."

57 See, for example, "Curves from an earlier era," *New York Times*, Dec. 6, 1987, p. 98; "New York feminine flourishes," *New York Times Magazine*, Oct. 25, 1987, pp. 70ff.

58 I am grateful to Patricia Fallon for this observation.

59 R. Coward, *Female Desires: How They are Sought, Bought, and Packaged* (New York: Grove Press, 1985).

60 I am grateful to Christopher Athas, Vice-President of the National Association of Anorexia Nervosa and Associated Disorders, for this information regarding the Hershey advertisement.

61 S. H. Murray, S. W. Touyz, and P. J. V. Beumont, "Awareness and perceived influence of body ideals in the media: A comparison of eating disorder patients and the general community," *Eating Disorders: Journal of Treatment and Prevention*, 4 (1996), pp. 33–46.

62 *Today* show (NBC), June 13, 1989.

63 For example, E. Stice and H. E. Shaw, "Adverse effects of the media-portrayed thin ideal on women and linkages to bulimic symptomatology," *Journal of Social and Clinical Psychology*, 13 (1994), pp. 288–308; C. R. Kalodner, "Media influences on male and female non-eating-disordered college students: A significant issue," *Eating Disorders: Journal of Treatment and Prevention*, 5 (1997), pp. 47–57.

64 Murray, Touyz, and Beumont, "Awareness and perceived influence of body ideals in the media." See also K. Hamilton and G. Waller, "Media influences on body size estimation in anorexia and bulimia: An experimental study," *British Journal of Psychiatry*, 162 (1993), pp. 837–40. This study showed that exposure to thinness imagery led a group of eating-disordered patients to significantly overestimate their body size more than normal controls.

65 A. E. Becker and P. Hamburg, "Culture, the media, and eating disorders," *Harvard Review of Psychiatry*, 4 (1996), pp. 163–7.

66 C. G. Fairburn, S. L. Welch, H. A. Doll, B. A. Davies, and M. E. O'Conner, "Risk factors for bulimia nervosa: A community-based case-control study," *Archives of General Psychiatry*, 54 (1997), pp. 509–17.

67 David Garner, presentation on "Challenging the Overvaluation of Thinness," Sixth Annual Conference on Anorexia Nervosa and Bulimia, sponsored by the National Anorexic Aid Society, Columbus, Ohio, October 1987.

68 See, for example, C. Steiner-Adair and A. Purcell, "Approaches to mainstreaming eating disorders prevention," *Eating Disorders: Journal of Treatment and Prevention*, 4 (1996), pp. 294–309; M. P. Levine, L. Smolak, and F. Schermer, "Media analysis and resistance by elementary school children in the primary prevention of eating problems," *Eating Disorders: Journal of Treatment and Prevention*, 4 (1996), pp. 310–22; S. Berel and L. M. Irving, "Media and disturbed eating: An analysis of media influence and implications for prevention," *Journal of Primary Prevention*, 18 (1998), pp. 415–30.

69 B. Barber, *Jihad vs. McWorld* (New York: Times Books, 1995)

70 A. Becker, *Body, Self and Society: The View from Fiji* (Philadelphia: University of Pennsylvania Press, 1995).

71 These findings were presented at the meeting of the American Psychiatric Association in May 1999. A. E. Becker and R. A. Burwell, "Acculturation and Disordered Eating in Fiji," American Psychiatric Association 1999 Annual Meeting. New Research Program and Abstracts, 1999. My thanks to Dr Becker for providing details and permitting me to cite her work.

72 B. Silverstein, B. Peterson, and L. Perdue, "Some correlates of the thin standard of bodily attractiveness for women," *International Journal of Eating Disorders*, 5 (1986), pp. 895–905; B. Silverstein, L. Perdue, B. Peterson, L. Vogel, and D. Fantini, "Possible causes of the thin standard of bodily attractiveness for women," *International Journal of Eating Disorders*, 5 (1986), pp. 907–16.

73 Silverstein et al., "Possible causes of the thin standard."

74 B. Silverstein and L. Perdue, "The relationship between role concerns, preferences for slimness, and symptoms of eating problems among college women," *Sex Roles*, 18 (1988), pp. 101–6; B. Silverstein, L. Perdue, C. Wolf, and C. Pizzolo, "Bingeing, purging, and estimates of parental attitudes regarding female achievement," *Sex Roles*, 19 (1988), pp. 723–33.

75 The theme has been developed in greater historical depth in B. Silverstein and D. Perlick, *The Cost of Competence: Why Inequality Causes Depression, Eating Disorders and Illness in Women* (New York: Oxford University Press, 1995).

76 These considerations have been elaborated further in N. Barber, "The slender ideal and eating disorders: An interdisciplinary 'telescope' model," *International Journal of Eating Disorders*, 23 (1998), pp. 295–307.

77 S. R. Dyrenforth, O. W. Wooley, and S. C. Wooley, "A woman's body in a man's world: A review of findings on body image and weight control," in *A Woman's Conflict: The Special Relationship Between Women and Food*, ed. J. R. Kaplan (Englewood Cliffs, NJ: Prentice-Hall, 1980), pp. 29–58.

78 G. Obeyesekere, *Medusa's Hair* (Chicago: University of Chicago Press, 1981).

Chapter Six   The War Against Fat: Obesity, Dieting, and Exercise

1 P. J. Brown and M. Konner, "An anthropological perspective on obesity," in *Human Obesity*, ed. R. J. Wurtman and J. Wurtman (New York: The New York Academy of Sciences, 1987).

2 J. R. Staffieri, "A study of social stereotype of body image in children," *Journal of Personality and Social Psychology*, 7 (1967), pp. 101–4.

3 A profession of vegetarianism is common among anorexics. See R. Kadambari, S. Gowers, and A. Crisp, "Some correlates of vegetarianism in anorexia nervosa," *International Journal of Eating Disorders*, 5 (1986), pp. 539–44. However, it is probably in most instances a secondary rationalization of caloric avoidance, not a primary philosophical commitment. A case of preadolescent anorexia nervosa that was triggered by an attempt to reduce cholesterol level was reported at a panel discussion on Preadolescent Anorexia Nervosa at the Third International Conference on Eating Disorders, New York, April 1988.

4 Meat avoidance was also common among nineteenth-century anorexics. See J. J. Brumberg, *Fasting Girls: The Emergence of Anorexia Nervosa as a Modern Disease* (Cambridge, MA: Harvard University Press, 1988). The magical and instantaneous transformation of food into body substance (fat into fat) is one of the bases of the infamous "Beverly Hills Diet" (see chapter 7).

5 The phrase is that of the English psychiatrist John Dally. On the weight and fitness preoccupations of the families of anorexics, see R. S. Kalucy, A. H. Crisp, and B. Harding, "A study of 56 families with anorexia nervosa," *British Journal of Medical Psychology*, 50 (1977), pp. 381–95.

6 J. A. Sours, *Starving to Death in a Sea of Objects* (New York: Jason Aronson, 1979), p. 325.

7 H. Bruch, *Eating Disorders: Obesity, Anorexia Nervosa and the Person Within* (New York: Basic Books, 1973), p. 95.

8 D. B. Herzog, "Bulimia: The secretive syndrome," *Psychosomatics*, 23 (1982), pp. 481–3; R. L. Pyle, J. E. Mitchell, and E. D. Eckert, "Bulimia: A report of 34 cases," *Journal of Clinical Psychiatry*, 42 (1981), pp. 60–4.

9 The families of bulimics in general are given more to oral pleasures and addictive behaviors; alcohol abuse is also commonly (although not always) a problem in the family. C. M. Bulik, "Drug and alcohol abuse by bulimic women and their families," *American Journal of Psychiatry*, 144 (1987), pp. 1604–6.

10 These issues have been discussed by S. Wooley and O. W. Wooley, "Intensive outpatient and residential treatment for bulimia," in *Handbook of Psychotherapy for Anorexia Nervosa and Bulimia*, ed. D. M. Garner

and P. E. Garfinkel (New York: Guilford Press, 1985), ch. 17.

11 R. J. Kuczmarski, K. M. Flegal, S. M. Campbell, and C. L. Johnson, "Increasing prevalence of overweight among US adults: The national health and nutrition examination surveys, 1960 to 1991," *Journal of the American Medical Association*, 272 (1994), pp. 205–11. See also the accompanying editorial by F. Xavier Pi-Sunyer, "The fattening of America," pp. 238–9.

12 J. C. Seidell and K. M. Flegal, "Assessing obesity: Classification and epidemiology," *British Medical Bulletin*, 53 (1997), pp. 238–52.

13 See Brown and Konner, "An anthropological perspective on obesity." See also C. R. Raymond, "Biology, culture, dietary changes conspire to increase incidence of obesity," *Journal of the American Medical Association*, 256 (1986), pp. 2157–8.

14 A. Furnham and N. Alibhai, "Cross-cultural differences in the perception of female body shapes," *Psychological Medicine*, 13 (1983), pp. 829–37.

15 See A. Stunkard, "From explanation to action in psychosomatic medicine: the case of obesity," *Psychosomatic Medicine*, 37 (1975), pp. 195–236; A. Stunkard, E. D'Aquili, S. Fox, and R. Filion, "Influence of social class on obesity and thinness in children," *Journal of the American Medical Association*, 221 (1972), pp. 579–84. J. Sobal and A. J. Stunkard, "Socioeconomic status and obesity: A review of the literature," *Psychological Bulletin*, 105 (1989), pp. 260–75.

16 G. A. Bray, "Effects of obesity on health and happiness," in *Handbook of Eating Disorders: Physiology, Psychology and Treatment of Obesity, Anorexia and Bulimia*, ed. K. D. Brownell and J. P. Foreyt (New York: Basic Books, 1986); G. A. Bray, "Pathophysiology of obesity," *American Journal of Clinical Nutrition*, 55 (1992), pp. 488S–494S; I. M. Lee, J. E. Manson, C. H. Hennekens, and R. S. Paffenbarger, "Body weight and mortality: A 27-year follow-up of middle-aged men," *Journal of the American Medical Association*, 270 (1993), pp. 2823–28.

17 J. E. Manson, W. C. Willett, M. J. Stampfer, G. A. Colditz, D. J. Hunter, S. E. Hankinson, C. H. Hennekens, and F. E. Speizer, "Body weight and mortality among women," *The New England Journal of Medicine*, 333 (1995), pp. 677–85.

18 R. P. Troiano, K. M. Flegal, R. J. Kuczmarski, S. M. Campbell, and C. L. Johnson, "Overweight prevalence and trends for children and adolescents. The National Health and Nutrition Examination Surveys, 1963–91," *Archives of Pediatrics and Adolescent Medicine*, 149 (1995), pp. 1085–91; R. E. Andersen, C. J. Cresp, S. J. Bartlett, L. J. Cheskin, and M. Pratt, "Relationship of physical activity and television watching with body weight and level of fatness among children: Results from the Third National Health and Nutrition Examination Survey," *Journal of the Ameri-*

can Medical Association, 279 (1998), pp. 938–42.

19 A. M. Prentice and S. A. Jebb, "Obesity in Britain: Gluttony or sloth?" *British Medical Journal*, 311 (1995), pp. 437–9.

20 See, for example, W. C. Willett and J. E. Manson, "Epidemiological studies of health risks due to excess weight," in *Eating Disorders and Obesity: A Comprehensive Handbook*, ed. K. D. Brownell and C. G. Fairburn (New York: Guilford Press, 1995), pp. 396–400; and F. X. Pi-Sunyer, "Medical complications of obesity," in the same volume, pp. 401–5.

21 This controversy is discussed by D. M. Garner, W. Rockert, M. P. Olmsted, C. Johnson, and D. Coscina, "Psychoeducational principles in the treatment of bulimia and anorexia nervosa," in Garner and Garfinkel, *Handbook of Psychotherapy for Anorexia Nervosa and Bulimia*, pp. 513–72.

22 Brown and Konner, "An anthropological perspective on obesity."

23 C. Ritenbaugh, "Obesity is a culture bound syndrome," *Culture, Medicine, and Psychiatry*, 6 (1982), pp. 347–61.

24 C. Bouchard, A. Tremblay, J. P. Despres, A. Nadeau, P. J. Lupien, G. Theriault, J. Dussault, S. Moorjani, S. Pineault, and G. Fournier, "The response to long-term overfeeding in identical twins," *The New England Journal of Medicine*, 322 (1990), pp. 1477–82.

25 J. Marx, "Obesity gene discovery may help solve weighty problem," *Science*, 266 (1994), pp. 1477–8.

26 M. Marinaga, " 'Obese' protein slims mice," *Science*, 269 (1995), pp. 475–6; M. Pelleymounter, M. J. Cullen, M. B. Bakler, R. Hecht, D. Winters, T. Boone, and F. Collins, "Effects of the *obese* gene product on body weight regulation in *ob/ob* mice," *Science*, 269 (1995), pp. 540–3; J. L. Halass, K. S. Gajiwala, M. Maffei, S. L. Coehn, B. T. Chait, D. R. Rabinowitz, R. L. Lallone, S. K. Burley, and J. M. Friedman, "Weight-reducing effects of the plasma protein encoded by the *obese* gene," *Science*, 269 (1995), pp. 543–6.

27 E. S. Valenstein, *Great and Desperate Cures* (New York: Basic Books, 1986).

28 For a critical discussion of the dangers and possible abuses of liposuction, see R. M. Henig, "The high cost of thinness," *New York Times Magazine*, Feb. 28, 1988.

29 A. M. Prentice, "Obesity – The inevitable penalty of civilisation?," *British Medical Bulletin*, 53 (1997), pp. 229–37.

30 H. Schwartz, *Never Satisfied: A Cultural History of Diets, Fantasies and Fat* (New York: Macmillan, 1986); see esp. pp. 77–84, 305–7.

31 C. Crandall, and M. Biernat, "The ideology of anti-fat attitudes," *Journal of Applied Social Psychology*, 20 (1990), pp. 227–43. See also S. Wooley and O. W. Wooley, "Should obesity be treated at all?," in *Eating and Its Disorders*, ed. A. Stunkard and E. Stellar (New York: Raven Press, 1984).

Particularly provocative is the negative evidence for the common belief that the obese overeat. On the stigmatization of the obese, see S. Millman, *Such a Pretty Face: On Being Fat in America* (New York: W. W. Norton, 1980).

32 C. S. Crandall, "Prejudice against fat people: Ideology and self-interest," *Journal of Personality and Social Psychology*, 66 (1994), pp. 882–94.

33 W. J. Cahnman, "The stigma of obesity," *Sociological Quarterly*, 9 (1968), pp. 283–95.

34 Brown and Konner, "An anthropological perspective on obesity." See also A. Sobal and A. J. Stunkard, "Socioeconomic status and obesity."

35 See S. Bordo, "Reading the slender body," in *Unbearable Weight: Feminism, Culture and the Body* (Berkeley: University of California Press, 1993).

36 Brown and Konner, "An anthropological perspective on obesity."

37 H. Canning and J. Meyer, "Obesity – its possible effect on college acceptance," *The New England Journal of Medicine*, 275 (1966), pp. 1172–4.

38 See, for example, L. R. Reskin, "Employers must give job applicants a chance," *Journal of the American Bar Association*, 71 (1985), p. 104.

39 M. R. Hebl and T. F. Heatherton, "The stigma of obesity in women: The difference is Black and White," *Personality and Social Psychology Bulletin*, 24 (1998), pp. 417–26.

40 In fact, one large scale study found a *greater* drive for thinness among black preadolescent girls in the United States than their white counterparts (R. H. Striegel-Moore, G. B. Schreiber, K. M. Pike, D. E. Wilfley, and J. Rodin, "Drive for thinness in black and white preadolescent girls," *International Journal of Eating Disorders*, 18 (1995), pp. 59–69). These authors speculate that black girls' drive for thinness may reflect a "realistic appraisal of becoming overweight." The relationship between drive for thinness and low self-esteem that was found for white girls was not in evidence for black girls.

41 D. R. Greenberg and D. J. LaPorte, "Racial differences in body type preferences of men for women," *International Journal of Eating Disorders*, 19 (1996), pp. 275–8.

42 S. Orbach, *Fat is a Feminist Issue* (New York: Berkeley Books, 1979).

43 S. Orback, *Hunger Strike: Anorexia as a Metaphor for Our Time* (New York: W. W. Norton, 1986).

44 L. Brown and E. Rothblum, "Fat oppression and psychotherapy: A feminist perspective," *Women and Therapy*, 8 (1989); E. D. Rothblum, " 'I'll die for the Revolution but Don't Ask Me Not to Diet:' Feminism and the continuing stigmatization of obesity," in *Feminist Perspectives on Eating Disorders*, ed. P. Fallon, M. A. Katzman, and S. C. Wooley (New York:

Guilford Press, 1994), pp. 53–66; and in the same volume, M. G. Hutchinson, "Imagining ourselves whole: A feminist approach to treating body image disorders," pp. 152–70; and D. Burgard and P. Lyons, "Alternatives in obesity treatment: Focusing on health for fat women," pp. 212–30.

45 The popular Christian literature linking dieting to salvation includes Deborah Pierce, *I Prayed Myself Thin* (1960), Ann Thomas, *God's Answer to Overeating* (1975): and K. Wise, *God Knows I Won't Be Fat Again* (1978). These and other references are cited in Schwartz, *Never Satisfied*, p. 439.

46 K. Lampson Reiff, "The fundamental flaw: Christianity and eating disorders," presented at Sixth National Conference on Anorexia Nervosa and Bulimia, sponsored by the National Anorexic Aid Society, Columbus, Ohio, October 1987.

47 T. Berland, *Rating the Diets* (Stokie, IL: Publications International Ltd, 1986).

48 M. Gladwell, "The Pima paradox," *The New Yorker*, Feb. 2, 1998, pp. 44–57. I have followed Gladwell's incisive analysis of *The Zone Diet*.

49 The hypothesis of the effects of yo-yo dieting on metabolic rate and subsequent weight loss is controversial, and has recently been criticized by Brownell, who originally proposed it. See K. D. Brownell and J. Rodin, "The dieting maelstrom," *American Psychologist*, 49 (1994), pp. 781–91. Evidence for an increase in morbidity from weight cycling was presented in L. Lissner, P. M. Odell, R. B. D'Agostino, J. Stokes, B. E. Kreger, A. J. Belanger, and K. D. Brownell, "Variability in body weight and health outcomes in the Framingham population," *The New England Journal of Medicine*, 324 (1991), 1839–44. According to Brownell and Rodin, however, there is also contradictory evidence for the notion that weight cycling brings about ill health.

50 J. R. Hirschmann and C. H. Munter, *Overcoming Overeating: Living Free in a World of Food* (Boston: Addison-Wesley, 1988); G. Roth, *Feeding the Hungry Heart: The Experience of Compulsive Eating* (New York: NAL, 1983).

51 R. Klein, *EAT FAT* (New York: Pantheon Books, 1996).

52 An overview of this work is contained in J. Polivy and C. P. Herman, "Diagnosis and treatment of normal eating," *Journal of Clinical and Consulting Psychology*, 55 (1987), pp. 635–44.

53 C. P. Herman and J. Polivy, "Restrained eating," in *Obesity*, ed. A. J. Stunkard (Philadelphia: W. B. Saunders, 1980, pp. 208–25).

54 J. Polivy, "Perception of calories and regulation of intake in restrained and unrestrained subjects," *Addictive Behaviors*, 1 (1976), pp. 237–43.

55 J. Polivy and C. P. Herman, "The effects of alcohol on eating behavior:

Influences of mood and perceived intoxication," *Journal of Abnormal Psychology*, 85 (1976), pp. 601–6.

56 C. P. Herman and J. Polivy, "Effects of an observer on eating behavior: The induction of 'sensible eating'," *Journal of Personality*, 47 (1979), pp. 85–9.

57 R. Larson and C. G. Johnson, "Bulimia: Disturbed patterns of solitude," *Addictive Behaviors*, 10 (1985), pp. 281–90.

58 J. Polivy and C. P. Herman, "Dieting and binging: A causal analysis," *American Psychologist*, 400 (1985), pp. 193–201.

59 M. R. Lowe, D. H. Gleaves, and K. P. Murphy-Eberenz, "On the relation of dieting and bingeing in bulimia nervosa," *Journal of Abnormal Psychology*, 107 (1998), pp. 263–71.

60 G. C. Patton, E. Johnson-Sabine, K. Wood, A. H. Mann, and A. Wakeling, "Abnormal eating attitudes in London schoolgirls – a prospective epidemiological study: Outcome at twelve month follow-up," *Psychological Medicine*, 20 (1990), pp. 383–94.

61 K. Schleimer, "Dieting in teenage schoolgirls: A longitudinal prospective study," *Acta Paediatrica Scandinavica Supplement*, 312 (1983), pp. 1–54.

62 An important study of the interacting risk factors for bulimia is that of C. G. Fairburn, S. L. Welch, H. A. Doll, B. A. Davies, and M. E. O'Conner, "Risk factors for bulimia nervosa: A community-based case-control study," *Archives of General Psychiatry*, 54 (1997), pp. 509–17. These researchers found that while factors such as adverse childhood events and childhood psychiatric symptoms were not unique to bulimia nervosa patients, a history of weight preoccupation as well as a family preoccupation with achievement coupled with parental detachment were specific risk factors for the disorder.

63 R. C. Casper, "Behavioral activation and lack of concern, core symptoms of anorexia nervosa?" *International Journal of Eating Disorders*, 24 (1998), pp. 381–94.

64 W. F. Epling, W. D. Pierce, and L. Stefan, "A theory of activity-based anorexia," *International Journal of Eating Disorders*, 3 (1983), pp. 27–46.

65 H. Green, *Fit for America: Health, Fitness and Sport in American Society* (New York: Pantheon, 1986).

66 "Shaping up: The worldwide fitness boom," *Newsweek* (International Edition), Sept. 10, 1984.

67 See J. Klemesrud, "Now, personal trainers push clients to new highs of fitness," *New York Times*, Style Section, Dec. 14, 1984, p. B18. See also "Coach, confessor, confidante: Is the personal trainer the therapist of our times?" *Self*, March 1989, pp. 95–9.

68 M. MacKenzie, "The distrust of pleasure in affluent societies: Anthropol-

ogy and the concept of culture in eating disorders," presented at Third International Conference on Anorexia Nervosa and Related Disorders, Swansea, Wales, September 1984.

69 P. J. V. Beumont, S. W. Touyz, and S. Hook, "Exercise and anorexia nervosa," presented at Third International Conference on Anorexia Nervosa and Related Disorders, Swansea, Wales, September 1984.

70 J. Chalmers, J. Catalan, A. Day, and C. Fairburn, "Anorexia nervosa presenting as morbid exercising," *Lancet*, Feb. 2, 1985, pp. 286–7.

71 See, for example, N. J. Smith, "Excessive weight loss and food aversion in athletes simulating anorexia nervosa," *Pediatrics*, 66 (1980), pp. 139–142; P. Zucker, J. Avener, and S. Bayder, "Eating disorders in young athletes," *The Physician and Sportsmedicine*, 13 (1985), pp. 88–106; J. S. Borgun and C. B. Corbin, "Eating disorders among female athletes," *The Physician and Sportsmedicine*, 15 (1987), pp. 89–95; J. Brooks-Gunn, C. Burrow, and M. P. Warren, "Attitudes toward eating and body weight in different groups of female adolescent athletes," *International Journal of Eating Disorders*, 7 (1988), pp. 749–57.

72 L. W. Rosen, D. B. McKeag, D. O. Hough, et al., "Pathogenic weight control behavior in female athletes," *The Physician and Sportsmedicine*, 14 (1986), 79–86. Also G. Dummer, L. Rosen, W. Heusner, P. Roberts, and J. E. Counsilman, "Pathogenic weight-control behaviors of young competitive swimmers," *The Physician and Sportsmedicine*, 15 (1987), pp. 75–84. In the latter study, the authors were surprised to find that even in swimming, in which the demands for weight and shape control are not as rigorous as in other sports, the level of pathogenic weight-control behaviors was quite high.

73 J. Sundgot-Borgen, "Risk and trigger factors for the development of eating disorders in female elite athletes," *International Journal of Sports Nutrition*, 3 (1993), pp. 29–40.

74 I. R. Tofler, B. K. Stryer, L. J. Micheli, and L. R. Herman, "Physical and emotional problems of elite female gymnasts," *The New England Journal of Medicine*, 335 (1996), pp. 281–3.

75 A good discussion of the kinship between running and anorexia is given in Sours, *Starving to Death*, pp. 259–60, 283–6.

76 G. Sheehan, *Running and Being: The Total Experience* (New York: Warner Books, 1978).

77 Ibid., p. 36.

78 Ibid., p. 38.

79 Sours, *Starving to Death*, pp. 282–6.

80 A. Yates, K. Leehey, and C. Shisslak, "Running: An analogue of anorexia?" *The New England Journal of Medicine*, 308 (1983), pp. 251–5. For a subsequent analysis with useful additional commentaries, see A.

Yates, "Eating disorders and long-distance running: The ascetic condition," *Integrative Psychiatry*, 5 (1987), pp. 201–11.

81 Yates, Leehey, and Shisslak, "Running," p. 252.

82 R. Coward, *Female Desires: How They are Sought, Bought, and Packaged* (New York: Grove Press, 1985).

83 See, for example, J. A. Blumenthal, L. C. O'Toole, and J. L. Chang, "Is running an analogue of anorexia nervosa? An empirical study of obligatory running and anorexia nervosa," *Journal of the American Medical Association*, 252 (1984), pp. 520–3; and L. M. Weight and T. D. Noakes, "Is running an analogue of anorexia?: A survey of the incidence of eating disorders in female distance runners," *Medicine and Science in Sports and Exercise*, 19 (1987), pp. 213–17.

84 A. Yates, *Compulsive Exercise and the Eating Disorders: Towards An Integrated Theory of Activity* (New York: Brunner Mazel, 1991). See also H. A. Slay, J. Hayuaki, M. A. Napolitano, and K. D. Brownell, "Motivations for running and eating attitudes in obligatory versus nonobligatory runners," *International Journal of Eating Disorders*, 23 (1998), pp. 267–76.

85 T. F. Heatherton, P. Nichols, F. Mahamedi, and P. Keel, "Body weight, dieting and eating disorders symptoms among college students, 1982–1992," *American Journal of Psychiatry*, 152 (1995), pp. 1623–9.

86 See, for example, Jane Brody, "For women who haven't gotten the message yet: Thin isn't necessarily in," *New York Times*, Health Column, March 18, 1987; Trish Hall, "Self-denial fades as Americans return to the sweet life," *New York Times*, Living Section, March 11, 1987; A. J. Britton, "Thin is out, fit is in," *American Health*, July 1988, pp. 65ff. But also, N. R. Kleinfield, "The ever-fatter business of thinness," *New York Times*, Sept. 7, 1986, Business Section, p. 1.

Chapter Seven   The Templates of a Disease

1 G. Devereux, "Normal and abnormal: The key problem of psychiatric anthropology," in *Basic Problems of Ethnopsychiatry* (Chicago: University of Chicago Press, 1980), p. 42.

2 Ibid., p. 34.

3 T. Szasz, *The Second Sin* (New York: Anchor Books, 1974), p. 105.

4 H. Ellenberger, *The Discovery of the Unconscious* (New York: Basic Books, 1970), p. 256.

5 A. Bandura, *Social Learning Theory* (New Jersey: General Learning Press, 1971).

6 H. Bruch, "Four decades of eating disorders," in *Handbook of Psychotherapy for Anorexia Nervosa and Bulimia*, ed. D. M. Garner and P. E.

Garfinkel (New York: Guilford Press, 1985), p. 11.

7 A. Silber, "Acquired pseudo eating disorder: An imitation or fabrication of anorexia nervosa," *Journal of Adolescent Health Care*, 8 (1987), pp. 452–5.

8 J. Yager and C. A. Hatton, "Anorexia nervosa in a woman totally blind since the age of two," *British Journal of Psychiatry*, 148 (1986), pp. 506–9.

9 A comparison suggested to me by Craig Johnson.

10 I am grateful to Dr Paul Kaunitz for sharing this observation from the days of his psychiatric training.

11 J. Dwyer, J. J. Feldman, and J. Mayer, "The social psychology of dieting," *Journal of Health and Social Behavior*, 11 (1970), pp. 269–87.

12 J. Rodin, L. Silberstein, and R. Striegel-Moore, "Women and weight: A normative discontent," in *Nebraska Symposium on Motivation, 1984*, ed. T. Sonderegger (Lincoln: The University of Nebraska Press, 1985), p. 290.

13 H. Bruch, *Conversations with Anorexics* (New York: Basic Books, 1988), p. 149.

14 Ibid., p. 150.

15 A. Liu, *Solitaire* (New York: Harper and Row, 1979), pp. 106ff.

16 J. J. Brumberg, *Fasting Girls: The Emergence of Anorexia Nervosa as a Modern Disease* (Cambridge, MA: Harvard University Press, 1988), p. 19.

17 P. N. Wold, "Family attitudes toward weight in bulimia and in affective disorder – a pilot study," *Psychiatric Journal of the University of Ottowa*, 10 (1985), pp. 162–4; J. E. Mitchell, D. Hatsukami, R. L. Pyle, and E. D. Eckert, "Parental factors related to bulimia nervosa," *Comprehensive Psychiatry*, 27 (1986), pp. 165–70.

18 A. Moreno and M. H. Thelen, "Parental factors related to bulimia nervosa," *Addictive Behaviors*, 18 (1993), pp. 681–9.

19 K. M. Pike and J. Rodin, "Mothers, daughters, and disordered eating," *Journal of Abnormal Psychology*, 100 (1991), pp. 198–204.

20 See Moreno and Thelen, "Parental factors related to bulimia nervosa." In fact, these authors suggest that it is not a history of overweight per se but rather the mother's direct encouragement of the daughter to lose weight which plays a critical role in the development of the eating disorder.

21 G. F. M. Russell, J. Treasure, and I. Eisler, "Mothers with anorexia nervosa who underfeed their children: Their recognition and management," *Psychological Medicine*, 28 (1998), pp. 93–108. See also A. Stein and H. Woolley, "The influence of parental eating disorders on young children: Implications for some clinical interventions," *Eating Disorders: Journal of Treatment and Prevention*, 4 (1996), pp. 139–46. The latter

documented the impact of the feeding patterns of anorexic mothers on the eating behavior of their one-year-olds. A chief area of difficulty for the mother is the child's making a "mess."

22 A. Stein and C. G. Fairburn, "Children of mothers with bulimia nervosa," *British Medical Journal*, 299 (1989), 777–8.

23 K. M. Pike, "Bulimic symptomatology in high school girls: Towards a model of cumulative risk," *Psychology of Women Quarterly*, 19 (1995), pp. 373–96. See also P. K. Keel, T. F. Heatherton, J. L. Harnden, and C. D. Hornig, "Mothers, fathers and daughters: Dieting and disordered eating," *Eating Disorders: Journal of Treatment and Prevention*, 5 (1997), pp. 216–38.

24 M. P. Levine, L. Smolak, and H. Hayden, "The relation of sociocultural factors to eating attitudes and behaviors among middle school girls," *Journal of Early Adolescence*, 14 (1994), pp. 471–90. See also M. P. Levine, L. Smolak, A. F. Moodey, M. D. Shuman, and L. D. Hessen, "Normative developmental challenges and dieting and eating disturbances in middle school girls," *International Journal of Eating Disorders*, 15 (1994), pp. 11–20.

25 F. Martin, "Subgroups in anorexia nervosa: A family systems study," in *Anorexia Nervosa: Recent Developments in Research*, ed. P. L. Darby, P. E. Garfinkel, D. J. Garner, and D. V. Coscina (New York: Alan R. Liss, 1983), pp. 57–65.

26 S. Squire, *The Slender Balance* (New York: Pinnacle Books, 1983), pp. 22ff.

27 See, for example, M. S. Gould and D. Shaffer, "The impact of suicide in television movies: Evidence on imitation," *The New England Journal of Medicine*, 315 (1986), pp. 690–4; and D. Phillips and L. L. Carstensen, "Clustering of teenage suicides after television news stories about suicide," *The New England Journal of Medicine*, 315 (1986), pp. 685–9.

28 The number of popular articles per year on anorexia nervosa listed in the *Reader's Guide to Periodical Literature* grew steadily from two in 1972 to 14 in 1983. The total number of articles during this period was over 50. Some representative titles include K. Lynch, "Danger! You can overdo dieting," *Seventeen*, 34 (1975), pp. 106–7; J. Ramsey, "Anorexia nervosa: Dying of thinness," *Ms*, 5 (August 1976), pp. 103–6; "When dieting goes wild," *US News and World Report*, 85 (1978), p. 62; B. Conley, "My sister and I tried to outdiet each other with some pretty scary results," *Glamour*, 77 (1979), pp. 38ff.; "My daughter was starving herself to death," *Good Housekeeping*, 194 (May 1982), pp. 73ff. On bulimia, see B. Stein, "Dangerous eat-and-purge disorder strikes young women," *People*, 16 (1981), pp. 47–8; M. L. Schildkraut, "Bulimia: The secret dieter's disease," *Good Housekeeping*, 194 (May 1982), pp. 239ff.; F. A. Bernstein, "Bulimia: A woman's terror," *People Weekly*, 26 (Nov. 17, 1986), pp. 30–

41. For article on "Golden Girls," see *Playgirl*, June 1975.

29 Lynch, "Danger! You can overdo dieting."

30 I. Johnson, "Starving for perfection: one girl's battle with anorexia," *Seventeen*, September 1986, p. 194.

31 C. B. O'Neill, *Starving for Attention* (New York: Dell, 1983).

32 C. B. O'Neill, *Dear Cherry: Questions and Answers on Eating Disorders* (New York: Continuum, 1985), p. 75.

33 J. Bode, *Food Fight* (New York: Simon and Schuster, 1997). I am grateful to Laura Hill for her review of this book in *Eating Disorders: Journal of Treatment and Prevention*, 7 (1999), pp. 66–9.

34 E. Levin, "A sweet surface hid a troubled soul in the late Karen Carpenter, a victim of anorexia nervosa," *People*, 19 (1983), pp. 52–4.

35 J. Fonda, *Jane Fonda's Workout Book* (New York: Simon and Schuster, 1981), esp. chapter entitled "A body abused."

36 For some current approaches to prevention, see a number of articles in *Eating Disorders: Journal of Treatment and Prevention*, 4 (1996): C. Steiner-Adair and A. Purcell, "Approaches to mainstreaming eating disorders prevention," pp. 294–309; M. P. Levine, L. Smolak, and F. Schermer, "Media analysis and resistance by elementary school children in the primary prevention of eating problems," pp. 310–22; N. Piran, "The reduction of preoccupation with body weight and shape in schools: A feminist approach," pp. 323–33; J. A. Graber and J. Brooks-Gunn, "Prevention of eating problems and disorders: Including parents," pp. 348–63; P. S. Powers and C. Johnson, "Small victories: Prevention of eating disorders among atheletes," pp. 348–63; and in the same journal, vol. 5 (1997), G. F. Huon, W. G. Roncolato, J. E. Ritchie, and C. Braganza, "Prevention of dieting-induced disorders: Findings and implications of a pilot study," pp. 280–93; D. M. Martz, K. D. Graves, and E. T. Sturgis, "A pilot peer-leader eating disorders prevention program for sororities," pp. 294–308.

37 T. Mann, S. Nolen-Hoeksema, K. Huang, D. Burgard, A. Wright, and K. Hanson, "Are two interventions worse than none? Joint primary and secondary prevention of eating disorders in college females," *Health Psychology*, 16 (1997), pp. 215–25.

38 J. C. Carter, D. A. Stewart, V. J. Dunn, and C. G. Fairburn, "Primary prevention of eating disorders: Might it do more harm than good?," *International Journal of Eating Disorders*, 22 (1997), pp. 167–78.

39 L. Cohn and M. Maine, "More harm than good," *Eating Disorders: Journal of Treatment and Prevention*, 6 (1998), pp. 93–5. See also, though, the rejoinder to this article in J. C. Carter, D. A. Stewart, and C. G. Fairburn, "Primary prevention of eating disorders: The dilemma and its denial," *Eating Disorders: Journal of Treatment and Prevention*, 6 (1998), pp. 213–16; and T. Mann and D. Burgard, "Eating disorder prevention

programs: What we don't know can hurt us," *Eating Disorders: Journal of Treatment and Prevention*, 6 (1998), pp. 101–3.

40 A popular book on the rice diet, which is a reputable method for the treatment of obesity, is J. Moscovitz, *The Rice Diet Report* (New York: Avon, 1986); The Diet Workshop Wild Weekend Diet is presented in L. Lindauer, *The Diet Workshop Wild Weekend Diet* (New York: Delacorte Press, 1985); for evaluations, see T. Berland, *Rating the Diets* (Skokie, IL: Publications International Ltd, 1986).

41 J. Mazel, *The Beverly Hills Diet* (New York: Macmillan, 1981).

42 Ibid., p. 114.

43 Ibid., p. 217.

44 "The Beverly Hills Diet," *Harper's Bazaar*, May 1981, pp. 72ff.

45 G. B. Mirkin and R. N. Shore, "The Beverly Hills diet: Dangers of the newest weight loss fad," *Journal of the American Medical Association*, 246 (1981), pp. 2235–7.

46 S. C. Wooley and O. W. Wooley, "The Beverly Hills eating disorder: The mass marketing of anorexia nervosa," *International Journal of Eating Disorders*, 1 (1982), pp. 57–68.

47 Ibid., p. 57.

48 Ibid., pp. 57–68.

49 J. Mazel, *The Beverly Hills Lifetime Plan* (New York: Bantam Books, 1983), p. 13.

50 Bruch, "Four decades of eating disorders."

51 Mazel, *The Beverly Hills Diet*, pp. 132, 134.

52 Ibid., p. 2.

53 J. Mazel, *The New Beverly Hills Diet Born Again Skinny* (Deerfield Beach: Health Communications, Incorporated, 1996); *The New Beverly Hills Diet Little Skinny Companion* (Deerfield Beach: Health Communications, 1997).

54 B. Sears, *The Zone: A Dietary Road Map to Lose Weight Permanently, Reset Your Genetic Code, Prevent Disease & Achieve Maximum Physical Performance* (New York: HarperCollins, 1995).

55 T. F. Heatherton, P. Nichols, F. Mahamedi, and P. Keel, "Body weight, dieting and eating disorder symptoms among college students, 1982–1992," *American Journal of Psychiatry*, 152 (1995), pp. 1623–9.

56 K. Halmi, comment at Symposium at Third International Conference on Eating Disorders, Center for the Study of Anorexia Nervosa and Bulimia, New York, April 1988.

57 C. Johnson, "A psychoeducational approach," presentation at Second Annual Conference on Eating Disorders, Center for the Study of Anorexia Nervosa and Bulimia, New York, November 1983.

58 S. Orbach, *Hunger Strike: Anorexia as a Metaphor for Our Time* (New

York: W. W. Norton, 1986), p. 15.

59   C. S. Crandall, "Social contagion of binge eating," *Journal of Personality and Social Psychology*, 55 (1988), pp. 588–98. For an informative discussion of the problem of bulimia in sororities, see Squire, *The Slender Balance*, pp. 73–7.

60   J. P. Cesari, "Fad bulimia: A serious and separate counseling issue," *Journal of College Student Personnel*, 27 (1986), pp. 255–9.

61   J. Chiodo and P. R. Latimer, "Vomiting as a learned weight-control technique in bulimia," *Journal of Behavior Therapy and Experimental Psychiatry*, 14 (1983), pp. 131–5.

62   G. Russell, "Bulimia nervosa: An ominous variant of anorexia nervosa," *Psychological Medicine*, 9 (1979), pp. 429–48.

63   Advertisement in *New York Times*, Aug. 26, 1987, p. C4.

64   G. Tillotson, *Responsible Bulimia: Is It Possible?* Privately printed, August 1987.

65   Tillotson, *Responsible Bulimia*, p. 28.

66   G. Tillotson, personal communication.

67   R. Barthes, "Towards a psychosociology of contemporary food consumption," in *European Diet from Preindustrial to Modern Times*, ed. E. Forster and R. Forster (New York: Harper and Row, 1975), pp. 47–59.

68   Much of this discussion draws on the ideas of Sidney Mintz. See S. Mintz, *Sweetness and Power: The Place of Sugar in Modern History* (New York: Viking, 1985), esp. ch. 5. On solo eating in public in the 1980s, see B. Miller, "Solo dining: New options in privacy vs. company," *New York Times*, March 5, 1986, pp. C1, C6.

69   An excellent discussion of the "empire of snacks" is contained in C. Fischler, "Food habits, social change and the nature/culture dilemma," *Social Science Information*, 19 (1980), pp. 937–53.

70   See, for example, R. C. Hawkins, "Meal/snack frequencies in college students: a normative study," *Behavioral Psychotherapy*, 7 (1979), 85–90. See also the study by Heatherton and colleagues, n. 55, above.

71   J. Wurtman, *Managing Your Mind and Mood Through Food* (New York: Harper and Row, 1988). Also see N. Jenkins, "For many young professionals, the way to eat is on the run," *New York Times*, Jan. 30, 1985, pp. C1ff.

72   R. Coward, *Female Desires: How They are Sought, Bought and Packaged* (New York: Grove Press, 1985), pp. 99–107.

73   A popular self-help approach to the problem of compulsive overeating is presented by Geneen Roth in *Feeding the Hungry Heart: The Experience of Compulsive Eating* (New York: NAL, 1983) and *Breaking Free from Compulsive Eating* (New York: Signet Books, 1984). Roth herself experienced both obesity and anorexia nervosa, and her approach is specifically

directed towards females with eating problems.

74 Studies document that about 80 percent of female and 50 percent of male college students engage in eating binges. See R. C. Hawkins and P. F. Clement, "Development and construct validation of a measure of binge eating tendencies," *Addictive Behaviors*, 5 (1980), pp. 219–26. This does not mean, of course, that all these students are bulimic, but it does suggest that binge eating is part of the American student "life-style."

75 D. Hoffman, *The Joy of Pigging Out* (New York: Warner Books, 1983).

76 For example, the replacement of regular with low-fat yogurt will typically involve a negligible real reduction in calories from fat, since the baseline already reflects a low level, while the replacement of regular peanuts with peanuts with reduced fat content will not accomplish much, because the baseline is very high (and therefore the reduced fat version moderately high).

77 This term was proposed by S. Holmgren, K. Humble, C. Norring, B. Roos, B. Rosmark, and S. Sohlberg, "The anorectic–bulimic conflict: An alternative diagnostic approach to anorexia nervosa and bulimia," *International Journal of Eating Disorders*, 2 (1983), pp. 3–13.

Chapter Eight   The Cultural Politics of Eating Disorders

1 These ideas about the social response to ethnic disorders were articulated in G. Devereux, "Normal and abnormal," in *Basic Problems of Ethnopsychiatry* (Chicago: University of Chicago Press, 1980), pp. 28ff.

2 I follow here a discussion by Roland Littlewood and Maurice Lipsedge, "The culture-bound syndromes of the dominant culture: Culture, psychopathology and biomedicine," in *Transcultural Psychiatry*, ed. J. L. Cox (London: Croom Helm, 1986), pp. 253–73. The reference to Turner's concept of "power of the weak" is theirs, but was originally discussed by Turner in *The Ritual Process* (London: Routledge and Kegan Paul, 1969).

3 Discussed in Littlewood and Lipsedge, "The culture-bound syndromes." The phenomenon of the Zar cult is discussed further in I. M. Lewis, *Ecstatic Religion: An Anthropological Study of Spirit Possession and Shamanism* (New York: Penguin Books, 1971).

4 Littlewood and Lipsedge, "The culture-bound syndromes."

5 C. Smith-Rosenberg, "The hysterical woman: Sex roles in 19th century America," *Social Research*, 39 (1972), pp. 652–78.

6 For an interesting discussion of the cultural significance of agoraphobia, see A. DeSwaan, "The politics of agoraphobia," *Theory and Society*, 10 (1981), pp. 359–82. DeSwaan sees the "fear of the marketplace" as an individual residue of the threats to the status of a woman who ventured

out alone in the city in the eighteenth century. The family dynamics of agoraphobia are discussed in R. J. Hafner, "The husbands of agoraphobic women and their influence on treatment outcome," *British Journal of Psychiatry*, 131 (1977), pp. 289–304. It should be pointed out, however, that the stereotypical picture of the agoraphobic marriage has not gone unchallenged. Indeed, the recent employment of the husband as "helper" in behavior therapy approaches seems to contradict the popular family-systems notion that the husband could not tolerate the wife's recovery, since it would upset his position of dominance.

7   J. H. Lacey, "Anorexia nervosa in a bearded female saint," *British Medical Journal*, 285 (1982), pp. 1816–17.

8   See C. Bynum, *Holy Feast and Holy Fast: The Religious Significance of Food to Medieval Women* (Berkeley: University of California Press, 1987), p. 194.

9   R. Bell, *Holy Anorexia* (Chicago: University of Chicago Press, 1985).

10 Bynum, *Holy Feast and Holy Fast*, pp. 220–4.

11 Ibid., pp. 46–7.

12 Ibid., p. 233.

13 On this point, see the illuminating afterword to Bell's book by William Davis.

14 On Simone Weil, see J. Petrement, *Simone Weil: A Life*, tra. Raymond Rosenthal (New York: Random House, 1976). Caroline Bynum in *Holy Feast and Holy Fast* rejects the notion of identifying Simone Weil as anorexic, as if this somehow detracted from her spiritual and literary accomplishments. However, the parallels between her life and her thinking and some of the central psychological themes characteristic of anorexia are too striking to ignore. For an illuminating discussion, see J. V. Herik, "Looking, eating and waiting in Simone Weil," in *Mysticism, Nihilism, and Feminism: New Critical Essays on the Anti-Theology of Simone Weil*, ed. T. A. Idinopolous and J. Z. Knopp (Johnson City, TN: Institute of Social Sciences and the Arts, 1984), pp. 57–90.

15 This material is drawn from E. N. Rogers, *Fasting: The Phenomenon of Self-Denial* (Nashville: Nelson, 1976).

16 Quoted in Rogers, *Fasting*, p. 77.

17 Bynum, *Holy Feast and Holy Fast*, p. 192.

18 H. Schwartz, *Never Satisfied: A Cultural History of Diets, Fantasies and Fat* (New York: Macmillan, 1986), pp. 132–4.

19 F. Kafka, "A hunger artist," in *Kafka: The Complete Stories* (New York: Shocken Books, 1976). Kafka himself may have been in the grip of an anorexic mentality, as suggested by M. M. Fichter, "The anorexia nervosa of Franz Kafka," *International Journal of Eating Disorders*, 6 (1987), pp. 367–78.

20 E. Showalter, *The Female Malady: Women, Madness, and English Culture, 1830–1980* (New York: Pantheon Books, 1985), p. 162.

21 See, for example, S. Orbach, *Hunger Strike: Anorexia as a Metaphor for Our Time* (New York: W. W. Norton, 1986); and "Accepting the symptom: A feminist psychoanalytic treatment of anorexia nervosa," in *Handbook of Psychotherapy for Anorexia Nervosa and Bulimia,* ed. D. M. Garner and P. E. Garfinkel (New York: Guilford Press, 1985), pp. 83–104; M. Boskind-Lodahl, "Cinderella's stepsisters: A feminist perspective on anorexia nervosa and bulimia," *Signs: The Journal of Women in Culture and Society,* 2 (1976), pp. 342–56; K. Chernin, *The Hungry Self* (New York: Times Books, 1986); and M. Lawrence (ed.), *Fed Up and Hungry* (New York: Peter Bedrick Books, 1987). For a critical view of the feminist interpretations of eating disorders, see L. Swartz, "Is thin a feminist issue?," *Women's Studies International Forum,* 8 (1985), pp. 429–37.

22 S. Srikameswaran, P. Leichner, and D. Harper, "Sex role ideology among women with anorexia nervosa and bulimia," *International Journal of Eating Disorders,* 3 (1984), pp. 39–44.

23 See S. Ross, *Fasting* (New York: Pan Books, 1978). On the notion of anorexia nervosa as addiction to starvation, see G. I. Szmuckler and D. Tantam, "Anorexia nervosa: Starvation dependence," *British Journal of Medical Psychology,* 57 (1984), pp. 303–10. See also H. Huebner, *Endorphins, Eating Disorders and Other Addictive Behaviors* (New York: Norton, 1993).

24 H. Bruch, *The Golden Cage* (New York: Vintage, 1978), p. 5.

25 The links between anorexia and asceticism have been noted by H. Bruch, *Eating Disorders: Obesity, Anorexia Nervosa and the Person Within* (New York: Basic Books, 1973), pp. 11–13 and A. H. Crisp, *Anorexia Nervosa: Let Me Be* (London: Academic Press, 1980), pp. 5, 10. More extended discussions are contained in S. L. Mogul, "Asceticism in adolescence and anorexia nervosa," *The Psychoanalytic Study of the Child,* 35 (1980), pp. 155–78; and D. Rampling, "Ascetic ideals and anorexia nervosa," *Journal of Psychiatric Research,* 2/3 (1985), pp. 89–94. Mogul cites one case in which a patient saw a parallel between her food restriction and the fast of atonement on Yom Kippur. Rampling, anticipating the later work of Bell, suggests direct parallels between the writings of Catherine of Siena and contemporary autobiographies, such as that of Cherry Boone O'Neill.

26 Rampling, "Ascetic ideals and anorexia nervosa," p. 94. Rampling suggests that the infrequency with which these parallels are discussed has to do with the difficulty that clinicians have in going beyond their own paradigms, a point with which I am in agreement.

27 This statement probably needs to be qualified. When a person becomes

270

actively anorexic, their behavior is typically frightening, frustrating, and maddening to those around them and may be sufficient in and of itself to provoke intense emotional reactions.

28 S. Minuchin, B. Rosman, and L. Baker, *Psychosomatic Families: Anorexia Nervosa in Context* (Cambridge, MA: Harvard University Press, 1978).

29 Although it should be added that we have little data to indicate that it will systematically and regularly do so. Minuchin's research has been criticized as being based on small samples and for confounding the effects of dramatic rituals like the family lunch session with more mundane procedures used by his treatment team, such as behavior therapy.

30 M. S. Palazzoli, "Anorexia nervosa: A syndrome of the affluent society," *Transcultural Psychiatric Research Review*, 22 (1985), pp. 199–204.

31 M. S. Palazzoli, S. Cirillo, M. Selvini, and A. M. Sorrentino, *Family Games: General Models of Psychotic Processes in the Family* (New York: Norton, 1989).

32 Ibid.

33 M. S. Palazzoli, "Towards a general model of psychotic family games," *Journal of Marital and Family Therapy*, 12 (1986), pp. 339–50. See also M. S. Palazzoli, "The anorexic process in the family," *Family Process*, 27 (1986), pp. 129–48.

34 This case is discussed in detail in P. Papp, *The Process of Change* (New York: Guilford Press, 1986), ch. 6.

35 Palazzoli et al., *Family Games*.

36 One should not get the impression, though, that such methods as described by Palazzoli are applicable in all or even most cases. They require a team working on each case, and they are extraordinarily difficult to teach. For further discussion of these and related methods, see C. Dare and I. Eisler, "Family therapy for anorexia nervosa," in *Handbook of Treatment for Eating Disorders (Second Edition)*, ed. D. M. Garner and P. E. Garfinkel (New York: Guilford Press, 1997), pp. 307–26.

37 M. P. Root, P. Fallon, and W. N. Friedrich, *Bulimia: A Systems Approach to Treatment* (New York: W. W. Norton, 1986).

38 Devereux, "Normal and abnormal," p. 31.

39 C. H. H. Branch and L. J. Eurman, "Social attitudes towards patients with anorexia nervosa," *American Journal of Psychiatry*, 137 (1980), pp. 631–2 .

40 See, for example, A. H. Crisp and R. S. Kalucy, "Aspects of the perceptual disorder in anorexia nervosa," *British Journal of Medical Psychology*, 47 (1974), p. 358.

41 A. Liu, *Solitaire* (New York: Harper and Row, 1979), p. 188.

42 For example, see the discussion of the patient Annette in H. Bruch, *Conversations with Anorexics* (New York: Basic Books, 1988), p. 62.

43 S. Sontag, *Illness as Metaphor* (New York: Farrar, Straus, and Giroux, 1978).

44 B. C. Meyer and L. A. Weinroth, "Observations on psychological aspects of anorexia nervosa: Report of a case," *Psychosomatic Medicine*, 19 (1957), pp. 389–98.

45 Sontag, *Illness as Metaphor*.

46 Little is known about the specific meanings of thinness to Victorian anorexics. For a discussion of the nineteenth-century imagery of thinness, see J. J. Brumberg, *Fasting Girls: The Emergence of Anorexia Nervosa as a Modern Disease* (Cambridge, MA: Harvard University Press, 1988), esp. ch. 6 ("The Appetite as Voice"), in which she argues that the romanticization of thinness was tied to notions of frailty, gentility, and passivity.

47 I. Story, "Caricature and impersonating the other: Observations from the psychotherapy of anorexia nervosa," *Psychiatry*, 39 (1976), pp. 176–88.

48 Such an argument has been made by Swartz, in "Is thin a feminist issue?" Swartz argues that anorexia nervosa has led to a "medicalization" of the problem of thinness, thereby deflecting attention from the more general cultural problem. However, it could easily be argued that the reverse is true – that is, that the public awareness about anorexia nervosa has led to a more general awareness in the public consciousness of the dangers of severe dieting.

49 S. Murray, S. Touyz, and P. Beumont, "Knowledge about eating disorders in the community," *International Journal of Eating Disorders*, 9 (1990), pp. 87–93. In this Australian study, the researchers found that over one-third of the subjects whom they interviewed found that their eating habits had been affected by their knowledge about anorexia nervosa, mostly in the direction of increased caution about dieting. However, a small number had incorporated weight-loss tactics.

50 Brumberg, in *Fasting Girls*, emphasized that this was the core of anorexia nervosa in nineteenth-century Victorian middle-class families. However, the dynamic also operates today, particularly on the individual level. The behavior often represents an attempt to specifically inflict punishment on the mother, particularly in so far as the mother represents the food-giving function in the family.

51 See, for example, Boskind-Lodahl, "Cinderella's stepsisters," and Orbach, *Hunger Strike*. See also H. Malson, *The Thin Woman: Feminism, Post-structuralism, and the Social Psychology of Anorexia Nervosa* (London: Routledge, 1998).

52 J. Dally and J. Gomez, *Anorexia Nervosa* (London: William Heinemann Medical Books, 1979). In fairness, Dally, a psychiatrist with long experience in the treatment of anorexics, advocated a far more sympathetic and

sophisticated approach than is indicated in this statement, which can be taken more as a characterization of the feelings evoked in the doctor than the advocacy of coercive treatment. For example, in his chapter on treatment, he suggests, like most contemporary therapists, that forced tube feeding is rarely necessary. See also P. E. Garfinkel and D. M. Garner, *Anorexia Nervosa: A Multidimensional Approach* (New York: Brunner Mazel, 1982), ch. 9; Crisp, *Anorexia Nervosa*; A. E. Andersen, C. L. Morse, and K. S. Santmyer, "Inpatient treatment for anorexia nervosa," in Garner and Garfinkel, *Handbook of Psychotherapy for Anorexia Nervosa and Bulimia*, pp. 311–43.

53 For a discussion of the complexities surrounding enforced treatment such as coercive feeding, see R. Dresser, "Feeding the hunger artists: Legal issues in treating anorexia nervosa," *Wisconsin Law Review*, 2 (1984), pp. 297–384. In a searching review of the relevant legal and moral issues, Dresser suggests that coercive treatment of anorexics is only permissible if the patient's life is immediately threatened. She concludes that:

> We live in a society that reflects inconsistency and ambivalence about the extremely thin feminine form. Sometimes the shape is revered, but if it represents severe anorexia nervosa, it is viewed with horror. Our culture is highly competitive, expecting certain of its young women to achieve not only the ideal appearance, but to perform well at work and at home. Some individuals intimidated by these demands of modern womanhood develop symptoms of anorexia. The specter of anorexia nervosa evokes uneasiness in its observers .... Because available evidence indicates that unrestricted forcible treatment confers little or no long term benefits upon anorexics, but instead can reduce their chances for full recovery, anorexics quite possibly would be better off if their audience were forced more frequently to confront their disturbing appearance. Perhaps their presence among us would constitute a compelling challenge to the social forces shaping the strange phenomenon of anorexia nervosa. (p. 374)

54 H. Bruch, "Perils of behavior modification in the treatment of anorexia nervosa," *Journal of the American Medical Association*, 230 (1974), pp. 1419–22. Bruch's critique seems to have had a significant impact. Although many treatment programs now use some form of systematic reinforcement of weight gain, in which patients gain more privileges as they approach their target weight, it is generally understood that such procedures will be ineffective and perhaps counterproductive in the long run if they are not complemented by a more comprehensive approach to the complexity of the patient's psychological problems. Unfortunately, this can make inpatient care an inherently lengthy process, a requirement that runs counter to expectations of managed health care for shorter and shorter patient stays.

55 Smith-Rosenberg, "The hysterical woman"; Showalter, *The Female Malady*.

56 The issue of the gender of the therapist has been raised frequently in discussions of the treatment of anorexia nervosa. For an enlightening discussion, particularly of the advantages and pitfalls for female therapists, see F. R. Frankenburg, "Female therapists in the management of anorexia nervosa," *International Journal of Eating Disorders*, 3 (1984), pp. 25–33. A case can be made for the notion that females may have some advantage over males, given their own inevitably experiential understanding of the cultural pressures on women to achieve, to please men, and to control body size. But there may be disadvantages as well. For example, the competitive mind-set of anorexic patients may pose problems for both the patient and her female therapist. These may be compounded for those anorexics who have a hostile and competitive relationship with their mothers, which may in turn be projected onto the female therapist. There seems to be little question that in order to become effective, male therapists need to develop sensitivity to the particular stresses of female development. But the psychological issues confronting anorexic patients, such as those of low self-esteem, autonomy, or the need to please others, are not bound by gender. To argue otherwise is to revert to nineteenth-century definitions of sex roles, in which each gender is characterized by an exclusive set of attributes.

57 M. Lawrence, "Anorexia nervosa: The control paradox," *Women's Studies International Quarterly*, 2 (1979), pp. 93–101.

58 A. A. Sallas, "Treatment of eating disorders: Winning the war without having to do battle," *Journal of Psychiatric Research*, 19 (2–3) (1985), pp. 83–8.

59 H. Bruch, "Four decades of eating disorders," in Garner and Garfinkel, *Handbook of Psychotherapy for Anorexia Nervosa and Bulimia*, p. 12.

60 It should be emphasized, however, that length of stay in the hospital for anorexic patients has been drastically shortened owing to insurance restrictions. Anorexics have also been victimized by negative attitudes on the part of some insurers, for example, by the notion that the disorder is "self-induced."

61 T. Cooper, "Anorexia and bulimia: The political and the personal," in Lawrence, *Fed Up and Hungry*, pp. 175–92.

62 See J. R. Kaplan, *Woman's Conflict: The Special Relationship Between Women and Food* (Englewood Cliffs, NJ: Prentice-Hall, 1980).

63 M. Dana and M. Lawrence, " 'Poison is the nourishment that makes one ill': The metaphor of bulimia," in Lawrence, *Fed Up and Hungry*, pp. 193–206.

64 It has been increasingly recognized that the use of groups is highly relevant for the treatment of bulimia. See, for example, D. Jones, "Bulimia:

A false self identity," *Clinical Social Work Journal*, 13 (1985), pp. 305–16; C. Johnson, M. Conners, and M. Stuckey, "Short term group treatment of bulimia," *International Journal of Eating Disorders*, 2 (1983), pp. 299–308; M. Boskind-White and W. C. White, "An experiential behavioral approach to the treatment of bulimarexia," *Psychotherapy: Theory, Research and Practice*, 4 (1981), pp. 501–7; and J. S. Lazerson, "Voices of bulimia: Experiences in integrated psychotherapy," *Psychotherapy: Theory, Research and Practice*, 21(1984), pp. 500–9. The approaches of Boskind-White and White and of Lazerson specifically incorporate feminist concerns in their group workshops. Boskind-White and White, for example, have periods where the female therapist meets with the group alone, with the male joining the group and serving as a target for various role-playing exercises.

65 H. Levitt, "A semiotic understanding of eating disorders: The impact of media portrayal," *Eating Disorders: Journal of Treatment and Prevention*, 5 (1997), pp. 169–83.

66 T. Gaudoin, "Body of evidence: Eating disorders and the media: We bite back," *Harper's Bazaar*, July 1993, pp. 74–8.

67 R. Johnson, "The body myth," *Vogue*, September 1996, pp. 653–8. The editor's introduction to the article complains that "hostility against thin people is at an all-time high and fashion models are taking the brunt of the criticism. Yet there's no evidence that images of models provoke eating disorders."

68 See Y. Ono, "Fashion's new queens: Heavy Teens," *Wall Street Journal*, July 31, 1998, pp. B1, B4.

69 Minuchin, Rosman, and Baker, *Psychosomatic Families*, p. 333.

70 K. Chernin, *The Obsession: Reflections on the Tyranny of Slenderness* (New York: Harper and Row, 1981), p. 100.

71 N. Wolf, *The Beauty Myth: How Images of Beauty are Used against Women* (New York: Dutton, 1991).

Index

Printed in the United States
130573LV00006B/9/P